Little
Rock

POLITICS AND SOCIETY IN TWENTIETH-CENTURY AMERICA

Series Editors
William Chafe, Gary Gerstle, Linda Gordon, and Julian Zelizer
A list of titles in this series appears at the back of the book

Little Rock

Race and Resistance at Central High School

Karen Anderson

PRINCETON UNIVERSITY PRESS   *Princeton & Oxford*

Copyright © 2010 by Princeton University Press
Published by Princeton University Press, 41 William Street,
Princeton, New Jersey 08540

In the United Kingdom: Princeton University Press, 6 Oxford Street,
Woodstock, Oxfordshire OX20 1TW

LIBRARY OF CONGRESS CATALOGING-IN-PUBLICATION DATA
Anderson, Karen, 1947–
Little Rock : race and resistance at Central High School / Karen Anderson.—
1st ed.
p. cm.—(Politics and society in twentieth-century America)
Includes bibliographical references and index.
ISBN 978–0-691–09293–5 (cloth)
1. School integration—Arkansas—Little Rock—History—20th
century.   2. Central High School (Little Rock, Ark.)—History.
3. African American students—Arkansas—Little Rock—History—
20th century.   4. African Americans—Education—Arkansas—Little
Rock—History—20th century.   5. School integration—Massive
resistance movement—Arkansas—Little Rock—History—20th
century.   6. Little Rock (Ark.)—Race relations.   7. Little Rock
(Ark.)—Politics and government—20th century.   I. Title.
LC214.23.L56A53 2010
379.2'630976773—dc22   2009022870

British Library Cataloging-in-Publication Data is available

This book has been composed in Adobe Garamond.

Printed on acid-free paper. ∞

press.princeton.edu

Printed in the United States of America

10   9   8   7   6   5   4   3   2   1

Contents

Illustrations

Acknowledgments

All scholars depend on the assistance of many others. I am grateful to all those individuals and institutions who have enabled me to shape and complete this project. My first debt is to the many colleagues at the University of Arizona, past and present, who have created a stimulating intellectual community for me and have provided wonderful examples of innovative scholarship. In addition, my colleagues in the Teaching Workshop in Women's History at UCLA have pursued an impressive range of topics, many focused on gender and race, over three decades of annual meetings dedicated to the serious intellectual work of teaching generously nourished with laughter. Finally, my graduate students at the University of Arizona, particularly those in women's history, have taught me a great deal through the years and have deepened my understanding of gender, race, and power.

Many archivists contributed to the success of *Little Rock*. I owe a special debt to Linda Pine at Special Collections at the University of Arkansas at Little Rock; Andrea Cantrell and Michael Dabrishus at Special Collections at the University of Arkansas, Fayetteville; and Jane Hooker at the Arkansas History Commission. In addition, archivists at the National Archives; the Dwight D. Eisenhower Presidential Library; the State Historical Society of Wisconsin; and the University of California, Santa Barbara provided essential assistance.

Many participants in the events of this book were willing to spend time with me in oral history interviews. I am grateful to them for their trust in me and for their insights into the events they helped to form. It saddens me to know that so many of them have passed away while I took my time on this project. I am particularly grateful to Georg and Wilma Iggers and to Lee Lorch for their generous hospitality on my research trip to Buffalo and Toronto.

The University of Arizona was generous in its support for my research trips. I received funds from the small grants program of the Vice President for Research, the Social and Behavioral Sciences Research Institute, and the Udall Center. Without these kinds of resources, humanists would be seriously impaired in their scholarly work.

Finally, those who read and edited the manuscript provided crucial insights and assistance. William Chafe, who proved to be a model of forbearance as well as insight, read all the drafts. Anonymous reviewers for Princeton University Press also read carefully and provided helpful advice. At the University of Arizona, Laura Briggs and Myra Dinnerstein read early chapter drafts. I also want to thank Sherry Smith for her work on the index. Finally, the editors at Princeton University Press worked hard to improve the manuscript. I particularly appreciate the assistance of Clara Platter and Ellen Foos in the late stages of the project.

Little
Rock

INTRODUCTION

Not Here, Not Now, Not Us

> Little Rock did not bring on disaster. Disaster was deliber-
> ately thrust upon a majority of progressive and law-abiding
> citizens by extremists and outsiders seeking to serve their
> own ends.
>
> —Little Rock School Superintendent Virgil Blossom[1]

> Well, Little Rock, we believe, was selected by those who were
> pushing for integration as a city to be made an example of,
> and all the forces of government and the forces of liberalism
> and all the forces of integration were sent to Little Rock to
> make this the battleground and fight it out, fight the issue
> out and settle it here, so as to place other school districts in
> the state and in the South in an indefensible position.
>
> —Rev. Wesley Pruden[2]

On the morning of September 4, 1957, 16-year-old Elizabeth Eckford awoke early, so keyed up about her first day at Little Rock's Central High School that she could hardly wait to be up. As she ironed the black and white dress she had made for the occasion, her brother turned on the television. A local newscast related that large crowds were gathering at the previously all-white school to prevent the entry of Elizabeth and eight other African American students scheduled to start school that day. Her mother, anxious about her daughter's safety, yelled from the kitchen for them to "Turn that TV off!" Her father paced throughout the house, unable to calm his fears. Before Elizabeth left for school, her mother summoned the family to the living room for a prayer.[3]

As she walked the block from the bus to her new school, Elizabeth was unaware of crucial decisions made by others. Because the Eckfords did not have a phone, state NAACP leader Daisy Bates had intended to send someone to their house that morning to notify Elizabeth where to meet the other black students and an interracial escort of ministers before entering the school. Distracted and exhausted, Bates had forgotten to do so. Isolated from the others, Elizabeth found herself on her own in a dangerous situation. Unbeknownst to her, Governor Orval Faubus had ordered the Arkansas National Guard to prevent the entry of the African American students.[4]

Elizabeth assumed that the soldiers were there to offer protection to her and to Central High's other black pupils. Believing that one of the Guardsmen had directed her to go to a particular entrance, she walked down the street between a hostile crowd of whites and the guards. She tried twice to cross the National Guard lines, but was refused access to the school. In the meantime, segregationist whites closed in around her, shoving and yelling epithets. One woman urged her to "go back where you came from," while others cried "Lynch her! Lynch her!" The frightened girl made her way to a bus stop, where a Guardsman ordered the crowd away from the bench. Grace Lorch, a white woman who belonged to the local NAACP chapter, stayed with her, fending off the crowd while Elizabeth waited for a city bus to take her to safety. Lorch told members of the crowd that Elizabeth was "just a little girl" and that "Six months from now you'll be ashamed at what you're doing." In a gesture that would make him a lightning rod for segregationist anger, *New York Times* reporter Benjamin Fine put his arm around the frightened adolescent and urged her, "don't let them see you cry." When a few segregationists tried to block entry to the bus, Lorch also threatened to punch them in the nose. She then rode the bus with the silent and terrified young woman, who got off at the School for the Blind, where her mother worked. There she found safety and comfort in her mother's arms.[5]

Elizabeth Eckford's ordeal received world-wide publicity. The picture of Central High School student Hazel Bryan, her face contorted with hate, taunting a frightened but dignified Eckford became a national and international symbol for racial politics in Little Rock. The *Arkansas Gazette* editorialized that the picture of Eckford in front of "the shouting white girl with her pretty face distorted by unreasoning hate and fear" spoke for itself. Central High School Vice Principal Elizabeth Huckaby described the pictures in her journal as reflecting "the dignity of the rejected Negro girl, the obscenity of the faces of her tormentors." One Central High alumnus wondered whether Bryan was "the flower of white Southern womanhood?" Gentility, as Beth Roy has noted, "was a deeply gendered act; men could be rough-and-tumble while women carried the torch of right behavior." Bryan apparently had dropped the torch.[6]

If southern white women had a special responsibility to embody and enact southern gentility, something was clearly amiss in Little Rock. The contrasting images presented by Little Rock's youthful antagonists threatened to undermine the historic associations between race and respectability for southern white women. With her shy demeanor and fashionable but proper attire, Elizabeth Eckford embodied an innocent, demure young womanhood. Bryan, by contrast, projected a disorderly and subversive womanhood, one that violated white middle-class taboos against *visible* manifestations of racial hatred and against provocative and disagreeable behavior by women. The day after the incident, Vice Principal Huckaby chastised Bryan for her role in the mob, beginning a series of highly class-based confrontations between school administrators and dissident students over the latter's role in segregationist protests. As the reactions to Bryan indicated, any form of public activism involved segregationist women in a troubling contradiction: they had to flout the gender conventions of southern society in order to strengthen them.[7]

The resistance to desegregation evidenced by the disorders at Central High School and by later segregationist actions makes Little Rock an especially illuminating case study of the problem of enforcing federal desegregation laws in the first ten years after the *Brown v. Board of Education* decision. Officials and citizens in Arkansas used many of the evasive strategies that characterized massive resistance to desegregation elsewhere. These strategies included the passage of myriad state laws whose constitutional validity was suspect, state and private harassment of the NAACP and of individuals associated with desegregation, foot dragging by local school officials, and interference from a state government intent on impeding any compliance with federal law.[8]

Little Rock was poised to become a singularly powerful regional, national, and international symbol of violent resistance to federal desegregation efforts and to racial change. After a federal court injunction forced the governor to remove the state troops from Central High, Little Rock police attempted unsuccessfully to prevent mayhem when the African American students entered the school on September 23, 1957. Confronted by a menacing segregationist mob that they did not believe they could control, local police removed the black students at midday. In order to enforce federal authority, President Dwight Eisenhower federalized the Arkansas National Guard and sent the 101st Airborne Division to Little Rock. With their assistance, the nine African American students entered Central High again on September 25, eight of them for the duration of the academic year.

Once Eisenhower ordered federal troops to Arkansas, Little Rock became *the* central symbolic event in the racial and sectional politics of the 1950s. For civil rights activists and other supporters of integration in the nation, it was a critical early site where the enactment of a violent and hateful resistance to African American advancement served as a foil for the display of a courageous and justifiable challenge to oppression by black citizens. For segregationists, the events in Little Rock represented a very different sort of morality play, one in which jack-booted federal authorities overrode the wishes and interests of the white majority as they sponsored a dangerous inversion of the South's "cherished traditions" and the nation's racial heritage.[9]

The law in question was that mandated by the U.S. Supreme Court in its 1954 decision in *Brown v. Board of Education of Topeka, Kansas*. In a short opinion, the justices unanimously held that segregated public schools violated the equal protection clause of the Fourteenth Amendment and were thus unconstitutional. Specifically, the justices declared that "in the field of public education the doctrine of 'separate but equal' has no place." That doctrine had become a revered ideal in the minds of many southern whites since the 1896 decision in *Plessy v. Ferguson*. In public schools, it was more honored in the breach than in the practice as the "equal" part of the principle fell into immediate and sustained disuse in southern law and policy.[10]

In 1954, the Court left the issue of implementation of its decision in *Brown v. Board of Education* to further arguments, which informed its decision a year later in a case dubbed *Brown II*. That opinion was vague about timetables, asking only that school officials proceed "with all deliberate speed" as they forged school systems "not based on color distinctions." The Court held that the trial courts would retain jurisdiction over districts under court orders "to consider whether the action of school authorities constitutes good faith implementation." The requirement that school officials create and implement "racially nondiscriminatory" practices provided great latitude for local authorities to define the meanings of "race neutral" laws and practices in postwar America. Because Arkansas cases were heard in the United States Court of Appeals for the Eighth Circuit, which included the plains states and none from the Deep South, they would be decided by judges who might be more supportive of the intentions of the first *Brown* decision.[11]

The fact that the school board in Little Rock had initially stated its intention to comply and in 1955 had drafted a plan for desegregation made the situation more promising there than in many southern communities. Ironically, the school board's victory in a 1956 lawsuit initiated by local NAACP officials meant that the district operated under a court-ordered desegregation plan, albeit one that moved much more slowly than the African American litigants would have preferred. That lawsuit also points to the critical role African American activists played in contesting segregation in Arkansas and in shaping the terms and outcomes of the struggle in Little Rock.[12]

The critical actions taken by NAACP leaders and African American citizens in Little Rock reveal the importance of local activism to the national organization's legal strategies and successes. The national NAACP's relationship to school desegregation in Little Rock was purely reactive; local leaders alone initiated the 1956 lawsuit that placed the Little Rock School Board under a court order to desegregate. Once Faubus put state troops around Central High School, local NAACP leaders consulted closely with the national organization about political and legal strategies to reopen the school on a desegregated basis and to protect the African American students enrolled there. Moreover, local activists and NAACP leaders worked together to contest the narrow formalism advanced by moderates seeking minimal compliance with the *Brown* decision. In Little Rock, grassroots activism and litigation were intimately related, not opposing points on a continuum between community-based militance and an elite politics of "polite protest" and legalistic approaches.[13]

When initially confronted with the need to accommodate the Supreme Court's mandate in the *Brown* cases, white Arkansans' reactions ranged from a reluctant and cautious acceptance to extreme hostility. After the situation exploded in the fall of 1957, most whites in Arkansas came to feel that they had been singled out for unwarranted hardships that included international misrepresentations, social conflict, violence, lost business, and significant disruptions to their daily lives and relationships. Many whites expressed the strong conviction that Little Rock was not the appropriate place to start school desegregation. Moderates claimed that Arkansas was a progressive state improving its race relations through a careful adherence to white voluntarism. They believed, however, that their ability to sustain continued racial progress required that they be allowed to do so "quietly" and on their own initiative. Staunch segregationists, by contrast, did not claim the mantle of racial "progress," largely because they touted a rigid system of racial segregation as the prerequisite for racial harmony.[14]

Moderates and segregationists alike advanced conspiratorial explanations for Little Rock's plight. After claiming that large numbers of outsiders had been ready to descend on Little Rock in September 1957 in order to prevent desegregation, the Rev. Robert Brown, Episcopal Bishop of the Diocese of Arkansas, concluded: "It would seem to those who know the South, and its attitude towards these problems, that Little Rock, a moderate city in the Southwest, was chosen by design to be the ground for the battle" because its moderation made it a target for each side and its significance would be far "bigger than Little Rock." In 1959, a committee of the Arkansas Legislative Council concluded that the fall 1957 events that had occurred in Little Rock were "planned, schemed, calculated and had as [their] motivating factor the international Communist conspiracy of world domination squarely behind the entire shocking episode."[15]

The idea of outside interference allowed locals to deny any responsibility for events occurring in their midst and to project racism and violence onto people from another place, social class, or political standpoint. The problem, in short, was "not us," but rather nameless outsiders seeking to fight their racial battles by proxy. This view not only enabled Little Rock residents to save face, it also allowed them to believe that their actions and political commitments were not at issue. For the moderates, it also justified a politics of inaction sustained by the conviction that outsiders had precluded effective action on their part. "Being southern," as historian Sheldon Hackney has observed, "inevitably involves a feeling of persecution at times and a sense of being a passive, insignificant object of alien or impersonal forces." As a result, southerners have "fostered a world view that supports the denial of responsibility and locates threats to the region outside the region and threats to the person outside the self."[16]

In fact, the crisis over school desegregation was constructed by multiple actors, inside and outside of Little Rock, who often worked together to secure their goals. However much some citizens wished for a complete autonomy from "outsiders," Little Rock was inextricably linked to other parts of the state, the region, the nation, and the world. Indeed, some of the individuals who most fervently wished for isolation on the issue of race had worked energetically to forge economic, political, and cultural ties to various "outsiders." The terms used by many in Arkansas, however, precluded acknowledging this or discussing how to operate in an interdependent world divided by race and other significant social and cultural fissures.

In Little Rock, as in many other places in the South, the most common white plea was for more time—time to adjust, time to secure more social acceptance of racial change. A segregationist, for example, wrote to the *Arkansas Gazette* in 1955 and, citing biblical arguments against integration, expressed his belief that "we should wait for this until nearer the end of time. We do not want something that will cause our hearts to almost stand still and ache." In 1957, Governor Faubus pointed to the state's segregationist legislation and asked for time "to litigate these measures to final conclusions in order that we may see clearly and unmistakably what is the law of the land—either state or Federal." The plea for more time was a panacea for individuals who believed that the postponements they sought might become, in fact, indefinite ones.[17]

In the meantime, conflicts over school desegregation generated a great deal of political heat. That heat derived not only from the disturbing effects of racial change but also from their relationship to other transformations in American society and culture. In the postwar period adult southern whites and the region's male civic leaders found their power imperiled by the unsettling effects of changes in economic structures, the rise of a youth culture, the increasing power of national media, changing sexual mores and practices, and dramatic shifts in gender and family relations. Moreover, these domains of social and cultural life were densely interconnected. African American campaigns for increased rights and opportunities threatened to destabilize not only the southern system of race but also the class compact among whites that the system secured. Women were entering paid employment in growing numbers and participating in the public world of volunteer associations and social movements even as the dominant ideology proclaimed that their only legitimate place was at home.[18]

In the postwar period, changes in teen dating patterns and sexual practices meant that high schools became a critical site where young people
found intimate partners and spouses. Consequently, as David Goldfield
observed, the prospect of the racial integration of public schools "aroused
deep-seated fears that propinquity would ultimately become intimacy." As
more adolescents formed intense heterosexual pairs and decided to "go
steady," parents worried that the relationships would lead to premarital
sexual intercourse and tried to control their children's social world. Their
anxieties were well founded. Teen pregnancy rates skyrocketed, reaching
their twentieth-century peak in 1957.[19]

When Elizabeth Eckford and the other African American students
sought to enter Central High School, they were defying more than Arkansas's state sanctioned inequality in educational opportunity. Similarly,
when Hazel Bryan and other white antagonists at the school challenged
the right of black students to be there, they were defending a social order
different from the one their parents had experienced or imagined in their
youth. The defiant behavior of white antagonists in school provoked a range
of reactions in their parents, from unequivocal support to hostility. In the
civil rights struggle in Little Rock, children became significant political
actors, sometimes serving as surrogates for their parents and sometimes
representing their own concerns and goals.[20]

For all social groups, the law became a crucial venue for political action.
Because American courts have the authority to decide whether laws conform to the requirements of the federal and state constitutions and can
invalidate those that do not, judges at all levels have played a crucial role
in American politics and political culture. The centrality of the courts in
the formation and legitimation of political claims and public policies
makes them sites for struggles over fundamental political questions and social values. The role of the courts in defining and enabling the rights, responsibilities, and benefits of citizenship places them at the center of debates regarding racial and other hierarchies and gives them a central ideological
significance in the nation's political culture.

This study examines Little Rock as a site for the creation of a class-
conscious thinking about race that would inform "color-blind" law in the
South and the nation long after the decision in *Brown v. Board of Education*. From the conception of the Little Rock school desegregation plan to
the application of pupil placement policies, Little Rock's school officials
and civic leaders helped to forge the post-*Brown* era of "race-neutral" law

that was suffused with racial meanings and racist intentions. The focus on law, society, and political culture distinguishes this study from Tony Freyer's scholarship on Little Rock, in that it focuses less on the formal language of court decisions and more on the social logic of the laws and policies being contested, the cultural meanings found in the testimony in court cases, and the role of law in reflecting, legitimating, and transforming political rhetoric and social relations. In particular, it examines the middle-class ideologies revealed and enacted in the school board's policies and legal strategies and in the political actions of the moderates.[21]

Recently, scholars have offered persuasive analyses of the complexities of the resistance of southern whites to the egalitarianism of the civil rights movement while examining the recuperation of racist assumptions and practices in the accommodations of southern whites to the legacies of that movement. They stress the self-conscious adoption of race neutrality as a political vocabulary and legal strategy in the South's responses to African American demands for greater rights and opportunities. Focusing their analyses on class differences among southern whites, these historians have documented the role of white elites and upwardly mobile suburbanites in promoting white flight from the central cities and their schools, the rise of modern conservatism, and the embrace of an ostensibly race-neutral law and politics in the region and the nation. Although this study, like the others, examines class relations as a systematic aspect of New South politics since the *Brown* decision, it differs in that it also analyzes gender and sexuality as critical aspects of southern responses to racial challenge.[22]

Along with the arch segregationists, Little Rock's moderates clogged the courts with cases designed to thwart progressive court decisions and laws, and both factions pioneered in the use of litigation as a conservative political tool. In addition, both groups paved the way in the use of law breaking as a fundamental tactic for disaffected conservatives, a successful strategy that would become a staple of conservative politics in the years to come. Little Rock's civil rights activists, by contrast, used litigation as a critical form of protest directed at undermining social and political hierarchies and redefining the terms of political and legal discussions. In particular, they contested the legal formalism and racist implementation practices embedded in the school board's desegregation policies.[23]

Little Rock's business elite faced multiple challenges in its quest for economic and political power. Dramatic changes in the economy of the postwar South had disturbed customary social, political, and demographic

patterns. The displacement of rural workers of both races by mechanization on the plantations created pressures on business and government leaders to provide industrial jobs for whites who moved into the cities of Arkansas in the postwar period. Indeed, business and government leaders
embraced development as a priority for their state. After World War II, the
economic elite of Little Rock, in alliance with the state government,
worked to attract new businesses and jobs from outside the South. Governor Faubus wholly endorsed this goal, signing a law creating the Arkansas
Industrial Development Commission, which became, in the words of historian James Cobb, "one of the most aggressive and highly visible industrial recruitment agencies in the South." Faubus also supported an amendment to the state constitution that enabled local governments to finance
land acquisition and build facilities for the companies they lured from out
of state. Clearly, the support of state government was an integral part of
the development plans of men intent on forging the New South economy
in Arkansas.[24]

The control of politics and the uncontested right to define the public
good were therefore essential to the economic ambitions of business leaders. Moreover, as Elizabeth Jacoway has noted, Little Rock's business elite
"had just launched a movement to clean up city government and make it
more amenable to the needs of the business community." Business leaders
viewed both objectives of this movement as equivalent goals. Not surprisingly, they were hostile to the idea of sharing public power in the workplace or in the polity. Their "imagined community" was not in fact a democracy of white men. It was instead a hierarchy in which a politics of
deference to elite white men enabled those men to secure profits for themselves and jobs for others. For the business leaders, economic development
in a context of political inequality was necessary and sufficient for the creation of a just economic order and political stability in the region. Indeed,
their conviction that they were apostles of progress justified an exclusionary politics and sanctified their efforts to retain power at all costs.[25]

The civic elite expected deference from working-class people in the
workplace as well as in the political arena. The promotional literature used
by the Little Rock Chamber of Commerce in the 1950s touted the tractability of the city's white labor force. The city's economic leaders assured
corporate leaders considering a move to Arkansas that the state's "freedom
to work" amendment and its "anti-violence law" contributed to the "har-

monious industry-labor relationship" they would find in the state. More-over, the oversupply of labor, caused by mechanization in the state's rural areas, meant that workers would accept lower wages. As a result, employers would benefit because Little Rock not only had a "tremendous *quantity* of workers seeking industrial employment" but also offered workers whose rural roots "had [instilled] in them an inclination to work conscientiously at whatever tasks are assigned to them." These workers were "native-born and quick to learn; they are not susceptible to radical ideas."[26]

The values embraced by business leaders anticipated those that would later be labeled as neo-liberal. Their system of beliefs and practices pro-moted economic expansion as a social panacea, solidified the political pri-ority accorded to growth politics in urban America, combined *laissez-faire* pronouncements with business subsidies from government, and placed worker subordination, opposition to unions, and low wages at the center of its development policies. Little Rock's civic and economic elite regarded the issue of racial justice as a political threat to more important goals and took for granted that development would provide African Americans with an appropriate level of economic opportunity.

Little Rock's business leaders generally tried to exercise political power from behind the scenes, thus distancing themselves from public visibility and accountability. In this way, they could deny the connections between their economic and political roles and minimize the risks to their busi-nesses entailed in public activism. The businessmen were socially conserva-tive and sought to avoid public association with controversial issues. They hoped to keep segregation because they believed in racial hierarchies and in particular because challenges to the racial order could destabilize the system of power they had created. In a time of dramatic economic change, racial discrimination in employment operated to cushion the strain of transi-tion for working-class whites and thus reinforced elite claims to power in the emerging new order.[27]

Business leaders' actions revealed the assumptions and operations of a managerial masculinity characterized by an unshakeable sense of entitle-ment to public power and an overt contempt for others who sought a voice in the community's affairs. As Deborah Kerfoot has noted, "those for whom masculinity resonates most loudly appear to be so preoccupied with 'fixing' the world around them and others in it as to detract from the pos-sibilities of other forms of engagement." The civic elite's use of secrecy, manipulation, and deception to achieve its goals reflected a deep-seated anxiety that more democratic processes would erode its economic and political power and introduce profoundly unsettling values and modes of interaction. Local civic and business leaders' claims to represent reason, moderation, and the public good masked the fear and egoism that often compelled their actions. However dispassionate their public language may have appeared, theirs was a politics of panic and timidity, bespeaking a radical discomfort with anything but uncontested dominance.[28]

The crisis over school desegregation undermined the desire of civic leaders for unchallenged power as working-class whites mobilized openly against integration, defied federal authority, and voted for segregationist politicians, particularly in elections to the school board. Significantly, working-class segregationists employed racial rhetoric to express class-based grievances and used symbols of the Confederacy to signal their fealty to a region whose heritage of slavery, localism, and rebellion they embraced. Their rhetoric, in the words of historian Pete Daniel, invoked "a flawed history that conflated segregation, the Lost Cause, religion, and sex." The idea that African Americans might claim greater rights and opportunities created a "confrontation between Little Rock's working-class blacks and whites, who were competing for jobs, education, and respectability in a decade of great social change." It also pitted working-class resisters to integration against the local establishment.[29]

The members of that establishment viewed quality public education as a critical element in their industrial recruitment plan. Without good public schools, they believed, northern companies would not relocate managers and their families to Little Rock. Segregationists' threats to the existence and quality of the public schools frightened local developers as much as the public disorders orchestrated by segregationists to sustain massive resistance. As with other elements of the local elite's growth agenda, education required support from all levels of government, including the federal. This need for government support was intensified when the children of the baby boom era and of the rural migration to Little Rock markedly increased public school enrollments in the postwar era.

Local business and civic leaders wished to profit from interdependence in a national economy while maintaining the South's political isolation from a national polity and its racial arrangements. They held to a general belief in states' rights, although they were more than willing to accept federal funding for education and other public services when it was available on their terms. In fact, their hopes for social stasis in the midst of economic changes were utterly chimerical. As Virginia Scharff has cogently noted, "Markets and nations are creatures of motion. They require the circulation of people and money, goods and ideas." The proliferation of televisions in America's living rooms reduced local elites' ability to maintain their autonomy by giving racial conflicts national and international visibility.[30]

This study seeks to focus on various actors in the Little Rock story in order to understand its meanings in a new way. In particular, a broader comprehension of the crisis in Little Rock means taking the activism of white women much more seriously when analyzing the terms of public debates over race and education and when interpreting the outcomes of the crisis over school desegregation. The segregationist Mothers' League of Central High School orchestrated not only the harassment of African American students at Central High by white racist students; its members also worked to mobilize segregationist resentment and resistance within the white community. Once state and local segregationists orchestrated the closing of Little Rock's public high schools in September 1958, a group of indignant middle-class white women entered the political fray organized as the Women's Emergency Committee to Open Our Schools (WEC). The organization soon became a formidable political presence throughout the state. The WEC worked with local civic leaders to support open schools and gradualism in desegregation, although its more liberal leadership ultimately developed an agenda that differed in important respects from that pursued by the male moderate establishment. The WEC's deference to male civic leaders propped up the men's power and doomed the progressive vision of some WEC leaders. Moreover, the WEC's middle-class political appeals and priorities ultimately limited not only its progressive political vision but also its social base, as did the leaders' commitment to trying to end segregation while excluding African Americans from their own organization.

Examining businessmen's actions more systematically in relation to local social relations than has previously been done illuminates the institutional and ideological bases for their success in maintaining their dominance over local politics despite the growing opposition to their policies. Focusing on the relationship of male business elites to working-class whites, middle-class white women, and African Americans also highlights the importance of local considerations in motivating activism for or against desegregation and in shaping political rhetoric, goals, and outcomes. As the Little Rock case suggests, local conflicts developed not only over what should be done with respect to desegregating the schools but also over the interrelated questions of who was to exercise power in the community and what kind of community should be created in postwar Little Rock.[31]

More elusively, this study also reveals the operation of gender in the politics and social relations enacted by men throughout the crisis over school desegregation. Historians and the general public have become accustomed to the idea that gender as a power relation and cultural script shapes women's consciousness and motivates their actions, albeit in complex and sometimes contradictory ways. Men, however, have remained the "invisible gendered subject," in the words of Stephen Whitehead. That invisibility has obscured the fact that "American men's ceaseless quest for manhood" formed American organizations, traditions, associations, public policies and political systems, as numerous scholars have documented.[32]

That quest for manhood has also shaped men's social and political disputes. The different social backgrounds, political affiliations, and attitudes to race of the white men involved in the Little Rock crisis created profound conflicts. These conflicts centered in part on whether men would claim political authority as proponents of an ideology of progress centered on the economic and educational development of middle-class whites, or as defenders of racial purity and white working-class respectability. At the same time, men at all levels in the political hierarchy sought ways to assert their wills and protect themselves from the humiliation, material losses, and disempowerment they all associated with public defeats. Joane Nagel has noted the entrenched nature "of such masculine preoccupations as honor, cowardice, strength, face-saving, and manliness" in domains of competition among men. In Little Rock, these preoccupations became central obsessions, especially for the segregationists, as men fought for dominance for themselves and their interests.[33]

Lurking under the surface of southern white men's encounters with federal authority was the memory of Civil War defeat. Although their honor had been propped up by almost a century of memorialization, the hundreds of statues of Confederate military leaders had not effaced the anxieties about confrontations with powerful outsiders just below the surface of their political consciousness. Male moderates used a rhetoric of victimization to express strong desires for a respite from the authority of others, for a system of impermeable boundaries that would protect them from "outsiders" to their world. Male segregationists' use of masculinist and martial rhetoric bespoke the politics of manhood enacted in their conflicts with federal officials and with Little Rock's moderates. Moreover, the intense preoccupation of southern white men with issues of dominance, submission, and honor fueled a political culture of anger and retribution that shaped their actions and public statements at critical moments.[34]

This study pays particular attention to gendered political rhetoric and iconography so as to examine more closely the values, strategies, and emotional cultures of various groups and organizations. Clearly, some white activists against integration and their allied politicians chose their language and symbols opportunistically and even cynically in order to appeal to or intensify popular fears and prejudices. Many of the ideas advanced by segregationists, however, revealed the gendered anxieties, values, and goals of both political leaders and constituents with particular clarity. This anxiety was not new in the postwar period. From the specter of black male rapists invoked to justify segregation, disfranchisement, and lynching in the Jim Crow era to the demonization of "welfare mothers" pioneered by Orval Faubus, gender has provided a vocabulary for the racial fears and prejudices of whites in the South and the nation.[35]

While segregationists relied on fundamentalist Protestantism to provide religious justification and emotional intensity for their racist views, moderates sought to marginalize the voices of liberal ministers and others who supported an egalitarian racial morality. For moderates, the introduction of new political actors and of different values (of "morality" itself) into the political economy was at odds with modern masculine identities whose ideals derived from marketplace goals and practices. Moreover, because masculine success was to be achieved primarily within dominant economic and political institutions, the performance of middle-class masculinity was inextricably linked with advancing the values and interests of those institutions.[36]

This book examines political disputes over race and schools in relation to interconnected social inequalities, the contested boundaries of political authority in a federal system, shifts in American law, and the rhetoric used by activists to interpret and shape the contours of their social worlds. It does so by understanding that social and economic class is important in shaping the perspectives and actions of both middle-class and working-class people, that men as well as women construct and reflect gender identities and relations, and that the construction of racial formations in the South involved whites and African Americans. Even as it offers a different view of the meanings and consequences of African American and NAACP activism in Little Rock and the United States, this book focuses mainly and deliberately on the ideologies, actions, and emotional investments of whites in Little Rock, the state of Arkansas, and elsewhere who failed to rise to the moral and political challenge posed by the efforts of African Americans to eradicate racial hierarchy.

This work differs significantly from studies by other scholars who have investigated many of the groups and issues involved in the crisis over desegregation in Little Rock, but who have not offered the kind of systematic and interconnected social and cultural analysis developed in this book. The Women's Emergency Committee and the Mothers' League of Central High School, for example, have been investigated separately by scholars but have not occupied a central place in their examinations of the political dynamics of the crisis over desegregation. Political historians have also treated segregationist activists, most of whom were working class, as the group responsible for mobilizing class identities and ideologies politically. C. Fred Williams and David Chappell have concluded that class was the primary issue for Little Rock's arch segregationists, but do not analyze closely the ways in which southern whites' class-based politics were linked to racial hierarchies in the postwar culture and politics of Little Rock, choosing instead to ask which social relationships were most important during the crisis. The politics and ideologies of business elites, by contrast, have been so taken for granted that they have not been investigated seriously as an expression of gendered class identities. In all cases, the emotional cultures of political movements have received little scrutiny as significant sources of insight into politics.[37]

The book begins by describing the murky origins of Little Rock's school desegregation plan and the exclusionary politics and social visions those origins reveal. The segregationist mobilization activated by the integration crisis in Hoxie, Arkansas in 1955–1956 and the resistance laws endorsed by Orval Faubus in 1956 and early 1957 provided the basis for the sustained campaign of massive resistance to desegregation in Little Rock that began in the summer of 1957. Chapter 2 focuses particularly on the segre-

gationist campaign and on the politics of confrontation with federal officials it provoked. Concerns about gender and sexuality were central to the
emotional culture, the rhetoric, and the actions of segregationists and thus
receive particular attention.

When segregationists shifted their resistance from the streets to the hallways of Central High School, they caused critical dilemmas for the moderate establishment. Chapter 3 analyzes the politics of school discipline as it
reveals the assumptions, goals, and tactics that characterized the efforts of
white moderate, segregationist, and African American activists to advance
their respective political goals. This chapter, in particular, demonstrates the
centrality of the Mothers' League of Central High School to the emotional
culture and politics of the massive resistance movement to desegregation in
Little Rock. The closing of the public high schools in the fall of 1958 raised
the stakes of the opposition to integration in the schools and led to the
mobilization of middle-class white women in Little Rock to reopen the
schools. Chapters 4 and 5 consider the political shifts that were revealed
and produced as segregationists directed their attacks against public school
administrators and teachers. The political shifts reveal the quest for social
legitimacy, moral authority over children, and political power that motivated segregationist activists and prompted some of their most significant
political blunders. Chapter 6 examines the contested politics of tokenism
and gradualism in integration that developed after schools reopened in
1959, focusing particularly on the dynamic nature of the politicization
that occurred as white women and African Americans sought greater power
in Little Rock politics.

The history of Little Rock's school crisis reveals the dense interconnec-
tions between various social inequalities and disputes over cultural values
and public policies. When segregationists defended white supremacy as necessary to sexual and moral order and white male moderates defended their
racial and gender privilege as the prerequisite for economic and social progress, they acknowledged the complex and contested social relations that
shaped their disputes. When African Americans and white middle-class
women sought to change the terms of public discussion and broaden the social basis of political power in Little Rock and Arkansas, they faced opposition
not only from arch segregationists but also from many male moderates.

The activism of African Americans, Women's Emergency Committee
leaders, and white liberals was suspect precisely because it threatened to

deploy a concept of political morality and the public good at odds with the values supported by the city's traditional male elite. The civil rights movement, its rhetoric based in democratic and Christian promises of human equality, offered one of the most powerful threats not only to racial hierarchy but also to the exclusion of alternative values and marginalized social groups from the public sphere. An analysis of the Little Rock crisis over school desegregation reveals how various actors and organizations interpreted and contested the meanings of legal equality in a context of political and social inequalities. It also reminds us that the past contained multiple possibilities and perspectives and examines why some perspectives received little opportunity for a hearing.

The moderates' great success in maintaining their power has masked their equally stunning failures of vision and courage. Racist assumptions and narrow economic perspectives informed all aspects of local governance in postwar Little Rock from the educational policies pursued by school superintendent Virgil Blossom and Little Rock's civic leaders to the development agendas embraced by business elites to the legal arguments pursued by local school authorities. Investigating the dynamics and outcomes of Little Rock's social conflicts discloses their formative role in the construction of America's late twentieth-century neo-liberal political order.

CHAPTER ONE

Mapping Change: Little Rock
Forges a Desegregation Plan

> With the confident air of a high pressure salesman Dr. Blos-
> som produced charts, maps and statistics describing where
> Negro and white high school pupils lived. He explained
> that... attendance areas could be developed which would
> result in maximum avoidance of the mixing of the races.
>
> —Rev. Colbert Cartwright[1]

In 1953, the Little Rock School Board hired Virgil Blossom, then director of schools in Fayetteville, as its new superintendent, a decision that
would profoundly shape the future direction of school politics in Little
Rock. A former football player, the tall and burly Blossom was physically
imposing. Willful, visionary, and ambitious, the school administrator could
project a daunting political presence. A former student at Fayetteville High
School, who had been sent to Blossom's office after one too many infractions, reported this encounter with his school's principal: "Mr. Blossom
just talked to me, but as he talked I started getting smaller and he started
getting bigger. By the time he got through, he was the biggest man I ever
saw." Regarding Blossom's "conference methods," another observer noted
that he had "played tackle on the football team of the University and he
still relies on power plays."[2]

Blossom used such strategies of domination in policy discussions as
well. Arkansas Council for Human Relations executive director Nathan
Griswold reported that school patrons often reported difficulty in "getting
through" to Blossom and that the superintendent "seemed quite uneasy in
any meeting where he was not in charge." When Blossom spoke before
community groups about Little Rock's school desegregation plan, for ex-

ample, he presented it as a given ("the way it's to be," in the words of businessman Grainger Williams) and managed to exclude differing views or
probing questions. At the same time, Blossom's verbal dominance often
masked deeply rooted insecurities and ambivalences. As Griswold noted,
he had "an ego that was hungrier than most." Blossom's contradictory tem-
perament would play an important role in his state's volatile politics of race
in schools, reflecting in microcosm the confidence and caution, hubris and
fear that characterized Little Rock's political and economic leaders in the
postwar era.[3]

Those contradictions marked moderate responses to the issue of school
desegregation from the local to the national level. From Virgil Blossom to
President Dwight D. Eisenhower, moderate white male leaders sought to
confine the legal, political, and social effects of the 1954 U.S. Supreme
Court decision in *Brown v. Board of Education* so as to maintain their own
authority. At the same time that they faced challenges from local African
Americans and civil rights leaders to realize the promise of equality entailed in the Court's ruling they also faced, throughout the South, immediate strong segregationist resistance to racial change. Those sources of opposition intensified the already fervent conservatism of moderates in Little
Rock and elsewhere.[4]

No group demonstrated their conservatism more than Little Rock's
business leaders, who were closely tied to Blossom from the beginning of
his tenure as superintendent. Indeed, they had played a critical role in recruiting him and working closely with him as he established his authority
in the school system and defined his role in the community. In December
1953, the leaders of the city's power structure hosted a dinner for Blossom
that featured Arkansas Governor Francis Cherry and Winthrop Rockefeller, chairman of the Arkansas Industrial Development Commission, as
speakers. Blossom reciprocated, speaking before men's civic groups, urging
them to provide "citizen leadership" for the public schools and offering his
support for the business development strategies advanced by local economic elites. In return for his efforts on their behalf, he was named the
Little Rock Man of the Year for 1955. Everett Tucker, Jr., manager of industrial development for the Little Rock Chamber of Commerce, con-
gratulated him on his "well deserved honor... that I and your many friends
in the Chamber of Commerce are delighted to see you receive."[5]

White businessmen also played a critical role in recruiting and raising funds for candidates to run for vacant positions on the school board. Although these business leaders believed that their activism was but an expression of their civic generosity, it is clear that they expected new school board members to share the views of Little Rock's power structure with respect to the operation of the schools. As a general rule, this business leadership was averse to taking risks and was convinced that race relations in Little Rock were generally positive. Throughout the desegregation process, board members would consult exclusively with those who had put them in office.[6]

Little Rock's business leadership had a contradictory relationship to the city's African Americans, acceding to their requests at times while excluding them from meaningful power over issues important to blacks. In 1950 Georg Iggers, a white professor at Little Rock's all-black Philander Smith College, wrote a letter to the editor of the *Arkansas Gazette*, asking that the Little Rock Public Library be integrated so that his students could have the books that were necessary to their studies. Neither the college library, which depended primarily on white donations for its support, nor the black public library, which had few books and was open only a few hours a week, was adequate. In response, the public library board met privately and agreed to allow African American adults access to the "white" library on an unrestricted basis.[7]

In response to his success in persuading the library board to integrate its facility, the local NAACP invited Iggers to join. Subsequently, he successfully negotiated with the owners of downtown department stores to remove the racial designations from their drinking fountains. The concession was important to African Americans because it removed a hated symbol of white disrespect and it also encouraged white moderates and liberals to believe that changes could occur without litigation or white backlash. For moderates, these changes exemplified white voluntarism, a keystone in their racial politics. For liberals, both white and African American, such reforms offered hope that school desegregation in Little Rock would also proceed smoothly. Historian John Kirk concluded that the changes were limited concessions designed "to enable whites to retain control over the segregated system by self-regulating reforms" and to avert more systematic changes enforced by federal courts.[8]

White voluntarism did not suffice to address African American concerns, especially those related to housing. Little Rock's business leadership actively supported racially based urban renewal policies opposed by many blacks. In a series of interrelated decisions beginning in the late 1940s, the city razed housing in African American neighborhoods and built public housing and recreational facilities for blacks on the far east side of Little Rock. As noted by the *Arkansas Gazette*, these decisions channeled "residential growth into the most desirable patterns," moving and directing the African American population to the east and the south in the interests of "natural expansion" while reducing "the chance of conflict with the rapid growth of white communities to the west." In short, city officials did their best to segregate neighborhoods by race during the period in which school authorities implemented school desegregation.[9]

When Little Rock's business leaders targeted a black neighborhood near Dunbar High School for urban renewal in 1952, African American women organized against the proposal. One woman wrote to the *Arkansas Gazette* protesting the city's plan to take her property and that of the other homeowners in her neighborhood in order to make the land available for private development and a new school and community center:

> We have given almost everything we have except our very life blood over a long period of years to pay for these homes, improvements and educate our children.... Is there a law anywhere in the United States that says one private property owner must sell what he has so another private owner can buy it to make a profit?

The protestors received support from the *State Press*, an African American weekly owned by L. C. and Daisy Bates, which accused city officials of trying "to centralize all Negroes in one area and forget about them while the city progresses in another direction." As this editorial implies, "progress" was a highly racialized notion in the postwar South. In this instance, as in others, African Americans paid the price for white advancement.[10]

The problem of providing adequate school facilities and programs for African American students occasioned continuous conflicts between civil rights leaders and the city's governing elite. The policies pursued by city leaders over the half century preceding the *Brown* decision typified those of the South in the era of segregation. While officials saw the provision of education to white children as a civic responsibility to be shouldered by southern taxpayers, they expected private philanthropies and African American parents to assume a significant proportion of the costs for educating black students. Over time, Little Rock's black parents grew tired of the burdens imposed by a system of partially privatized, poorly funded, and segregated black schools and sought improvement through both equalization and integration.

For decades, Little Rock school officials had relied on northern philanthropy and fundraising efforts by local blacks to supplement inadequate public funding for African American schools. When Dunbar Jr./Sr. High School was built in 1929, part of its $400,000 cost was provided by a grant from the Julius Rosenwald Fund. Little Rock High School (later renamed Central High School), which was built in 1927 at a cost of $1,500,000, was fully funded by local and state taxpayers. Public funds bought more books for the Little Rock High School library than for the Dunbar High School library, which had a more vocational curriculum than that offered at Little Rock High. Dunbar lacked the science labs, equipment, gymnasium, band instruments, and other resources that school officials funded for Little Rock High.

African Americans in Little Rock started asking for a gym and health center for Dunbar High School in 1938. In 1944, school authorities suggested that they seek private funding. In 1949, officials finally provided public money for the facilities. A survey of Dunbar alumni in 1981 reveals the deep anger felt by blacks who were compelled to volunteer their time and labor when school authorities denied adequate funds for the school: "Staff, students, and parents had to spend too much time raising money and collecting student fees for needs that the district should have supplied." As this statement indicates, the systematic "privatizing" of America's public schools began with the South's historic refusal to assume public responsibility for the education of black children.[11]

In 1951, the Little Rock School Board had closed the African American Gibbs Elementary School, calling it a "dangerous fire trap," but had not provided for its replacement. The board also refused to build a school for children of African American families removed to the Granite Mountain housing project as a result of urban renewal, claiming that the county should provide the school. Meanwhile, the board spent $250,000 to build a new field house for Little Rock High School. Board member Edwin Barron said that much of the money from the last two bond issues had been spent on black schools and that the money to build a school for the housing project residents would come at the expense of white schools and students. The state, however, disagreed, passing a law placing the proposed school for the Granite Mountain housing project within the boundaries of the Little Rock school district.[12]

African American leaders and white liberals formed the interracial Little Rock Council on Schools and issued a report in 1952 documenting the poor state of public schools for Little Rock's black children. The report focused particularly on the situation at Dunbar Jr./Sr. High School and concluded that the school's facilities, staffing levels, curriculum, and budget were inferior to those in white schools. In 1950–51, for example, the state and the local school board spent $164.21 per pupil at Dunbar High School and $225.17 per pupil at Little Rock High School. As a result of inadequate funding, African American students, whose achievement test scores in second grade were nearly as high as those of white Little Rock second graders, lagged substantially behind whites by the sixth grade. After that, the gap widened even further.[13]

According to the drafters of the study, equalizing the spending for all students would be inefficient, expensive, and insufficient to the goals of equal educational opportunity. Providing Dunbar High School students with the staffing and equipment necessary to duplicate the courses at Little Rock High School and at Technical High School, an all-white vocational school, would entail prohibitive and unnecessary costs. The report went further, indicting segregation itself as a barrier to equal educational opportunities. Black children's separation from "the cultural advantages of the privileged majority" impaired their ability to acquire "that part of education which the white child learns not necessarily through formal instruction but acquires more indirectly from fellow students and teachers."[14]

Its report completed, the Council on Schools proposed informally to the Little Rock School Board that it consider opening some classes at Little Rock High School to selected African American students. The council, along with the local NAACP branch, hoped that such informal negotiation would enable it to persuade the board to begin the process of dismantling segregation without a lawsuit. For reasons that remain unclear, local NAACP branch president Thad D. Williams announced the proposal to the press, stating that the NAACP planned to end school segregation in

Little Rock through "peaceful negotiation." The school board, which was extremely reluctant to discuss racial issues in public, then declined to hold a private meeting with representatives of the Council on Schools scheduled for February 20, 1952.[15]

Instead, school superintendent Harry A. Little wrote a letter to the school board on that date, taking issue with some of the conclusions drawn by the Council on Schools. He justified the broader curricula at Little Rock High School and Technical High School by noting that Dunbar offered courses not available at the two white high schools, including bricklaying and trade laundry. The differences in per pupil expenditures, he claimed, derived solely from the fact that some black teachers had lower salaries because they had not completed degrees at accredited colleges. He further attributed black students' failure to achieve at the same scholastic level as white students solely to factors within the African American community: irregular school attendance, "poor home conditions," and inadequate instruction by black teachers. Little further claimed that "many of the colored teachers who are average teachers for their race could not qualify for teachers in comparison with our white schools." A few months later, the board met formally with representatives of the interracial council, but in a closed session decided not to adopt its recommendations, in part because Little was so strongly opposed to any integration.[16]

In response, the local NAACP chapter voted to file suit against the Little Rock Board of Education. The national office of the organization, however, opposed this action, urging the Little Rock branch to await the decisions in the promising cases that were in litigation and that would eventually form the basis for the Supreme Court's historic finding in 1954. The local NAACP leadership agreed to rescind its resolution to file suit, suggesting the reciprocal relationship and the potential for conflict between grass-roots activism and national civil rights leadership over the issue of school desegregation. This early activism by local leaders gives the lie to the later assertion by segregationists that the national NAACP foisted its desegregation goals on southern blacks who would otherwise have been content with their lot.[17]

When the United States Supreme Court held unanimously on May 17, 1954 that public school segregation violated the constitutional requirement that all citizens be treated equally before the law, public authorities in Arkansas generally stressed the necessity of compliance. Governor Francis Cherry dissociated his state from the talk of massive resistance developing elsewhere in the South. Carroll C. Hollensworth, speaker of the Arkansas House of Representatives, concluded that "it is immaterial whether we agree with the court's decision or not. We are confronted with the necessity of making our laws conform."[18]

Little Rock School Board President Foster Vinyard reacted with surprise, claiming that the Supreme Court ruling had caught the board off guard because it had "been working on the idea of equal facilities." Indeed, the school district was in the process of implementing a costly school construction program predicated on equalizing racially segregated facilities and meeting the increase in school population caused by the postwar baby boom. School superintendent Virgil Blossom claimed that their "position at the present time is probably one of the best in the South." In short, they had come closer than others in the South to complying with the 1896 decision in *Plessy v. Ferguson*. They had done so, of course, in response to the NAACP's national success in litigating and threatening cases based on segregated "equality."[19]

Once the high Court outlawed racial segregation in schools, Blossom determined that Little Rock would become the model for southern compliance with the new standard, a decision rooted equally in his limited progressive vision and in personal ambition. On May 20, 1954, the Little Rock School Board decided to abide by the decision as soon as the Supreme Court had developed more specific guidelines. The board also stated that it would begin conducting research to assist its desegregation efforts and that it would develop school attendance areas "consistent with the location of white and colored pupils" for its current and future schools. At the outset, then, the board envisioned desegregation within a system whose schools would retain racial identities, defined in part by patterns of residential segregation and in part by school administrators' decisions regarding school locations and attendance areas. In its public statement, the board praised Little Rock's citizens for having "the understanding and tolerance required to solve any difficult problem" and solicited their assistance in the "creation of an integrated school program required as a result of the Supreme Court Decision."[20]

From the beginning, however, the school board members indicated that they were initiating desegregation efforts only because the federal court ruling left them no choice. The board members' open distaste for desegregation created an atmosphere in which only African Americans and a few white ministers were willing to offer an ethical justification for compliance. Ultimately, the school officials' rationale of forced compliance to federal law left them vulnerable to the politics of resentment that would feed the segregationist South's twentieth-century "lost cause" and provided them with no argument for even gradual desegregation when Arkansas whites, including many in Little Rock, decided that federal authority could be resisted successfully.[21]

The school board's reluctance to initiate desegregation also fostered conflict with African American leaders. As early as August 1954, Wiley Branton, a lawyer who served as the chair of the Arkansas NAACP Legal Redress Committee, asked for a public meeting with the Little Rock School Board to discuss its desegregation plans. The school board refused the request for a public meeting, but did meet with the committee privately on September 9. Branton and others in the local branch of the NAACP assured the board that they did not plan to initiate a lawsuit, but petitioned the board to begin desegregation "as speedily as possible" and offered their assistance in the process. Worried that the school board would adopt the "wait and see" approach endorsed by Governor Cherry, Branton observed that "we can make plans and studies forever," an assertion that annoyed Blossom, who stated that the board would announce its policies and timetables after it had completed its studies. While he denied any intentions to delay, school board member Edwin Barron said that they could not "be pushed in this matter, because we are waiting on the U.S. Supreme Court to tell us how and when to end segregation."[22]

However reluctant school officials in Little Rock were to move forward, they offered more promise for change than their counterparts in the plantation areas of eastern Arkansas. There, local landowners and the politicians they helped to elect had ensured that black schools were woefully underfunded. By 1955, eastern Arkansas elites were in a quandary: they knew that equalizing black and white schools in their areas would be quite costly, but hoped that pressures for integration might abate if black schools were improved significantly. They tried to get the state of Arkansas to increase the sales tax and use the money to benefit those areas that had been most negligent in funding African American schools. The state legislature refused to do so, instead passing a law requiring that property tax rates—which were especially low in eastern Arkansas—be assessed at the same rate across the state. A March 1955 editorial in the *Arkansas Democrat* had justified the legislative initiative by accusing Mississippi County and others like it in eastern Arkansas of evading "its fair share of school financing."[23]

Even worse, eastern Arkansas was exporting its educational problems as it mechanized its system of farm labor. A reduced demand for workers sent many families to the cities of Arkansas and to other states. Little Rock received many impoverished and poorly educated migrants from rural areas of eastern Arkansas. In March 1955, social workers provided information to the Little Rock School Board regarding the problems presented by the large number of needy children who had moved to the Little Rock district in the previous few years. Because migrant families were often ineligible for unemployment compensation or for welfare, their poverty was dire. The caseworkers saw both possibilities and serious obstacles for students from these displaced families:

> Many of these children show a keen desire to learn, but each faces many difficulties in his school life such as failure to be accepted by his peers, changing schools, non-nutritious lunches, or none at all, inadequate clothing. It naturally follows that these children present many disciplinary problems.

Since so many of the migrant families were African American, there was a greater tendency for school officials to equate poverty and poor academic preparation with race. In retrospect, it is surprising that the problems created for urban school districts by rural displacement received so little public attention.[24]

Arkansas officials continued to hope that a decision to obey the constitutional principle asserted in the 1896 ruling in *Plessy v. Ferguson* would obviate the need to comply with the *Brown* decision. In August 1955, for example, Richard B. McCulloch, attorney for the Hughes Special School District, told school superintendents at the Arkansas Education Association meeting that they could not simply "stand by and do nothing." He said that attempts to defy or change the Supreme Court's decision would be futile but that if local people could decide for themselves and "outside agitators stay out," then "Negro children will be provided facilities that are entirely adequate." He urged the school superintendents to consult with "leading citizens" of both races and then "carry out the advice." A quintessential moderate, McCullough continued to believe that African Americans in Arkansas would not press the issue of school desegregation or anything else opposed by white leaders. Ultimately, McCullough and other Arkansans would find that it was not wise to build public policies on such racial fictions.[25]

As Arkansas leaders had been pointing out for quite some time, equalizing facilities was no simple matter. In the fall of 1953, the Arkansas Education Department had estimated that it would cost $21 million to equalize black facilities. Indeed, the day after the decision in *Brown v. Board of Education*, the *Arkansas Gazette* ran a story emphasizing the high costs of equalization and the difficulties of achieving it, given the poverty of the South. Arkansas, for example, ranked eighth in the nation in percentage of income devoted to education, while coming in just ahead of Mississippi (which finished last) in personal income. Its resources already stretched thin, Arkansas still lagged behind most of the nation in school funding. Given this context and the likelihood that federal courts would not allow southern officials to adopt separate but equal as a default strategy, those superintendents who shared McCullough's beliefs and followed his advice might find themselves incurring unanticipated costs and risks.[26]

Because the Little Rock school district was the largest and most politically visible in the state, its desegregation decisions would likely serve as models and provide a political barometer for the state. In late 1956, a school superintendent from Union County expressed the anxiety of officials in Arkansas who wanted to resist the *Brown* decision, stating that he did not "like to see a leading community like Little Rock take the lead too fast... In the end, other communities will have to follow suit." Indeed, by August 1957 the Citizens' Councils of Arkansas, its anxieties heightened by the impending desegregation of Little Rock's Central High School, petitioned Governor Faubus to use the State Sovereignty Commission to prevent integration in that school because integration there would serve as a significant precedent for other districts in the state. Ultimately, segregationists' fears about integration would sound the death knell for the autonomy from state interference initially promised by Faubus.[27]

Like many moderates in Little Rock and elsewhere, President Eisenhower was uncomfortable with the overt social conflict engendered when African Americans sought educational rights through federal court orders. Although he expressed an abstract commitment to equal rights and supported school desegregation in Washington, D. C., the president never spoke favorably about the decision in *Brown v. Board of Education.* Moreover, he often wished that a "change in heart" had preceded that landmark judgment and expressed sympathy for southern whites who were emotionally wedded to segregation. In 1953, for example, he said to South Carolina Senator Jimmy Byrnes that he did not believe "that prejudices, even palpably unjustified prejudices, will succumb to compulsion." As a result of his conviction that prejudice was the fundamental problem, Eisenhower was reluctant to sponsor or use what he called "punitive legislation" to eradicate discrimination.[28]

In these statements, President Eisenhower echoed the desires of many whites for change to come only as they themselves willed it and after an indeterminate process of "education" in which they were to assume no role. His solicitousness of white feelings went beyond a political expediency rooted in a nascent southern strategy of the Republican Party. It also reflected his close personal and professional ties to southern white men, men with whom he had served in war and with whom he worked in the White House. According to Frederic Morrow, the president's sole African American adviser, when Eisenhower was inclined to act on civil rights, his old friends would persuade him otherwise. The power of discussions in "close personal surroundings or in the intimacy of a bridge game" meant that his views on race were "colored by his background and his friends."[29]

Eisenhower faced continuing pressure to meet with African American leaders and to use the moral authority of his office to advance school desegregation. As southern resistance to desegregation made blacks vulnerable to economic coercion and violent reprisals, these pressures increased. Eisenhower, who did not share African Americans' sense of urgency, put off their requests for meetings until civil rights became less salient as a public issue. Furthermore, he refused to denounce the violence that haunted black lives, citing the responsibilities of his office as his reason for not speaking out against racial violence. Implicitly, he took the position that black safety would have to be subordinated to institutional and national priorities he deemed more important.[30]

Eisenhower also received frequent requests to place the moral stature of the presidency behind interracial meetings focused on school desegregation. In 1956, the president said that he would not do so "because mere discussion was not enough, and that action was necessary after that kind of discussion." Frederic Morrow expressed the administration's preoccupation with its image in a later diary entry, noting that it was still weighing the risks and benefits of such a meeting: "If the dignity of the Presidential office were loaned to such an occasion, and the occasion failed, this could mean a very serious loss of prestige and dignity." Morrow accurately reflected the Eisenhower administration's reasoning on race in the 1950s. Eisenhower viewed the maintenance of the credibility and power of the presidency as more important than (and in conflict with) the prerogatives of the office of the president to advance public school desegregation in the south.[31]

When segregationists used violence to thwart school desegregation in Clinton, Tennessee and Mansfield, Texas in 1956, Eisenhower responded by claiming that "extremists on both sides" were preventing "reasonable, logical" progress toward the "equality of men." According to Eisenhower, the resistant segregationists and "the people who want to have the whole matter settled today" were equally responsible for drowning out the voices of "people of goodwill." In a measured but angry rejoinder, Thurgood Marshall wrote to Eisenhower, stating that he was certain that the president did not "mean to equate lawless mobs with federal courts as 'extremists.'" Marshall noted that the conflict was a "question of unlawful violent opposition against the orders of duly constituted federal courts. These are the only 'two [sides]' involved."[32]

The president also declined to intervene in either Tennessee or Texas, despite the violence that had developed. In Tennessee, state and local officials used strong law enforcement measures and put down the violence. Desegregation of the schools proceeded peacefully thereafter. In Texas, by contrast, Governor Allan Shivers used the Texas Rangers to stop desegregation and restore order. Because local officials had not sought court injunctions to protect the desegregation process and, as a result, no district court had requested federal enforcement assistance, the Eisenhower administration believed it had little authority to act. Attorney General Brownell believed that an intervention outside the strict requirements of *Brown II* might have led to a federal court decision opposed to such intervention and would have cost the administration credibility in school cases.[33]

Historian Michal Belknap, however, has concluded that the Civil Rights Acts of 1866, which protected citizens from conspiracies to deny their civil rights, provided the administration with sufficient authority to act in Mansfield, Texas and similar cases. He noted that Shivers had been "defying federal authority" by impeding the "implementation of a desegregation order from a federal court." The administration's position that states should assume the responsibility for enforcing civil rights and ensuring public safety ignored the "fact that southern authorities repeatedly failed to protect blacks from violent interference with the exercise of rights supposedly guaranteed them by the federal Constitution." Eisenhower feared that someday court decisions and southern resistance would necessitate his action. When the federal courts mandated the desegregation of the bus system in Montgomery, Alabama in 1956, Eisenhower privately worried that "Eventually a district court is going to cite someone for contempt, and then we are going to be up against it."[34]

In the meantime, the Little Rock School Board went ahead with its desegregation initiative, referred to by supporters and opponents alike as the Blossom Plan. This reflected the crucial role the superintendent played in formulating it as well as his conviction that its success would provide the measure of his own worth. Business leader Everett Tucker said later that "Mr. Blossom was sort of a loner, and I don't mean this in a critical way, but I think Mr. Blossom evolved this plan pretty much on his own." He further concluded that if the pressure to desegregate had come from "a different type [of] personality [than Blossom], I rather doubt that the School Board . . . would have insisted" on implementing the plan. Race relations leader Nathan Griswold noted the desegregation plan's importance to Blossom: "To defend it, to implement it, to anticipate the plaudits it should bring gave him a sense of mission." Forrest Rozzell, director of the Arkansas Education Association, agreed: "The Blossom Plan—he could see it in headlines and quotation marks."[35]

Until the Little Rock School Board had to present its desegregation proposal in court early in 1956, the plan lacked specificity and did not circulate publicly in written form. Even after the 1956 trial, the language of the desegregation plan remained vague on critical points until the board was forced to implement it. Prior to its formal submission in court, its contours were revealed in private meetings and public talks given by Blossom. In those conversations, Blossom apparently presented divergent interpretations of the desegregation plan and expressed different concerns to different audiences, promoting an initial optimism in the African American community regarding his intention to support meaningful change.[36]

The Little Rock School Board's early discussions with whites reflected the anxieties of moderates forced to take risks in a freighted situation. These conversations, always held privately, focused on creating a desegregation plan acceptable to the courts and to local whites while keeping as much power in the hands of the board as was politically possible. From the beginning, Blossom feared that a violent opposition to desegregation might develop unless the board proceeded slowly. After he conveyed his concerns in a meeting with the then all-white Little Rock Ministerial Alliance in 1954, the Rev. Colbert Cartwright urged him not to delay desegregation too long out of "an unconscious white bias," adding, "I find as a white person that often I tend to want to go even more slowly in race relations than events later indicate was necessary."[37]

Blossom, however, was from the outset determined to do as little as the law permitted. Although an early proposal suggested that Little Rock's process of desegregation might begin in 1956, it also required that the new high schools under construction—one designated for blacks and another in the affluent western part of the city—be completed before desegregation would begin. The latter school, later named Hall High School, would have only whites in its original attendance zone. At the outset, Blossom based his plan on a class-based gradualism that protected Hall High School as an all-white middle-class institution. Whatever the start date, Blossom and the board made it clear that they would not adopt any desegregation policy until the Supreme Court had handed down its implementation decision in *Brown II*.[38]

By the summer of 1955, Virgil Blossom had apparently devised a formal plan for desegregation to submit to the Little Rock School Board. The question of when and how the proposal was approved, however, remains open. In all formal court documents and testimony, the school board claimed it had endorsed the proposal in a meeting held May 24, 1955. If so, the board held a closed session and did not announce its results publicly. Indeed, Blossom said in an interview in the *Arkansas Democrat* on June 1 that the board was still working on its desegregation plan and was not ready to reveal it. The day before, the same paper reported that the board was "unofficially" working on a desegregation plan just in case the courts should ask it to present one. The claim that the proposal was approved on May 24 enabled the board to assert in court that the desegregation plan had been designed before the Supreme Court endorsed the principle of "all deliberate speed" in its *Brown II* decision.[39]

Moreover, the moderates on the school board apparently decided not to seek the consent of Dale Alford, the only staunch segregationist on the board, for their proposal. The approval of the desegregation plan became a campaign issue in 1958 when Alford ran for the United States Congress on a platform endorsing massive resistance to desegregation. When moderates supporting the incumbent Brooks Hays confronted Alford with his "record" in support of the Blossom Plan, he denied any such support. In fact, Alford said he did not remember any meeting convened to discuss the desegregation plan and charged that the others on the school board often failed to notify him of meetings. Indeed, when the school board provided a copy of the plan to the federal court in 1956, the names listed at the bottom were those who had served on the board before Alford was elected in March 1955. When the FBI requested a copy of the plan in 1957, the school board sent the same one. Even under legal compulsion to reveal the names of the board members who had approved the desegregation plan, the board did not include the name of the segregationist.[40]

As Blossom and the school board developed the desegregation plan, they incorporated into the plan their concern that desegregation not impair the educational experiences of white students (usually expressed in terms of the best education for all students) and made changes in response to some white fears. The most important concession to the latter involved the decision to begin desegregation at the high school level and then move gradually to junior high schools and finally to elementary schools. According to Paul Fair, an administrator in the school system, some white parents of grade school students expressed the fear that their children would experience violence at the hands of African American students. The belief that high school students would be better able to defend themselves justified the decision to begin at that level, although the board's belief that the small number of high schools involved would make the process administratively easier also informed its reasoning.[41]

Starting with the high schools would also minimize the number of African Americans who would be entering previously all-white schools. School board members believed this would serve two interrelated goals: maintaining educational standards for whites and minimizing political mobilization against the desegregation plan. According to one board member, when they mapped residency patterns by race, they found that blacks resided in neighborhoods containing several white elementary schools and that "solving the problem by attendance areas was thus rendered impossible." The board adopted the Blossom Plan because with it "we could hold the number of negroes down, screen them carefully, and meet with less violent objections on the part of the [white] parents." The board also developed an unpublicized policy of allowing students to transfer from schools in their attendance area to the nearest school in which their race was in the majority. According to Blossom, the board devised this policy in order to "give each child the best education in the light of his individual ability and achievement." Some board members apparently hoped that placing a small number of African American students in a student body of almost two thousand at Central High would create such a sense of isolation for the black students that they would voluntarily return to Mann High School. Virtually at the outset, then, tokenism played a critical role in the board's political and educational strategies.[42]

As a result, in 1955 the school board designed a plan for a gradual if not glacial process of desegregation to begin in the high schools. Soon after the *Brown* decision, the board decided that the new secondary school for African Americans it had been planning would be a high school rather than a junior high school, a move that would enable whites to claim that blacks had a better high school than Central. While the plan dismantled one form of boundary setting—that based on a rigid system of race—it created in its stead another that literally used school boundary and construction policies to institute a system explicitly designed to secure race-based class hierarchies in education.[43]

A quintessential New South educator, Blossom embraced education and economic development as the twin pillars of southern progress while implementing the dominant educational practices of his period. Those practices, which would form a critical element in his planning for desegregation, provided mechanisms for the construction and maintenance of hierarchies based on race and class in decisions involving school locations, facilities, and curriculum. As Nathan Griswold observed, Blossom was not only "the author of one of the earliest plans for school desegregation in the South; he was at the same time guardian of its built-in, submerged features which provided a way for schools in the South to avoid the dreaded consequences of integration."[44]

Blossom's plan, in fact, followed national practices for the avoidance of social mixing in schools almost to the letter. In a 1947 article in *The School*

Review, for example, Los Angeles County administrator Alexander Frazier offered advice to "schools under attack by minority or other militant groups" on "How to 'Keep Them in Their Place.'" A reaction to "well-meaning 'sentimentalists' [who] advocate that... students be thrown together indiscriminately for the dubious benefits of interaction," Frazier's commentary suggests placing schools in minority neighborhoods at the center of their attendance areas, while locating those in Anglo neighborhoods at the peripheries when that served to distance them from racial ethnic populations. Within schools, Frazier recommended the use of "ability grouping" based on "the really not too reliable I.Q. index," teachers' evaluations of students, and achievement scores. This, he said, was "one of the most satisfactory methods of separating students of what may be called 'differing' backgrounds." Combined with tracking, work experience programs, vocational schools, and suitable counseling, "ability grouping" would maximize the separation of students from different backgrounds. Once this was achieved, administrators could deliver different curricula to various social groups and thus "preserve... the standards of learning that once obtained in all secondary schools."[45]

Blossom believed, though he did not state it directly, that "ability grouping" would best serve all students and that students who were white and middle class were more "able" and would advance faster educationally than working-class whites and virtually all African Americans. Although he was aware that the education gap between blacks and whites created problems for compliance, Blossom did not devise any curricula or other strategies to address it. Convinced that mass public education would work only if teachers had students of homogeneous social backgrounds and academic aptitudes (which he conflated), Blossom devised a plan that deliberately delayed desegregation until 1957 when the two new high schools would be completed. Desegregation would begin at Central High, which seemed destined to become the city's high school for most working-class whites. In order to secure funding for the new white high school, which was to be located a long distance away from African American neighborhoods, the board agreed to apply for federal aid to education under Title III of Public Law 815.[46]

By late 1954, Blossom had begun giving talks before community groups and discussing desegregation with interested individuals. Once the school

board had agreed generally on its desegregation plan in the summer of
1955, Blossom started a more systematic program of lectures on the topic.
Despite the pretense of democratic consultation, these meetings were not
designed to solicit alternative views from the community or to invite direct
community participation in preparing for such a significant change in social relations. The Rev. Colbert Cartwright, a liberal critic of the tokenism
employed by the board, accused Blossom and the board in 1957 of having
"taken an autocratic approach" in relation to the community. He noted
that various citizens' groups, including the Ministerial Alliance, had offered to provide public support for desegregation, but Blossom had declined their assistance. After noting that Blossom "had a tremendous ego,"
Nathan Griswold reported that the superintendent had ordered principals
not to speak about the desegregation plan because he wanted to be the
only one to do so. In meetings with speakers from other southern communities that were implementing desegregation, Blossom expressed open
disdain for the idea of genuine community involvement.[47]

Blossom's extreme efforts to control public discourse reflected not only
a strong will to power but also a fundamental anxiety regarding his ability
to keep resistance at bay and succeed in a highly public arena. Blossom's
tactics exemplified the managerial masculinity described by Deborah Kerfoot: "management practices are concerned, at all times, to control the
unpredictability of social interaction and render it 'safe' within the confines of a pre-designated script such as is offered by 'modern' management
practice." As R. W. Connell has noted, men's ability to maintain political power depends to an important degree on their "ability to impose a
definition of the situation, to set the terms in which events are understood
and issues discussed, to formulate ideals and define morality." Virgil Blossom's intense resistance to the participation of others in matters he reserved
for himself reflected his desire to keep a strict control over both ideas and
actions.[48]

In November 1955, the African American Interdenominational Ministerial Alliance, headed by the Rev. Roland Smith, requested to meet with
the school board so the alliance could lobby the board members to form an
advisory committee for desegregation, modeled on one in Chattanooga,
Tennessee. Such a meeting apparently took place, but Blossom wrote to
the Rev. Smith in January 1956 that the board believed "that it is not best

at this time to set up such a committee." They did not provide reasons for their decision, although the desire to control public discussion of the issue was clearly important to them.[49]

At public forums and in private meetings, Blossom expected that he would speak while others heeded his words. Forrest Rozzell, head of the Arkansas Education Association, later observed, "Mr. Blossom wasn't the kind of person you conferred with. Mr. Blossom was the kind of person you listened to." Wayne Upton, who was elected to the school board in March 1957, described the superintendent as "a very intense man. He was... a very determined person, a man who liked to have his own way." Moreover, as the Rev. Robert Brown noted, in talking primarily to those of his own social class, Blossom "talked chiefly to himself."[50]

Blossom's desire for uncontested control derived as much from fear as from his outsized ego. This was particularly true with respect to dealing with African American and white leaders in the NAACP, including state president Daisy Bates. Harry Ashmore, editor of the *Arkansas Gazette*, remembered urging Blossom to give blacks a voice in the planning process:

> Virgil Blossom was a tower of jello and Virgil, despite all my urging, I said you've got to deal with Daisy Bates, you can't put this damn thing over just addressing the Rotary Club. I never could get him to be more realistic. Daisy, of course, was just raising hell. She wouldn't really accept the plan and she'd come in and give me hell for supporting the Blossom plan. I kept saying well, it's all we can get, and it's better than nothing.[51]

When speaking before civic groups, Blossom generally received a favorable hearing, in part because he delivered a message they were willing to accept. Charles B. Pyles, the president of the Greater Little Rock Junior Chamber of Commerce, wrote to Blossom following a talk he had given before the organization. He praised him for the "best considered and thought out [integration] plan of any that has come to my attention," adding that he was "confident that this opinion was shared by others in your audience."[52]

Not all whites agreed, however. Many disempowered working-class whites saw Blossom's plan as a way for affluent whites to impose desegregation on them while protecting their schools from racial change. Teacher Elizabeth

Williams noted that the audiences "listened politely," but that throughout 1956 she had

> heard many resentful expressions at this familiar coddling of Heights residents [an affluent white community]. I never discounted this social resentment—felt it was real, with a foundation in feelings, if not in fact—but I never found anybody willing to discuss it further. Several times I heard people declare that Superintendent Blossom had promised the Heights people that they wouldn't have to go to school with the Negroes.[53]

Before white audiences, Blossom outlined a program of minimalist compliance with court-ordered desegregation that involved using school location decisions to ensure that very few African American students would attend "white" schools. Cartwright described a typical presentation to whites as follows:

> With the confident air of a high pressure salesman Dr. Blossom produced charts, maps and statistics describing where Negro and white high school pupils lived. He explained that by the conversion of an already proposed Negro junior high school building into a Negro senior high school, the speedy erection of a new senior high school building in a white residential area, and the conversion of the present Negro [junior high and] high school to a junior high school, attendance areas could be developed which would result in maximum avoidance of the mixing of the races.[54]

However satisfied some whites were with the desegregation plan, local African Americans harbored serious doubts regarding the willingness of the Little Rock School Board to comply fully with the *Brown* decision. Despite internal differences over whether to proceed with legal action against the board, the local NAACP decided late in 1955 that the Blossom Plan was so limited that officials would be likely to move forward with desegregation only if confronted with a court order. In particular, local activists objected to the board's decision that the new Mann High School be designated a black high school and with the lack of any specific timetable for ending segregation at the elementary and junior high school levels.

Their call for black parents to attempt to enroll their children in white schools in January 1956 elicited a surprisingly strong response from the African American community. As Tony Freyer has noted, African Americans' reliance on litigation as a political strategy "also facilitated black community mobilization." Local leaders, however, discouraged some black parents from enrolling their children in white schools because the parents were vulnerable to white retribution and could lose their jobs.[55]

When school officials refused to allow the black children to attend white schools, the NAACP filed suit. The school board, resolved that it and not the NAACP would determine the timetables and extent of desegregation in Little Rock, decided to fight. In addition to its regular lawyer, Archie House, the board hired four attorneys who represented various opinions on the *Brown* decision to assist it in court. Even House, who strongly supported desegregation and understood the need for African Americans to exert pressure to secure it, responded with hostility to the lawsuit, believing that it had been inspired by national NAACP leadership. Given the division among local blacks about filing suit, he suspected that "local conditions [had] been subordinated to the aggressiveness of the national leaders." House's reaction shows the intense resistance of elites to anything perceived as African American pressure and it emphasizes their assumption that blacks in Little Rock would not aggressively pursue their rights.[56]

In fact, as House soon found out, local activists did initiate the lawsuit. Thad Williams, an attorney for the local chapter of the NAACP, objected that a court decision upholding the Blossom Plan could put its stamp of approval on inadequate policies throughout the region. Although the national NAACP acquiesced in the decision to sue, it told Little Rock chapter leaders that they had to raise the funds to pay their own lawyers. NAACP members Georg Iggers and Lee Lorch, both professors at Philander Smith, raised the money from local and national sources. When Williams and J. R. Booker declined to take the case, local NAACP members hired Wiley Branton of Pine Bluff, who agreed to charge only for legal expenses.[57]

By the time the trial date arrived, however, the national NAACP decided to pay Ulysses Simpson Tate to argue the case on behalf of the national organization. Adopting the policy of the national leadership, Tate declared immediate and systematic desegregation as the goal of the suit. This, however, was not the strategy desired by local NAACP leaders, who had wanted African American students to have the right to enroll in previ-

ously all-white schools on the basis of their residence in those schools' attendance areas. They argued for this strategy despite their recognition that
school authorities had engaged in significant gerrymandering when they
drew the attendance area lines. Even with the high level of residential segregation in Little Rock, the local litigants' strategy would have achieved
significant desegregation in certain schools and would have undermined
the racial logic of the Blossom Plan.[58]

The national NAACP's insistence on immediate and widespread desegregation in Little Rock struck fear not only in die-hard segregationists but
also in moderates. Indeed, by the time the trial began, Blossom and some
members of the school board had decided that they would resign their
positions rather than comply with a court order to integrate fully and more
rapidly. House shared Blossom's worries about "the overnight program
sponsored by NAACP," concluding that the question was "whether the
courts will require slow and orderly desegregation or whether they will require prompt action with a disregard of the economic and educational
factors involved and the possibility of violence." The moderates who defined school policies viewed the crisis through the lens of class as much as
that of race. They feared the destruction of educational opportunities for
middle-class children and the erosion of their political credibility should
violent opposition to desegregation develop in Little Rock.[59]

Thus it is not surprising that Blossom testified in a hearing in the summer of 1956 that integration, if it was "unwisely done or hastily done,"
would lower standards in the schools. Citing differences in average scores
by race on IQ tests, Blossom asserted that "centuries of culture and opportunity" had given white students an advantage. Concerned lest whites
be held back academically in mixed classrooms, Blossom stated that it was
important to "group children with enough homogeneity for efficient classroom management and planning" in order for teachers to plan curricula
and for students to learn. To do so, the school board would have to devise
"school attendance areas consistent with the location of white and colored
pupils with respect to present and future physical facilities in the Little
Rock School District."[60]

Although Blossom maintained in court that the school board's policies
were based on socio-economic differences, not racial ones, he systematically conflated the two to justify the minimal desegregation plan he was
defending. In the hearing, school board attorney Leon Catlett tried to as-

sist Blossom in his testimony, stating that the superintendent was just trying to bring out that the new westside high school would be designed for
college-bound students while Mann High School would have a different
mission. NAACP lawyer Tate then asked Blossom how it would impair the
goal of student homogeneity to have equally qualified black students who
did not intend to go on to higher education attend Technical High School
with white students who were also not college bound. The superintendent
evaded the question, asking the plaintiffs' lawyer whether he was asking
school officials "to downgrade our program to integrate." His response
suggests not only the racism but also the fear that grounded his approach
to desegregation—that it entailed huge risks to white students and, therefore, to his reputation and priorities as a progressive educator. Blossom
could either gain acclaim as a southern school administrator who delivered
quality education for whites while managing token compliance with federal mandates or infamy as the administrator whose plan for compliance
led to the degradation of Little Rock's white schools. His lack of concern
for improving educational opportunities for black students through desegregation reveals the degree to which he understood the public good in
terms of white interests.[61]

In August 1956, District Court Judge John E. Miller accepted Blossom's
race-based reasoning regarding educational quality in the schools and held
that the Little Rock School Board was acting in good faith. According to
Miller, the school board's gradual plan for integration was essential "to
provide information necessary for public understanding, acceptance, and
support, and to provide a 'teachable' group of children for each teacher."
Because the board had declared its intention to admit students "on a nonracial basis as soon as practicable" and had begun planning for it, the court
found that it had made a "prompt and reasonable start toward full compliance with the requirements of the law." The decision of the district court
meant that the Little Rock School Board was under a federal court order
to proceed with its desegregation plan. Failure to do so could result in
convictions for contempt of court for school board members who impeded
compliance.[62]

The decision in the case heartened many whites in Little Rock, who saw
it as a victory for their interests. Teachers at the Centennial School wrote
to Blossom expressing their appreciation for the "court victory you accomplished for us and for our community." Other correspondents invoked a

masculine politics of resistance to all desegregation. Marvin Hamilton, for example, wrote to the school board members that he was "truly glad that we have at least a few school boards that have the manhood and courage to stand for the right, and try to protect the rights of the white people." One letter from an anonymous "Citizen of Little Rock" declared that "as long as there is life and power in my body" he would "see to it personally" that his five daughters would not attend school with African Americans. The author further concluded that it was the "young bucks that has been in the army and came back" who were "the main ones that is putting this corruption in the heads of the younger class of negros [sic]." Significantly, almost everyone who wrote to the school officials ignored the fact that the district court decision required that Little Rock begin its gradual process of desegregation the very next year in 1957.[63]

In the eastern Arkansas town of Hoxie, however, segregationists were left frustrated and angry. Segregation had been costly for Hoxie, which operated a one-room grade school for blacks and paid tuition and transportation costs for its African American high school students to attend a black school in Jonesboro. In 1955, school officials there faced a looming budget deficit. Equalizing facilities for the twenty-five black students in the district, which also had one thousand white students, would have been prohibitively expensive. So the Hoxie School Board decided to integrate its schools because, as one official put it, "It's the law of the land, it's inevitable, it's God's will, and it's cheaper." In July 1955, at the beginning of the split session common in cotton-producing areas, black students attended the public schools of Hoxie for the first time. Despite some local complaints, the experiment began peacefully.[64]

Then *Life* magazine featured the integrated schools in a story that touted the small town of Hoxie as an example of a white community that had made "a 'morally right' decision" to accept racial change, eliciting a powerful segregationist backlash. That backlash derived from the determination of southern whites that districts that desegregated not receive favorable national and regional publicity. In response to the article in *Life* magazine, segregationists from Hoxie and elsewhere, including Jim Johnson of Crossett and Little Rock attorney Amis Guthridge, mobilized a repertoire of tactics that would soon become familiar in Arkansas, including inflammatory racial rhetoric and intimidation directed at supporters of desegregation. When the Hoxie School Board refused to meet with segregationists regarding its policy of full integration, local resistance intensified. Speaking at a protest rally in Hoxie, Johnson told the crowd that he feared sending a child to an integrated school because "I'm afraid I might see the day when I'll be bouncing a half-Negro on my knee and have him call me Grandpa."[65]

His fear—that desegregation portended a loss of patriarchal control so serious that it could lead to consensual interracial sex on the part of one's own children—was broadly shared with other segregationists, giving emotional power to their states' rights arguments and justifying extreme measures. Curt Copeland claimed that "Smith and Wesson, Colt, and whoever made the grass rope have kept the nigger out of the white bedroom. If you integrate your schools, you invite the niggers to marry your daughter." He further asserted that he had helped lynch a black accused of raping a white woman in Mississippi, adding that "I have no apologies [for that], because in the end the power of the government is with the people." Amis Guthridge said he would not take the responsibility should someone throw a rock through a school board member's windshield, blinding him. A Hoxie minister told his congregation that God would overlook violence committed in defense of white racial "purity," thereby providing religious sanction for a politics of threat and intimidation. Segregationist rhetoric in the Hoxie crisis revealed the centrality of a sexualized and patriarchal racism to calls for states' rights, local control, and violence in response to the twin perils of federal authority and racial change.[66]

The involvement of segregationists from other parts of Arkansas and outside the state revealed the symbolic importance of the conflict to the region. Six leaders from Hoxie, for example, went to Mississippi in mid-August to meet with Senator James Eastland, who offered to speak in Hoxie in September. Accusations by the *Arkansas Gazette* that "outsiders" were interfering with an otherwise peaceful process of integration in Hoxie did not discourage local segregationists from working with others to rally resistance. The decision of the Hoxie School Board to consult only with "leading citizens" about its integration policy and its refusal to meet with local critics of that policy more than likely exacerbated the conviction of local segregationists that they had been turned into "outsiders" in their own community and therefore required support from others.[67]

In the meantime, the Hoxie School Board, aided by Jonesboro lawyer Bill Penix, who was handling the case without pay, entered federal court seeking injunctions against individuals and organizations interfering with the execution of federal constitutional doctrine. Penix had asked the U.S. Justice Department to enter the case with an *amicus* brief, but it refused to do so. Department attorneys, however, did offer Penix, who was receiving anonymous threats to his safety, considerable assistance in drafting his brief. On October 31, 1955, federal judge Thomas C. Trimble granted a temporary injunction against several named defendants, prohibiting them from interfering with the school board's efforts to secure the civil rights of black students in the district. On January 9, Judge Albert Reeves granted a permanent injunction, finding that the defendants had created "an undercurrent of menace and threat of harm to those responsible for desegregation" and to those who supported the decision to integrate the schools. According to Reeves, anxious parents had withheld their children from school and the board members feared harm if they exercised "their sacred right" to exercise their authority in conformity to the U.S. Supreme Court decision in *Brown v. Board of Education*. The judge also warned the defendants that they "should not complain against an injunctive order that restrains them from doing things that might result in criminal prosecutions and civil suits against them."[68]

Despite this apparent legal protection, Hoxie School Board President Howard Vance was assaulted by a person not named in the permanent injunction. Penix asked the federal government to bring criminal charges against the attacker under the 1866 Civil Rights Act, but it refused to do so. The FBI did launch an investigation, prompting *New York Times* reporter Cabell Phillips to conclude that there was little basis in federal law for the federal probe, which he characterized as "largely a strategy of 'counter intimidation' engineered by Penix." Mississippi Citizens' Council leader Robert Patterson charged that the NAACP had pressured the federal government into the probe "in order to intimidate those who disagree with their radical aims." The school board asked for local police protection for its meetings. It was refused. Penix wrote to the Justice Department that a "handful of friends of the school board came to the meeting and provided their own frontier-type protection and there was law and order at the meeting." Finally convinced that "conditions [had] degenerated" in Hoxie, the Justice Department filed an *amicus* brief for the appeal process, but still refused to bring criminal charges against Vance's attacker. Acting informally, U.S. Attorney Osro Cobb called two segregationist leaders and the assailant to a meeting with the Hoxie school superintendent and told the segregationists that they would be dealt with sternly if they defied the injunction. After the Eighth Circuit Court of Appeals upheld the injunction in October 1956, resistance dissipated in Hoxie.[69]

The injunction, which was used to buttress a threat to expel any students who created trouble in the schools and to forbid interference by those named in the injunction and their supporters, ultimately succeeded in coercing community cooperation with the policy of full integration. What accounts for the ultimate success of Hoxie officials in restraining violence and proceeding with desegregation? No doubt the courage and conviction of a majority of school board members and the pro bono work of a team of lawyers enabled officials in Hoxie to continue the legal battle against the segregationist opposition. Federal judges enforced the *Brown* decision and the Justice Department offered informal assistance and an *amicus* brief in the injunction to prohibit interference with the school board's efforts to secure the civil rights of black students. On balance, however, the federal executive's response was minimal and timorous. Eisenhower made no public statements about the conflict.[70]

According to legal historian Michal Belknap, Hoxie officials should not have had to go to the courts for protection because in conspiring to deprive citizens of their civil rights the defendants violated the 1866 Civil Rights Act. The Eisenhower administration, however, decided not to seek indictments, relying instead on district court judges to grant injunctions in such cases and to ask for federal investigations in cases of suspected violations of those injunctions. In short, the Eisenhower administration insisted that the federal judiciary take the lead on enforcement whenever possible.[71]

The declaration of Arkansas Governor Faubus that Hoxie was a local matter left him vulnerable to charges that he was "weak" on the question of integration. Jim Johnson, who would use the issue of desegregation in his 1956 campaign for governor, charged that Faubus had been supine in the face of federal "tyranny" in Hoxie. A charismatic race baiter and arch conservative, Johnson became the state segregationists' most important leader and spokesman. He liked to claim that his politics of resistance would create such a dilemma for federal authorities that "there wouldn't have been enough jails to hold all the resisters!" Although he was not named in the injunction, he did not continue to generate resistance to integration in Hoxie. Like Faubus, Johnson was unwilling to risk a charge of collusion with those named in the injunction and a term in jail for his principles. In the civil rights struggles of the 1950s and 1960s, it was African Americans, not white segregationists, who willingly sacrificed individual freedom in large numbers for their cause. As Adam Fairclough concluded, when it came to filling the jails with dissidents, the segregationists' "huffing and puffing was so much hot air."[72]

Johnson stayed out of Hoxie but he did not construe the Hoxie conflict as a defeat. Instead, he and other segregationists used it as a rallying cry and a precedent for future mobilization. Segregationists advanced a con-spiratorial view regarding the forces they confronted. Guthridge, for ex-ample, claimed later that events in Hoxie were "all a setup" in which those supporting segregation were "predestined to lose." The rhetoric of honor and power invoked by the segregationists in this and other conflicts with federal authority reinforced active resistance in the face of the setbacks they experienced. While a sexually freighted fear of racial change aroused moral outrage, segregationists' ideology of victimization by federal authorities provided additional emotional impetus for resistance by associating defi-ance with manhood. That defiance would be more successful in Little Rock, where the school board members demonstrated much less courage and conviction than the Hoxie officials.[73]

Absent the moral courage evidenced by Hoxie school leaders, black pe-titioners in Little Rock would have little recourse but to take the risks, mobilize their communities' scarce resources, and hope that they could hold out until their legal challenges to segregation made their way through the courts. Then they would be forced to rely on the dilatory procedures established by the Eisenhower administration to stop the intimidation and reprisals orchestrated by segregationists. Hoxie's "battle in a test tube" re-vealed that the federal government would be a reluctant warrior in future conflicts over the *Brown* decision. The Eisenhower administration's resort to bureaucratic and legalistic enforcement procedures reflected its unwill-ingness to use its authority even when local officials were prepared to pro-ceed with desegregation. In other areas of the South, where federal judges had little enthusiasm for enforcing the law and racial violence was more likely, efforts to desegregate schools would be even more dismal.

Segregationist mobilization continued in the aftermath of the Hoxie case as more whites in Arkansas joined the fight against integration. They orga-nized first in White America, Inc. and then formed chapters of the White

Citizens' Council. Jim Johnson and segregationist firebrand Curt Copeland began publishing *Arkansas Faith*, a racist periodical that Faubus called
"one of the vilest, most dissolute, neo-pornographic publications it has
ever been my disgust to see." Indeed, that publication often reflected the
sexualization of race relations at the heart of the segregationist cause. The
November 1955 issue featured a cartoon of an attractive white woman at-
tired only in a scarf bearing the words "southern civilization" strategically
placed across her lower body. She hung from a cross, held by nails labeled
"white (?) politicians," "NAACP," and "Supreme Court Ruling." The erot-
icized image rested uneasily with the image of innocence that segregationists normally attributed to white women.[74]

It is sometimes hard to disentangle sincere convictions from opportunistic rhetoric in the segregationist vocabulary. Some segregationists, like
Johnson's campaign advisor Phil Stratton, understood the political utility
of violent threats and appeals to anti-Semitism but opposed their use because they alienated more mainstream voters. In Johnson's 1956 primary
campaign for governor, Stratton urged his candidate to tell Curt Copeland
that "[in] the future there will be no, repeat NO, reference to killings, lynch-
ings, whippings or violence except in the negative sense." In the South, the
Citizens' Councils discouraged overt anti-Semitism as a threat to their
image "as the respectable face of segregation," although anti-Semitism remained a critical aspect of the South's racist political culture. After the
Arkansas Democrat condemned the anti-Semitism of Johnson's supporters,
Stratton worried that the media could "easily pick up an isolated quote and
butcher us with it." Although he maintained that it was important that the
Johnson campaign be conducted "on high ground," Stratton was willing to
reap the political advantages of demagoguery. He allowed that in the two
weeks preceding the primary "Curt can say anything he damn well pleases
so long as it is not on the same platform with Jim." Stratton's willingness
to tolerate Copeland's bigotry and threats of violence at the end of the
campaign reflected his candidate's right-wing views as well as his respect
for Faubus's political skills.[75]

Those skills were honed in the crucible of poverty that Orval Faubus
endured in his early years. Raised by a radical father and a quiet, cautious
mother in the hill country of northwestern Arkansas, Faubus experienced
early the hard labor and hard luck that was the lot of the people there.
From his outspoken and opinionated father, Sam Faubus, he acquired a

love for learning, a respect for the power of language, and a keen interest in politics. He also discovered that unpopular views invite public scorn and determined to avoid appearing foolish at all cost. As his father noted later, "Orval never liked to be looked down on." The younger Faubus carried a suspicion of urban elites and a resentment of their class pretensions with him throughout his political career.[76]

As he grew older, Faubus resolved to find a way out of a life that was becoming more difficult as the value of the land and its resources declined through over cultivation. Doing so would not prove easy. The future governor worked as a migrant farm laborer and a schoolteacher for part of the year. His service during World War II fueled his ambitions even as it distanced him from his wife and his young son, Farrell. His tendencies to self-absorption and caution combined with his aspirations made Faubus a wily and effective politician. In the words of his biographer, Roy Reed, for Faubus "ambition for public office became a kind of greed." In time, political success would feed his need for approval and authority while allowing him a broad canvas on which to make his mark. His fear of failure would also lead him in 1957 to the Faustian deal that would undermine his national ambitions.[77]

Facing the challenge from Jim Johnson in the 1956 gubernatorial campaign, Governor Faubus felt compelled to devise strategies to counter white supremacist support for his opponent. Ironically, the power of the strongly segregationist eastern Arkansas leaders, who were wary of outsider participation in local politics, enabled Faubus to adopt a "moderate" position on school desegregation. The efforts of Johnson and other segregationist outsiders in the area prompted a sheriff to declare that local residents were "getting along fine without anybody stirring up trouble." Faubus, who had been providing state positions and other forms of patronage to secure his base in the plantation areas, appointed several leaders from eastern Arkansas to a delegation he sent to Virginia to examine that state's resistance strategies. The members of the delegation included Marvin Bird, chairman of the Arkansas Board of Education, Richard McCullough, who had written the state's brief for the *Brown II* case, and Bex Shaver, a lawyer from Cross County. They returned and advised Faubus to introduce an interposition resolution weaker than the one previously introduced by Johnson.[78]

Straddling the fence between an endorsement of local authority in matters of desegregation and outright opposition, Faubus declared that "no

district will be forced to mix races as long as I am Governor" and that the
retention of segregated schools offered "the surest way to safeguard our
public school system at present for all citizens." As Nathan Griswold later
astutely noted, the governor's statement in fact reflected his intention to
defend resistant school districts but leave those seeking to comply with the
Brown decision on their own. Ultimately, Faubus's control over state politics, his alliance with eastern Arkansas interests, and his moderate stance
carried the election, but not before Johnson and his supporters gave him a
good scare.[79]

Johnson's interposition amendment and the weaker one initiated by
Faubus were both approved by the electorate, along with a pupil placement act instigated by Faubus. The pupil placement law combined the
politics of classroom homogeneity pursued by progressive educators with
the fears, threats, and assumptions that grounded massive resistance. It
provided that school districts, which could not use race overtly as a cate-
gory for assigning students, could take into account the consequences of
transfers for "established or proposed academic programs," the "academic
progress of other students," or for "the morals, conduct, health and personal standards of the pupil." In addition, school districts could take into
account individual students' "academic preparation for admission to a particular school and curriculum," relative scores on IQ and similar tests, "the
maintenance or severance of established... relationships with other pupils
and with teachers," and parents' wishes as they considered black students'
request to transfer to previously all-white schools. The criteria for the pupil
placement law incorporated the sexual and moral fears of segregationist
resisters as well as their conviction that white parents should consent to the
assignments of their children. The law's focus on academic preparation and
standards articulated the deepest fears of moderates in the Little Rock establishment and gave its school board the authority to pursue a politics of
tokenism. The pupil placement law epitomized the development of a "race
neutral" legal framework suffused with racist assumptions and designed to
sustain white supremacy.[80]

The electorate that supported these pupil placement laws, however, included African American sharecroppers coerced into voting for the proposals by landowners in eastern Arkansas. The absence of a secret ballot in
Arkansas translated economic power into electoral power in a most direct
fashion. Although the lack of a secret ballot made any claims of popular

sovereignty questionable, Faubus would maintain that he had to enforce state laws on the grounds that they represented the will of the people.[81]

Faubus later pointed to the Southern Manifesto, endorsed by the vast majority of southern senators and congressmen in 1956, as a sign of the political pressures faced by southern politicians placed in political jeopardy by the *Brown* decision. Proclaiming that the Court's decision was "a clear abuse of judicial power," the signers of the Manifesto pledged themselves "to use all lawful means to bring about a reversal of this decision" and "to prevent the use of force in its implementation." Faubus responded to critics who later charged him with a lack of political courage by blaming the federal government:

> Do you see, in all that situation, for the federal government to issue an order like that and place all the burden on the state authorities or local authorities and say, "Go ahead, and (looking at it from the pragmatic standpoint) commit political suicide now. We're aloof from it." I didn't think it was proper. I didn't think it was honest. I didn't think it was courageous.

As Anthony Badger observed, what Faubus "conveniently ignored was the role he himself played in creating that pressure." Significantly, Brooks Hays claimed later that Faubus had persuaded him to sign the Manifesto so that they could strengthen the position of moderates. If that was their goal, they fell wide of the mark. Their actions in fact narrowed the choices available to other moderates as the credibility and popularity of resistance to desegregation increased.[82]

Moreover, in 1956 Faubus forged a political compromise that enlisted the state of Arkansas on the side of defiance of the *Brown* decision. The governor supported laws to protect segregation, which were especially important to legislators from eastern Arkansas, in exchange for votes for an increase in the sales tax that he needed to provide additional state funding for public schools. This decision reflected Faubus's reluctance to "commit political suicide" and his conviction that educational improvement and economic development would benefit all Arkansans. Laws passed in early 1957 established a Sovereignty Commission with broad investigatory powers to assist the state in resisting desegregation; the laws gave parents the right to refuse to send their children to desegregated schools and autho-

rized school districts to use their funds to meet the costs of fighting desegregation lawsuits. Finally, the laws targeted the NAACP by requiring certain organizations to disclose membership and financial data. The only
public opposition to the new laws came from a small group of clergymen,
who objected that they gave too much power to the Sovereignty Commission and were being used to undermine federal law. The clergymen found
then, as later, that their moral authority carried little weight with Arkansas
politicians.[83]

In the meantime, the Little Rock School Board sought consensus among
whites in order to protect the stability of class relations and the power of
the business leaders from whom its members were drawn. The glacial pace
of the Blossom Plan was designed precisely to sustain the support of moderate whites hostile to integration but fearful of the consequences of defying federal authority. Blossom solicited their support by promising them
that the plan provided for the least integration to be achieved over the
longest period of time allowable by the courts. Blossom's decision to present his ideas primarily to middle-class activist audiences derived from his
unquestioned assumption that they constituted those "who counted" in
Little Rock politics. At the same time, the school board's recourse to secrecy and deception as it adopted the plan revealed its deep-seated anxiety
that candor would activate a latent but pervasive opposition. The school
board's position lacked moral content, evaded the issue of race, and fueled
resistance from those who saw federal authority as a threat to their dignity
and independence.[84]

For the arch segregationists, resistance to the courts bolstered a southern
pride battered by the moral condemnation implicit in the federal court's
decision that segregation defied not only the U.S. Constitution but also
the nation's commitment to equality. Their resistance also expressed and
allayed the sense of disempowerment that southerners, especially men, felt
when "Yankees" told them what to do. Indeed, Little Rock's moderates
were as likely as the members of the White Citizens' Council to rail against
federal actions.[85]

In Little Rock as elsewhere, segregationists linked states' rights and racial hierarchy. Such a connection was manifest at the symbolic level for the
Citizens' Council, which became the main vehicle for southern resistance
to racial change after its formation in 1954. The council's emblem, which
featured intertwined Confederate and American flags and the words "States'

Figure 1. Emblem of the Citizens' Council.

Rights" and "Racial Integrity," perfectly represented the densely connected nationalist, regionalist, and racial claims of the massive resistance movement to desegregation. The longing for racial integrity, however, required the strict sexual containment of white women and fueled the "moral panic" at the heart of the movement. The adamant assertion of states' rights as a principled constitutional position not only provided a salve for racist consciences, but also expressed men's fears that their sexual and familial authority was waning.[86]

The propensity to resistance was exacerbated by the fact that those "Yankees" were allied with African Americans. Despite white convictions that "outsiders" generated legal challenges to Little Rock's segregated school system, the activism of local blacks and their white allies in the Little Rock NAACP was critical to the litigation that forced the school board to act on school segregation. Although the 1956 lawsuit did not force the board to abandon tokenism, it revealed the depth of support for change in the Little Rock black community and left school officials legally bound to implement the Blossom Plan.[87]

In June 1957, segregationists attended the school board's regular meeting to question the legality and desirability of integration. Citing the state's segregation legislation, spokesman Amis Guthridge asked the board to abandon "forced integration" and to provide separate schools for white students who did not wish to attend school with blacks. He ended his appeal with questions regarding black participation in certain extracurricular activities. He wondered, for example, whether African Americans would be allowed to attend the school dances and, if so, would African American "boys be permitted to solicit the white girls for dances?" In school plays, would parts involving "the enactment of tender love scenes ... be assigned to negro boys and white girls without respect to race or color?" Citing an ostensibly "high venereal disease rate among negroes," he asked "if the white children will be forced to use the same rest rooms and toilet facilities with negroes?" Deliberately provocative, his questions crystallized the political positions defined in the preceding months and years and set the stage for future conflicts. Despite the continued optimism of the Little Rock School Board regarding the possibilities for a relatively peaceful transition to token compliance with *Brown*, the politics of confrontation would intensify dramatically by September.[88]

The ensuing conflicts among whites would reveal the ways that racial change generated fear not only because it asked whites to reconsider their relationship to blacks but also because it required whites to reexamine their political and other connections to each other. In particular, white men differed in the racial ideologies, identities, and privileges they sought to enforce through law. Many working-class men stressed their roles as protectors of white women and children while middle-class businessmen and politicians forged a neo-liberal claim to power based on their economic roles and interests. Their bitter clashes would occur on the overlapping grounds of gender, race, and class.

CHAPTER TWO

"Occupied Arkansas": Class, Gender, and the Politics of Resistance

We are now an occupied territory. Evidence of the naked force of the federal government is here apparent in these unsheathed bayonets in the backs of school girls.
—Orval Faubus[1]

I feel like a damned fool—protecting 2,000 white high school students from nine colored students.
—Unnamed Arkansas National Guardsman[2]

In August 1957, as the city of Little Rock prepared to desegregate its schools by admitting a few African American students to previously all-white Central High School, its citizens became increasingly anxious. Fearful that desegregation would involve violence and unwilling to have her daughter attend school with black students, Carol Thomason called Little Rock School Superintendent Virgil Blossom to request that her daughter Louise be allowed to transfer. He refused her request. Thomason, described by another segregationist as "a sweet little thing but a very stern person in the things she believes," called him back repeatedly. He did not return her calls.[3]

His silence typified the assumptions and strategies of Little Rock's leaders when they contended with segregationist complaints and pressures. The moderates believed that they could defuse the situation by stonewalling their opponents and avoiding public comment on race and the schools. Moreover, the middle-class leaders held the working-class segregationists in considerable disdain, an attitude not lost on their adversaries. In fact, the moderates' tactics only intensified the segregationists' class resentments and motivated their activism, as the formidable Thomason would soon make evident.

An employed working-class mother, Thomason reacted with anger at Blossom's indifference to her fears. On August 27, she filed suit in Pulaski Chancery Court asking for a temporary injunction against the integration of the Little Rock schools. Although she clearly did so in collusion with Arkansas Governor Orval Faubus, she also acted for her own reasons. In her interview with the Federal Bureau of Investigation, she alleged that Blossom not only ignored her calls but also that he "met at least twice a week with various Negro groups." Interpreting her political marginality in racial terms, she conveyed the segregationists' anger that their whiteness did not result in political inclusion by white officials.[4]

This chapter begins with the story of the segregationists' efforts to stop school desegregation with both legal maneuvers and violent opposition while the Little Rock School Board tried to salvage the Blossom Plan, which it was legally obligated to implement, and to preserve the city's image as a peaceful community with harmonious race relations. When the actions of segregationists and civil rights activists imperiled both goals, the school board tried to find a legal way out of its responsibilities. Together, public officials at all levels created a political culture of buck-passing that heightened the threat of violence and retarded racial change by encouraging the beliefs that federal court decisions lacked legitimacy and that defiance could be effective.

The chapter then moves to an analysis of the rhetoric and symbols employed by segregationists to deny their association with violent behavior and to depict whites, particularly white women, as the victims of school desegregation and of violence at the hands of the federal government. It also examines the segregationists' use of threat and intimidation as political tools and the response of Little Rock's moderates to those tactics. Caught between the considerable economic and political power wielded by the governor and his allies and the need to maintain public order and shore up their own political legitimacy, the moderates vacillated. Although they complained about the bullying tactics used by the segregationists, business leaders also used coercion to silence other moderates and liberals who disagreed with their priorities and actions. As a result, virtually no whites stepped forward to support any form of racial change.

After her rebuff from Superintendent Blossom, Carol Thomason joined with other segregationist women to organize the Mothers' League of Central High School. Its membership consisted primarily of working-class women, some of whom had children assigned to attend Central in the 1957–58 school year. The organization immediately began to mobilize local opposition to desegregation by calling mothers of Central High students to condemn integration as a threat to public order and white well-being and to spread rumors that armed students would turn the school into a battleground. The members of the Mothers' League fueled fears that violence would accompany any attempts to admit African American students to Central High. They encouraged protestors to converge at the high school and to pressure the governor to bar the entry of black students in September 1957. One anonymous mother wrote that:

> Parents of children were frightened out of their reason with the claim that their children would be half-murdered if they were not sent to school prepared to meet violence, that mob gangs were being formed; the parents were urged to deluge the governor with letter upon letter, urged to get on the phone and warn others before it was too late.

As her letter suggests, the segregationists saw both opportunity and danger in the threats of violence. The Mothers' League members expressed and intensified a threatening sense of imminent violence, hoping that a politics of fear would prompt Governor Faubus to interpose the power of the state between the federal courts and the community.[5]

In fact, nothing would have given the governor more pleasure than successfully defying the federal government. Fiercely proud and independent, Faubus experienced the negative judgments and the authority of others as an intensely humiliating form of subjection. As his biographer Roy Reed observed, "It was as if Arkansas in the mid-twentieth century had become his personal battleground in still another engagement of the Civil War." At the same time, Faubus knew that the federal government would ultimately have its way. His politics of defiance had to enable him to impede desegregation while eluding legal accountability for his actions, to appear lawful

while breaking the law, to accede ultimately to federal authority while
avoiding a humiliating capitulation, and to invoke the threat of violence
while distancing himself from its roots.[6]

Deeply embedded in southern culture and history, the rhetoric of violence provided a language for expressing the fears associated with dramatic
social change, for conveying the intensity of political convictions, for mobilizing supporters and discrediting opponents, and for arguing about and
describing power relations. Historians of the Little Rock crisis have reduced the complexity of the meanings and uses of a rhetoric of violence to
questions about whether the threat of violence was "real," whether Faubus
lied about the degree of threat to justify his actions and orchestrated the
disorders to serve his purposes or was the dupe of segregationists using
scare tactics. This chapter will focus not only on the instrumental uses of
violent threats by segregationists but also on the real fears that segregationists articulated through the rhetoric of violence, their contradictory relationship to the idea of violence, and the ways that gender relations and
ideologies shaped the emotional culture, legitimation strategies, and social
visions of massive resistance in Arkansas.[7]

Using political symbols and language that invited Arkansans to right
the wrongs of the Civil War and return the state to a halcyon "golden age"
of race relations, the segregationists claimed a virtual monopoly on public
discussions of race. Moreover, Faubus and many of his supporters used a
powerful rhetoric of invasion and emasculation to express their convictions regarding the harmful effects of federal authority in matters of race.
State autonomy came to represent the possibility of impermeable political
borders, which would offer some protection to men who exercised and
sought power in a competitive system.

The desire of southern whites for strict political boundaries, however,
was undone as much by the mobility of capital, ideas, and images as it was
by Eisenhower's decision to intervene. When Faubus called out the National Guard to keep nine African American students from entering Central High School, many Americans reacted with horror to the images they
saw on television and in newspapers. For them, the images affirmed and
generated moral disgust at southern whites for being disorderly, racist,
and contemptuous of legally constituted federal authority. The much-
publicized violence and the racial hatred evidenced by the hostile crowds
on the school grounds created a national mandate for enforcement of the

Brown decision. This national response produced a crisis of legitimacy for local segregationists, who invoked ideas about gender to distance themselves from the threats of violence that they themselves had generated and to claim that whites were the victims of an undemocratic politics of "forcible integration."[8]

As participants in the school controversy filed a spate of lawsuits, most designed to impede desegregation, litigation became a central form of political discourse and strategy. This morass of lawsuits in various courts created legal incoherence, much of it intended, and encouraged the belief that federal court decisions could be evaded. Almost all public officials, including Governor Faubus, tried to shift responsibility for the effective enforcement of school desegregation onto others. In the meantime, moderates and segregationists alike solicited his support for their agendas and legal strategies.[9]

In the hearing on the Thomason lawsuit, segregationists made their first attempt to use the threat of impending violence to block integration. On August 29, Thomason testified that "violence was brewing" in Little Rock but refused to name the sources for her conclusion. Employing a remarkably lax view of the requirements of legal procedure, Pulaski Chancellor Murray Reed, a Faubus appointee, agreed that she would not have to reveal her sources until she had gotten their permission. Faubus offered similarly unsubstantiated testimony regarding impending disorders, asserting that "a crowd can assemble with the best intentions and become a mob just because of two or three hot-headed people." His testimony implied that local and state law enforcement officials would be unwilling or unable to handle the firebrands. Faubus and his lawyers then walked out of the hearing. Despite the absence of any concrete evidence to support the witnesses' assertions of imminent violence, Reed granted a temporary injunction against desegregation in Little Rock. The next day, U.S. District Court Judge Ronald Davies threw out the chancery court's order and enjoined "all persons" from interfering with the Little Rock integration plan previously approved by the district court.[10]

In the weeks before school was to begin, school officials sought ways to get others, most notably District Court Judge John E. Miller and Governor Faubus, to take responsibility for preventing disorders occasioned by desegregation. In late June, Justice Department attorney Arthur Caldwell met with Archie House, attorney for the Little Rock School Board, and

Judge Miller to discuss the issuance of injunctions that would place segregationists under court order to refrain from interfering with desegregation.
Miller, who was violating professional ethics by talking to litigants in a case
before him, said that he did not have the authority to issue injunctions
unless the school board or the NAACP petitioned for them and provided
evidence for their necessity. If this was done, he would grant the injunctions and, he further volunteered, if asked for a declaratory judgment on
new state segregation laws, he would find them unconstitutional. House
stated that the school board would be "extremely reluctant" to begin such
a proceeding.[11]

On the issue of injunctions, the school board's political caution reinforced a policy of legal timidity. According to school board member Wayne
Upton, the board believed that criminal prosecutions would have been
more effective than injunctions, given the size of the opposition to desegregation in Little Rock. Had the school board obtained injunctions, "something would have broken out in some other place" and school officials, he
claimed, "could have very well been involved in an almost endless effort to
obtain injunctions." In addition, board members were afraid that their
adversaries would bring suit.[12]

Subsequently, Blossom and the school board met with Faubus and his
counsel, William Smith. Although accounts of this meeting are contradictory, self-interested, and incomplete, it appears that Blossom hoped that
Miller would make a quick decision against the state segregation laws and
tried to get Faubus to agree that, should Miller do so, he would make a
public statement supporting the school board's obligation to obey district
court orders. The governor, however, wanted to use state laws and state
courts to delay or avoid desegregation and refused to support compliance
by the board if the Arkansas segregation laws were declared unconstitutional in federal court.[13]

Noting that the use of injunctions for contempt of court appeared "to
be the only penalty available" in school desegregation cases, school board
attorney Archie House concluded that "no Federal Judge sharing the sentiments of the Citizens Council is going to be alert in applying that kind of
penalty." When House concluded later that District Court Judge Miller
could not bring himself to "put his heart into trying to enforce *Brown v.
Board of Education*," his words applied as much to the school board as they
did to the judge, particularly if Justice Department attorney Arthur Cald-

well's accounts of his conversations with House and Miller were accurate. In the final analysis, neither the judge nor the members of the Little Rock School Board were willing to take responsibility for the issuance of an injunction against the segregationists. In courage and commitment to federal court decisions, they were not equal to the judge in the Hoxie case and the Hoxie school board members.[14]

Segregationist mobilization peaked in the two weeks before school was to begin, intensifying the pressure on Governor Faubus to resist federal law. On August 22, 1957, Little Rock's Capital Citizens' Council brought Georgia Governor Marvin Griffin and regional citizens' council leader, Roy Harris, to Little Rock to speak. They told their audience exactly what it wanted to hear: desegregation was optional if Arkansas politicians would follow the example of resistance provided by other southern leaders. Griffin claimed that Georgia had devised a workable plan of resistance to the *Brown* decision based in part on a voucher program to fund students in segregated private schools. He added that Arkansas could do the same if its political leaders would stand behind the wishes of whites. Moreover, he urged them to do so in defense of politically unassailable moral values: "our way of life is constitutional, American, Christian and scientific." Faubus refused to attend the rally, but did invite Griffin and Harris to stay in the governor's mansion that night. Clearly influenced by their visit, he told Blossom that Griffin's speech had achieved more than "anything else that has happened to solidify public sentiment against school integration." The governor's silence, of course, contributed to that outcome.[15]

Meanwhile, segregationists sought out the governor to reinforce the message that integration meant violence. Jim Johnson and other Citizens' Council activists persuaded Faubus that groups of angry whites from the rural areas of Arkansas would converge on Little Rock to stop integration at all costs. Although they greatly overstated the likelihood of violence, Little Rock segregationists did work with like-minded people throughout the state in an attempt to make it a reality. The statewide citizens' councils planned to bring a motorcade to Little Rock on September 3, but abandoned that idea three days earlier when they heard that the Arkansas State Police would be called out to keep black students from entering the school and to preserve order. Faubus or the state police may have revealed the governor's decision to the citizens' councils before it was made public. Hugh Adams, president of the Mississippi County Citizens' Council, told reporter L. R. Luker that he "could raise a regiment in Eastern Arkansas to surround the school and keep the Negroes out." When interviewed by the FBI, Adams said that he "had meant that we could get shotguns or other weapons and do whatever would be necessary to keep the Negroes from attending the school." Neither the FBI nor state and local law enforcement agencies investigated these threats further.[16]

Even as Little Rock Citizens' Council leaders stressed the inevitability of violent white resistance and acted to turn it into a self-fulfilling prophecy, they disavowed the use of violence by their organization. Indeed, they worked to position themselves as the reasonable alternative to more violent groups. Capital Citizens' Council President Amis Guthridge told Blossom in February 1957 that he knew a group of men who would not join the Capital Citizens' Council because it was nonviolent, "but at the proper time, [this group of men] would take over with guns and pistols." In a letter to Faubus, Guthridge assured the governor that he had told his members that anyone who participated in violence would be removed from the organization. He also predicted that desegregation would cause "blood shed" [sic] and worried that it would be blamed on the Citizens' Council. On September 9, 1957, L. D. Poynter, president of the Association of Citizens' Councils of Arkansas, told the FBI that his group was trying to achieve its goals legally, but that if they failed, he believed that "other more drastic organizations would be formed to work in an underground manner." He disavowed any intention of *leading* such an effort. Divided within and among themselves, the arch segregationists disclaimed and desired violence in equal measure.[17]

Under intense contradictory pressures, Faubus tried to find out what role the federal government intended to play as the veiled threats of violence mounted. He met with Arthur Caldwell of the Department of Justice on August 28. Caldwell tried to persuade the governor that legal means could be used to prevent violence in a context of desegregation, pointing to the successful use of injunctions to quell resistance to desegregation in Hoxie in 1956. According to Faubus, Caldwell then stated, "we can't do a thing until we find a body." Faubus told Caldwell that his information regarding threats of violence "was much too vague and indefinite" to be useful to the FBI or to local law enforcement agencies. The governor had little interest in pursuing the Hoxie strategy in Little Rock. At the same time, he expressed concern that opposition to integration in Arkansas had intensified in the wake of the visit of Harris and Griffin, with the result that even "respectable" citizens believed that they could maintain school segregation without adverse consequences.[18]

Federal authorities, committed to respecting state law enforcement authority, wished to allow Faubus to use his power on behalf of peaceful compliance with a federal court order. Their inaction in the wake of mounting threats of violence only encouraged Faubus's resistance to federally mandated desegregation. In a later interview, Faubus stated that the federal government "refused to help in any way, refused to send anybody, refused to discourage violence, refused to say what the penalties would be, made no statements." What he meant, of course, was that the federal government refused to take actions that would relieve him of responsibility for maintaining order in the state he claimed as his own.[19]

Faubus's position was fraught with contradictions. He condemned the federal government for its failure to take over complete responsibility for the police powers that, as he had claimed repeatedly, were exclusively in his domain of legitimate, autonomous power as the governor of a state. At the same time, the rhetoric of "forcible integration" used by Faubus and his segregationist allies meant that compliance with federal court orders would never achieve legitimacy in Arkansas. As the governor's critics pointed out then and later, it was difficult to promote law and order while undermining the authority of the judiciary.[20]

As the opening day of desegregated classes approached, the school board instructed Blossom to get a statement from Faubus that he would call out the state police to preserve the peace. In a meeting at the governor's home on September 1, Blossom tried to persuade Faubus to use his authority to discredit and suppress violent resistance to integration. Blossom told the governor of threats directed against him and his family, adding that violence could be averted only if the governor acted in support of peaceful desegregation. Faubus, however, interpreted Blossom's remarks as evidence that violence would inevitably accompany efforts to admit African American students to Central High School. The governor, who had a considerable penchant for hearing only what he wanted to hear, claimed later that Blossom "gave me more information than anyone else on impending violence and disorder." He stated that the superintendent had told him of school officials taking guns and knives from students, many of them African American. When Blossom did not sustain Faubus's allegations about

impending violence in court, the governor was enraged at what he felt was
a profound betrayal.[21]

Following the federal court's dismissal of the Thomason suit, the governor took his case to the court of public opinion in Arkansas. In a prime-
time televised speech announcing his decision to send the National Guard
to Central High School on the opening day of classes, Faubus stated that
he had no choice but to intervene because the rise in [white] hostility to
integration posed a great risk to public safety and the fact that the segregation laws of Arkansas had not been tested in the courts called into question
the authority of any recent federal court rulings. Those segregation laws, he
noted, had been passed by overwhelming majorities in the Arkansas legislature. He did not say, as he had in his private conversation with Arthur
Caldwell, that if tried in federal court those same laws would most likely
be declared unconstitutional. He insisted that Arkansas was a progressive
southern state being pushed too far, too fast by autocratic outsiders willing
to disregard completely "the overwhelming sentiment of the people of the
area."[22]

He stated that the opposition to integration contained an imminent
threat of violence evidenced, he alleged, by large numbers of weapons sales
to blacks (including gangs of young blacks), and some to white students.
His claims displaced responsibility for the possibility of violence onto
blacks and young whites, when, in fact, the real threats came from white
adults. Faubus, however, asserted that white adults organizing to demonstrate against integration operated within the domain of legitimate, peaceful protest. These adults included the segregationist women who were
"calling upon the mothers of white children to assemble peaceably upon
the school grounds" alongside segregationists coming in "caravans . . . from
many points in the state." An FBI report, however, stated that Faubus interpreted the Capital Citizens' Council's denunciation of violence as actually meaning that the organization "was laying the ground work for possible violence."[23]

In order to sustain the legitimacy of his position, Faubus invoked the
idea of a spontaneous popular racism that exceeded the capacity of state
and local law enforcement to contain. The idea that a propensity to racist
violence operated independently from the governor's actions was succinctly
stated by the pro-Faubus *Arkansas Democrat* when it concluded that the
governor could not "turn the resistance to integration on and off like a

water faucet." Faubus bemoaned the apparent fact that state authority was powerless in the face of an unpredictable white resistance to integration but, according to former governor Sid McMath, Faubus staged the protests at the school and "then called out the Guard in order to put down the mob which he [himself] had organized." If Faubus had reliable information regarding threats to public safety, his refusal to pass on that information to the Justice Department or to use state law enforcement authority against those making threats was, in fact, highly irresponsible and quite at odds with his professed commitment to preserving the peace.[24]

In the meantime, employing various screening processes, Superintendent Blossom had reduced the number of African American students permitted to enter Central High School to nine. He restricted transfers to black students who lived in the Central High School attendance zone (about two hundred); asked black school administrators to screen applicants for ability, achievement, deportment, and attitude; and then interviewed those students who remained to reduce their numbers further.[25]

The result, as Henry Louis Gates, Jr., later noted, was a group of children who "were all well scrubbed and greased down, as we'd say.... Starched shirts, white, and creased pants, shoes shining like a buck private's spit shine." His father had concluded that "They hand-picked those children. No dummies, no nappy hair, heads not too kinky, lips not too thick, no disses and no dats." As Gates remembered, those students and their adversaries had high visibility in the African American community: "We watched it on TV. All of us watched it.... I mean *all* the colored people in America watched it, together, with one set of eyes." The television had become "the ritual arena for the drama of race."[26]

Those watching also included President Eisenhower, who responded to the governor's defiance cautiously, saying that he could not react to Faubus's actions until he consulted with Attorney General Herbert Brownell. With unintentional irony, he urged Americans "to bring about the kind of America that was visualized by our forebears." Noting the depth of the opposition among many southern whites, he went on to express his sympathy for them and his skepticism regarding the use of law for purposes of social change: "But there are very strong emotions on the other side. People that see a picture of [the] mongrelization of the race, they call it. There are very strong emotions, and we are going to whip this thing in the long run by Americans being true to themselves and not merely by law." The president's willingness to wait until southern whites were "ready" for integration meant a slow pace indeed for racial change. Then as later, Eisenhower did nothing to dispel the fears of southern whites and offered no support for racial justice.[27]

Despite the president's unwillingness to support court-ordered integration unequivocally, Faubus realized he was in trouble. Judge Davies had ordered an investigation to determine who was responsible for the evasion of a federal court order. Much of the national media portrayed Faubus as a racist rube, and his position with Arkansas moderates who supported compliance with federal law was deeply strained. Faubus did not find uncritical approval at home either: his father, sister, wife, and son all opposed the position he had taken. Indeed, his father wrote letters to local newspapers, under a pseudonym, condemning his son's actions. It was unclear whether there would be a face-saving way out for him. Called a "slightly sophisticated hillbilly" by *Time*, his claims of impending violence were greeted with mocking skepticism in the national press. That skepticism increased when he refused to provide evidence to reporters that integration would endanger the public safety.[28]

Many of Little Rock's moderates also responded to Faubus's claims with incredulity. They were convinced that Faubus had an integral role in the mobilization of violent dissent and in managing dissent for his own political ends. As school board member Wayne Upton put it later, "the fire he was seeking to put out was the fire that he himself had built." Elizabeth Huckaby, the vice principal for girls at Central High, concluded in a letter to her brother that "Governor Faubus is playing a very low sort of politics, it seems to me, aimed at enlisting East Arkansas support. What information he had about guns and knives I suspect was hearsay from scared segregationists." Former political ally Henry Woods later mournfully concluded that Faubus "sold his soul, it was kind of a Faustian deal because he knew better."[29]

Arkansas Gazette editor Harry Ashmore and other moderates observed that the threat of violence was critical to Faubus's political agenda. The *Gazette* editorialized on September 6:

> National guardsmen in effect protect and encourage the whites who assemble daily at Central High School. Yet the terrible truth is that this unseemly spectacle is essential to the position Mr. Faubus has taken in his calculated course of direct defiance of the federal govern-

ment. In order to sustain his position the governor must have a threat of violence. If the impasse continues long enough the chances are he will have it in fact.[30]

Reeling from adverse publicity and fearful that he would be enjoined to obey federal law or jailed for contempt of court, Faubus hurled wild charges against federal officials, accusing them of "unwarranted interference." In a telegram to President Eisenhower, he claimed that he had dependable information that federal authorities in Little Rock had tapped his phone and had been considering plans to "take into custody by force the head of a sovereign state," that is, to arrest him. The president denied this, but noted that the Justice Department was investigating the obstruction of a federal court order. Stating that he could no more "surrender [his] rights" in the dispute than Eisenhower could his, Faubus personalized the confrontation between state autonomy and federal power in which he was embroiled.[31]

The rhetoric of states' rights and gubernatorial autonomy employed by Faubus bespoke his identification of state supremacy with his own power as governor and his personal claim to immunity from subjection to federal authority. As school board member Wayne Upton remembered it, Faubus was "hellbent on letting the whole wide world know that he was in charge of this state and the federal government just wasn't going to interfere with him and with his operation of the state of Arkansas." Although Faubus's fears regarding the consequences of his choice to violate a federal court order were not entirely groundless, they were quite exaggerated and indeed a bit hysterical. Legally dubious, his assertions of personal sovereignty made more sense as political posturing and as a politics of masculine protest powerfully linked to his southern identity. His claim to political "sovereignty" resonated with the independence and dignity associated with hegemonic masculinity in postwar American culture and carried a particular weight with southern politicians in the post-*Brown* era.[32]

Because of the governor's interference, the school board asked the federal court for a temporary delay in implementing the desegregation plan. On September 7, U.S. District Court Judge Ronald Davies refused the request. Attorney W. Wilson White of the Justice Department informed Attorney General Brownell that the FBI investigation discovered no evidence of excessive weapons sales; the investigation report therefore concluded that Faubus had deliberately flouted federal law and the orders of the district court. Presidential adviser Sherman Adams stated that the president wanted to give Faubus the chance "to make an orderly retreat" but could not himself consider any "compromise or capitulation... on this issue."[33]

As events careened out of his control, Faubus sought a meeting with Eisenhower in order to find a face-saving way out of his dilemma. Arkansas Congressman Brooks Hays and Sherman Adams intervened with the president on his behalf, hoping to ward off disaster. Attorney General Brownell, who believed that the governor "had 'soiled' himself badly," advised against the meeting. Nonetheless, the president decided that a conference with the wayward governor would offer a good chance for a solution to the impasse.[34]

In that conference, Eisenhower told Faubus that he did not object to calling out the National Guard to preserve the peace, but he believed that the governor had given the troops the wrong order. The governor, thought Eisenhower, should simply instruct Guardsmen to allow the admission of the African American students. Eisenhower reminded Faubus that in this kind of conflict between a state and the federal government, the state could not win and that he "did not want to see any Governor humiliated." At the conclusion of their conference, the president believed that Faubus would do as he had asked within the next few hours.[35]

After the meeting, Eisenhower stated publicly that Faubus had expressed his willingness "to give his full cooperation in carrying out his responsibilities in respect to [federal court] decisions." Although the president acknowledged "the inescapable responsibility resting upon the Governor to preserve law and order in his state," he made it clear that he expected Faubus to do so while supporting "the orderly progress of the [desegregation] plans" devised under the federal court order. For his part, Faubus issued a statement declaring that he knew he had to "harmonize" his actions under Arkansas law "with the requirements of the Constitution of the United States." He further allowed that the decision in *Brown* was "the law of the land" and had to be obeyed. At the same time, he expressed his hope that federal officials would "act with understanding and patience in discharging their duties" as the changes they required could not "be accomplished overnight." Thereafter, the recalcitrant governor backed off from his promises to the president. He hoped to secure a delay in Little Rock's desegregation plan and continued to defy federal authority.[36]

Faubus later commented that the president's advisers thought he was "a country boy" who would defer to their orders, but they were wrong if they saw him as their subordinate. Linking his appeal to masculine independence with national values, he asserted: "Well, I'm not made of that kind of material. The country wasn't built with that kind of people, either." Faubus continued to demonstrate his contempt for federal judicial authority, first by refusing to honor a summons in a case brought by African American ministers in Little Rock against segregationist legislation and then by trying to get Judge Ronald Davies dismissed from the NAACP injunction suit on the grounds that the federal judge was not objective.[37]

By then Eisenhower had lost all patience. He felt the same contempt for Faubus as he would have felt for an insubordinate and duplicitous junior officer. His belief that Faubus was motivated solely by sectarian political advantages intensified his disdain for him. As Eisenhower deliberated what to do should Faubus continue his defiance, he told Attorney General Brownell that "he wished someone would tell Brooks Hays just how low the Governor [had] fallen in [his] estimation." For his part, Hays said that he "felt like a sparrow that flew into a badminton game."[38]

Predictably, Judge Davies enjoined Faubus and the Arkansas National Guard from any further interference with a court order. In response, Faubus proclaimed, "Now begins the crucifixion." Unwilling to declare war on the federal government, Faubus declared that "tensions... had lessened to a considerable extent" and withdrew the National Guard from the school, leaving it to others to protect the African American students. The Little Rock Police Department had to assume full responsibility for maintaining order and ensuring the safety of the black students as they entered Central High School on September 23.[39]

City authorities put assistant police chief Gene Smith in charge. Marvin Potts, the segregationist chief of police, stayed away. Worried that his police officers shared the sentiments of the crowd, Smith threatened to shoot any officer who failed to perform his duties. To show them that he meant business, Smith walked behind the police cordon around Central High School with his gun drawn. Edwin Dunaway, a liberal local lawyer who took a behind-the-scenes role in the conflicts, concluded later that the shift in assignments had been fortunate because "Marvin was an absolute milquetoast; Gene was not afraid of a buzzsaw."[40]

Once the crowd got the news that the African American students had entered the building, the level of rage intensified and the promise of violence was unleashed. Cries of "the niggers are in" joined with exhortations for white students in the high school to come out. Carol Thomason shouted, "My daughter's in there with those niggers." Angry whites turned on a small group of African American newspapermen, yelling "Kill them, kill them." They kicked Alex Wilson of the Memphis *Tri-State Defender* and hit him on the head with a brick. Onlookers and journalists reported that Faubus surrogate Jimmy Karam orchestrated the resisters' actions and encouraged their attacks on white and black journalists and on others. Members of the mob understood their role in sustaining Faubus's claims that violence would accompany desegregation. They asked reporters: "Well, do you believe that there will be violence now? The Governor was right. You can see that." Faubus claimed afterward that "The trouble in Little Rock vindicates my judgment."[41]

On-the-scene broadcasts from a segregationist radio station claimed that violence had broken out in the school itself. In response, worried parents converged on the school grounds demanding the right to remove their children. They were allowed to do so. As the menacing crowd threatened to break through the police lines, the situation grew more dangerous. The parents of the African American students, who had been asked by school officials to stay away, could only worry from afar. Police Chief Gene Smith decided at midday that his officers had to remove the black students to ensure their safety. The mob had won—for the moment.[42]

In the meantime, President Eisenhower received confused information from local observers and authorities. They noted that no one seemed to be in charge, that local leaders were not speaking publicly or advancing solutions to the disorder, and that U.S. Attorney Osro Cobb, who was charged with handling the situation in Little Rock for the federal government, was "a weakling and incompetent." The president, who had already decided that he would use federal troops if the disorders continued the next day, released a statement that federal laws and court orders "cannot be flouted with impunity by any individual or any mob of extremists." When mobs again assembled at Central High the next morning, Eisenhower ordered federal troops into Little Rock.[43]

Little Rock's citizens reacted with strong but mixed emotions. Some saw the presence of the troops as an unthinkable and oppressive threat to states' rights and white freedoms, an invasion evoking ancient memories of federal occupation almost a century before. Others, including many moderates, viewed the troops as an unpalatable but necessary means to the restoration of public order. All waited anxiously for the first signs of federal action. Blossom, who shared the moderates' view, described the scene: "There was a rumble of heavy wheels outside in the darkness.... The grim procession could be seen in sharp outline as the vehicles lumbered past a huge and brightly lighted commercial billboard... [with] the words: 'WHO will build Arkansas IF HER OWN PEOPLE DO NOT?'"[44]

Most Little Rock residents, however, were hostile to school desegregation and opposed to the president's decision to intervene. Despite this hostility, Eisenhower took care to create the impression that the request for federal troops came from local authorities. Indeed, Little Rock Mayor Woodrow Wilson Mann had been communicating his fears to the White House in the preceding days. At the prompting of the White House, Mann sent a telegram to the president declaring that the crowds were larger than the previous day and that the "mob is armed and engaging in fisticuffs and other acts of violence." He stated that only federal troops would "restore peace and order and compliance with your proclamation."[45]

The use of public violence posed a critical problem for segregationist organizations: how to maintain public sympathy for their cause and how to deny a direct connection to a politics of threat and violence when others charged that their supporters had caused the disorders. In response, the segregationists used representations of gender to recast themselves as the victims of federal violence and as victims of the purported dangers involved in racial change. To pressure the governor to defy federal authority, they linked "capitulation" to federal authority with masculine dishonor. To discredit supporters of desegregation, they claimed that they had subversive connections and intentions.

The meanings of the mob scenes at Central High School were not self-evident; neither were they fully controlled by Faubus, the media, or other political actors. News stories reflected the politics of their ownership and locality. The stories represented segregationist crowds as Christian law-abiding folks or as poor whites looking for a pretext to vent their racial hatreds. Gender perceptions shaped observers' interpretations of the meanings of violence, although it did so in contradictory ways. Many described women at the scene either as unruly and dangerous hysterics or as loving mothers protecting their children.[46]

Representations of women as mob participants reveal the intense ambivalence experienced by many observers who analyzed the role of women in the violent confrontations. Segregationists interpreted these white women as victims of integration and of the violence that accompanied it in Little Rock. Mainstream media, as well as critics of violent resistance to desegregation, often described women's behavior in the crowds as both hyperfeminine in its extreme emotionality and as unfeminine in dress, in demeanor, and in its hatefulness and unruliness. Mob violence itself was feminized, described as "belligerent, shrieking and hysterical." In Benjamin Fine's front page *New York Times* story on the September 23, 1957 disorders, women screamed and men yelled: "Hysteria spread from the shrieking girls to members of the crowd. Women cried hysterically, tears running down their faces." The story also noted that some of the women in the crowd used a rhetoric of gender to provoke more violent resistance by the men, taunting them by questioning their masculinity: "Are you men?" and, from a woman who had failed to break through the police lines, "Where's your manhood?" Their words also suggest that some women felt unable to use the force that they believed necessary.[47]

While the women's actions were not entirely pacific, for some observers the participation of women endowed the mobs with benign intent. Reporting for the *Arkansas Democrat*, Bascom N. Timmons discounted the potential danger of the crowds at Central High School by peopling them with innocent mothers and children:

> But some of the Little Rock "mob" were school children, armed with nothing more lethal than school books. And there was a preponderance of women. One does not ordinarily think of the raw material for mobs as coming from mothers who bear children, nurture them to school age, sacrifice for them, wish them trained and educated in the best environment.[48]

The Mothers' League reinforced this view of childhood innocence and self-sacrificing maternal love by speaking out against violence. In an August 1957 meeting of the Mothers' League, a man wanted to know how many would show up at Central High School when desegregation began so that they could "push back" any blacks who dared to enter. When he added that he "[imagined] there are a few shotguns in Little Rock, too," Mrs. O. R. Aaron, president of the Mothers' League, told him that the members of her organization were "trying to keep down violence."[49]

In their interviews with the FBI and in other statements, Mothers' League leaders repeatedly said that the threat of violence came from high school students of both races and from the provocative presence of blacks in "white" spaces. One woman who expressed sympathy with the Mothers'

League stated that she thought violence would occur when African American students participated in school social activities, thereby naturalizing the connection between sexual fears and violent responses. Even as they sought to repress white violence in their ranks, they rationalized and tacitly encouraged it. They did so by advancing the view that the ultimate cause of violence was desegregation and not the resistance to it.[50]

The strategy of mobilizing large numbers of segregationist women to converge at Central High School as desegregation began resonated in high places. By early October 1957, FBI Director J. Edgar Hoover advised the Eisenhower administration to take no further legal action to enjoin the segregationists to obey federal law on the grounds that the crowds had included large numbers of ministers and women. Hoover believed that the FBI would lose legitimacy in Little Rock if it targeted ministers and white women. With the FBI director, the Mothers' League achieved its goal of cloaking massive resistance to desegregation with respectability.[51]

The Mothers' League sought to legitimize segregationist actions by employing maternalist rhetoric about the safety and welfare of their children. They called themselves a "group of Christian mothers opposed to violence," even as they fanned white fears and, once desegregation had begun, orchestrated the harassment and intimidation of African American students at Central High. The women's organization helped segregationists to deny the centrality of violence to their political position. Their mobilization around a Christian identity, whether it was an appeal to an encoded anti-Semitism or to an unspecified religious solidarity with other whites, was designed to render their values and actions unassailable.

Mothers' League members' claims to a maternal authority were based on an ideology of sexual propriety defined within a racist system. Their rhetoric focused on themes of sexual (and other) dangers posed to whites by integration. Their mobilization strategies concentrated particularly on recruiting the mothers of girls attending Central High. Acting with the Capital Citizens' Council, Mothers' League members deployed vintage stereotypes of African American men as violent sexual predators. They focused constantly on the dangers of interracial dating and marriage, dangers that stemmed as much from their daughters' sexual agency as from the actions of African American males.[52]

The Mothers' League and other segregationists thus fanned popular fears about student violence, hoping that the threat of disorder would justify a refusal to comply with the *Brown* decision. Their conviction that integration was unthinkable and their fear that public officials would compromise their cause meant that the arch segregationists needed and wanted the threat of violence. Most of them also recoiled from the implications of their embrace of violence, routinely projecting violent feelings and impulses onto others, usually unnamed "students." The arch segregationists' claim to "respectable resistance" required that they maintain the appearance of lawfulness. That appearance also served their efforts to elude legal accountability for attempting to obstruct the execution of a federal court order.[53]

At the same time, the power of the segregationists' dissent rested upon their apocalyptic vision of the consequences of racial change—consequences so ominous that they had to be prevented at all cost. In their view, racial change threatened untold harm to whites, to "civilization," to the meaning of America—in short, to the moral order they embraced. It also threatened their children by undermining the authority of segregationist parents over their children's values, associations, and behavior.[54]

Segregationists alleged that whites were the real victims of the politics of integration and they played on the fears about interracial sex that southern whites had long associated with integration. After President Eisenhower sent federal troops to Little Rock to support lawful desegregation in late September, Faubus declared to the citizens of Arkansas that "We are now an occupied territory." Claiming that several whites had suffered bayonet wounds inflicted by federal soldiers, he added that "evidence of the naked force of the federal government is here apparent in the unsheathed bayonets in the backs of school girls." As Phoebe Godfrey has noted, the powerful rhetoric deployed by Faubus relied on "a clear sexual image reverberating no doubt back to Civil War fears of the Yankee rapist."[55]

In a speech before the Capital Citizens' Council in January 1958, council leader Roy V. Harris of Georgia stated that whites throughout the South were grateful to the resisters in Little Rock as they confronted ostensibly abusive federal troopers:

> Pictures flashed all over the world of innocent young high school girls being pushed along the sidewalks of your city by the bayonets of paratroopers. Pictures flashed all over the world showing a man in your town with blood streaming down his face while under arrest by the federal troops.[56]

Figure 2. "Remember Little Rock" political icon.

White southerners used the photograph of federal troops following young white girls at Central High captioned with the words "Remember Little Rock" as a political icon. This representation, appearing on envelopes, fliers, and other documents, had great resonance in the South. The slogan "Remember Little Rock" became a rallying cry for massive resistance to desegregation. The *Arkansas Democrat*, the pro-Faubus newspaper in Little Rock, used similar pictures and headlines such as "Spectator Bayoneted, Another Clubbed by Tough Paratroopers" and "CHS Emptied by Bomb Scare Shortly after U.S. Troops Force Integration" in its coverage of the arrival of the federal troops. These images reinforced the message that the intent and actions of the federal government were violent and coercive while the people in the crowds around the high school were peaceable spectators.[57]

When Governor Faubus claimed that FBI agents in Little Rock had taken into custody adolescent schoolgirls who had been "held incommunicado for hours of questioning while their frantic parents knew nothing of their whereabouts," he expressed and played on parents' fears regarding the vulnerability of their daughters to racial change. As Phoebe Godfrey perceptively noted, "Faubus's genius was to seal the two fears together—federal authority and miscegenation—in one sizzling and politically efficacious package." Parents were especially fearful of their daughters' budding cultural and sexual autonomy when it occurred within the context of racial integration. The parents' inability to exercise power over school politics in Little Rock combined with the "moral panic" engendered by changes in sexual mores and in the family structure to fuel a powerful politics of rage evidenced by the women and men of the segregationist movement.[58]

While segregationist white girls and women enacted the role of passive and nonviolent "victims" of integration, their male counterparts assumed the role of "protectors" of white women and defenders of segregation. Paradoxically, this allowed white women to assume critical roles in organizing segregationist politics in Little Rock without apparently violating southern white gender norms. At the same time, it displaced men's sense of victimization and thus of masculine failure onto female figures. Otherwise the figures of federal troops—associated in history with southern men's defeat in the Civil War—might have carried a different message. As David Goldfield and others have concluded, southern defeat was redeemed only through representations of planter culture as the height of genteel civilization and of Reconstruction as the epitome of a jackbooted military and social oppression of whites. In Little Rock, where bumper stickers with the words "Occupied Arkansas" proliferated, white men transformed their fear of victimization into a righteous defiance of tyrants and denied that fear through the iconography of feminine victimization they circulated throughout the South.[59]

Sexual fears were not the only concern of those who opposed racial change. In an anonymous letter, one segregationist wrote to Virgil Blossom that African Americans were not "working for equality but supremacy—with *your* help, they will get it." The message was written on a comic strip depicting a future inversion of class relations between blacks and whites. In that world to come, a white man worked either as a chauffeur, a shoe shine, or a policeman for blacks whose economic supremacy was signified by their affluent attire and their ability to secure service and deference from whites. One frame depicted an African American man marrying a white woman (labeled "Blossom's daughter" by the letter's author) while her hapless father watched. White men suffered complete loss *as men* in this vision of the future. Their losses included not only economic privilege but also sexual control over white women and social esteem that derived from that economic privilege. The stakes of the desegregation struggle therefore included white manhood itself.[60]

The cartoon, moreover, revealed that segregationists occupied a rule-or-be-ruled racial order. The comic strip pictured "The White Man of Today" standing hat in hand under a tree defying a bird to drop a load on him with the words "Go ahead, I've let everyone else." The message was obvious enough—white men facing racial and political challenges from African Americans and the federal government could choose either supremacy or capitulation. Within this worldview, forged equally from class oppression and racial privilege, white men's freedom required black people's oppression.[61]

A belief in the moral superiority of whites heightened the sense of injustice that arch segregationists felt when blacks acted to secure their rights. This sense of injustice was expressed in part through claims that African Americans were unable to support themselves or secure advancement without the assistance of whites, whose ostensibly advanced state of civilization and personal generosity enabled the very survival of blacks. Segregationists' conception of themselves as responsible and industrious workers and of blacks as parasitic dependents underwrote white claims to economic preference and political dominance. Many hate letters to Arkansas NAACP leader Daisy Bates expressed white moral superiority and contained threats to discontinue accustomed acts of "generosity," including the provision of employment. Carol Woods of Pine Bluff, for example, wrote that her tax dollars had provided good schools for blacks and that "NEVER AGAIN WILL I DO ONE THING FOR THE NEGRO RACE NEVER." From the point of view of Woods and many other segregationists, African Americans who did not play their roles according to white scripts evidenced ingratitude and threatened a dangerous racial inversion.[62]

Many middle-class whites, in contrast to the arch segregationists, were more concerned about the social disorder that characterized opposition to racial change than they were about moral and economic threats. They interpreted local conflicts through the lens of class rather than race. Some middle-class whites in Little Rock concluded that the governor had enabled the rule of poor whites. Adolphine Fletcher Terry, for example, wrote: "For days I walked about, unable to concentrate on anything, except the fact that we had been disgraced by a group of poor whites and a portion of the lunatic fringe that every town possesses. I wondered where the better class had been while this was being concocted." *Arkansas Gazette* owner, J. N. Heiskell, who favored segregation, supported the decision of his publisher, Hugh Patterson, and editor, Harry Ashmore, to oppose Faubus because he was unwilling "to let those kind of people (rednecks) run my town." His views were widely shared by the media, which often depicted violent resistance to integration as a predominantly working-class affair.[63]

The stress on the racial violence of the working class ignored the support, tacit and overt, given to the working-class resisters by "the better class" in Little Rock. Although the crowds that gathered at Central High were predominantly working class, their leaders included ministers, lawyers, and merchants. As one Little Rock businessman later told reporter

Gertrude Samuel: "I have no use for Faubus or Guthridge. Yet I feel a bit of comfort whenever a roadblock is thrown up to stop the plans of the N.A.A.C.P., and they're the biggest roadblocks to have come along."[64]

That businessman's willingness to allow working-class segregationists to do the public dirty work of opposing integration was widely shared with others of his class. Henry Woods later noted the silence of the business leaders: "In fact, the vast majority of them were so blinded by prejudice and by the fact that they didn't want that high school integrated, period—they were sympathetic with whatever would be done to delay it or stop it. Now, I'm not saying that they liked the idea of a mob, I don't think they liked that." But, according to Woods, they did believe that white resistance to desegregation discredited the very idea of racial change. Elizabeth Huckaby attributed middle-class silence to intimidation:

> Unfortunately, many people not in their [the mob's] class—much above it, in fact—are using this violence feeling [*sic*] as an excuse for defending the governor's actions. The parallel with Hitler... is too close for comfort: the leaders in school and town silenced by physical threats, principally to children, and by economic boycotts; second-rate professional people doing the big talking for the rough and rather inarticulate mob—inarticulate except for the usual epithets.[65]

The politics of class and race enacted in Little Rock were therefore quite complex. Most whites preferred to retain segregation, but many in the middle class were deeply distressed at the disorders and repressions that attended massive resistance to desegregation in Little Rock. Although membership in the Capital Citizens' Council and Mothers' League was relatively small, the membership's working-class roots and the rhetoric they employed bespoke the political mobilization of a racialized class consciousness that would later result in electoral support for segregationist candidates in working-class neighborhoods.[66]

Enraged at the violent defiance of federal authority by the demonstrators in Little Rock, President Eisenhower wasted no time in denouncing their behavior as "disgraceful" and promising that he would use the "full power" of his office to prevent any further obstruction of the law in Little Rock. Speaking from the Southern Governors' Conference in Sea Island, Georgia, Faubus denied that Eisenhower had the authority to use federal troops without a request from him. The scene was set for a historic confrontation until Little Rock's lame-duck mayor, Woodrow Wilson Mann, asked presidential assistant Maxwell Rabb on September 24, 1957 for federal troops to restore order. Having provided the administration with cover by issuing a local request for federal troops, Mann also urged Eisenhower to federalize the Arkansas National Guard to prevent Faubus from employing state police to fire on federal troops. Rabb instructed the mayor to send a telegram requesting federal forces in order "to clear our files" and Mann promptly did so.[67]

On the night of September 23, President Eisenhower relaxed by watching the Walt Disney animated film *Song of the South*. The next day he directed troops from the 101st Airborne Division to go to Little Rock to protect the legitimacy of federal authority. Faubus reacted to the president's action with a military metaphor: "I feel like MacArthur. I have been relieved of my command." Eisenhower intervened, not because he wanted to stop violence or because he opposed massive resistance to desegregation, but to protect the authority and prestige of the presidency and the international prestige of the country in the face of a state government in open insurrection against federal courts.[68]

Many segregationists, however, experienced federal presence itself as violence. Shortly after Eisenhower's order, Margaret Jackson, another of the leaders in the Mothers' League, filed suit to have the federal troops removed. She alleged that the troops "did intimidate, mutilate, bayonet and bludgeon private citizens" and "endangered the lives and safety of the petitioners." Taking up a theme already employed by Faubus, she worried that young people who were "impetuous and excitable" might "at an unguarded moment, say... or do something that would cause them to be bayonetted." In February 1958, Everett Barnes, a science teacher at Central High who opposed desegregation, told the Arkansas State Police that he found it difficult to teach "with the 'ring of steel around the school'" and further that "the feeling of being constantly watched became 'sickening.'"[69]

Faubus and other segregationist men used a powerful rhetoric of invasion and emasculation to describe the harmful effects of federal authority in matters of race. Faubus, moreover, understood that segregationists saw his inability to find a face-saving way to avert federal intervention as both a shameful capitulation to the South's enemies and as the occasion for his own abasement. The rhetoric of states' rights and gubernatorial autonomy that Faubus employed expressed both the White South's historic support for states' autonomy and an attempt to shore up his own dignity.[70]

After the federal court enjoined Faubus from interfering with integration, Jim Johnson, speaking for the states' arch segregationists, begged Faubus "not to humiliate" the state *and himself* by submitting to the jurisdiction of the court. According to Johnson, "Such action of submission will be an unwarranted surrender of rights reserved to the states." In a later discussion of his uneven power struggle with the president, Faubus said that he did not "believe in degrading anyone or putting anyone in a subservient role to another." *Arkansas Gazette* editor Harry Ashmore wrote that after the meeting between the governor and the president "there remained some doubt as to who emerged with whose sword." Once federal troops arrived, however, no doubt remained. The language of submission and surrender, indeed the common recourse to military metaphors to describe the encounter, suggests that federal-state confrontation also involved a contest for manhood, one that Faubus (and the South) had apparently lost, at least for the moment.[71]

At this point, some segregationist leaders decided that winning the contest for manhood would require assistance from "outside agitators" equally dedicated to maintaining segregation. In December 1957, the Rev. Wesley Pruden revealed at a Mothers' League meeting that he had met with segregationists from Mississippi, Louisiana, and Alabama and that they assured him they would use violence in Little Rock if violence was necessary to prevent school integration. Whether he urged them to renounce such tactics is not clear, but seems unlikely. The FBI, which apparently monitored the Mothers' League meeting, did not investigate the matter further.[72]

Faubus shared the segregationists' conviction that deference to federal authority signified a loss of masculine honor, but he also knew that resistance was futile after the federal court issued an injunction prohibiting him from impeding desegregation. According to Tony Freyer, Faubus got "what he needed" when he withdrew the state National Guard under a federal court order because "he had made a show of defiance and had made it appear that his retreat was being forced by a higher authority." In fact, what Faubus wanted was impossible because he and his supporters believed that a forced retreat signified a loss of white manhood and southern honor. As with the Hoxie setback, masculine redemption could be secured only with continued defiance. Ironically, the presence of federal troops provided a perfect symbolic foil for the segregationists' political culture of victimization and righteous retribution.[73]

Clearly, the segregationists' defiance had to take different forms to be effective after the federal troops arrived. From the beginning, supporters of massive resistance in Arkansas tried to silence or eliminate those who advocated for integration, token or otherwise. As was true elsewhere in the South, the linchpin of these efforts was a legal and ideological assault on the NAACP. Beginning in 1957, Arkansas Attorney General Bruce Bennett filed a series of suits that were intended to obtain membership and donor lists and other records of the organization in order to enable segregationist reprisals against NAACP members and supporters. He and other conservatives in the state charged that the NAACP was thick with Communists who were using it to advance a Soviet agenda of world domination. They devised various state and local laws to discredit and marginalize all who supported desegregation and to deploy a politics of fear intended to drive potential members away from specific organizations and ideas. This monitoring of acceptable political thought and action served to narrow the terms of discussion and reduce the available political solutions.[74]

Within a few weeks of her action to protect Elizabeth Eckford from the dangerous mob at Central High School, Grace Lorch, a member of the NAACP, received a subpoena to appear at a hastily organized hearing before the U.S. Senate Internal Subversion Committee. She declared publicly that she was called to appear only because of her protective actions on behalf of Ekford, a charge that irritated some members of the committee. Lorch refused to answer their questions, stating that she had been subpoenaed with very little notice and had been denied her constitutional rights, including the right to counsel. In a letter to the editor of the *Arkansas Gazette* in February 1958, she decried the committee's tactics in denying her the right to speak and noted the importance of "the right to assemble peacefully... and to discuss common problems without fear of persecution" particularly with "attempts to change the old patterns of economic backwardness and racial discrimination."[75]

Although Indiana Senator William E. Jenner, himself a committee member, denied the racial motivation for interrogating Grace Lorch, the committee's actions in her case and others demonstrated the centrality of red-baiting to the South's campaign of massive resistance to desegregation. As Jane Cassels Record noted in the summer of 1957, the idea that the civil rights movement was the product of a pervasive Communist influence over credulous African Americans allowed southern whites to continue to believe that blacks in the South were content with their lot even in the face of evidence that many southern blacks were actively challenging segregation. The anti-Communist posturing of southerners in Congress also exemplified the power of the South in the federal government and the persistence of "McCarthyism" in the late 1950s. As white southerners demonized the federal government for the *Brown* decision, they helped to create an oppressive national state designed to discredit activists and their causes, to monitor political thought, and to limit policy alternatives.[76]

In the postwar South, anti-Communism and anti-Semitism provided interlinked ideologies for white attempts to uphold the South's existing racial order. As Clive Webb has noted, "The desegregation crisis sparked the largest explosion of anti-Semitism in southern history." In Little Rock, anti-Semitism was conspicuously evident in Jim Johnson's 1956 campaign for governor and in the widespread distribution of literature claiming that Jews were behind the entire civil rights movement. This view was concisely articulated in a hate letter sent to Daisy Bates: "This NAACP you are president of in Little Rock is a Communist organization sponsored [*sic*] by a bunch of Jews, and a bunch of illiterates."[77]

Racist red-baiters extorted a particularly high price from Grace Lorch's husband, Lee, whose civil rights activities, radical affiliations, and Jewish identity made him a potent symbol for the segregationists. Lee Lorch was a professor of mathematics at Philander Smith College in Little Rock. His wife's assistance to Elizabeth Eckford and the accusation that she was a Communist motivated white donors to put enormous pressure on the African American college to fire him. The college president did not ask for Lorch's resignation but did tell him that continuing in his job would result in the closure of the school for lack of funds. When Lorch left Philander Smith, it was the fourth time he had lost an academic job for his civil rights activism since finishing his World War II military service. In the North, his opposition to housing segregation led to his ouster from the City College of New York and the Pennsylvania State University. At Fisk University, an African American college in Nashville, and at Philander Smith, his support for school desegregation led to donor pressure to fire him. Lorch's political activism also led the House Committee on Un-American Activities to subpoena him in 1954 and threaten to indict him for contempt when he refused to answer questions about his political affiliations. He was ultimately forced to seek employment in Canada.[78]

As a result of the media exposure received by the Lorches nationwide, national NAACP leaders became anxious about Lee Lorch's prominent role in the Little Rock NAACP. In mid-September 1957, Daisy Bates assured Gloster Current that she had "had a long, long conference [with the Lorches] early in the game about that... I told them not to project themselves in the forefront... [because] this is too important." According to Lee Lorch, local NAACP leaders did not ask for his formal resignation, despite pressure by national leaders to remove him.[79]

Although he himself had been accused of Communist affiliations in the 1954 gubernatorial race, Faubus was not above using McCarthyite tactics when they served his purposes. He found the Lorches to be a convenient foil in his efforts to keep abreast of his followers in demonizing those advocating for school desegregation in Arkansas. In a May 1959 speech denouncing a recall election directed at the segregationists on the Little Rock School Board, he claimed that Grace Lorch had been a delegate to a state communist convention. He also used the Arkansas State Police to place under surveillance certain integrationists and some Arkansas citizens whose interracial associations violated racial norms. Acting under the aegis of the Arkansas Legislative Council, the state police also interviewed some teachers and administrators at Central High in early 1958 regarding desegregation in the school. As with Bennett's red-baiting campaign, these tactics were designed to intimidate and silence any who dissented from the South's racial orthodoxies.[80]

The politics of threat claimed its share of success. When the state police appeared at the door of a meeting of the Arkansas Council on Human Relations, two of the men in attendance decided to make a quick exit through the back. Charles Johnston, who worked for a savings and loan company, described the scene: "What did Fred Darragh and I do—duck out the back window. I had to push him over the fence in the back yard.... That's my comment on white man's courage—when push came to shove, we cowarded out."[81]

Little Rock's moderate leadership vacillated between pious protestations of its regard for lawful and orderly public behavior and silence on the critical issues facing the community. Many business leaders had strong economic ties to Faubus and state government; others feared the loss of

customers through segregationist boycotts. Most shared the resisters' belief
in segregation, although they did not generally accord it the same level
of priority in their political goals. As Irving Spitzberg pointed out, Blossom "had directed his appeal to exactly those men who held the community's power during the crisis, and he had persuaded them to acquiesce to
his plan." Acquiescence, however, was not enough to generate the vision
and courage required in the heated political climate of Little Rock in the
fall of 1957. Blossom had bet on the wrong horse.[82]

From the beginning of the crisis, Little Rock's business leadership sought
to promote its views on "law and order" and avoid public discussion of
race and desegregation. On October 2, 1957, twenty-five business leaders
issued a statement affirming their belief that Little Rock's citizens, "regardless of their feelings on the subject of integration" were "dedicated to government by law and order," hated violence, and were willing to use "democratic legal processes for [the] settlement of differences." They asked the
public to support law enforcement, "condemn violence or the threat of
violence or the encouragement of violence," and pray for "guidance and
counsel" for their leaders. This attempt to sever the issues of race and political order proved both timorous and futile.[83]

The caution of Little Rock's business leaders mirrored that of its religious leaders. Even though some clerical authorities privately supported
desegregation and a courageous few championed a racially egalitarian
Christian theology in their churches, most who said anything merely urged
their congregants to support "law and order." Rev. Robert Brown, who
believed "the right to speak and to be heard on the social issues of life" to
be one of the most pressing concerns of the ministers, wrote despairingly
that he had "to admit the staggering conclusion that as clergymen they
were largely without influence in the time of trouble." He surmised that
the "casualness with which these people accept the pragmatic values of the
business and social world should have warned them [clergy] that the ministry was looked upon as something of an anachronism." Many ministers
in Little Rock experienced significant disagreements with their congregants over fundamental values:

What they [clergy] were proclaiming as sacred, many of their own
church members rejected as impractical and unrealistic. What they
witnessed as the Gospel, the average man would not accept. What

they insisted was truth, not a few disavowed as moralism and senti-
mentality.

The result, according to Rev. Brown, was that the laity "reserved the right
to make a cafeteria approach to the Gospel."[84]

In October 1957, an interracial group of Arkansas clerics from various
faiths issued a joint call for a day of prayer on Columbus Day. According
to Rev. Brown, who was an organizer for the event, the day of prayer would
enable the restoration of the communication within congregations that the
clergy believed was necessary for any long-term solutions. Each religious
group was to meet in its own segregated church or synagogue and pray for
a solution to the problem of desegregation. The day of prayer received ring-
ing endorsements from Eisenhower, Faubus, the school board, and numerous community leaders, all of whom agreed on "the need for humility, the
guidance of God and the necessity of prayer and discussion." Faubus lauded
this effort at reconciliation within and between congregations, concluding
that it was not a time "for recrimination or blame-placing," even as he
continued condemning the Little Rock School Board, the federal government, the NAACP, and numerous others for their actions in support of
compliance with constitutional law.[85]

Some liberals thought the clergy's efforts at this time lacked moral content or a substantive plan for change. According to Nathan Griswold, the
day of prayer became so vague a concept that almost anyone could support
it. Griswold criticized the compromise at the heart of the focus on creating
white unity: "Bishop Brown said this was an effort at reconciliation. You
see, it was reconciliation without ethical discrimination."[86]

The ministers' approach reveals the impossibility of solving the problem
of segregation from within the institutions, ideologies, and modes of interaction forged by segregation. Their commitment to the construction of
harmony within white congregations and among their clergymen precluded any action and left the ministers in the same position as the local
elites whom some of the ministers had criticized for a similar paralysis.
Operating from the premises of the "progressive mystique" so perceptively
described by William Chafe, the ministers believed that they could not
speak or act in public until all of them had agreed to a specific plan. According to Rev. Brown, they could not answer the question, "Is this the
Church's task?" The ministers' ideology of moderation and reconciliation

within their churches ceded power to conservative and moderate members of their churches, who could use threats to leave the church or withdraw financial support to great effect, even in churches ostensibly committed to racial change.[87]

Some women parishioners, however, urged the clergy to greater resolve and themselves condemned Faubus's actions publicly. On September 9, 1957, the Council of Church Women of Little Rock and North Little Rock published a resolution condemning the governor for using the state police "to defy the order of the federal court instead of upholding the law of the land." They declared that it was their "Christian conviction that enforced segregation of any group of persons because of race, creed or color is a violation of Christian principles." They also worried that Faubus's actions would endanger "the effectiveness of those who represent us in mission posts throughout the world." Sociologists Ernest Campbell and Thomas Pettigrew reported that many of their informants in Little Rock had stated that "many of the church women were 'far ahead of' their ministers and the men of the churches" and were asking for explanations from their ministers when the ministers did not "take bold positions."[88]

The Rev. Colbert Cartwright also dissented from the culture of consensus embraced by most of his peers. Determined to take a forthright stand with his congregation and the community in support of integration, he not only spoke publicly but also wrote about the crisis in Little Rock in national publications. Moreover, unlike some proponents of obedience to court orders, he was willing to criticize the school board and other moderates for their failure to advocate for integration on moral grounds and for the tokenism that they enacted in school policies.[89]

His forthright action caused deep schisms in his congregation and prompted some parishioners to leave and others to express their disappointment in his performance of his pastoral role. Cartwright met with members who disagreed with him but would not alter his position or consider leaving his post. He found that the most important challenges in his church came from the moderates, "those timid souls ... who think the end of the world has come when disagreement does appear." One irate parishioner noted that if he ever left the church it would not be because he disagreed with the minister's views but because he was "tired of strife and turmoil and intolerance of intolerance."[90]

Cartwright's efforts to persuade his fellow clergymen to follow his lead met with a similar response. When he complained privately in the fall of 1957 that no community leaders were working to gain public support for desegregation, he included the clergy, noting that they shared in the moderate conviction that "any positive action will only 'stir things up.'" After reading an article Cartwright wrote in the *Christian Century* excoriating the Little Rock School Board for its policies of gradualism and tokenism, Virgil Blossom called the minister and threatened to damage his public reputation. According to Nathan Griswold, "The arrogant tone and abusive language [used by Blossom] were those ordinarily associated with rabid racists, not with the cultured superintendent of a city school system." Cartwright wrote to friends in December 1957 that Blossom had "sought in rather desperate and ugly ways to discredit me, and he [had] succeeded with most of my fellow ministers."[91]

For the Rev. Brown, however, the strategy of reconciliation perfectly expressed the "moderate" position in politics. He believed that only with open and respectful conversations among those who were "tempered and temperate; restrained and composed; patient and tolerant" could workable solutions be found. Moderates, he claimed in a speech, possessed "faith in man's ability to work out his problems for they have a prior faith in God's willingness to assist him in doing so." In his draft of the speech, Brown crossed out the word "equitably" after "problems," indicating through omission the insignificance of justice in moderate approaches to social issues, the priority of process over substance. As was true of other self-designated moderates, Brown understood his position in relation to extremists, who were defined as emotional idealists who refused to consider problems in all their complexity or to "broaden their base" to accommodate "the sincere moderate—the 'man of good will.'" Local elites used the contrast between dangerous "extremists" (a code word for arch segregationists and civil rights activists) and beleaguered moderates to construct the boundaries of acceptable political discourse and action in racial politics.[92]

After the day of prayer, law enforcement authorities at all levels made no effort to identify and punish the September rioters at Central High. By December, local authorities had either dropped the charges or suspended the fines for those arrested by the Little Rock police for their actions in the September disorders. Federal officials had likewise decided against prosecutions. Business leaders issued no complaints that lax enforcement of the laws in these cases would diminish popular respect for law and order, although the worsening situation at Central High offered substantial evidence that this was so. The silence of the moderates grew positively deafening. They kept silent even though the city's political strife and the uncertain future of its schools were scaring off potential business investors.[93]

Concerned that the costs of Little Rock's political conflicts were too high, the moderate leadership came up with a legal strategy that it hoped would secure white consensus and social peace. On February 20, 1958, a business group chaired by Walter Guy wrote a letter to the school board urging it to go to court to secure a delay in implementing its desegregation plan. The committee of business leaders, which had conferred with Faubus, the school board, federal officials, and others as it considered the issue, said that it had "endeavored to approach the problem from an impersonal, non-political, legal and on a non-partisan basis." The delay would, the business leaders averred, "bring about a higher degree of unanimity in the thinking of our citizenship."[94]

As it sought that consensus, the business group claimed to have consulted with unnamed African American leaders, not including Daisy Bates or the parents of the black students then attending Central High School. Characterizing the NAACP as a source of public turmoil, Guy said that he saw "no point in talking to groups we knew were obdurate and willing to forsake law and order to gain their point." He further stated that they had also chosen not to talk to the "counterparts" of the NAACP, by which he meant the Capital Citizens' Council and the Mothers' League. Given that his committee had conducted a poll, which revealed that 86 percent of whites wanted the black students removed from Central High and 85 percent of blacks wanted them to stay, it is clear that some white moderates fully realized that local African Americans did not and would not consent to their solutions.[95]

On the same day that the Guy committee released its letter to the school board, the board filed a case in U.S. District Court requesting a delay in implementing its desegregation plan. In its petition, the board claimed that "in its respect for the law of the land," it had been "left standing alone" because of the opposition of state government and "apathy on the part of the Federal Government." The petition noted that opposition to the desegregation plan had created so much unrest at Central High School that it had disrupted educational programs and it asked that desegregation be delayed "until such time as it may be accomplished without an impairment of educational standards." Although Blossom drew attention to the fact that the school board had developed its petition before the Guy committee sent its letter to the board, it was clear that once again school officials and business leaders together decided school policies.[96]

In its petition to the court and in its public statement, the school board chastised the NAACP as an adversary of quality schooling and an exponent of immediate and systematic integration. Claiming that the 1956 lawsuit by the NAACP had sought "total integration in all schools... [to] be accomplished immediately," the school board asked for a delay until it could "offer all students, white and Negro, the quality education which was made available to them prior to September, 1957." The *Arkansas Gazette* argued that the school board's actions showed that it was "more interested in educating the youth of Little Rock than in serving as an agency of the federal courts to enforce integration." The moderate daily thus endorsed not only the school board's decision to return to court but also its refusal to seek injunctions against segregationist leaders.[97]

Whites from across the political spectrum were quick to praise the school board's decision, although Governor Faubus did so grudgingly, claiming that he had repeatedly urged board members to take the course they were finally pursuing. Significantly, Citizens' Council leaders used the language of dominance and submission as they praised the school board's action. Casting the realm of politics as a domain of competition in which "losers" suffered humiliation, Amis Guthridge sought to reassure school board members that "the people I represent" would not see their decision as a "capitulation" or consider it in relation to "who beat whom." His disavowal nonetheless reinforced the idea that political conflicts conferred dignity or debasement as much as they determined particular policy and electoral outcomes.[98]

At the same time, *Arkansas Gazette* editor Harry Ashmore publicly criticized President Eisenhower for his "failure of leadership" on civil rights. In a speech at Harvard University, Ashmore said that the Eisenhower administration had made only "token efforts to pass stringent civil rights legislation," but "at no time did Mr. Eisenhower attempt to use the great moral force of his office to persuade Southerners of the justice of the course the Supreme Court required of them." Eisenhower's failure to provide moral leadership, he concluded, left "the Little Rock School Board the entire burden of carrying out the court order against impossible odds." In his role as editor, however, Ashmore himself had not provided a moral case for school desegregation, although he supported compliance with court orders on legal grounds.[99]

When Ashmore published an expanded version of his speech in *Harper's* in June 1958, he excoriated the Eisenhower administration for backing away from its initial support for the inclusion of a section to increase federal authority in civil rights cases in the 1957 Civil Rights Act. As the president signed the watered-down bill on September 9, he was in the middle of his historic confrontation with Faubus without the weapons his original proposal would have given him. The president's public deference to the power and perspectives of southern legislators was as important in signaling federal weakness as was his decision to authorize an inadequate law. Ashmore also accused the Republican administration of cutting a Faustian deal with southern Senators in return for their approval of William P. Rogers as the new United States Attorney General. Despite the South's ire over the federal government's intervention in Little Rock, not one member of the Senate committee, which counted Senator James Eastland of Mississippi in its ranks, asked even one question regarding Little Rock. This occurred, Ashmore assumed, as a result of "what must have been one of the most singular political deals in recent years." Given Eisenhower's record, Ashmore predicted continued federal weakness in the face of rising southern resistance.[100]

In a later interview, Ashmore also faulted the business elite for its timidity. Concerned with advancing the values and interests of the institutions they served, business leaders would only go as far in preserving public order or advancing racial change as they believed necessary to serve those interests. For them and for Faubus, personal success and political courage were quite at odds. As Ashmore put it:

Well, I think you will find, at any time today or that day, the leaders of the business community are gutless. Their bottom line is don't offend the customers and so anything that gets very controversial, they are going to run for cover. Now usually they are pleased to have something like the *Gazette*, which is ready to take the fire, to keep them from looking so bad.

As new outside investments in Little Rock dried up, the business elite retreated to the Country Club.[101]

In the summer of 1958, Justice Department attorney Arthur Caldwell wrote to school board attorney Archie House to lament the lack of "men of courage" in Little Rock. Of the Little Rock School Board and its travails, he noted that "compared to the hardship and trouble suffered by the school board in Hoxie their harrasment [*sic*] and difficulties were minor indeed." Caldwell worried "about the future of our form of government, state and federal," commenting that "Our country was not founded by cowards and cowards will not preserve it." House defended the board members, declaring that the responsibility for enforcing federal court orders rested with the government that had issued those orders. E. Frederick Morrow, the lone African American in the Eisenhower administration, agreed that the president avoided his responsibilities, concluding that "civil rights in the Eisenhower Administration was handled like a bad dream, or like something that's not very nice, and you shield yourself from it as long as you possibly can, because it just shouldn't be."[102]

At the time, public officials at all levels of government sought to hand off responsibility for the enforcement of peaceful desegregation to others, in part to avoid accountability for advancing civil rights, in part from racist commitments to the existing social order, in part from an ideological allegiance to a particular parsing of authority in a federal system. Faubus, who claimed that the federal government was accountable for the enforcement of federal court orders, denounced that government when it sent troops to Little Rock to do exactly that. He then rode massive resistance to four more terms in office. Eisenhower, who was unduly influenced by his southern white friends in the military and Congress and who was wedded to an unnecessarily limited view of his own authority, believed that local authorities and federal judges should assume responsibility for the enforcement of the *Brown* decision.[103]

The Little Rock School Board, which was arguably the most supine of all the major actors in the crisis over desegregation, knew that it would receive support from Judge Miller and the Justice Department if it sought injunctions against Little Rock's segregationist leaders, but refused to do so. To seek injunctions, however, would have meant the abandonment of the political "safety" of a spurious middle ground. Locked into an alliance with the business community, whose interests and perspectives it represented, the school board predictably chose a path of timorous evasion in service to those interests.

The political impasse that developed was also the logical outcome of Eisenhower's desire to require others, particularly southern whites, to take responsibility for dismantling school segregation. Under the president's policy, which required federal judges to initiate proceedings for injunctions if local officials were unwilling to do so, there was, as Archie House observed, "no solution other than having a strong Federal Judge who will use the contempt procedures unsparingly." Given the veto power accorded locally based politicians, particularly U.S. senators, in the naming of federal judges, House rightly concluded that it looked "as if the politicians will obstruct the appointment of the right kind of a man."[104]

Repeatedly, Faubus and other segregationists deployed a majoritarian rhetoric based on white opposition to school desegregation to justify resistance. Although the opponents of desegregation raised serious issues about the difficulties of enforcing laws that lacked popular support, they ignored the undemocratic practices on which their own politics rested. Political repression and private intimidation were critical to their political strategies, as were threats of violence. The rhetoric and apocalyptic imagery they used and the sheer force of their desire to avert integration made credible the rumors of weapons, gangs, and impending violence, and made violence seem inevitable. Moreover, as labor lawyer James Youngdahl noted, "the new populism of Orval Faubus, defined as including an appeal to all interests of the lower income majority, may be the new look in Southern racism." The politics of class were inextricably tied to white supremacy and cannot be understood outside the context of race.[105]

Those who served as visible symbols of white support for racial change became the objects of public vilification, economic retaliation, and physical threat. Virgil Blossom and other school officials received death threats against themselves and their families. Teachers suspected of supporting desegregation or assisting black students faced intimidating inquisitions from the Arkansas State Police. Because it adamantly supported obedience to federal court orders and thus the implementation of the Blossom Plan, the *Arkansas Gazette* experienced a substantial loss of advertising and subscription revenues. Ministers who publicly espoused the view that Christian beliefs included racial equality endured enormous pressures from their congregants, especially the wealthy donors; some clerics were transferred to positions in other cities.[106]

For their part, the segregationists believed themselves to be on high moral ground. They fortified the notion of white supremacy by representing themselves as the defenders of patriarchal family relations and as the guardians of white women's sexual purity. By constructing white men as reliable providers and protectors and characterizing African Americans as economically and sexually irresponsible and dangerous, they gave emotional fuel to their cause. By casting the federal government in the role of an occupying army, they pressured public officials to defend the honor and manhood of the South through continued resistance. The segregationists' defense of a sexual and gender orthodoxy (not yet labeled "family values") crowned their cause and its tactics with the halo of an irreproachable moral stance. Their fundamentalist religious culture transformed a politics of threat and intimidation into one of righteous retribution against their class enemies in a morally based race war.

Segregationists' intense class resentments focused particularly on Little Rock's civic elite, whom they successfully cowed in the fall of 1957. Although it had technically won as the Blossom Plan received support in the courts and desegregation proceeded at Central High School, the local establishment was in fact in total disarray. Intimidated by the economic, political, and physical threats posed by their adversaries, business leaders retreated as far as they could from the cause of desegregation and silenced those in their ranks who disagreed. In Little Rock, the politics of coercion cut in many directions.

Establishment whites, however, were not the only ones who stood in the way of the segregationist cause. In Little Rock, nine black students demonstrated a militant idealism and physical courage that sometimes belied their "respectable" image. Along with their families and supporters, they paid a disproportionate share of the costs of racial change. As the next chapter demonstrates, those costs were imposed not only by the segregationists, who tried to drive these black students out of Central High School, but also by Little Rock's moderates who tried mightily to stand in the shadows of history.

Uncivil Disobedience: The Politics of Race and Resistance at Central High School, 1957–1958

The worst aspect of the situation was the hour-by-hour and day-by-day TENSION. What bomb threat would prove to be real? Which one of the nine black students would get a switch-blade in the gut? Or acid in the face?

—J. O. Powell, Vice Principal for Boys,
  Central High School[1]

There wasn't much trouble inside the school.

—R. A. Lile, Little Rock School Board[2]

In mid-December 1957, Minnijean Brown cracked under the pressure of the daily harassment she was experiencing at Central High School. In the cafeteria, which was often the site of minor provocations engineered by a cabal of racist white students, she had her way blocked by a chair. Believing that the incident had been intentionally provocative, Minnijean took her tray and dumped its contents, including a bowl of chili, on two boys sitting in the vicinity. Confused, she missed the student who had deliberately moved the chair to block her path. She "had been provoked previously in the same location" and had warned those responsible that "they might get something on them." The two boys she "souped," who had not been involved in racial incidents at school, sympathized with her. One of them said that he "knew she'd been through a lot of strain recently and could be expected to pop off." School officials suspended her until early January.[3]

Temperamentally more spirited and more openly rebellious than the other African American students at Central High School, Minnijean believed that she should be able to participate fully in student life and that she deserved to be treated with respect without fear for her personal safety. The latter conviction led to conflicts with her white antagonists, school officials, and the military as she occasionally talked back to hostile students and demanded that the guards do a better job of protecting African American students. She pushed the boundaries by seeking to participate in Glee Club and other activities in order to showcase her talent as a singer and win acceptance from other students. In the charged atmosphere at Central High School, her personality, her conviction that she was entitled to decent treatment, and her ambitions were an explosive combination.[4]

In order to cope with the constant racial epithets and harassment, Minnijean believed that "you have to feel like you're better than they are in order to keep your morale up high because it makes you feel kind of low when they are always doing something." Her public bravado and her resistance to the limitations placed on her by school officials, however, were interpreted by many of her white classmates as insolent insubordination. One remembered Minnijean as having "a haughty, snotty, look-down-your-nose-at-me attitude." Another recalled that Minnijean "walked the halls as if she belonged there." As Beth Roy concluded, moderate white students were willing to tolerate the presence of African Americans in "their" high school, but not when those students "acted like they were there by right, not by generosity." At the time, whites viewed such behavior as evidence of racial insubordination.[5]

This chapter examines the politics of race at Central High School in 1957–58 in order to illuminate the role of children as political actors, to show the complex relationships between those children and adults in the community, and to examine the ways in which public officials and activists politicized the question of school discipline. In the process, it reveals the importance of the Mothers' League in the creation of segregationist tactics, rhetoric, and ideologies. The interactions of League members and segregationist parents with school officials became the stage on which a racialized politics of class authority and class resentment were enacted. The actions of Daisy Bates and the parents of the African American students demonstrate their determination to make desegregation work while protecting the children from threat and harm. As this chapter makes clear, the indifference of public officials to the concerns of black parents was rooted not only in racism but also in the priorities of the white officials.[6]

As soon as desegregation began in the fall of 1957, Central High School became a theater in which many of Little Rock's students enacted the city's politics of race, usually without the subterfuges adults used to disguise their motives and palliate their critics. With the assistance of adults in the community, some of the city's white adolescents explored the limits of acceptable violence and assumed highly public roles in the conflicts between segregationists and school officials. Most of the school's white students, however, adopted the politics of silence and avoidance favored by the city's adult moderates, encouraged to do so by frightened parents and school officials. Some did so because they shared their parents' views on race, others out of fear or deference to peer pressure, others out of complex motives related to class or gender identities. Melba Pattillo told one administrator that "many white students had [initially] been friendly [to the African American students], but that they had explained that they were [as] afraid of the 'tough' students as the negro students [were]." The inaction of these white students enabled the violence and intimidation directed at the nine African American students by the segregationist hard core at Central High.[7]

Thus isolated, the African American students faced their tormentors without peer support from outside their small beleaguered group. Neither the federal troops nor sympathetic teachers and administrators could offer them systematic protection or an alternative to the politics of racial subordination that was the precondition for their role in desegregation. As a result, the students faced what Melba Pattillo Beals later described as a "haunting aloneness" as they braved the hallways and classrooms of Central High.[8]

The vulnerability of the African American students derived from policies defined by school administrators at all levels as well as those pursued by state officials and the Eisenhower administration. In order to appease local segregationists, Superintendent Virgil Blossom and the Little Rock School Board enforced the school's disciplinary policies against defiant segregationist students with great caution, a policy the school board labeled "restrained mildness." Initially, only incidents witnessed by a teacher or school official would result in any action. Even in those cases, offending white students faced repeated "warnings" or, occasionally, suspensions. Later, school authorities allowed federal troops to serve as witnesses. When faced with adverse publicity and the threat of lawsuits, administrators backed off from expelling repeat offenders. Expulsions remained the rare exception, even when a student's record was littered with documented violations of school rules. The troops stationed in the school could interfere only to protect students' safety and at the beginning of the year school authorities refused to allow them to serve as witnesses to misconduct. Moreover, the Eisenhower administration, under intense pressure from southern politicians to remove the federal troops, sought to minimize the presence and visibility of those troops as soon as it could.[9]

Even before the year began, school officials made it clear that they expected that some white students would insult and persecute African American students, but that black students were never to talk back to their tormentors or act in any way that might antagonize them. Black community leaders reinforced this message in a public meeting held a week before classes were to begin. Panelist Frank W. Smith, for example, urged black students entering white schools to remember that "it is not cowardly to ignore slurring remarks. The Scriptures tell us to turn the other cheek." Blossom later labeled the meeting "constructive," noting that the speakers "discussed all phases of good citizenship and the responsibilities of the students, from scholarship to hygiene," emphasizing "the importance that would be attached to the conduct of the Negro community generally in the next few weeks." Nonetheless, attorney and civil rights activist C. C. Mercer also told the members of the audience to "support the School Board, but speak up if you don't like what it's doing."[10]

Just before classes started in the fall, the African American students attended a workshop on nonviolent resistance given by the Rev. James Lawson of Los Angeles. According to Ernest Green, it was designed to give them strategies on "how we were going to survive in a body of 2,000 plus students and there were only nine of us." They would find the training they received that day relevant throughout the school year as they served a larger cause by stoically enduring the abuse they faced.[11]

By contrast, the staff, faculty, and white students at Central High had received no formal preparation for desegregation. Superintendent Blossom consistently sought to maintain control over all public discussions of school politics, hoping to prevent the emergence of dissent on the issue. The approach taken by school principal Jess Matthews, which was compatible with that of Blossom and perhaps dictated by Blossom, reflected the desire of moderates to manage the situation through silence. J. O. Powell, the vice principal for boys, blamed "the principal's acute sensitivity to the climate of public opinion—which was something less than favorable to any degree of school desegregation" for Matthews' inaction during the crisis.[12]

Despite this policy of silence and inaction, Elizabeth Huckaby, the vice principal for girls at Central High, remained optimistic about school administrators' ability to handle any situation that might arise in relation to school integration. A few days before classes started in 1957, she wrote to her brother that "whatever happens is likely to be outside, not inside, our school. We have always had our pupils under pretty good control and aim to keep them that way." Up to that point they had also had community and parent support for discipline in the school. This was about to change.[13]

After confronting angry menacing crowds in their first two attempts to begin classes at Central High, the "Little Rock Nine" entered the school successfully under the protection of federal troops on September 25, 1957. Years later Ernest Green related his reactions to those experiences: "at that time, and in that atmosphere, for somebody, anybody, to do something to protect black people gave us a tremendous sense of feeling at last that we were somebody." Melba Pattillo "felt proud and sad at the same time," concluding that there was "a reason that I salute the flag." The trauma and triumph that marked those days would continue to characterize the black students' experiences as interracial pioneers in the American South.[14]

Arkansas NAACP leader Daisy Bates felt alienated from her country as she witnessed the rage, hostility, and threats that accompanied school desegregation in early September 1957. "If I could have lifted the Cotton Curtain and walked behind the Iron Curtain," she commented, "I would have told America to go straight to hell because I felt absolutely no justice anywhere in America." Bates later disclosed that she had "been angry all my life about what has happened to my people."[15]

In the fall of 1957, her sense of alienation diminished with the arrival of federal troops and as the ongoing school crisis gave her a sense of mission. Throughout the year, Bates worked long hours to host and manage the press, keep national NAACP leaders informed of local events daily, boost the morale of NAACP members and leaders in Arkansas as they faced intimidation from state government, and marshal support for desegregation in the community. As the Little Rock Nine confronted threats and harassment from an organized group of white students at Central

High, Bates offered daily counsel and assistance to the black students and their families while working assiduously to pressure public officials to discipline the students' tormentors. Likening the situation to a war, Bates said: "I realize now how a general feels when he sends his troops into battle. You are deeply concerned for every one of them every single minute."[16]

From the racial epithets they directed at African American students daily to their public actions, white segregationist students at Central High revealed the decisive role that race played in their resistance to school desegregation. When white students walked out after the entry of the African American students on September 23, 1957, they wrote on the school's sign-out ledger that their reason for leaving was "niggers." They then turned their departure into an impromptu pep rally for segregation, chanting "2–4–6–8—we're not going to integrate." However much some of their elders claimed then and later that states' rights was the founding premise of their dissent, white students clearly understood that race was *the* issue.[17]

Segregationists, both adults and children, engaged in a variety of activities designed to disrupt the normal operation of the schools to such a degree that desegregation would be abandoned. Even before African American students walked through the doors, Central High staff received an anonymous call reporting the presence of dynamite in the school. School administrators, in an effort to conceal the bomb threat, told students to empty their lockers and leave the locker door open before leaving that day because the school planned to have exterminators come in. Such ruses, which fooled no one, would become routine over the academic year. Some parents removed their children when bomb threats were reported. Only the resolve of school administrators and the fact that no bombs actually detonated in the school allowed the school to operate.[18]

After the African American students returned to school on September 25, 1957, with protection from the 101st Airborne Division of the U.S. Army and from the recently federalized Arkansas National Guard, resistant white students began a long-term war of attrition designed to drive the black students from Central High. Taking advantage of the vast size of the school building and grounds, they orchestrated a campaign of verbal threats, name-calling, and physical harassment that ranged from shoving and tripping to spilling ink on students' clothes and putting broken glass on the floor in the gym's shower room. J. O. Powell called it "a kind of Chinese torture, over a long period of time." His counterpart on the distaff side, Elizabeth Huckaby, concluded that "the negro children there were under constant threat" all year.[19]

The task of maintaining discipline inside the school, however, rested primarily with teachers and administrators. Principal Jess Matthews seemed to hope that bulletins urging students to avoid arguments on controversial issues would cause them to focus on schoolwork and approved activities. On September 4, he issued a bulletin announcing that integration would proceed and instructing teachers that the bulletin was "to be read without discussion" in their homeroom classes. It urged students to avoid being "drawn into any disputes or disputing groups." As school officials antici-pated the imminent entry of the black students on September 23, Mat-thews again reminded the white students that if they avoided "arguments on controversial issues... the tensions of the past weeks should disappear."[20]

Throughout the fall semester, the principal urged the teachers to stand at their classroom doors in order to monitor the hallways between classes and prevent students from "congregating in groups and clusters in the halls." Heightened teacher vigilance alone, however, was not sufficient to the task of protecting African American students when a sizable number of white pupils were determined to drive them from the school. As Huckaby later noted in a letter to her brother, there were "a hundred ways of making the Negroes miserable without being detected. As one person put it, it's hard to put these Negro children—the best-reared of their group—up against our near-delinquents."[21]

Although most teachers behaved professionally in the tense situation, a few sympathized with those resisting racial change at the school and others simply could not manage recalcitrant students effectively. Elizabeth Eck-ford reported later that one of her teachers "would take up money for the 'Weekly Reader,' but she wouldn't take mine; I had to put it on the teach-er's desk because she didn't want me to touch her." Melba Pattillo found that teachers sometimes lacked control over their classes or could not mon-itor everything that students said or did in the classroom. As a result, she was subjected to whispered racial epithets and other covert forms of bully-ing in some of her classes. Ernest Green concluded that "events propelled outside of [the teachers'] ability to control them, for certain."[22]

Neither the teachers nor the troops could prevent or witness every inci-dent that occurred. In crowded hallways, white students relied on the ano-nymity provided in a school of almost two thousand students as they seized the opportunity to walk on the heels of African American students, give them a quick shove, or knock their books away. The troops were barred from certain spaces, including restrooms, classrooms, and gym classes, and among their numbers were homegrown Guardsmen who had little enthusiasm for their assignment. Indeed, as early as October 2, 1957, Powell concluded that the "federalized guards were seeing everything but doing nothing." The eventual decision to reduce the number of troops in the high school and to end the practice of assigning personal guards to individual students increased the vulnerability of those students.[23]

So, as the African American students went to school daily, a cadre of white students greeted them with racial epithets, kicks, shoves, death threats, and other forms of physical harassment and intimidation. Terrence Roberts, for example, remembered that his year at Central High included "a lot of insanity" like "being cast into the showers with all the hot water jets turned on, or being hit on the head with a combination lock, or being threatened with a baseball bat on the playing field." Most of the African American students found it frightening and emotionally wearing to face unknown dangers and racial hostility as they attempted to meet the rigorous academic standards at a new school and to negotiate the extreme attention of the public on them. They sometimes found that their relationships with their families, neighbors, and friends were also strained by the situation. Their parents faced job loss or the threat of job loss, the stresses associated with the necessity of mediating with white officials regarding their children's well-being at school, and fears for their families' safety.[24]

On October 3, 1957 over one hundred white students staged a walkout to oppose the desegregation of Central High, some wearing Confederate hats and pins to signify the "southernness" of their protest. Orchestrated in part by the Mothers' League, the demonstration represented the first significant confrontation between school officials and segregationist activists over authority relations in the school. Students who lacked a valid excuse for being absent faced suspension for truancy and had to undergo interviews with school authorities before being readmitted. Their parents also received a stern warning letter that read: "This reinstatement is on a probationary basis for the rest of the school year, which requires the best citizenship in all actions on the part of /your child/, each day of the school year." Soon thereafter the school board decided to expel a white student for his previous harassment of black students, participation in the walkout, "slanderous remarks made in his homeroom," and "violent demonstrations plus attempts to mislead everybody concerned."[25]

Despite these demonstrations of disciplinary resolve, one staff member remained skeptical that school officials would have any authority over students whose parents encouraged unruly behavior in support of white supremacy, predicting that the "only understanding most of those kids'll ever have is just what their parents tell 'em they ought to have; and that's to run the niggers off." Indeed, most of the student dissenters who later engaged in disorderly behavior would face reprimands and counseling rather than suspensions or expulsions.[26]

A humorous exchange during the October 3 walkout simultaneously illuminated the possibilities for amicable interracial relations and the efficacy of school and perhaps parental authority in the lives of some students. According to the *Arkansas Democrat*, "one white boy turned to another and asked: 'You goin' out?' No, I'm chicken.' The first boy turned to a Negro boy. 'You goin' out?' he asked. 'No, I'm chicken, too,' said the Negro. All three grinned."[27]

Those same white students, however, were also "chicken" in the face of peer pressure to ostracize the black students and turn a blind eye to the violence those students were experiencing. Although segregationist students targeted the black students for the most overt persecution and intimidation, they also bullied any white students who offered friendship to their African American peers. In early October, Elizabeth Huckaby noted in her journal that segregationist activists in the student body had successfully intimidated those white students who had initially been inclined to be friendly to African American students. She added that "With the 'protection,' one forgets the submerged violence. Negro children being actively ignored, it seems."[28]

Segregationist students also participated actively in a war of images and words designed to discredit desegregation and its advocates, spreading rumors and lies in the process. When the African American students first entered Central High School on September 23, white students left the school and told radio reporters at the scene that there was widespread violence in the school. This opening salvo of deception in the long war of words to come hit its mark by staging the volatile social conflicts at the high school as "inevitably" violent. After panicked parents went to Central High to insist that their children be allowed to leave the school, Huckaby

called their removal a "scandalous and humiliating experience." Some of
the students who left, she wrote in her journal, were "hysterical with hate
by the time they reached the corners." Throughout the crisis over desegregation, resisting white students had extensive access to the media, particularly the *Arkansas Democrat*, which relayed their accusations of unfair treatment at the hands of school officials, often sustaining the credibility of
their charges without investigating their basis in fact.[29]

From the beginning of the school year, the principal administered by
bulletin. At first, his bulletins to the students emphasized the harsh pun-
ishments disorderly students might face. On September 4, for example, he
warned them sternly that anyone "interfering by word or action with the
orderly carrying out of a direction from the Federal Court may be judged
in contempt of the Court" and could face arrest and prosecution. Such
interference, he explained, could include "name calling, demonstrations,
or similar disorder." The next day he asked for silence on matters related to
desegregation, declaring that "The less we discuss these matters, the better." Apparently he assumed that the legitimacy of his requests for discipline and obedience would be more secure without classroom discussions
of the issues that occasioned student resistance. Events would prove him
wrong.[30]

Within a month, school principal Matthews was once again calling for
white students to stop their intimidation of African American students,
threatening this time that they would face school authorities, not officers
of a federal court. Huckaby described October 2 as a "*really* rough day" for
the black students, virtually all of whom experienced repeated episodes of
violence following a substantial reduction in the numbers of troops at the
school. In response to the heightened violence, Matthews issued a bulletin
the next day decrying students who "gave Central High School a real black
eye yesterday when they *attempted to* [emphasis added] harass Negro students" and threatening "disciplinary action" against any "who deliberately
heckle, shove, or otherwise intimidate in any fashion any student in school."
The efficacy of such warnings, of course, would depend on the ability of
school administrators to identify and punish students caught engaging in
harassment.[31]

The principal's warning was a response to African American complaints
that the Arkansas National Guardsmen at the high school were ignoring
incidents of violence against the black students and that General Edwin

Walker, who commanded the federal troops assigned to the high school, would not meet with African American parents concerned about their children's safety. Bolstered by a phone conversation with Daisy Bates, the black students informed school administrators at the end of the day on October 2 that they would not stay at Central High unless they could be guaranteed protection. Bates then contacted two of Walker's aides and threatened that the parents would complain directly to Washington if Walker did not speak with them and direct the troops at the school to protect the students. Virgil Blossom, who was noncommittal when Bates met with him on the issue earlier in the day, called her later to say that the students would receive greater protection and urged her to let them stay at Central High.[32]

Clarence Laws, who represented the national office of the NAACP in Little Rock at the time, worried that school officials had defaulted on their responsibility to discipline unruly white students. He recognized that the segregationist resistance had moved from outside the high school to its interior and that the harassment signaled a "concerted attempt to conduct a war of nerves to force the Negro kids to get out." At this point, it was already clear that certain white students were repeatedly attacking the black newcomers. One student had been given a three-day suspension for kicking black students. Within two days of his return he hit an African American boy in gym class in the morning and kicked a girl in the afternoon. Because no adults witnessed the assaults nothing was done.[33]

The rule that an adult had to witness an assault was designed to relieve school administrators of the responsibility of determining which student to believe when accounts of events diverged. It thus made the safety of black students depend on the vigilance and political will of numerous officials. In particular, the division of authority between military guards and school officials and the efficacy of the communication between the two would affect student safety. At the outset, military and school officials working together limited the authority of the troops in the school. They ordered soldiers to leave discipline to school officials and decided that students could be disciplined only when schoolteachers or administrators had witnessed their misconduct. Matthews defended such policies on the grounds that he could not "see how we can make an airtight case against one of our kids just because one of these good old Arkansas farm boys says he saw somebody sticking a match in a locker."[34]

According to J. O. Powell, Matthews needed and resented the troops in equal measure. The military presence on the school grounds and the requirement that everyone entering the school provide identification, the injunctions against Faubus and the state police to obey federal law, brought calm to the school grounds. The troops also prevented total chaos inside the school, but segregationists resented school administrators' cooperation with the federal "invaders," who symbolized state power being mobilized in support of black aspirations and goals. Matthews' ambivalence may explain his reluctance to involve the troops more directly in disciplinary matters or to tell General Walker that he was reducing the numbers of soldiers at the school too fast. When African Americans protested to the principal about lax military protection, Matthews responded that he would not tell the general "how to run his business."[35]

Minnijean Brown was not as reticent on the matter. When she complained directly to federal troops regarding their lack of vigilance in the school, army officials protested to U.S. Attorney Osro Cobb that it was not her place to tell them how to do their job. Cobb in turn called L. C. Bates to relay the military's unhappiness about Brown's remarks. In the meantime, white students took every opportunity to taunt the troops for their inability to identify those among them who harassed black students. In response, school officials decided that soldiers who witnessed or heard about incidents of harassment should intervene and bring those responsible to the principal's office.[36]

Nonetheless, resistant white students soon realized that they could express their contempt for the troops with considerable impunity. Powell observed later that their actions grew "progressively hostile," prompting Matthews to issue bulletins in early October alerting students that school administrators would not tolerate "hoodlum tactics, such as wisecracks to soldiers." In fact, resistant students did not stop at words and took advantage of "areas of concealment" in the school to engage in "ambush tactics" against black students with whatever objects they could find.[37]

The actions of these segregationist students reflected a deep southern hostility to Eisenhower's decision to send troops to Little Rock. From the start, the president faced intense political pressures from southern leaders and citizens to remove the soldiers. Keenly aware of those feelings, Eisenhower moved as quickly as he could to diminish the number and visibility of federal troops in and around the school. As a result, identity checks of people entering the school were compromised. Strangers intent on trouble could enter undetected, increasing incidents of vandalism and other disruptions inside the school.[38]

Administrators, parents, and African American leaders all worked to ensure that the black students at Central High followed the school district's warnings that they were not to respond either verbally or physically to their harassers. In early October 1957, NAACP leaders noted that some of the Little Rock Nine were talking back to their tormentors. Clarence Laws counseled them to ignore their harassers completely, pointing out the risks of getting into a war of words with those intent on disparaging them. To others in the NAACP he worried that "you have to handle [the black students] so as to not break their spirits, and try to steer them on a course which will precipitate less trouble."[39]

Nothing worried administrators and others trying to make desegregation work more than the possibility of contact between African American boys and white girls attending Central High. So when Matthews noticed that Ernest Green had been having lunch frequently with a white girl, he told Elizabeth Huckaby to talk to the girl. The principal also brought the African American boys into his office and warned them against being seen with white girls. Ernest Green's grandfather reinforced the warning by telling him that he had to break off the friendship. When Jefferson Thomas asked to study in Huckaby's outer office during his lunch hour, she asked J. O. Powell to allow Thomas to study outside his office instead so that the black student would not be sitting in close proximity to two white girls.[40]

Media attention to the African American students distracted them from their schoolwork and kept them in the public eye. Controlling press access to the students and managing public relations thus became an important concern of local and national NAACP leaders. They worried that students faced reprisals at school after talking to the press and that they were likely to make offhand remarks that would not reflect well on them or the goal of desegregation. In and out of school, then, black students were expected to walk a thin line; their words and conduct would have great bearing on the respectability of their community and the legitimacy of the cause they hoped to advance.[41]

In order to maintain parental authority, some segregationists were willing to foster their children's rebellion against teachers and administrators. Deception would play an important role in that effort. When large numbers of resistant pupils missed school on the same days, some parents signed notes stating that their children had been ill or at the dentist. Similarly, a few parents kept up a litany of complaints that their children had been attacked, insulted, or otherwise harmed by African American students. These complaints kept administrators busy consulting everyone involved, writing reports, informing other parents, and handling the emotional and political fallout from allegations of incidents that had no adult witnesses. Parents' willingness to air their charges in the press demoralized many teachers and administrators.[42]

Segregationist students spread rumors—many of them without foundation—regarding events at the school. In early October 1957, for example, Governor Faubus charged that federal soldiers were following girls at Central High into their dressing room for gym class. According to an FBI report, Capt. Alan Templeton of the Arkansas State Police was the source of the rumors. He, in turn, had apparently gotten his information came from the daughter of a Mothers' League leader and a woman who was active in that organization. These and other charges against U.S. military personnel infuriated President Eisenhower and army leaders and prompted Huckaby to wonder, "How silly can Faubus get?"[43]

The failure of public officials to prosecute those involved in the September disorders conveyed the message that local law enforcement did not take segregationist violence seriously, as did their unwillingness to seek injunctions against those interfering with a federal court order. The moderates' segregationist sympathies and political caution that led to the failure to prosecute or seek injunctions also shaped decisions regarding discipline, or the lack of it, at the high school. In November 1957, for example, school superintendent Blossom refused to allow a lawyer to speak to a student assembly about court prosecutions for segregationist students who interfered with black students' right to attend Central High School on the grounds that such a speech "might inflame matters." Resistant students therefore could continue their harassment of African American students without fear of prosecution

Vice Principal J. O. Powell, who objected strenuously to lax discipline at the school, described the operant principle adopted by school principal Matthews as follows: "Musn't get out on any limbs.... Musn't rock the boat.... Musn't do anything impulsive.... Sit tight and say nothing.... Our position is precarious enough." Powell's impatience was fueled by the knowledge that the silence and caution of the school administration was met by a barrage of inflammatory charges from partisans of segregation and by a concerted public campaign to undermine the authority of teachers and administrators associated with the desegregation process. Indeed, by early October, Vice Principal Huckaby experienced the effects of this campaign when she saw white students congregate at the front entrance to the school in order to harass black students as they entered. She tried without success to get them to disperse and noted despairingly that it was "the first time I've ever had youngsters just not pay any attention to what I said."[44]

In late October military officials and school administrators met to discuss what they might expect once the troop numbers were reduced. They shared a strong and reasonable fear that discipline would deteriorate. Military leaders believed that the student ringleaders should be disciplined sternly, but some school officials feared that if they did so it would make "martyrs" of them. In fact, the segregationists' sense of victimization required the creation of martyrs. Little Rock's arch conservatives used the media to accuse school officials publicly of discriminating against white students whenever authorities attempted to discipline white racist students for their bullying behavior. Because they refused to discipline offenders with authority, school officials found that their timorous politics of discipline would occupy them the entire year. Resistant students continued their campaign of intimidation against African American students, encouraged by adults in their families and the community and by the permissive policies in place at Central High.[45]

As the numbers of military guards inside the school diminished in November, Margaret Jackson of the Mothers' League told the press that there was "great resentment against the Negroes inside the school. The white children are determined to get them out of there. There will be bloodshed if all the troops are taken away." Her organization, of course, worked actively to stoke that white student resentment, to defend violent students against school administrators who tried to discipline them, and to insist that the troops be removed.[46]

The segregationists had apparently underestimated the resolve of the African American children. In early November, a white boy knocked Jefferson Thomas unconscious. After the assault, Thomas told his mother: "Mom, I'm going back there as long as I'm able to walk." Blossom, who knew better, denied the existence of a campaign of intimidation against African American students, claiming instead that the school was operating smoothly.[47]

By the end of the semester, episodes of harassment directed at African American students at Central High had developed a certain pattern. In addition to the hallways, places of physical and social intimacy—gym classes, restrooms, and the cafeteria—had become particularly freighted sites of racial conflict. Girls found racist graffiti written in lipstick on the mirrors of the restroom. By mid-October, Melba Pattillo had stopped eating lunch because the cafeteria had become "the main place for them to get me." Jefferson Thomas also skipped lunch to avoid harassment, often studying in Huckaby's outer office. In the gym shower rooms, the boys experienced innumerable incidents, ranging from broken glass scattered on the shower floors to flogging with wet towels.[48]

As the academic year wore on, the African American students faced continuing threats, harassment, and physical intimidation. Early in the second semester, the usual group of white students conducted an intensified campaign of persecution while their elders heightened the political pressures on school officials and teachers. At the same time, federal officials reduced the number of troops, limiting their duties to the lunch period and the hours before and after school. School administrators at all levels found themselves immersed in the politics of school discipline as the "psychological warfare" they faced all year intensified. However ineffectual they were, attempts of school officials to reform their troubled and troubling students elicited class resentment from parents.[49]

As the African American students experienced their own kind of warfare, their parents tried to get officials to act more effectively against the children's antagonists. When Elizabeth Eckford reported that several girls in her gym class had been singing songs to denigrate her, her father met with school officials about it. Superintendent Blossom suggested that the best solution would be for her just to ignore it, and "she agreed this would be the best remedy." Two white boys received suspensions for their witnessed assaults, mentioned earlier, on Minnijean Brown. Shortly after Brown's return to school following her suspension, a boy poured soup on her in the cafeteria. He told a teacher that she had called him "white trash." The teacher responded, "So you [had] to prove it, did you?" A crowd of between one hundred and one hundred fifty students converged in the hall to cheer his feat. In a second assault on Brown that occurred on January 29, Richard Boehler kicked her and pulled a knife on her. Captain Leon Stumbaugh of the federalized National Guard reported that it took three Guardsmen to keep him from stabbing her. Brown's mother tried to get criminal charges brought against Boehler but failed.[50]

As school officials coped with escalating disorder, state government agencies from the Legislative Council to the governor's office worked to undermine the authority of the Little Rock School Board, the staff at Central High School, and superintendent Blossom. They did so in response to charges from white students, the Mothers' League, and others opposed to desegregation that school officials were discriminating against white students simply because those students opposed "race mixing." All of the Little Rock Nine were still enrolled at Central High at the start of the second semester and thus the sense of urgency felt by arch segregationists heightened, fueled by the fear that they were on the verge of failure and a deep-rooted anger at those whose actions enabled African Americans to attend school with white children.[51]

The Mothers' League, the resistant students, and the Arkansas State Police coordinated their efforts to discredit desegregation and those who advanced it at Central High. The Mothers' League conducted "interrogations" of students who claimed they were being mistreated by school officials and used various media to publicize those charges. On January 20, 1958, the Mothers' League announced that it would hold a public meeting in which the Rev. Wesley Pruden, a Citizens' Council leader, would discuss "What the Race-Mixers Are Planning for Us." Seeking to expand its network of student "informants," the Mothers' League invited Central High students to attend.[52]

The Mothers' League's meetings with students and their public criticisms of school administrators provided ideological ballast to a campaign based on a sense of white racial victimization. By keeping the level of anger at white heat intensity they helped to forge political community and motivate resistance. The segregationists' sense of grievance about the treatment of white students spoke to the disrespect and class hostility they felt in their encounters with school officials. In December 1957, members of the Mothers' League had sent a letter to Central High School Principal Jess Matthews alleging that in "every incident of violence between a white and negro student, you suspend, dicipline [sic] or otherwise humiliate the white child and exonerate the negro." They claimed that he had granted Daisy Bates the "right of cross examination of our children... when fights or trouble" occurred. The segregationist mothers further complained that the principal's "sympathies and love are altogether on the side of the negroes," protesting that the "common decencies of one white person to another are being outraged—to say nothing of the respect a white child has a right to expect of a white school official." The letter apparently infuriated the principal, prompting him to announce at a teachers' meeting on January 17 that they had to "get tough" at school in response to the lies segregationists were telling about them.[53]

When the school board threatened to expel segregationist students for their disruptive behaviors, local segregationists mounted a public relations and legal campaign to stop it. For them, the harassment campaign directed against the African American students at Central High constituted a form of legitimate political speech. Its repression undermined freedom of political expression as well as parental authority over children. To persuade others of that view, the Capital Citizens' Council ran an ad decrying the school board for forcing integration "with bayonets in the backs of the students and armed guards in the classroom." They charged that those troops were forcing children who had "been reared to believe in a segregated society" to accept "a way of life foreign to their training, contrary to their convictions and nauseating to their esthetic being." The threat that student resisters would be expelled from school constituted an ultimatum to their parents: "The crackdown on our children has started. The school board gives us only one choice—*Submit*. And that's a terrible word for a red blooded American."[54]

A critical issue for the dissenters involved the right of students to carry and disseminate segregationist literature in school. The students circulated a variety of political messages, the "Remember Little Rock" slogan being a particular favorite. After Minnijean Brown was expelled in February 1958, students distributed "ONE DOWN EIGHT TO GO" cards. As Beth Roy has noted, the printed cards evidenced "a network of planners, writers, printers, and distributors" that had to include adults. An unnamed FBI informant reported that high school student Sammie Dean Parker had admitted to circulating segregationist materials at school and claimed that someone from the Arkansas State Police had delivered cards to her home. Believing that such literature heightened tension at the school and hampered their ability to teach *all* students, school officials warned students against displaying or distributing segregationist propaganda and disciplined them when they did so.[55]

Segregationists expressed their sense of racial disempowerment relative to blacks and their sense of class dispossession in relation to white officials in various ways throughout the crisis over desegregation. This sense of marginality reflected a partial truth: protecting African American students from their white harassers did absorb administrative and faculty energies and some faculty, especially vice principals Powell and Huckaby, did hold a low opinion of the students who resisted desegregation. Powell's unpublished narrative of the crisis, for example, contains countless mean-spirited depictions of white adults and students engaged in segregationist activities.[56]

The segregationists' sense of disempowerment was revealed in their conviction that blacks had excessive and illegitimate public power, stated most often in charges that NAACP leader Daisy Bates was allowed to interrogate white students or to influence school decisions about discipline. A Citizens' Council flier, for example, showed police mug shots of Daisy Bates and her arrest record (for her civil rights activities and for "gaming") and charged that she was the "unofficial 'principal' in charge of lecturing white students at Central High who 'cross' any of her 'brave' nine Negro students." The flier further alleged that Bates was allowed to "cross examine" any white students who had conflicts with black students and that she had free access to school principal Jess Matthews. As Huckaby noted, the aim of this propaganda was "guilt by association, the school officials with a 'criminal.'" The juxtaposition of Bates' police record with the allegation that she was actually running Central High conveyed the segregationists' sense that blacks' access to any public power constituted an illegal and morally dangerous racial inversion. The flier helped make credible the vicious propaganda against Bates.[57]

In late January, the Arkansas Legislative Council decided to launch an investigation of Central High School focusing particularly on teachers and administrators. When Matthews announced at a faculty meeting in February that they were all subject to subpoena in the inquiry and that the Arkansas State Police would be conducting the interrogations, many teachers interpreted it "as a crude attempt at intimidation." Powell, never one for understatement, concluded that it was another event in the "current ideological war at hand—in homes, in schools, and in communities—for the control of free men's minds all over America." The school board provided a court reporter for the interviews with Matthews, Powell, and Huckaby to forestall any distortion of their words by opportunistic politicians.[58]

Teachers found that their power over students was declining. One teacher brought a white boy to the office for spitting on two of the black students—in front of her. The episode caused Huckaby to conclude that "the segregationists were getting bolder—with the assured backing of state authority." Discouraged over student defiance and ineffective disciplinary procedures, teachers (and guards) reported fewer offenders in the second semester, concluding that to do so was a waste of time. Teacher Susie West had a rock thrown through her apartment window. Around it was a note with the words "Nigger-loving bitch." After the episode, she moved in with friends. On February 10, Huckaby wrote in her journal: "Not much change at school. Lockers tampered with, obscenities written, names called, and authority defied."[59]

Segregationist boldness was evidenced in the aftermath of school officials' decision to suspend Darlene Holloway for pushing Elizabeth Eckford on the stairs. Mrs. Fred Gist, the mother of the suspended student and a member of the Mothers' League, went to the press with her case. She threatened to sue if that was required to get her daughter back into Central High. She expressed her resentment of "Blossom's attitude toward her daughter," stating that she had gone "to see him but found him most obstinate and unreasonable. He gave a deaf ear and had a closed mind to my pleas." She further claimed that Blossom had "favored" Eckford in the episode. He responded that her account of her daughter's behavior differed significantly from that of school officials.[60]

Indeed, the school's reports indicate that the incident had not only been witnessed by a guard but that Darlene had admitted her guilt while complaining that other students who did the same thing were not disciplined. Moreover, in the fall semester Darlene had been disciplined for truancy and for "public disrespectful and vituperative language to a Negro student." During an interview with school administrators, Darlene claimed that she could say anything she wanted to black students. When threatened with suspension, Darlene and her mother agreed that she would avoid any further difficulties if she could remain in school. Despite her record, the school board decided to allow her to return rather than face a lawsuit. In March, the recalcitrant student withdrew from Central High.[61]

At the same time, a policy statement from the Little Rock School Board appeared in the local press. Addressing student disruptions in the school as well as segregationist propaganda charging the board with bias, the statement promised that when disciplinary action was being considered, "[e]ach student will be judged on his or her conduct." The board promised that a student's views on integration would not be considered but also declared that "[a]ny student whose conduct is unsatisfactory [would] be expelled." The Holloway decision, however, cast doubt on the board's resolve in dealing with defiant white students, even repeat offenders.[62]

As African American children faced escalating harassment, thefts from lockers, and threats to their safety, their parents grew increasingly concerned. In February 1958, they asked for a meeting with school administrators. At that meeting, Ellis Thomas, Jefferson's father, reported that he had called the parents of several of the students who were harassing the blacks. Some had agreed to cooperate in controlling their children and some had not. He suggested to the administrators that they hold a student assembly and "lay down the law" to the student body. School officials believed it would do no good.[63]

Meanwhile, Little Rock's white moderate leadership, itself deeply conflicted over what to do, worried that the escalating crisis could permanently damage public education in Little Rock. Despite the mounting violence and disorder in the high school, the business community's response was to focus on the city's public image. The Chamber of Commerce, for example, engaged in a letter-writing campaign to persuade the public that the reports of problems were quite exaggerated and that the school was in fact operating smoothly. While claiming that all was well at the school, however, business leaders also privately urged the school board to file a suit seeking a delay in the implementation of desegregation in Little Rock on the grounds that the presence of blacks at Central High had impaired school administrators' ability to keep order and provide quality education. They displaced responsibility for disorder onto African Americans and implicitly denied the board's responsibility for maintaining discipline at the school. In February 1958, the school board went to court petitioning for permission to delay desegregation for two and a half years. Liberal Nathan Griswold concluded that it "[a]lmost seemed as if [the school board] wanted it to get bad so that they could get a court order to delay. They just some-how didn't have the stomach to discipline these brats that were really mak-ing the trouble."[64]

The assertion by school board member R. A. Lile in his 1971 oral his-tory interview that "[t]here wasn't much trouble inside the school" echoed the official position taken by many civic leaders at the time and later. In 1958, however, Lile wrote to presidential adviser Sherman Adams express-ing his concern that the problems at the school were so severe that they threatened to cost the district some of its best faculty. Moreover, he feared the school board members' conviction that they could not operate ef-fectively in the face of segregationist resistance would result in their resig-nations followed by a takeover of the school board by segregationists.[65]

Ultimately, school principal Matthews failed to delegate to his subordi-nates authority commensurate with their responsibilities. According to Powell, several groups, including civic club members and "(most signifi-cantly, by unwritten and strictly unofficial innuendo)... the military," urged the principal to weed out the troublemakers. The principal, however, be-lieved that appeasement was a better policy because the segregationists might raise volatile questions in board meetings and might initiate litiga-tion. Powell blamed Matthews more than Blossom and the school board for the lax discipline and concluded that the principal's concern with pub-lic relations "outbalanced the board's promise of support, and the hooli-gans stayed on to heckle in Central High." Nonetheless, the board members also shared Matthews' concern with public relations as well as his reluc-tance to impose order at the school.[66]

Within weeks of her return to Central High, Minnijean Brown again found herself the object of continuous harassment and once again broke the school board rule prohibiting black students from engaging in any form of retaliation against their tormentors. After being followed for sev-eral days by a group of students taunting her with "nigger, nigger, nigger," she found one of them blocking her entrance to a classroom. Minnijean turned on her and said, "Will you please stop talking to me, white trash." The white student then threw her purse at Minnijean. A guard took both of them to Huckaby's office.[67]

It turned out to be a busy day for Central's principals. Before her inter-view with Matthews, Minnijean went to lunch. There she found herself on the receiving end of yet another bowl of soup, this one administered by a boy then on probation for numerous offenses, including harassing black students and cutting classes in which black students were enrolled. On the same day, the school received two bomb threats. Even though there was no public acknowledgment of the threats, numerous parents called requesting to remove their children from the school, suggesting that the threats were part of a larger plan orchestrated by adults to disrupt the school. In the wake of the cafeteria episode, a mob of students formed outside the principals' offices yelling cheers for the student who "souped" Minnijean. Matthews suspended Minnijean and the boy responsible for the cafeteria incident. The girl taunting Minnijean, who was already under a "peace bond" to refrain from segregationist activities at school, decided to withdraw from Central High. Administrators wrote reports.[68]

On February 17, 1958, the school board announced that it had decided to suspend Minnijean for the rest of the semester because she had shown an "inability to adjust to a difficult situation." Elizabeth Huckaby, who had a divided mind on the question, supported the board's decision. She believed that the feisty student's continued presence would be "a hazard to the other Eight," but that her ejection "was an admission of defeat on our part." The parents of the nine African American students at Central High disagreed. On behalf of those parents, Ellis Thomas, father of Jefferson Thomas, wrote to Blossom that Minnijean's permanent suspension "would only give aid and comfort to the lawless elements within the school" and "increase the intensity of their harrassments [sic] against the remaining students, with the hope of provoking them to commit an incident which would precipitate their expulsion." They also met with the superintendent to advocate for Brown, to draw attention to the number of repeat offenders among the black students' harassers, and to try to get greater protection for their children at school.[69]

Some observers questioned the necessity for Brown's expulsion, pointing particularly to the unfair burden of restraint imposed on the African American students in the face of systematic abuse at the hands of some white students. One citizen, for example, wrote to school board chair Wayne Upton that the "[l]ack of discipline in the school over a long period of time would produce retaliation in any individual." She added that "those of us who have never been victims of a similar situation . . . are unable to know just how we would react." The *Chicago Daily News* disagreed with the decision to expel Brown based on the fact that she had violated "an agreement not to fight back against white students' harassment!" Pointing to the racial basis of the policy, the paper called it "one of the most unfair, humiliating and discriminatory prohibitions ever imposed in a free country. It suggests that the harassment is expected, even if not condoned, and there have been no suspensions for it. Are any white students ordered to take abuse without resistance?"[70]

In the June 1958 hearing of the school board's suit to defer desegregation, NAACP attorney Thurgood Marshall queried Blossom about the board's decision to remove Brown from school. Blossom responded that "Minnijean Brown was a person that lacked the ability to adjust to a difficult situation. Not only the welfare of Minnijean was involved, but the welfare of all the students." Moreover, he claimed, she created animosity and did not listen to school authorities regarding her own role in the difficulties: "Because of her own actions and her own inability to adjust in a difficult situation, Minnijean Brown had more counselling [sic], more good advice, that didn't take than any one student of the 2,000 in Central High School." When Marshall asked whether those students included Sammie Dean Parker, a ringleader for the segregationist students, the superintendent affirmed that they did. Ultimately, what Blossom labeled Minnijean's failure "to adjust" derived from her legitimate desire to be accepted by her peers, acknowledged for her positive attributes, and allowed to participate fully in high school life.[71]

Within days of her expulsion, Minnijean received a scholarship to the New Lincoln School in New York City, where she finished her high school education. Finally free to speak her mind, Minnijean gave a press conference in New York regarding the racial harassment she experienced. Admitting that she had finally lost patience in the face of persistent persecution at the hands of some white students, she noted that "They throw rocks, they spill ink on your clothes, they call you 'nigger,' they just keep bothering you every five minutes." Elizabeth Huckaby confirmed that "What she said was a fair report."[72]

From the start, Sammie Dean Parker was the most visible and active of all the resistant students. On September 4, 1957, she walked beside Hazel Bryan as the latter taunted Elizabeth Eckford for attempting to enter the white space of Central High School. She accused *New York Times* reporter Benjamin Fine of trying to get some white boys to start a fight with blacks. On September 23, 1957, she urged other students to leave Central High after the African American students had entered it and was arrested later that morning for fighting with a police officer on the school grounds. It was not the last time she left the school without securing the permission of school administrators.[73]

Parker was also involved in innumerable hostilities directed at black students ranging from stepping on their heels to shoving to using racial epithets and other insults to distributing and wearing proscribed literature. The latter included "Remember Little Rock" stickers and the "One Down Eight to Go" cards distributed after Minnijean Brown's expulsion. One of the guards reported that she had even lifted her skirt in the hallway in order to show her friends the "Remember Little Rock" sticker attached to her panties. She joined others in expressing her disrespect for those attempting to enforce civil behavior in the school, calling a white federal trooper "nigger" and disregarding the authority of teachers.[74]

In addition, she cultivated the approval of segregationist leaders and continually sought media attention for her role in local resistance. A few days after the African American students entered Central High, for example, she was pictured in the newspaper hugging Governor Faubus at a gathering for the Mothers' League. Soon thereafter she appeared on a local radio show with other students to discuss segregation and schools. She told a school counselor that she reported regularly on events at the school to a state policeman, and if her statement is to be believed then it demonstrates the importance of the support of state officials to the students' continuing misconduct at school. She also claimed that she met frequently with the governor.[75]

Sammie Dean Parker was simultaneously rebellious against adult authority and eager for the approval of adults. In a later oral history interview, she stated that she had been "raised under [her] parents' thumb." At the time of the crisis over desegregation she had relied heavily on them and on segregationist leaders for ideological and political support. It was the latter, however, whom she credited later for providing encouragement and assistance to her resistance: "I had the White Citizens Council ... the support of all these people. I mean, wonderful, loving, caring, we're talking family, churches, you know." Her egocentrism and sense of entitlement fed her belief that she was being singled out for unfair and discriminatory treatment. Her emotional investment in the idea of her victimization in part derived from (as it stoked) the conviction of segregationists that racial change required the oppression of ordinary whites. She reveled in the sense of importance and celebrity status that her role as an informant to segregationist leaders gave her, noting later that "parents played such a big part in it, you know, the meetings were held and they wanted the right information about what was going on in the school." An aspiring actress, Sammie Dean found an outlet for her theatricality and her desire for attention by becoming the symbol for girls' vulnerability during desegregation. At the same time, the deliberately sexual image that she projected and her emotional volatility made her a troubling symbol for adolescent innocence and conventional femininity.[76]

School officials spent much time with Sammie Dean, counseling her about the rules and attempting to instill a modicum of manners in their unladylike charge. School officials also prohibited her from some public speech class activities until her behavior improved. When they decided in February 1958 to suspend her for distributing segregationist materials in defiance of the school's well-publicized policy, administrators waited until late in the school day to confront her in order to avoid disruption at school. Mindful of her penchant for contacting segregationist leaders and the local press when aggrieved, they also delayed so that the story would not appear that day in the noon edition of the *Arkansas Democrat*.[77]

On February 21, 1958 the school board decided to suspend Sammie Dean for two weeks and place her on probation for the rest of school year. Blossom had asked Huckaby before the hearing whether they had sufficient evidence to expel her, but Huckaby reported that they did not. The board further stipulated that Sammie Dean's reinstatement would occur only after "a satisfactory conference [had] been held relative to an improvement in her attitude," especially outside of classes, and she had demonstrated that she had decided to accept "full citizenship responsibility at all times." At that conference, however, the recalcitrant student denied that she needed to change her behavior in any way except to refrain from distributing cards at school.[78]

When Huckaby and Matthews left the conference, Mrs. Parker and her daughter ran after them. According to Huckaby, Mrs. Parker, "screaming that she was going to get me now," pulled the glasses from the face of the surprised vice principal while her daughter seized her umbrella. Matthews intervened, declaring that "you can't hit a lady." As Huckaby retreated into a nearby office, she heard Mrs. Parker say that "two hundred women have called me and said they'd be glad to pay my fine if I'd hit her!"[79]

It surely came as no surprise to Sammie Dean's family and friends when, the next day, school officials decided to suspend her for the rest of the year. They stated that her attitude made her "unable to conform to the standards of conduct requisite for high school pupils and this inability to conform, due to its deep-rooted causes, [could not] be remedied in the ensuing term." It seems equally likely that school officials expected Sammie Dean's immediate emergence as a full-blown martyr of the segregationist cause.[80]

As segregationists retold and revised the story of the Parkers' confrontation with Huckaby, Sammie Dean emerged as a heroine who had grabbed Huckaby's umbrella and chased her with it. That retelling was soon commemorated in cards that circulated inside and outside the school, depicting a pony-tailed teenager, umbrella in hand, giving chase to the vice principal. The caption read "Communism on the run." Soon after the incident, demonstrations of support for Huckaby's humiliation by a student were seen as honking cars bearing "Sammie Dean" signs circled the school. Students who championed the actions of teachers and administrators, however, did not demonstrate their support for fear of segregationist retribution.[81]

Anticipating Sammie Dean's suspension by school authorities, Capital Citizens' Council attorney Amis Guthridge went to Pulaski County prosecutor J. Frank Holt seeking to remove Blossom and the members of the school board on the grounds of their "malfeasance." Several students, including Sammie Dean and Richard Boehler, who were both under suspension at Central High, accompanied Guthridge and provided testimony. Some were wearing "One Down Eight to Go" buttons. Their actions signified the segregationists' conviction that the white students should be allowed to harass black students with impunity. Holt refused their petition, citing a lack of evidence to support their charges.[82]

In response to her suspension, Sammie Dean appeared on a Little Rock television program with local segregationist leaders Wesley Pruden and Amis Guthridge. During the course of the show, she related the details of her arrest during the September 23, 1957 melee. After leaving the school, she had attempted to reenter it, despite police warnings that she was not allowed to do so, in order to tell other students to walk out in protest. She alleged that police officers "bodily attacked" her and, after she ran from them, were "pretty well messing me up" before they put her in a paddy wagon. She cried when asked about her suspension, saying she "would give anything else in this world to go back to Central High School and finish my education."[83]

As they had done before, male segregationist leaders presented a young white girl as the iconic victim of integration while positioning themselves as her protectors. Alleging that the school board had "announced a get rough policy" that was "designed to smite into silence and to intimidate and to beat into submission every child and every parent" who did not support integration, Pruden claimed that they had chosen Sammie Dean as an example for the rest of the student body. He finished by threatening to go to court to "challenge every move that is made against this child."[84]

If his goal was to secure broader public support for his cause, he failed. The station that aired the program received a great number of phone calls objecting to its content. Letters to the editor of the *Arkansas Gazette* noted in particular the appeal for money made by Pruden. One viewer, who thought the production made "an excellent Class 'C' movie," suggested that viewers send Confederate money to the segregationist leader. Another viewer, noting that at "the right moment the mother and Sammie Dean broke into hot tears," wondered what Pruden planned to do with the money he received. The school board also broke its silence about her case, noting that her suspension "was fully justified" because she and her mother had physically attacked "a lady staff member." Guthridge called the assertion a "vicious untrue charge."[85]

The future of Sammie Dean Parker was not settled in the court of public opinion, however. On March 7, Jay Parker filed suit in Pulaski Circuit Court claiming that the Little Rock School Board had suspended his daughter without "just cause" and asked that she be readmitted immediately. Otherwise, the suit claimed, she would lose a year in her academic program and the students at Central High would suffer "irreparable damages." Within a few days, Sammie Dean had written a letter promising to abide by all school rules and the board had agreed to reinstate her. It did not ask that she admit to her wrongdoing or apologize. According to Powell, the decision to readmit Parker was not interpreted satisfactorily to the military or to staff at Central High. Many teachers wondered: "Why discipline a kid at all? Even if he does get suspended, which isn't likely, he'll be back in a few days to cause more trouble." As a result, morale among the staff "hit an all-time low."[86]

Reactions to Sammie Dean's return were mixed. For her part, Elizabeth Huckaby was relieved that she would not have to face a trial over the merits of Sammie Dean's suspension. She wrote to her brother that she "was glad to have her return rather than face a day in court being heckled by the unscrupulous Amis Guthridge." Some students gathered at the entrance to school on the day of her return to let her know she was unwelcome.[87]

After her conditional readmission, Sammie Dean took care not to violate school rules and kept her overt segregationist activities off campus. In late April, for example, she spoke at a Citizens' Council rally. Earlier that month, she engaged in various efforts to charge Ernest Green with making sexual advances toward her. Jay Parker, her father, called the school to accuse Green of winking at his daughter at school and of having "brushed against her with a familiar remark" at a downtown department store. A teacher provided Huckaby with a substantially different version of Sammie Dean's relationship to Ernest: "You should have seen Sammie Dean in the cafeteria today. She paraded to and fro past Ernest Green four times, staring hard at him each of the eight times she passed his table. Ernest never raised his eyes." Thereafter, green cards circulated accusing a black student of pulling a white girl's curls. According to a New York newspaper, Sammie Dean "plopped herself almost on the lap of one of the Negro boys [Ernest Green]" after a radio appearance with him in late April.[88]

On March 8, 1958, Elizabeth Huckaby sent an anonymous letter to the editors of both local newspapers to vent her anger at the troublemakers who were filling her days with needless work and frustration. Addressed to the "Parents (REAL Parents) of Central High Students," it asked those parents who had raised their children with "proper respect for law and order" to speak up against anyone responsible for the disruptions at the school. Directing her message to those parents who did not want their "sons and daughters to indulge in [the] food dumping, tripping, shoving, bodily assault, bullying, spitting name-calling tactics" that she believed the Mothers' League encouraged, the nameless writer asked readers to "tell the School Board and the school staff that we appreciate what they have done and are doing to protect and teach our High School students." Huckaby was disappointed that she did not receive a strong response of support from her former students and the community. In her 1980 book about the crisis at Central High she surmised that maybe she had "expected too much from a culture in which noninvolvement [was] an ideal."[89]

As the academic year drew to a close, the persecution of black students waxed and waned. As before, the persecution was often designed to terrify the students while distancing the white resisters from responsibility for their actions. At one point, segregationist students spread rumors that some boys would bring water pistols filled with acid to school and use them against the African American students. One student warned Gloria Ray to stay away for her own safety. The next day a boy pulled a water pistol and shot her in the face. Fortunately, the toy pistol contained only water. As Ernest Green noted, "that kind of thing is psychologically unnerving. It's a little bit like guerrilla warfare." Despite this and many other episodes, the remaining eight black students persevered through the end of the year. In late May, Ernest Green became the first African American to graduate from Little Rock's Central High School.[90]

The politics of school discipline at Central High School in 1957–1958 reveal in microcosm the social politics at play throughout the Little Rock crisis. Looking closely at the policies of school officials, for example, discloses the role of the moderates in enabling the regime of abuse directed at the African American students. The latter paid a disproportionate part of the social costs of racial change because white moderates pursued a strategy of conciliating segregationists, who themselves abetted the violent and hateful behaviors of their children at school. The relationship between the Mothers' League and the resistant students, all central actors in the segregationist movement, illuminates the emotional culture of massive resistance as well as its ideologies and tactics. Encouraged by their parents and other segregationists, the children expressed and fueled the adults' sense of victimization and their politics of righteous anger.

Girls occupied a central role, symbolically as well as behaviorally, in the racial confrontations at Central High School in the first year of desegregation. The association of white girls with innocence and vulnerability resonated strongly with segregationists, whose investment in the South's sexualized racial ideologies required corroboration from narratives of female victimization. For them, the extreme emotionality displayed by some girls in reaction to the presence of African American students at their school

evidenced the pain and harm occasioned by racial change. The white girls'
defiance at school registered their refusal to countenance any compromise
with segregation. Moreover, the girls were more willing than the boys to lie
about their behavior, either to shield themselves from the consequences of
their actions or to fortify their image as the politically necessary victims of
a school administration hell bent on "race mixing."

The boys, by contrast, displayed a penchant for open defiance. Several
admitted to their actions, virtually daring school officials to do something
about them. Some boys defended their actions on the grounds that the
student they assaulted was "a nigger" and thus deserved it. In several cases,
their defiance led to suspensions. A sizable number of the boys had also
committed numerous infractions unrelated to desegregation, including
truancy, smoking in the restrooms, forging notes, and disruptive behavior
in class. Many had poor academic records. A few had tangled with juvenile
authorities and had been charged with gas siphoning, vandalism, or theft.
Two boys who had participated in the harassment campaign against African American students left school in early March after being arrested for
stealing motorcycles. The boys' gendered behavior, in short, made them
poor poster children for white oppression.[91]

The resistant girls' actions, however, violated deeply held conventions
regarding the proper behavior for genteel young women. As Beth Roy perceptively noted, they engaged in conduct labeled "[w]hite trash behavior"
by their contemporaries, including "rowdiness in public, loose sexual
mores, [and] racist speech." That some of Sammie Dean's classmates saw
her as a "girl about town" reveals the strong association drawn by whites
between women's public conduct and their sexual reputations. In the words
of Roy, for a girl "to be 'good' meant to be both politically silent and sexually demure." Those who ran afoul of the former injunction therefore
risked the loss of sexual reputation as well.[92]

Ultimately, school officials failed to develop an adequate disciplinary
response to the politicized rule breaking orchestrated by a sizable cabal of
students. The practice of allowing multiple suspensions, each followed by
promises of future good behavior on the part of troublemakers, especially
irked Powell, who observed that the resistant students "also proceeded with
the comforting knowledge that the worst that could happen to them (if,
perchance, they were caught in an act by someone in 'authority') would be
another short reprieve from schedules, classes, and school." Parents' will-

ingness to threaten lawsuits and moderates' fear of segregationist backlash deterred administrators from expelling chronic offenders.[93]

African American parents, students, and community activists also pressured school officials regarding disciplinary decisions. Even as they grew discouraged over administrators' failure to handle dangerous students, the Little Rock Nine continued to report attacks and threats to their parents, Daisy Bates, teachers and principals, and the military. Parents and grandparents of the African American students called and met with school officials many times to demand that they implement more successful disciplinary policies. Daisy Bates sometimes accompanied students and parents and often acted independently to publicize the harassment and to pressure authorities to safeguard the students more effectively.[94]

Over the course of the school year, the dangerous and disruptive activities of segregationists in and out of school extorted a high cost. Officials coped with forty-three bomb threats, about thirty nuisance fires, systematic and repeated damage to lockers, and countless other acts of vandalism while also trying to deal with daily incidents of harassment against the black students. As they confronted attacks on their authority, classroom disruptions, and disquieting challenges to their values, teachers as well as administrators became demoralized.[95]

At the same time, Little Rock's moderate leaders nurtured a growing sense of victimization, attributing their plight not only to segregationists but also to the federal government and state leaders. This was particularly true of the moderates on the school board, who could not abandon integration without being vulnerable to prosecution for contempt of court. Despite President Eisenhower's decision to deploy federal military force in support of the school district's desegregation plan, board members remained convinced that his administration had abandoned them to handle the issue of enforcement alone. They also worried that the Capital Citizens' Council, the Mothers' League, and the NAACP alike were a menace to the quality of education in Little Rock. Moreover, they feared that the growing popularity of massive resistance to desegregation threatened their legitimacy as community leaders as well as their development investments and dreams. With so much at stake, moderate leaders chose a path of extreme caution.[96]

Elizabeth Huckaby wrote later that the school board's sense of victimization ignored the price paid by the black students and by teachers and

administrators at Central High during that tumultuous year. Some teachers, including J. O. Powell, would decide to quit teaching or to leave Central High rather than face again the school problems engendered by massive resistance. For the African American students and their families, the
price would be paid not only then but later. Most found their lives disrupted. Some families had to move when breadwinners lost jobs or when
closed schools forced them to look elsewhere for their children's education.
It is impossible to assess the emotional costs paid by the teenaged students
who confronted their adversaries daily. Their courage and dignity and the
ultimate success of their cause should not obscure the fact that white power
elites inside and outside of Little Rock imposed most of the burden of racial change on these black teenagers and their families.[97]

Segregationists remained convinced that school officials at all levels had
singled out resistant students for their politics rather than their behavior.
Their anger at what they saw as a despotic and discriminatory vendetta
against segregationists would simmer, barely contained, until the spring of
1959, when they would seek vengeance against those they held responsible
for their pain. In the meantime, they would finally succeed in closing Central High and the other public high schools in Little Rock. As the next
chapter demonstrates, their victories would sow the seeds of their ultimate
defeat.

Figure 3. The first African American to graduate from Little Rock's Central High School, Ernest Green stands alone among white students as they wait to begin the commencement ceremony in May, 1958. Will Counts Collection: Indiana University Archives.

Figure 4. In November, 1957 Daisy Bates organized a pre-Thanksgiving dinner for the Little Rock Nine in order to publicize their gratitude, patriotism, and religiosity. Newspapers across the nation carried pictures of the event. The visibility of the press in this photograph reveals the importance of public relations to the civil rights movement. Will Counts Collection: Indiana University Archives.

Figure 5. Thurgood Marshall, the chief counsel for the NAACP, holds the door to the Federal District courtroom in Little Rock as Daisy Bates, Gloria Ray, and Minnijean Brown leave after a hearing on their case. As southern states passed laws designed to destroy the NAACP and deny it access to the courts, keeping the courtroom door open for African Americans was a central challenge for the civil rights organization. Will Counts Collection: Indiana University Archives.

Figure 6. The nine African American students enter Little Rock's Central High School under military escort. Will Counts Collection: Indiana University Archives.

Figure 7. In the fall of 1958, Governor Orval Faubus closed the public high schools of Little Rock under a law passed by segregationist legislators. Their supporters then placed a sign in front of Central High School blaming the federal government. Moderates and liberals in the community used the misspelling of "goverment" to ridicule their opponents on the right. Will Counts Collection: Indiana University Archives.

Figure 8. White students at Raney High School, Little Rock's short-lived segregationist academy, protest desegregation. By claiming that their opponents lacked manly courage, the signs demonstrate the centrality of gender ideologies to segregationist political rhetoric. Will Counts Collection: Indiana University Archives.

Figure 9. Segregationists converge on the Arkansas Capitol Building to protest desegregation in August, 1959. The flags and signs demonstrate segregationists' identification of white supremacy with Americanism and anti-Communism. Will Counts Collection: Indiana University Archives.

Figure 10. Arkansas Governor Orval Faubus holds a press conference regarding events in Little Rock. The crowd of photographers reflected the intense national and international media interest generated after Faubus placed himself at the center of massive resistance to desegregation. Will Counts Collection: Indiana University Archives.

Figure 11. This iconic picture of Central High School student Hazel Bryan taunting Elizabeth Eckford as she tried to enter the previously all-white school circulated around the world in September, 1957. Her face contorted with hate, Bryan came to symbolize the visible racism that made Little Rock an epithet outside the U. S. South. Will Counts Collection: Indiana University Archives.

Figure 12. The Little Rock Nine gathered to commemorate the 40th anniversary of desegregation at Central High School. From the left, they are Melba Patillo Beals, Elizabeth Eckford, Ernest Green, Gloria Ray Karlmark, Carlotta Walls LaNier, Terrence Roberts, Jefferson Thomas, Minnijean Brown Trickey, and Thelma Jean Mothershed Wair. Will Counts Collection: Indiana University Archives.

CHAPTER FOUR

The Politics of School Closure: Massive Resistance Put to the Test, 1958–1959

> Like most parents, my first concern is for my own children. We have a son who is a senior in Central High. He has already lost three weeks of schooling. He does not want to join the 300 students who have transferred to other schools. He wants to graduate from Central High.... Through the years its graduates have shown that they can compete in the best colleges and universities with the top students from the best high schools and prep schools.... It is *these students* who are the real losers in this squabble and who stand to lose the most if we reject *education* in favor of segregation.
>
> —Mrs. Charles Stephens[1]

The graduation of Ernest Green in May 1958 meant not a resolution to the crisis over desegregation in Little Rock, but rather the end of its first stage. Indeed, citizens were still haunted by the specter of federal troops in their midst and the open racial conflict and disorder in schools that had characterized the first year of desegregation. Few whites in Little Rock were committed even to the token efforts at integration achieved in the 1957–1958 academic year and most sought ways to evade the spirit and intent of federal court decisions while successfully claiming compliance. The result was a tangled web of legislation and litigation, culminating in the closing of the Little Rock public high schools for the 1958–1959 academic year and intensified debate over the purpose and the future of public schools in the South and the nation.

This chapter will explain the court decisions that pushed Arkansas officials, including the governor, to support the closure of public schools as a
means of avoiding desegregation. It will also look closely at the varied responses of the community, including women, to the closing of public high
schools. Little Rock's failed experiment with a publicly funded private
school for white students will also receive attention as the school's existence revealed stark differences in how the predominantly working-class
segregationists and middle-class leaders and activists understood education. Most important, the chapter will focus on the Women's Emergency
Committee to Open Our Schools (WEC), a group organized by white
moderate women who entered the public fray once the public high schools
were closed. Their participation in Little Rock's political life shifted the
terms of public discussion and reconfigured the political landscape. Over
time, their participation revealed significant gender differences in the political perspectives and priorities of middle-class white women and men as
well as critical areas of agreement.[2]

The WEC's founders originally intended to form a women's organization dedicated to racial change. Velma Powell, who worked for the interracial Arkansas Council on Human Relations and was married to Central
High School Vice Principal J. O. Powell, wrote to Adolphine Terry: "Always in any crisis in Little Rock, you've been there to do something about
it. Where are you now?" Terry decided that it was "high time for the moderates to be heard from." She met with Powell and Vivion Brewer on September 12, 1958 and decided that they should form a group to discuss race
relations and civil rights. Terry, who had spent over fifty years as a civic
activist in Little Rock, wanted to model it on a group she had joined many
years before to oppose lynching, no doubt the Association of Southern
Women for the Prevention of Lynching.[3]

When the organizers met a few days later with a larger group, however,
they found that some of the fifty-eight white women in attendance were
afraid to form a civil rights organization and that others were hostile to the
idea. One of the women at the meeting expressed the urgency she and others felt about closed schools: "This is all very fine, but what are we going to
do now, *now*? My two boys must have an education and they have already
lost two weeks of school. I think we have to do something now to open our
schools." Thus prodded, the leaders decided to focus their efforts on making open schools the most important priority for Little Rock voters. They

faced a tough task, as the war between Arkansans and the federal courts had intensified in the months before they organized.[4]

In June 1958, the federal district court considered the school board's request for a two-and-a-half-year delay in implementing its desegregation plan. The district court judge, Harry J. Lemley, had started his law practice in Hope, Arkansas in 1912. The grandson of a Confederate soldier, Lemley had once said of his region, "I love the South so much that it is almost a religion with me." Lemley's values and his long career in Arkansas had made him a respected figure in white establishment circles in the state. A. F. House, the school board attorney, described Lemley as an "honest, courteous and conscientious judge" who was "the finest kind of man."[5]

In the course of the hearing, the events of the past year were debated by the official parties to the suit. Once again, they discussed the connections between white opposition to integration and public disorders inside and outside the school, drawing contradictory conclusions regarding the implications of those disorders for compliance with the decision in *Brown v. Board of Education*. The school board argued that the political climate had shifted since August 1957, so that it could no longer preserve order or provide an adequate education for children while attempting to comply with the federal court order to implement the Blossom Plan. In support of its contentions, the board offered testimony from teachers and administrators at Central High School attesting to the tensions that affected students, teachers, and others in the first year of desegregation. Central High School mathematics teacher W. P. Ivey testified that stress created by "the presence of the Negro students" had impaired teaching and learning in his classes to such an extent that grades declined from previous years and that grades in classes with African American students were lower than those in other classes. Vice Principal J. O. Powell called the previous year one of "chaos, bedlam and turmoil from the beginning."[6]

The school board asked that it be allowed to defer desegregation for two and a half years, arguing primarily that by then Orval Faubus would no longer be governor and therefore public opposition would somehow wane. The school board placed a disproportionate amount of the blame for massive resistance to desegregation in Little Rock on Governor Faubus and assumed that his removal from office would almost automatically solve the crisis. The testimony of school superintendent Virgil Blossom and other teachers and administrators inadvertently buttressed the position taken much earlier by Faubus by corroborating his contention that violence would inevitably attend integration.[7]

For its part, the NAACP questioned whether the school board had adequately acquitted its responsibility to ensure order at Central High and claimed that allowing the delay would only encourage violence as a tool of resistance to federal court orders. It brought in expert witnesses from New York to testify that student troublemakers had been treated too leniently, thereby encouraging continued disruptions at the school. Dr. David G. Slaten, superintendent of the Long Beach, Long Island schools, for example, said that he would have followed the recommendations of vice principal Powell that certain students be suspended. Not surprisingly, Richard Butler, attorney for the school board, attempted to discredit the expert witnesses by noting their "lack of first-hand knowledge of the Little Rock situation" and implicitly raising the question of whether northerners could adequately assess southern social relations. School board president Wayne Upton testified that "if we had operated with an iron fist we would have been in for more trouble than we would have prevented." When pressed by NAACP attorney Wiley Branton about the board's failure to seek injunctions against those disrupting the schools, Upton stated that the board did not believe it had sufficient proof for such action.[8]

The testimony of vice principals J. O. Powell and Elizabeth Huckaby, who handled most of the day-to-day discipline at Central High, differed from the official school board position in subtle ways. Both blamed policy decisions rather than integration per se or the opposition to it for the difficulties at the school. Powell stated that he believed that order could have been maintained if the students who were leading the disorders had been suspended for the year. Huckaby testified that court action against the groups "directing the trouble" outside the school would be necessary if the school were to avoid a repetition of the past year. Moreover, she stressed the danger and harm to the African American students caused by white dissidents.[9]

The Little Rock School Board, although it asserted that all students had been damaged by the difficulties of the previous year, conflated the interests of white students with the public good. Blossom claimed that black students received equal educational opportunities at Mann High School and would not be harmed by a return to a segregated system, disregarding the issue of their constitutional right to a nonsegregated education. This

was not a new position for the school board, as it had always justified desegregation on the grounds of the need to comply with court decisions
rather than on its educational benefits for black students. Blossom's testimony, however, may not have been an accurate statement of his real views.
In a book published soon thereafter, Blossom stated his belief that the
teachers in Little Rock's African American schools were poorly trained and
not equal to those in white schools. Those teachers, of course, were the
product of the segregated system that Blossom was defending.[10]

On June 20, 1958 Judge Harry Lemley announced his decision to grant
the delay requested by the school board. In order to justify his finding,
Lemley had to distinguish it from earlier federal court decisions in school
desegregation cases that had declared that public hostility to a decision was
not sufficient justification for the failure to enforce constitutional rights.
According to Lemley, Little Rock opposition was "more than a mere men-
tal attitude; it has manifested itself in overt acts which have actually damaged educational standards." Such opposition, however, did not derive
from malice toward the African American students at Central High, but
rather from opposition "to the principle of integration" and the conviction
that "the Brown decisions do not represent the law of the land" and could
be evaded. Although he concluded that the use of troops to enforce court
orders was "disrupting to the educational process," Lemley frequently attributed the problems in the schools to "the presence of the Negro students, and all that went with it." The delay, he decided, was necessary in
part so that segregationist legislation passed in Arkansas to challenge the
Brown decisions would receive judicial review.[11]

The Lemley decision temporarily unified white sentiment in Little
Rock, drawing praise from the school board, Orval Faubus, the *Arkansas
Gazette* and many other whites anxious for a reprieve from the conflict and
confusion occasioned by social change. They reiterated the faith expressed
by Eisenhower and Faubus in the fall of 1957 that somehow an unspecified process of public education would create the conditions necessary for
voluntary compliance. As before, whites offered no plans for such an educational effort, relying apparently on the idea of inevitable progress to pave
the way for public acceptance of integration. In short, their legal stance
was based on the assumption that the situation would right itself in time
without their actually having to act affirmatively to change public opinion.
As the *Wall Street Journal* put it in its editorial on the decision, "But time,

too, is useless if men put it to no purpose." Lemley, however, did not require that those persons seeking the reprieve spell out their plans for paving the way to community acceptance of integration. Indeed, Blossom had
testified that the school board did not intend to use the time to change
public opinion.[12]

The Justice Department found the decision deeply disturbing, concluding that the acceptance of Lemley's legal reasoning by the courts "would
undoubtedly encourage similar lawlessness" by those opposed to integration in other communities and would effectively kill efforts to desegregate
public education everywhere. At the same time, Justice Department attorneys knew that enforcing integration orders in Little Rock would not be
easy. In July, an internal memorandum on school desegregation warned
that if Lemley's decision was overturned, "considerable disturbances must
be expected at Little Rock" and federal assistance might be necessary to
support court decisions. By August, the Justice Department had apparently decided to file an *amicus* brief in the case and to seek injunctions
against any organizations and individuals for whom there was proof that
they were "creating or inciting disorder" or helping to undermine the district court's order for integration at Central High School.[13]

Within days of the Lemley decision, the long-deferred meeting between
President Eisenhower and African American leaders took place. The leaders, A. Philip Randolph, the Rev. Martin Luther King, Jr., Roy Wilkins,
and Lester Granger, were already disaffected with the president's failure to
offer meaningful support for school integration. King had sent a telegram
to Daisy Bates to ask for suggestions from her with respect to possible executive action in the Little Rock situation. Ike's concern that holding a
meeting with black leaders would lead to the expectation that the executive
would actually act to improve the situation for black students was therefore about to be realized. When the four leaders met with Eisenhower, they
came with a list of suggested executive actions on civil rights. These actions
included a statement by the president that he would use the "total resources at his command" to enforce the law, a White House conference on
compliance with the *Brown* decision, the enactment of a civil rights bill
that would allow the attorney general to enforce constitutional rights other
than voting rights, and action by the Department of Justice to protect voting rights. They told the president of their deep concern that the district
court decision would provide incentives for segregationists to use violence

as a means of flouting the law. According to E. Frederic Morrow, Eisenhower "listened with deep attention, and this in itself was reassuring to the delegation." He did not, however, make any public statements on the Lemley decision or the issues it raised and, as Morrow later concluded, "business went on as usual."[14]

For Eisenhower, the meeting was particularly frustrating because he believed that the African American leaders did not know how to communicate on his terms. He complained that they acted as though they were talking to their constituents rather than to him. Indeed, their message that black disaffection with white temporizing was reaching crisis proportions struck him as exaggerated and polemical. When they stated that the government could deal with moderate leaders like themselves at that time or with urban disorders and militant spokesmen later, he reacted with complete disbelief. Eisenhower's inability to grasp their point of view was hardly without precedent. As Morrow observed: "You also have to realize, if you know the history, that the Negro has been mis-read for 300 years."[15]

That misreading continued in the state of Arkansas. On July 29, Arkansas Democrats turned out in record numbers for the primary election, renominating Faubus for his third term as governor by a wide margin. In Arkansas at this time, Republican candidates did not stand a chance in the general election so that winning the Democratic nomination was the equivalent of winning the election. Faubus carried every county in Arkansas and received 70 percent of the vote. He claimed that his victory signaled "a condemnation by the people of illegal Federal intervention in the affairs of the state and the horrifying use of Federal bayonets in the streets of an American city and in the halls of a public school." Faubus had nearly reached the crest of his popularity and power in the state. He would use his mandate and his power to advance the cause of massive resistance.[16]

Immediately on the heels of Faubus's victory, however, on August 18, 1958, in a 6–1 decision, the Eighth Circuit Court of Appeals reversed the Lemley determination. It strenuously disagreed with Lemley's conclusions that the presence of the African American students caused the difficulties at Central High. Instead, it found that opposition to their presence caused the problems and faulted the school board for not seeking injunctions against the troublemakers in the community and for inadequate discipline in the school. To sustain the district court's findings would only invite further violence in defiance of legitimate court orders: *"We say the time has not yet come in these United States when an order of a Federal court must be whittled away, watered down, or shamefully withdrawn in the face of violence and unlawful acts of individual citizens in opposition thereto."*[17]

As the next school year approached, warring whites in Arkansas sought to set the terms of the debate over desegregation. By limiting the ways in which the issue could be discussed and understood (and by excluding blacks from the dialogue), various parties tried to define the options available in ways that would persuade the public that the solutions recommended by them were the only viable ones. From the beginning, the Little Rock School Board consistently advocated for a program of minimal integration to be implemented very slowly, telling white school patrons that although they had no choice but to comply with federal court decisions the fewest number of blacks possible would be admitted into previously white schools in any given year. By contrast, the architects of massive resistance in Arkansas cleverly sought to depict the school board plan as one that involved massive integration in the very near future and to reassure citizens that federal court orders were illegitimate usurpations of power they could safely ignore. Indeed, Faubus and his allies, knowing that it would strengthen resistance to desegregation, tried to use state powers to ensure that compliance with the *Brown* decision would mean integration in all schools. They represented the situation as an "all or none" fight between immediate, full-scale integration in all schools or the preservation of a racially segregated public school system.

In a speech given in response to the reversal of the Lemley decision, for example, Faubus falsely accused the Little Rock School Board of going to court in 1957 to secure support for a plan of total integration of the public schools. He asked whether the school board intended to follow that course or to "fight in every legal way possible the integration by force, with such dire consequences for education in the affected school, and the peace of the community." He also asked questions designed to create the impression that large numbers of blacks would be entering previously white schools in Little Rock in the near future. About Central High, he wondered: "when will the number be raised to 90 or 900, the latter figure being the number eligible to attend Central High School under the board's complete integration plan?" His "full-scale integration" or "full-scale resistance" line precluded the gradual evolution toward integration anticipated in the

Brown II decision and deliberately undermined any efforts by others to engender white acceptance of the necessity (much less the benefits) of school desegregation.[18]

Faubus consistently invoked "democratic" principles (understood as simple majority rule), stating that any actions by the school board had to have the support of the majority of the (white) citizens affected. He also alluded to "secret board meetings," implying that the school board was orchestrating a covert cabal to subvert popular wishes. Faubus's appeal to a "conspiratorial populism" resonated with the feelings of powerlessness that his white working-class constituency in Little Rock had experienced with the school board and other political bodies. Although Faubus was right that the school board made most of its important decisions in private discussions among board members or with Little Rock "power brokers," he was wrong (and willfully so) in his reading of their intentions. In fact, the school board wished nothing more fervently than to defer to white opinion in this case. Months of legal and moral equivocation on the necessity of compliance by the school board had fed the very resistance that it deplored, thereby heightening the board members' feelings of frustration as they found themselves caught between the federal courts and the local segregationists whose resistance was enabled by the government of the state of Arkansas.[19]

In anticipation of the Supreme Court's decision, Faubus convened a special session of the Arkansas legislature in August 1958 in order to secure the passage of new laws modeled on the "Virginia Plan" for massive resistance to desegregation. On the eve of the special session, Faubus claimed that "deep seated popular opposition in Little Rock to the principle of integration" and the widespread belief there that the Supreme Court decision could be evaded meant that the courts could not legitimately ask for compliance. Thus, while raising the important question of the relationship between public sentiment and law in a democracy, he also substituted a form of wishful thinking for any reflection on the appropriate means of dissent. Instead, he simply stated, in effect, that whites did not have to obey laws they did not like.[20]

Blacks, by contrast, were expected not only to obey laws but also to renounce their right to use the courts to advance their interests. Faubus claimed that the NAACP had "instigated and promoted the continued integration efforts" in Little Rock. He urged the school board to meet with

NAACP officials and the parents of the black students so that the latter would withdraw their objections to the two-and-a-half-year delay "in the interest of harmony and the greater good of the whole community." Once again, the governor advanced the view that black acquiescence in systems designed by and for whites was the price of and means to racial harmony. That the "whole community" to whom he referred was white was the unstated racial subtext of his appeal. In response to his address, the NAACP sent Faubus a telegram stating that the organization had assisted the parents of black students in Little Rock in securing their constitutional right to "non-segregated public education" and had advised them that the proposal that they voluntarily delay implementation was "a request that they surrender their rights as American citizens and one which cannot in honor be granted."[21]

For his part, the governor returned to a familiar refrain, alleging that it was necessary to call a special session of the state legislature because forced integration would cause "almost certain disorders" and because representative government must be used to define the course that the state would take. Although the violence he predicted and threatened would have come from members of the white community, their willingness to resort to violence did not diminish their claims on the polity. In his speech to the legislature, he claimed that his reliance on elected state representatives (as opposed to locally elected school board members) made his position the only legitimate one.[22]

In the special session, he and the legislators focused particularly on laws enabling the state to close the public schools rather than allow them to be integrated under a federal court order and on authorizing the use of public school moneys for private segregated schools. Act 4, which Jim Johnson had suggested to Faubus in the fall of 1957, allowed the governor to close any or all schools in any school district under federal court orders to integrate if he believed that federal troops would be used to enforce the order, violence would occur, or educational efficiency would be impaired. The schools would remain closed, pending the outcome of an election in which citizens would vote for or against the integration of *all* schools in the district. It is important that the timetable for integration constructed in Act 4 was much more rapid than that anticipated in the federal court-sanctioned Blossom Plan or in the *Brown II* decision, which allowed school districts to proceed with desegregation "with all deliberate speed." Under Act 4, if a majority of those eligible to vote (rather than those who actually chose to vote) cast their ballots for integration, then the schools could integrate and would remain open. Otherwise, the governor could keep them closed indefinitely.

Act 5 required that the unexpended public funds occasioned by the school closures be given on a per capita basis to schools, public or private, that the displaced students then chose to attend. Other laws required that school districts provide segregated classes to any student who requested them and enabled the transfer of students from integrated to segregated schools. This elaborate edifice of new laws, which passed through the legislature with only one dissenting vote, was designed to ensure that whites would never have to attend school with African Americans against their will.[23]

The legislature also passed several bills intended to undermine the ability of the NAACP and other organizations to organize effectively or to use the courts to advance civil rights. Staunchly supported by Arkansas Attorney General Bruce Bennett, who believed that all civil rights activism was Communist inspired, these laws prohibited the NAACP from financing legal costs for lawsuits and required that the organization provide the state with information about its membership. Act 10 required that state employees, including public school teachers, file affidavits listing the organizations to which they belonged and their financial contributions to such groups. Bennett was straightforward about the purpose of such laws, admitting that they were "designed to harass" civil rights organizations. Act 115 required the state to fire any employee who belonged to the NAACP. As Nathan Griswold noted later, the "meanest member [of the legislature] was now free to vent his spleen on 'all enemies of Southern people,' to use the current phrase."[24]

Without apparent irony, Faubus and his supporters declared that the new laws were necessary to preserve the quality of education and to retain democratic governance. Even as he closed the public high schools of Little Rock, the governor justified his actions in terms of the long-term interests of white students in "maintaining our form of government" and "preserving the great freedoms and privileges which we have known." In the statement he issued after signing the laws, Faubus claimed he was doing so to "avoid the impending violence and disorder which would occur" if he allowed desegregation to proceed and stated that "evidence concerning disorder and violence" could be found in the testimony of school officials in the June 1958 trial. Because they relied on threats of violence to sustain their politics of massive resistance, Faubus and his allies implicitly condoned its use as a political tool.[25]

While Faubus and the legislature maneuvered to prevent even moderate desegregation plans from being implemented, *Newsweek* reported that President Eisenhower had told friends that he thought that the school integration process was moving too rapidly and that he wished that the *Brown* decision had not been made. Thurgood Marshall responded to the president's statement by observing that, "If we slow down any more, we will be going backward." When questioned by reporters, Eisenhower admitted that he had said that he believed desegregation was occurring too rapidly because "we have got to have reason and sense and education, and a lot of other developments that go hand in hand . . . if this process is going to have any real acceptance in the United States." At the same time, he denied any statements regretting *Brown* and claimed that the *amicus* brief the Justice Department would be filing the next day in the Little Rock case fully reflected his views. In the meantime, the Supreme Court called an unusual special session to decide the case before the high schools of Little Rock were scheduled to open.[26]

On the eve of the Supreme Court decision, U.S. Attorney General William P. Rogers served notice that the federal government would see to it that federal court orders were obeyed. He announced that the Justice Department would send additional Deputy United States Marshals to Little Rock in order to assist local officials in the maintenance of law and order. The marshals would not usurp local law enforcement functions, but would, according to Rogers, "perform their proper functions to assist in the execution of the orders of the United States Courts." He also noted that additional lawyers from the Department of Justice were already in Little Rock to provide assistance with any legal matters relating to the implementation of federal court orders. For his part, Faubus charged that the marshals would be met with "cold fury" in Arkansas.[27]

In November 1958, at a celebration of "Orval Faubus Day" in Tiptonville, Tennessee, Faubus claimed that if the president had sent marshals or FBI agents to enforce desegregation in 1957, he would have had them arrested for interfering with his troops. The *Arkansas Gazette* responded to the governor's posturing with an editorial stating that his remarks had "more than abstract interest, since it can fairly be taken as revealing Mr. Faubus' present state of mind." The editorial noted that the campaign of massive resistance was running out of strategies as the federal government was not backing away from its support of the *Brown* decisions and the private school experiments in Arkansas and Virginia were showing "how inadequate such a school system is going to be." The only alternative to the South would then be armed insurrection against the national government.[28]

On September 12, 1958, an angry U.S. Supreme Court responded to the Little Rock School Board's request for a delay in compliance with the *Brown* decisions by agreeing with the school board that resistance to federal court decisions in Arkansas had been instigated by Governor Faubus and the state legislature. The Court held in *Cooper v. Aaron* that state officials had been "actively pursuing a program designed to perpetuate in Arkansas the system of racial segregation" that the Court had outlawed. Because the disorders in Little Rock had been caused by state actions, the Court concluded that "law and order are not here to be preserved by depriving the negro children of their constitutional rights." Moreover, the Court explicitly argued against the contentions of Faubus and the legislature (and many others in the South) that the *Brown* decisions were not binding on them by delivering a lecture on the "settled [constitutional] doctrine" that the Constitution was the supreme law of the land.[29]

After the ruling of the Supreme Court, Faubus went on television and claimed that the Supreme Court decision "promises 'the risk of disorder and violence that could result in the loss of life—perhaps yours.'" He also signed the new bills into law and closed the public high schools of Little Rock. Faubus saw the Supreme Court decision as a challenge to his personal power and autonomy as well as his position as governor, vowing: "I will not surrender to federal integration orders or to the NAACP." Moreover, his statement advanced the shop-worn notion that the legal power deployed by blacks in the courts was an illegitimate collusion between two "outside" forces: the NAACP and the federal government. His stance prompted a letter from Senator Strom Thurmond, who expressed the conviction that "the South can no longer confine its fight to the Courts." As a result, Thurmond resolved to call on "the Southern people to oppose integration orders regardless of Federal force."[30]

Faubus's response should have come as no surprise to the Eisenhower administration. Not only had his intentions been clear since August, but

Arkansas Congressman Brooks Hays had written to presidential aide Sherman Adams in early September warning that Faubus would close the schools if the courts required that integration go forward in Little Rock. When apprised that officials in Arkansas and Virginia planned to close some of the public schools rather than have them integrated, Eisenhower responded cautiously that he would await the actions of local citizens committed to open public schools before taking further legal action. Attorney General Rogers described local decisions to close schools rather than comply with federal court decisions as "inconceivable," but added that legal methods alone were not sufficient to resolve the situation. Having been informed that PTAs and other school organizations in Virginia and Arkansas were organizing against the closings, Eisenhower, who hoped that the federal government would not have to intervene, decided to await the actions of local citizens affected by the closing of public schools.[31]

In Little Rock, the citizens most likely to take action against school closings were those who joined the Women's Emergency Committee to Open Our Schools. Some of the women who organized the WEC followed a family tradition of community building and for them the crisis provoked deep concern regarding the reputation and future of Little Rock. Vivion Brewer, the first president of the WEC, noted that she had worried through the whole previous year "about what was happening to the city which my father had played such a leading role in developing. And with the threat of closed schools I worried about the children, our future citizens, who would be denied an education.... I worried about their being taught total disregard of law and order." Adolphine Terry, the grand dame of Little Rock civic volunteerism and the founding mother of the WEC, said that "When Little Rock became an evil word around the world, I felt that my own world had collapsed."[32]

The disaffection of these women with Faubus and his allies bespoke class and other divisions among whites over the meaning of the desegregation crisis. As David Chappell has noted, many people in the middle class faced a dilemma created by shifts in the political context within which social relations were organized in the south. Suddenly, they found that social values and institutional arrangements that had been compatible in the past were in conflict. No longer could they expect to build a community based simultaneously on legal segregation, law and order, public education, and economic development. The working-class segregationists simply assumed that a monolithic white interest in maintaining segregation would mean a willingness to sacrifice these other goals to maintain historic racial arrangements. In fact, however, southern whites varied in the meanings they attached to racial segregation, the ways in which they saw it articulating with other institutional arrangements, and the priority they assigned to segregation in relation to their social and political values. For the WEC, those differences created a cultural and political space for the articulation of an altered set of priorities in their community.[33]

The precarious predicament of Little Rock's power structure also contributed to possibilities for change. The crisis over desegregation had paralyzed the male business elite. Even the closing of public schools had not prompted business leaders to oppose Faubus and his policies publicly. Indeed, Virgil Blossom charged later that members of the state legislature were afraid to oppose the governor because their businesses would suffer. In response, Brewer, Terry, and other Little Rock women decided to fill the political void created in part by the inability of the established male leadership of Little Rock and Arkansas to offer viable solutions to local and statewide dilemmas. As Terry reputedly put it, "I see the men have failed again. I'll have to send for the young ladies."[34]

In sending for the ladies, she enlisted them in a cause that would test the possibilities of white dissent in the south. The fate of whites who supported integration in its first year in Little Rock offered warning enough for any who dared to question the wisdom of massive resistance. For white middle-class women to do so meant transgressing various dogmas about southern womanhood. It meant challenging the expectation that women would defer to men in politics, particularly with regard to issues central to economic development and partisan politics. To engage in a public controversy of this magnitude also challenged women to overcome their socialization to place people at ease and to create harmony, not conflict. This was particularly difficult when much of the conflict took place within families.[35]

Most important, supporting integration publicly involved rethinking their position as white women in a social order predicated on the idea that white women had to exchange their subordination to white men for protection from the bodily threats perceived to come from the mere presence of African American men. Many of the women who became publicly identified with the WEC received anonymous letters warning of the sexual dangers of school integration. One purported friend of Adolphine Terry wrote (anonymously) to her alleging that a very large proportion of blacks had venereal diseases and concluded: "It is a horrible thing to think of one's grand children sharing the rest rooms with them." Pat House reported that she received much hate mail accusing her of faulty morals because she advocated for opening the schools even if it meant gradual integration.[36]

For some southern white women, however, traditional ideologies of racial peril and privilege were no longer persuasive. Some WEC leaders said that their exposure to egalitarian educational or religious values facilitated their break from conventional beliefs. Adolphine Terry, for example, remembered a conversation in her dorm room at Vassar years before that transformed her thinking:

> . . . I made the statement, which I had heard all of my life, although not from my father, that if a black man assaulted a white woman he should be lynched on the spot. Lucy Burns, who came from Brooklyn and had more experience than I, looked at me with perfect horror, and I can still remember her exact words: 'For the sake of taking revenge on one poor wretch, would you destroy the very foundations of law and order in your community?' Well, I just sat back and thought about that. I knew she was right, and it really has affected my entire life.[37]

Women joined the WEC for various reasons. Terry, for example, had worked on behalf of African Americans in Little Rock for over forty years. Velma Powell worked for the Arkansas Council on Human Relations, an interracial group formed in the postwar period to advance social equality. Many of the members were drawn by a combination of concern for their children, civic pride, and a desire to restore peace and stability to their community. A substantial proportion of the membership preferred that segregation be retained, but were not willing to sacrifice public schools to do so. Moreover, mothers of displaced high school students (about 20 percent of the membership) saw the connections between public policy and private lives very clearly. They had the primary responsibility in their families to see to the education of their children and many felt keenly the loss of family integrity when their children were forced to attend school outside of Little Rock.[38]

The women who joined the WEC were affluent and very well educated relative to the general population of Arkansas. They resembled others in the New South community in being long-term residents of Little Rock or the South and belonging to a church. In a state characterized by low levels of education, at least 80 percent of WEC members had attended college, 21 percent for over four years. Almost three out of four owned their own homes, where they raised baby-boom era families. The typical member was a middle-aged married woman with two or more children. Her husband was a professional or businessman but with a few exceptions not likely to be from the business or political elite of Little Rock. Only 23 percent of those surveyed worked for pay outside the home. Their social identity as middle-class white women who did not engage in wage work was critical to their ability to mobilize resources, particularly their own time and labor, on behalf of their cause.[39]

Although most WEC members received crucial assistance with housework, primarily from African American women employed as domestics, their families' responses to their absences from home varied; some resented their activities, others pitched in to help with housework and childcare. One WEC member wrote to Vivion Brewer that her mother stayed for a few days to do her ironing and mending for the month so she could focus on WEC work, adding that "the family plumbing etc. can wait."[40]

As they had in other cities, white middle-class women in Little Rock claimed a role for themselves in civic work on behalf of cultural development, children, and, on occasion, economic development. They were densely connected to each other through a variety of women's clubs and civic organizations. The WEC was in fact a "Who's Who" of activist women in the community. It drew women from the League of Women Voters (most of whom joined the WEC), the American Association of University Women, the Parent Teacher Associations, and a large number of other groups. In women's history, the question of when, how, and why previously apolitical networks become politicized is critical to an understanding of women's political roles and contributions. In Little Rock, women who had never worked in political campaigns or lobbied for legislation rapidly found themselves giving prodigious amounts of their time in these kinds of activities as they took on the most controversial public issue in the history of their community .[41]

The leaders of the new organization brought to it the respectability of their connections to prominent Little Rock families and their impeccable credentials as southern "ladies" who had contributed much to their communities over the years. Vivion Brewer was the daughter of a former mayor of Little Rock. Adolphine Terry was the granddaughter of a Confederate officer and the wife of a former Congressman. When the seventy-six-year-old Terry decided to call in fifty years' worth of civic service "IOU's," many women in Little Rock felt compelled to respond. Later the *Pine Bluff Commercial* concluded that Mrs. Terry had "invested education with her own unquestionable propriety." Moreover, the fact that the WEC board met in Mrs. Terry's antebellum mansion made the group's connections to the slaveholding South material.[42]

Virtually from the outset, WEC members determined to mobilize white middle-class women and men in support of opening the public schools. They worked to impart their sense of urgency to other women in the community, telling them that "we feel a little like a person whose house is on fire," and asking "Do you continue the bridge game, the housework—the whatever? No, you drop everything else and grab a bucket of water to put out the fire. Right now our public school system seems to be the only thing that matters here."[43]

The election on school integration in Little Rock was scheduled for September 27. Although the ballot did not explicitly say so, a no vote on school integration was a vote in favor of closing public schools. Indeed, because of the way the law was written, staying at home on voting day was the same as voting to close the schools. Realizing that the majority of Little Rock whites supported segregation, the WEC set about to persuade voters that the issue was not integration but rather the future of the public schools. Moreover, they had less than two weeks to get the job done and they faced an opposition campaign orchestrated by a popular and politically astute governor.[44]

Faubus and his allies promised white voters that they did not have to worry about closed schools because private schools paid for with public funds would be available to their children. They even floated a plan to lease Central High School to a private school in order to evade court-ordered integration in that school. Faubus also stated that these arrangements would withstand legal challenge. In effect, the governor was promising whites that they would have to make no sacrifices in the quality of their children's education in order to retain segregation. This was a promise that legal experts knew he could not keep. Sixty-three lawyers in Little Rock signed a newspaper advertisement warning the voters that the use of tax money for private schools was unlikely to withstand the scrutiny of the courts and that "the alternative of no public school system is even more distasteful" than a "limited integrated school system pursuant to Court orders." The lawyers' ad was noteworthy because it broke the code of silence operating in the business and professional community. One of the signers, Ronald May, reported to Vivion Brewer that some lawyers had faced significant reprisals for signing the ad.[45]

Faubus went on television on September 18 and used a segregationist-inspired Congressional report on integration in the public schools of Washington, D. C. to heighten white fears that integration would cause a substantial decline in educational quality, would increase disciplinary problems in the schools, and would expose white students to moral dangers. In addition, he assured Arkansas citizens that his plan to use public funds to support private schools was constitutional and feasible. Using the Little Rock School Board's legal position in order to undermine support for compliance with integration orders, he noted that the board had admitted in court that it could not provide an environment conducive to learning in desegregated schools. He also denied that the school board members would be vulnerable to prosecution for contempt of court if they failed to follow a court order.[46]

The WEC had stated in its initial recruitment efforts and its first political campaign that its members were "dedicated to the principle of free public school education. We stand neither for integration nor for segregation but for education." The organization thus launched a campaign against Faubus's contention that private schools equal in quality to existing public schools could be opened (with taxpayers' money no less) rapidly. They asked voters to "Preserve Your Public Schools—Your First Class School" and warned them that they could have "ONE FIRST-CLASS PUBLIC SCHOOL SYSTEM" or "SECOND-RATE SUBSTITUTES." They told the voters that "although it may be extremely distasteful for you to mark your ballot 'FOR RACIAL INTEGRATION,' this is the only choice the ballot allows if the schools are to be reopened."[47]

In the first of two television programs it organized before the election, the WEC showcased the themes that it would emphasize in the following years. Moderator William Hadley, Jr., a former radio and television reporter in Little Rock, began the program by saying that "Segregation is not the question tonight. Integration is not the question. Our question is EDUCATION." Attorney Edward Lester explained that public funds could not legally be used to operate segregated private schools. Several other participants, including Mrs. Charles Stephens, the immediate past president of the Central High School PTA, discussed the value of public schools. Stephens, whose son was supposed to be complete his senior year at Central High that year, stressed the opportunities provided at Central for college-bound students, noting the school's strong academic reputation and the college scholarships won by its graduates.[48]

Pat House concluded later that "the main thing the Women's Emergency Committee accomplished, I feel, was that they shifted the issues away from the controversial, deeply, very emotional deep gut issue of integration, refused to discuss that. We simply said that it has nothing to do with integration, it has to do with education. This got the women, because it's their bailiwick." The schools were women's "bailiwick" because they were the ones responsible for overseeing their children's education and contributing their own labor as homeroom mothers, fundraisers, active PTA members, and family liaisons with teachers and other school officials. In short, they helped to police the boundary that the schools occupied between public institutions and private aspirations. According to Pat House, the focus on education also provided a comfortable political vocabulary for conservative southern women who were otherwise reluctant to disagree or cause trouble. The WEC's shift of focus from integration to the preservation of public schools also deflected attention from the question of the education of African American children to that of white children. It thereby went straight to the concerns of the majority of white mothers in the community, thus enabling their recruitment and providing an issue that kept the members committed to the WEC.[49]

On September 27, 1958, however, the enormity of the political task they had undertaken became clear to WEC members and supporters of public schools. Large numbers of citizens in Little Rock turned out to vote. The absence of a secret ballot in Arkansas meant that voters showed each other their marked ballots to assure one another that they had voted against integration. The large turnout did not hearten Elizabeth Huckaby, who wrote in her journal that "people seemed to be coming out of *gutters* to vote." In fact, the segregationists tried to draw numbers to their cause by having an African American couple and their two children picket in front of Hall High School with a placard asking voters to "Please Vote for Integration to Help Us Have Equality." Their picture appeared in the afternoon newspaper. The final tally was 19,470 to 7,561 against integration and in favor of closing the high schools.[50]

As David Wieck pointed out, the ballot did not ask voters "how much does [segregation] mean to you?" The results of the election, however, would ask many citizens to consider that very question. Even as they marked their ballots, some voters had not yet squarely faced the implications of the referendum. Jim Childers, for example, a long-time employee of the state legislature, did not vote in the election (a decision that was the equivalent of voting against integration and for school closings) because she did not believe that Faubus would actually allow the schools to remain closed. The result was that she and her husband then had to scramble to find a school for their daughter to attend.[51]

The people who were most affected by the election—the children scheduled to attend the closed schools—were also the ones most opposed to the outcome. One poll of 501 junior and senior students at Hall High School found that 71 percent wanted the schools open even if they were to be integrated. Sixty-five Hall High School students signed a petition asking that their school be opened. At Central High School, some members of the student council tried to secure a meeting with Faubus to persuade him to change his position. The student who claimed he could arrange such an appointment kept putting them off, however. Clearly many of the affected students were not in accord with their parents on the question of closing the high schools.[52]

Except for the fact that they lost badly, this campaign typified the role that WEC members would come to play in their community and state. They mobilized a large number of women to work on the political education of their community and on getting out the vote for their position; they organized media events in support of their position; they sought allies, particularly in women's organizations; and they worked to shift the terms of the discourse about school desegregation. Their efforts then and later caused them to be vilified and harassed and caused enormous discord with close friends and family.[53]

As would be true for some time to come, they also had difficulty securing the assistance of men in their efforts. As Adolphine Terry acerbically explained it, the school election occurred "when many of the menfolk were either panicky themselves or taking an impartial stand between education and ignorance." Irene Samuel said the situation was so bad at first that "We couldn't even get our own husbands to speak out." As a result, it was difficult for WEC members to offer opposing viewpoints when they secured television time before the election. Few community leaders were willing to appear on television in support of their position and few who did could compete with Faubus's media skills. In addition to the lawyers, only a few ministers, two church boards, and AFL–CIO chairman Odell Smith spoke for the public schools in this election.[54]

The moderate males' desire to control the terms of public discussion so that they could protect their business interests put them at odds with the growing women's movement. In her role as president of the WEC, Vivion Brewer approached business leaders to seek their public endorsement of the organization's goals. These leaders, however, continued to be wary of taking a public stance in the controversy. One banker told her that no one had been harmed by the closing of the schools, concluding: "You women ought to leave this thing alone. You are the ones stirring up trouble." Velma Powell directly linked the unwillingness of traditional community leaders to speak out during the crisis to their focus on issues related to industrial development and a new form of city government designed to advance their business goals: "Possibly, this very idea of progress caused some silence in the beginning of Little Rock's troubled times."[55]

At the same time, WEC activists knew that they needed public support and assistance to achieve their objectives. As Irene Samuel put it later: "the reason we tried to push the men is because they were in the driver's seat. And we couldn't drive." They continued working behind the scenes with businessmen, some of whom provided them with money and political expertise. They worked actively to get male leaders to make public statements in favor of open public schools even if it meant desegregation, and tried unsuccessfully to form a statewide organization that included men and women to advance their cause. For the first four years, they also deferred to the men over the choice of candidates for the school board, despite the occasional rudeness and their continued marginalization at the hands of the men they had assisted.[56]

In the meantime, the legal and political maneuvers of the opposition continued. On September 23, Faubus asked the Little Rock School Board to transfer control of the public schools to the recently chartered Little Rock Private School Corporation. The school board members refused, in part because the Justice Department dissuaded them from doing so. Informed by its lawyers that Act 5 and the private school scheme touted by Faubus and his allies would likely be declared unconstitutional, the school board offered instead to lease Central High to the Private School Corporation in order to test the validity of the action and, it was hoped, to protect board members from being found in contempt of a court order. The NAACP petitioned the court, asking that the Little Rock School Board be barred from making the transfer. Although the court did not solicit an *amicus curiae* brief from the Justice Department, the department decided to support the NAACP's petition with one, a departure from its previous policy of submitting such a brief only at the request of the court. The Justice Department asserted that the state's involvement in the private schools was clear, as was its intention to discriminate on the basis of race. Therefore, the "private" schools were, in fact, agents of the state and of the school board, which would be in violation of a federal court order if they proceeded with the transfer. Indeed, when it was presented with the issue of leasing Central High to a private school, the Eighth Circuit Court of Appeals agreed with the NAACP and the Justice Department. On September 29, the court issued a restraining order, directing the school board and all its agents (including the teachers) to have no part in the leasing arrangement.[57]

Orval Faubus, however, had no reservations about using state power to support the operation of the all-white private high school in Little Rock and other segregated private schools. He provided per capita tuition vouchers to schools in Arkansas, public and private, that took in students from the closed high schools and he raised a large sum of money on behalf of the all-white private high school. Renamed Raney High School, it opened on October 20, 1958 with a group of hastily recruited teachers who offered a limited curriculum in a substandard facility, despite receiving over $71,000 in state funds and a reported $300,000 to $400,000 in outside donations.

Little Rock School Board member Wayne Upton later stated that Raney High employed "innumerable misfits" as teachers. *Time* concluded that the teachers recruited for the new school were "as varied as a Foreign Legion Battalion, ranging from competent to questionable." Raney's faculty generally lacked the educational background of the teachers in the closed schools and few had any teaching experience. Raney offered no classes in foreign languages, general math, music, or art. Its only vocational courses were typing and shorthand. In order to obtain books for a library, the new school made public requests for book donations. Volunteer labor helped to make desks and other items of furniture. Clearly, the quality of education had become a secondary concern for many whites in Little Rock. Despite its many shortcomings, Raney High School was accredited by the state of Arkansas on January 13, 1959. Without consulting local officials, state administrators also withdrew Little Rock's public high schools from membership in the North Central Association of Colleges and Secondary Schools (NCACSS), whose accreditation was important to admission to colleges outside of Arkansas.[58]

From the perspective of Little Rock's middle-class leaders, Raney High was academically and socially unacceptable. Its lack of accreditation from NCACSS meant that graduates would have difficulty getting into colleges outside of Arkansas, an important goal for middle-class parents in Little Rock. Its predominantly working-class student body and its reputed lack of discipline gave it the nickname of "Hood High." An informal inquiry by the WEC, for example, elicited reports that profanity and fights in the classrooms and outside the school were not uncommon. Teachers reportedly wanted the principal to take a tougher stand against disruptive students, but he took the position that they could be educated and should be kept in school. Whether these reports were true or not, they were credible to some middle-class parents, who felt compelled to find other schools for their children.[59]

As a result, many parents in Little Rock frantically tried to secure an alternative school in order to ensure continuity in their children's education, and various institutions and individuals offered makeshift solutions. Mothers of displaced students, who assumed most of the responsibility for finding schools for their children, called Elizabeth Huckaby at Central High for her suggestions. Some Little Rock churches opened or expanded private schools. A Baptist congregation voted to open an interim school assisted by Ouachita Baptist College. The University of Arkansas offered extension courses while other school districts in Arkansas opened their doors to Little Rock's high school students. Many parents implored relatives near and far to take their children in for the year so that they could attend schools that were not in commuting distance to Little Rock. Some parents rented apartments in North Little Rock so that their children could go to school there. A few were able to use connections to get their children into private schools elsewhere despite the fact that their applications were late and classes had already started. One segregationist couple ended up sending their son to an integrated school elsewhere. They later wrote the Little Rock School Board imploring it to open the schools on an integrated basis.[60]

The smaller private schools suffered many of the problems that plagued Raney High—great difficulty recruiting qualified teachers, poor facilities, and an inadequate curriculum. Some private schools apparently also had problems with discipline. Moreover, these schools charged tuition and usually admitted only students from the religious faith that had established the school. Some seniors in these schools transferred to other schools at midyear, worried that they would not be able to gain admission to college with degrees from unaccredited schools. According to Wayne Upton, one public official had become deeply concerned about the closing of the public schools when his son, who had struggled in the public schools to make passing grades, made straight As without studying in a church school. The father said he would go to Hall High School and shoot anyone who attempted to keep it closed. Parents with children enrolled in public school systems some distance from Little Rock worried about their children having to drive long distances "in heavy traffic and icy dangerous weather."[61]

Many parents were very distressed by family separations necessitated when their children had to leave Little Rock in order to go to school. Jim Childers, whose daughter lived with relatives while she attended school in Fordyce, Arkansas, reported that she "felt cheated that I had lost her a year early." One woman moved to a nearby city so her only child could enter high school there. Her husband commuted from Little Rock on weekends to be with them. Other parents had children in schools very distant from each other. The children felt conflicting loyalties as they made new friends in new places. The WEC would turn this parental concern for the integrity of the family into a political appeal to open public schools in Little Rock. A typical flier implored: "Let's keep our children—our hope of the future—at home and returning home."[62]

For the children themselves, the consequences of moving to go to a new school varied, depending in part on the degree of social acceptance they experienced. Carol Ervren, who transferred to a private religious school in Searcy, Arkansas, desperately missed her old friends: "We were looking forward to the senior year. We did things together, had a lot of fun, and then, wham, here we are in practically every state there is." Her difficulties were compounded by the strict rules at her new school, which she experienced as repressive: "I didn't realize... until about twenty years after I got out of high school... what a stunt that experience had put on my spontaneity or my personality." By contrast, her childhood friend Linda Childers Suffridge found it easier to adapt when she transferred to a public school in Fordyce. Although she "was devastated at first," she soon made friends and adjusted well. Within a few weeks, she had stopped going home for the weekend.[63]

For African American students, the vast majority of whom were scheduled to attend Horace Mann High School that year, simply finding another school to attend was a challenge. Raney High School was closed to them and, because of the long legacy of racial discrimination in school funding in Arkansas, many of the other black schools in the state were overcrowded and not able to take in large numbers of new students. As a result, only about 210 of the 765 black children of high school age in Little Rock entered Arkansas schools outside Little Rock, while over 100 entered schools out of state. Some of the more than 400 students who remained out of school worked during the school closures. The NAACP was adamant that segregated private institutions not be established for the remaining students, because it believed that this is exactly what segregationists hoped they would do and that it would enable segregationists' resistance to court orders. The organization was willing, however, to accept and allocate donations so that black students could pay tuition for correspondence courses and to assist those students who were eligible to enter college early. In three cases, black students enrolled in colleges to complete their high school credits.[64]

Locally, the NAACP arranged for the black students who had been applicants for Central or Hall High School for the 1958–1959 school year, including five who had been at Central High the previous year, to meet five mornings a week at the Dunbar Community Center. They secured tutors for them and, with the assistance of Mrs. Terry, they identified WEC members who were willing to grade students' papers. With the help of the Congregational Church and the Friends Church, they were able place a small number of the other black students in private schools elsewhere. The NAACP tried to monitor the situation to ensure that the students were well situated and sent only the top students to live in white homes. They were probably as careful about the placement of African American students in integrated schools as the Little Rock School Board had been about the placement of African American students in integrated schools the fall of 1957. Even with these efforts, large numbers of African American students in Little Rock remained without access to education.[65]

Some whites, including representatives of the American Friends Service Committee who visited Little Rock, believed that Bates or the NAACP were using the displaced black students as a political symbol. Roy Wilkins, Executive Secretary of the NAACP, disagreed. In an address in Little Rock on November 2, he conceded that "It is hard to watch some of the white students getting some little education while your own high school students are shut out of school by your governor," but added that if they set up temporary schools on a segregated basis they would "be defying the law" and "selling out the youngsters who endured persecution at Central High School" and betraying all black children who sought equal educational opportunity. He added that "makeshift schools are of no benefit to the white students and must collapse." In January, Daisy Bates said: "It disturbs me that almost half of the Negro children still are unable to get into any school. But I've talked with many of their parents and they agree that an interruption in their education is a small price to pay for the eventual victory."[66]

Congressman E. C. Gathings, who represented the First District of Arkansas, also expressed concern about the lack of arrangements for displaced African American students. He worried, however, because he thought it would reflect adversely on the segregationist cause. He wrote to Governor Faubus, warning him that his focus on private schools for whites might alienate those "good colored people not affiliated with the NAACP" and call into question the South's intentions regarding blacks. He urged him to work hard to place black students in black schools. Faubus apparently disregarded the advice, concerned only with minimizing the costs to whites of massive resistance in order to retain their political support.[67]

Of the nine black students who had attended Central High the previous year, five took correspondence courses and two, Terrence Roberts and Gloria Ray, attended classes out of state. Roberts attended school in Los Angeles while his parents remained in Little Rock. They later decided to leave Arkansas and join him in California. Ray went to live with relatives in

Missouri for the year and completed her senior year in that state. Four of the students who remained in Little Rock had to take summer school courses in 1959 to make up for lost credits. They did so with assistance from local NAACP chapters in Chicago, where Melba Pattillo attended summer session; in Michigan, where Carlotta Walls went to the Ferris Institute; and in St. Louis, where Thelma Mothershed and Elizabeth Eckford took classes.[68]

A study by Harvey Walthall demonstrates that the closing of schools had particularly adverse effects on white working-class students, African American students, and students with poor academic records. Of the 2,915 white students closed out of their schools, 1,282 (44 percent) were in private schools in Little Rock; 1,034 (35.5 percent) were in public schools elsewhere in Arkansas; 275 (9.4 percent) were in schools out of state; 116 (4.0 percent) had entered college before graduation; and 208 (7.1 percent) did not attend school. Of the 750 black high school students, 277 (36.9 percent) attended public schools in state; 91 (12.2 percent) attended schools out of state; 6 (.8 percent) were in college; and 376 (50.1 percent) were not in school. Over half of the students with poor academic records were not in school. Not surprisingly, they contributed to a sizeable increase in the high school dropout rate. In the 1959–1960 school year, an estimated 1,142 of the 4,279 students of both races expected to enroll in high schools in Little Rock decided to attend school elsewhere or had dropped out.[69]

Race and social class dramatically affected students' experiences during the year of school closure. Parents who were very affluent and well educated sent their children to private schools out of state. While white middle-class parents tried to avoid Little Rock's private schools, white working-class parents made them their schools of choice. The absence of private schools for African American children—the product of white indifference, black poverty, the history of poor funding for black schools in the "separate but equal" era, and African American commitment to desegregation in Little Rock—contributed to the high rate of nonattendance for black students. Indeed, the NAACP leaders' insistence that black students not attend private schools in Little Rock while the public schools were closed signifies the willingness of African American parents and children to sacrifice for the gains they hoped to achieve through the eradication of racial segregation.[70]

Whether Little Rock's citizens would decide that the costs borne by students and their families would be worth the perceived benefit of retaining segregation would be determined in the months ahead. Segregationist resisters—their power at its high mark—would continue to fight to consolidate power in the school board and to ensure the retention of racially separate schools at all cost. Their strategy of resistance by litigation, however, was rejected after the U.S. Supreme Court stated decisively its commitment to the enforcement of school desegregation. Even as he temporized, President Eisenhower knew that he might again be forced to support the Court's mandate. The liberal leaders of the WEC and African American voters and activists would continue to advocate for change in Little Rock. Moderates, including the business leadership and the rank and file members of the WEC, would continue to hope that open schools could be attained without significant social or political change. In the political conflicts to come, the new strategy that the South employed in its massive resistance to desegregation would itself be put to its most important test.

CHAPTER FIVE

The Politics of Fear and Gridlock

> White women in the south have always been a little subversive. Perched on the pedestals where men placed them as long as they performed well in their half-person roles, they had a commanding view of the social landscape. It was not a pretty picture.
>
> —Sara Murphy, WEC activist[1]

William Hadley, Jr., who moderated the first Women's Emergency Committee television program, started losing business at his newly established public relations and advertising firm soon after the broadcast of the program. He continued to lose accounts after he made statements in support of racial change in private business meetings. His participation in interracial groups, his early and consistent support for open schools under the minimal desegregation provided by the Blossom Plan, and his profession and prominence in the community made him an easy target for segregationists and moderates anxious to police the white political community. Eventually, he and his family were driven from Little Rock.[2]

Hadley became a public and telling example of the use of fear and threat to intimidate and punish anyone who antagonized either the segregationists or the local business elite. Businessmen in Little Rock who were more conservative or less principled than Hadley played their part in his tribulations, withdrawing their accounts from his firm and distancing themselves from him politically. Indeed, Hadley's fate demonstrated the moderates' retaliation against any individual who broke the silence on race in the schools that they sought to enforce. It did not take many William Hadleys to convey the message that anyone who challenged politics as usual in Little Rock would pay a high price. Ultimately, as this chapter establishes, however much the moderates were intimidated by the segregationists, the moderates were themselves the authors of their own discontent.

A few years after he left Little Rock, Hadley wrote to Daisy Bates describing his family's experiences as racial traitors to the segregationist cause. Everyone in his immediate family had faced conflict and loss in critical personal relationships. His children lost friends and his wife's relationship with her extended family in Arkansas was severely strained. The family was plagued by harassing phone calls. He struggled to weigh the costs to all of them: "I couldn't sleep. I didn't sleep—for weeks at a time. I'd doze, then wander through the house at night. I was fighting a battle within myself: is this worth it, worth crucifying my family, myself? Why should I do this to myself, to my family?" He contemplated suicide, but finally decided to relocate his family away from the pressure instead. After three moves, they were established and happy in Washington, D.C. He had declared bankruptcy and was trying to pay back his creditors. The memories remained painful: "As you know, I have avoided talking about the 'Little Rock Case'; even the family has learned to avoid the subject. The deep, depressive periods of melancholia I suffered through have now gone, however, and I doubt if any set of circumstances could bring them back."[3]

As Hadley's experiences suggest, the constraints on white men's ability to support either open schools or racial change derived to an important degree from their family responsibilities and their economic and political roles. In a postwar culture that viewed family breadwinning as solely men's duty and economic success as a reflection of a man's individual worth, the business failure and economic stresses experienced by Hadley threatened not only his family's well being but also his ability to enact his primary role and to see himself in a positive light. As C. Wright Mills wrote in 1951, "If men are responsible for their success, they are also responsible for their failure." Hadley's status as a nominally independent entrepreneur, a fast disappearing and particularly venerated economic status for American men, did not protect him from the politics of retribution so central to Little Rock's massive resistance movement or from the internal disciplining essential to the moderate politics of caution.[4]

The caution of the businessmen derived not only from the solidarity of fear that kept them from acting in large numbers but also from their conviction that they were proper custodians of the public good. While the maintenance of masculine identities tied to income, power, and prestige in the public sphere kept many men from taking risks for the sake of political convictions, other men conflated personal interests and civic welfare. For many of the business elite, the idea that economic development constituted progress and social well being confirmed a belief that protecting their businesses and their political power was a socially responsible act as well as an egoistic one.[5]

Segregationists did not share that view. Emboldened by the closure of the public high schools in Little Rock in the fall of 1958, they launched an all-out campaign to use economic intimidation and electoral clout to seize power in Little Rock. With sufficient political power, they intended to eliminate moderates and liberals from positions of authority within the schools and the city. Their rage at their adversaries remained intense, fueled by an explosive mixture of religious zeal, sexual fears, and class resentment. The emotional culture of their movement wrought a politics of repression and retribution devised to discredit and punish its numerous enemies. This punishment not only served segregationists' tactical interests but also enacted the politics of vengeance central to their conspiratorial populism.

The supporters of segregation tried to intimidate anyone who advocated integration, token or otherwise, and to deny them the fundamental rights of citizenship. In October 1958, Attorney General Bruce Bennett announced new strategies for his campaign to drive the NAACP out of Arkansas and block its access to the courts as a source of remedy for racial discrimination. He called for Congress to eliminate the NAACP Legal Defense Fund's tax exempt status, he asked that lawsuits be brought in Arkansas against anyone who filed integration lawsuits and anyone who would "recruit or urge others" to do so, he asked that civil rights workers who came to Arkansas be arrested, he asked that economic boycotts be used against anyone who supported integration, and he asked that laws be enacted requiring organizations like the NAACP to disclose their finances and membership. His pairing of economic retaliation with disclosure laws communicated his intent quite clearly. The new laws he proposed included one to prohibit nonprofit organizations like the NAACP from participation in Arkansas politics and another to prevent the NAACP from practicing law in Arkansas as a corporation.[6]

Over time, Bennett and his allies also devised various state and local laws designed to discredit and marginalize all who supported desegregation, including the all-white WEC, and to deploy a politics of fear intended to drive potential members away from specific organizations and

ideas. These actions particularly revealed the ways in which the construction of the legitimate political community was linked to the limitation of
acceptable political thought and action.[7]

Bennett's ideological offensive culminated in December 1958 with
hearings by the Special Education Committee of the Legislative Council of
the Arkansas State Legislature on the role of Communist-inspired "subversion" in the Little Rock crisis. These hearings included all the elements of
vintage postwar red baiting combined with a southern white understanding of race: a repentant ex-Communist denouncing the desired targets,
guilt by association, and the implication that racial conflict could only be
explained in terms of external agitation. According to Bennett, race relations in the South were the best "in the entire history of the civilized world"
until the Communists and their sympathizers, who had targeted Little
Rock decades before, had succeeded in creating racial conflict over school
desegregation in the late 1950s. For those people already persuaded that
southern whites and blacks would maintain affectionate and peaceful race
relations if left to themselves, the hearings offered a comforting confirma-
tion of the subversive roots of the current crisis. They also served to justify
the political demonization of those who challenged that view.[8]

In September 1958, Governor Faubus had used similar tactics when a
group of Presbyterian ministers publicly opposed his policies, accusing
them of being leftists, "brainwashed by left-wingers and Communists."
Some Arkansas citizens sent letters to the governor indicating their disap-
proval of his efforts to discredit the ministers. Others supported his stance.
One copied the governor on a letter he had written to columnist Drew
Pearson, complaining that "some clergy are attempting to inject themselves into political and controversia [sic] matters which properly are NOT
IN THEIR SPHERE. They are supposed to teach THEOLOGY and not pro-
pound their own philosophy, psychological thinking or sociological thinking from pulpits." After stating his conviction that God had created the
races separately and intended that they be segregated, he concluded that
"the clergy [should] stick to GOSPEL teaching, visiting the sick and dying,
etc., and let the taxpayers decide how we want our schools and children,
homes and social life."[9]

Soon thereafter, Presbyterian officials transferred Dunbar Ogden, the minister who had served as one of the clerical escorts for the Little Rock Nine
in September 1957, to a church in West Virginia. Ogden had previously

engaged in publicly reported activities designed to enlist religious authorities in the cause of peaceful desegregation. He wrote to two hundred and fifty Arkansas ministers and religious leaders on the eve of school opening in 1957, asking them to appeal for orderly conduct. In mid-September, he had joined thirty-four other ministers in signing a statement expressing "deep concern" and asking for prayer regarding racial issues in the community. When he was forced from Little Rock, the message was not lost on other ministers in the city or elsewhere in the South. However much the moderates might have blamed segregationists for the repression experienced by Ogden and others, they themselves were the critical parishioners who worked for the minister's removal.[10]

The Arkansas State Police helped in the campaign against liberal ministers by providing routine investigation and surveillance of interracial groups and others whom the governor believed to be critical advocates for desegregation, especially the NAACP and the WEC. State police reports often included the names of the employers and supervisors of those whose associations raised suspicions. The Mothers' League assisted the state police by attempting to crash WEC meetings and reporting the license numbers of the women they saw attending or the people seen visiting the homes of WEC activists. The support that the Arkansas Education Association gave to the effort to keep schools open prompted an investigation of its executive director, Forrest Rozzell, apparently to discredit or blackmail him into political submission. According to Roy Reed, "The bloodhounds of the state police were merely one small part of a vast political apparatus that carried information to the governor's office and then, when necessary, carried favors, threats, or penalties back down the line."[11]

In Little Rock, the Mothers' League began a recall campaign against the five school board members who continued to support the Blossom Plan. Apparently, however, they were not able to get the required number of signatures on the petitions. Despite pressures from the men of the Citizens' Council, they did not file the petitions. It is not completely clear why the women of the Mothers' League, who had community sentiment on their side, were unable to secure the required number of signatures. More than likely, they lacked the time for volunteerism and they did not get the kind of informal assistance from their male allies that WEC members could count on. They also did not have access to the political advice and the money that the WEC was able to raise. However sympathetic he might be to their cause, Faubus did not deploy his resources on behalf of the Mothers' League recall campaign, either because he thought public opposition to integration would almost automatically generate electoral success for the efforts of the Mothers' League or because he preferred to act covertly in local elections.[12]

Moreover, some members of the Mothers' League spent a lot of time in support of the petition campaign for the "States Rights' Amendment" authored by Faubus's political nemesis, Jim Johnson. The amendment's provisions included the establishment of a states' rights commission to "protect the sovereignty of the State of Arkansas and her sister states" from the federal government and foreign governments and from mechanisms to close public schools under federal court orders to desegregate. Mrs. Abby Edwards, a member of the North Little Rock Mothers' League, wrote to Johnson that the women working on his behalf operated on a "shoe string" and made up for their lack of money with their labor: "Oh! Those ladies are doing such a valuable job. All of them were so tired, each had worked 8 hrs. Had not had supper." She added that the women "never sleep hardly. They are out early to hail the working men on their job at 6 a.m. to get them to sign petitions." She added that her work on behalf of segregation made her feel "just like Vera McQuigg Norris and Susan B. Anthony did."[13]

Segregationists also rallied behind the Congressional campaign of Dale Alford, the lone segregationist on the Little Rock School Board, who had decided to run a write-in campaign against incumbent Brooks Hays. Because of his role in mediating between Faubus and Eisenhower in the fall of 1957, Hays faced segregationist retribution at the polls in 1958. After Citizens' Council leader Amis Guthridge failed to wrest the nomination from Hays in the Democratic primary, Alford stepped forward. Alford's campaign speeches relied heavily on denunciations of the U.S. Supreme Court, the NAACP, and Communism—which were viewed as linked threats to the freedom and well being of white Arkansans. Meanwhile, Governor Faubus took the opportunity to exact his vengeance on the man he associated with his defeat at the hands of Eisenhower. By endorsing Alford and making his allies available to his candidate, Faubus lent critical support to Alford and the segregationist cause. The campaign also surmounted the disadvantage normally experienced by write-in campaigns when it provided stickers printed with Alford's name for voters to attach to ballots on election day.[14]

After Alford's victory, Hays accused Faubus of turning "the powerful forces of his office against me" despite an agreement between them to stay out of each other's campaigns, adding that "the South loses when moderates are pilloried and men like Governor Faubus try to drive us out." Hays suffered from the reluctance of many in the Little Rock business community to offer their open support to his bid for reelection. After his defeat, Senator J. William Fulbright wrote to him, calling his defeat "a sad development" and worried about "the people of Little Rock who have been caught up in this emotional hysteria and seem now to have an urge toward self-destruction." Fulbright, who had been unwilling to go out on a limb on behalf of Hays, believed that it was more important that he preserve his position in the U.S. Senate than take a stand on school desegregation.[15]

From the outset of the crisis over desegregation, in fact, Arkansas moderates had taken seriously the advice of those who thought Faubus had gained an unassailable political advantage in the state and in the South when he used state troops to bar African American students from Central High School. Fulbright refused to oppose Faubus publicly despite pressure from moderates like Harry Ashmore to support law and order in Little Rock and despite pressure from his sister, Anne Teasdale. She reminded him that the student exchange program named for him, which was the U. S. government's flagship program in international educational exchange, implied "feelings about the importance of understanding and appreciation of other races and cultures and the necessity of learning to live together."[16]

Teasdale accurately identified the contradictions at the heart of Fulbright's position. In order to stay in the Senate and speak on behalf of different policies toward the new nations being formed by anti-colonial forces in the Third World, Fulbright kept silent in the face of a similar revolution in political consciousness in his own nation. Like Little Rock's civic elite, he convinced himself that protecting his career and his political goals in other areas necessitated silence on human rights and other key issues raised by the crisis in Little Rock.

The Alford victory, which clearly revealed the segregationists' political muscle and the moderates' fear, gave Little Rock School Board members every reason to feel politically isolated. They were required to comply with federal court decisions but had little political support to do so. Despite the Mothers' League's failed attempt at a recall election of the moderates on the school board, they knew that they did not even have the political authority to keep the schools in their district open. On November 10, the Eighth Circuit Court of Appeals confirmed this when it formally overruled the plan to enroll students in private schools and ordered the school board to execute its integration plan. The three-judge federal court decision also condemned the state government of Arkansas and stated that the school board was not acting in good faith. According to R. A. Lile, the school board members had "just about had a bellyful by then" because "the federal courts were running the schools and they didn't need us."

Wayne Upton stated that the problem of the school board was closer to home and that the board members were "tired of being Governor Orval Faubus' whipping boys." Convinced that they were beset by opposing forces they could neither control nor contest, board members Upton, Lile, William G. Cooper, Harold Engstrom, and Frank Lambright decided to resign. Prior to resigning, the school board moderates dismissed superintendent Virgil Blossom without cause, enabling him to claim the salary from the rest of his contract. They then declared their intention to resign to the Chamber of Commerce at a dinner at the Little Rock Country Club, thus indicating their sense of accountability to the business elite. On November 12, they made their resignations public, leaving the community less than a month to identify candidates and mount campaigns prior to the December 6 school board election.[17]

As David Wieck observed generally of the failure of leadership in Little Rock, "one can act heroically only on grounds one has wholeheartedly accepted." The Little Rock School Board, immobilized by its own sense of victimization and too uncertain of its own principles to take on the task of the community education it had claimed was necessary in its recent court appearances, could muster no more political conviction or courage than many of the constituents it sought to represent. The business community refused to step forward. According to Irving Spitzberg, Faubus's economic power and the successes of the Citizens' Council "completely closed all possibilities for political protest. Protest would require leadership, and leadership would require guts."[18]

The crisis occasioned by the school board resignations led to frantic attempts by some in the business community to deploy a slate of candidates acceptable to local business leaders. An effort orchestrated by E. Grainger Williams, executive vice president of the Chamber of Commerce, to get professionals to run quickly failed. Then some business leaders tried to get the presidents of the six leading banks in Little Rock to run for the school board on the assumption that if they all ran no one would face a boycott by local customers. But the bankers would not agree, primarily because they were afraid of losing the accounts they received from large depositors in eastern Arkansas. According to Virgil Blossom, one of the businessmen at a meeting held prior to the resignations said: "you had all just as well recognize we are living in a police state." Another added: "I never before understood how it was that Hitler and Mussolini were able to exercise dictatorial power over so many people. Now I know from experience how they took over." What some scholars have described as the paralysis of the business class, members of the civic elite experienced as oppression at the hands of a tyrannical governor. In such a climate of fear, it is no wonder that large numbers of businessmen refused to run for the school board.[19]

Little Rock's business leaders found that economic interdependence and political isolationism were hard to reconcile. As they tried to exercise political control without taking political responsibility, they found that their position in an interdependent economy, crisscrossed by dense ties across the state, region, and nation, foiled their efforts. Local politics simply could not be disconnected from the political interests of businessmen located elsewhere. The bankers' fear of retribution from eastern Arkansas agricultural interests also attests to the importance of planter class racism in state politics. However easy it might be to note the racism of poor white tenant farmers, they were not the ones in a position to thwart the designs of Little Rock bankers. The businessmen's failure to recruit candidates to the school board frustrated WEC president Vivion Brewer: "Once more we hungered for action from the men of our town. Why could not the bankers find strength in togetherness and produce a slate?" With the assistance of the WEC, which called potential candidates to secure their consent, the business class finally managed to put forward a list of candidates. The list included one woman, Mrs. Charles W. Stephens, only because Adolphine Terry insisted that a woman be included on the moderates' slate of candidates.[20]

Everett Tucker, who was the industrial development manager for the Little Rock Chamber of Commerce, volunteered himself as a candidate and recruited realtor W. F. (Billy) Rector to run as well. They were joined by Stephens, a civic activist and former president of the Central High School PTA; contractor Russell Matson; and advertising executive Ted

Lamb. Nat Griswold later stated that Tucker was willing to run because he "grew up without any economic want, with plenty and still has, and this makes him fearless about what people can do to him." The candidates' experience or expertise in school matters was not uppermost in the minds of those who recruited "moderates" to run for the board. Indeed, Stephens' work for the PTA was the only education-related qualification any of the moderate candidates could claim. Everett Tucker later noted: "I suppose probably none of us had even been in the school headquarters building." The business coalition decided not to seek a candidate to run against segregationist Ed I. McKinley because "he was a lawyer and a member of the country club, so [they] thought he would not cause any trouble." Little Rock's "kingmakers" believed that a particular class status served as a proxy for pragmatism in racial matters. In McKinley's case, they would find that they were dead wrong.[21]

The "moderate" ticket for the board ran as segregationists, but in the words of Everett Tucker, they conceded "that it was going to... involve some degree of integration, if the schools were to be opened." While moderate candidates stated that they would not "voluntarily" integrate the schools, they did promise "to preserve the stability and integrity of our public school system." The segregationist slate—Ed I. McKinley, Jr., an attorney; Ben D. Rowland, Sr., a lawyer and retired school administrator; C. C. Railey, the business manager for Plumbers and Steamfitters Local 155; Mrs. Pauline Woodson, a real estate executive and reportedly a member of the Mothers' League; Mrs. Margaret Morrison, a housewife; and R. W. Laster, a municipal judge—ran explicitly as allies of Governor Faubus. Dr. George P. Branscum, a segregationist who had broken from the Capital Citizens' Council, ran as a third candidate in the race that also included the moderate Ted Lamb and segregationist Pauline Woodson.[22]

The segregationist campaign was hampered by divisions within its leadership. The leaders of the Mothers' League had begun to question the motives and actions of some of their most important male allies. In November 1958, Howard Chandler of the Arkansas State Police reported to Alan Templeton, his supervisor in the Criminal Investigation Division, that the Mothers' League believed that Wesley Pruden and Amis Guthridge had failed to turn over money raised for the private school to its officials and had instead deposited it in an account belonging to Pruden. According to an unsigned report on Arkansas State Police letterhead, Mrs. Curtis Stover reported that their suspicions extended to Jimmy Karam, Claude Carpenter, and others associated with the Capital Citizens' Council and Faubus. They believed that Branscum had withdrawn from the Citizens' Council out of disaffection with Pruden and Guthridge. By January, some members of the Mothers' League were fearful that these divisions, which had been exacerbated by gendered conflicts over who to support for the school board, would cause the demise of their organization.[23]

As before, the line between the moderates and the arch segregationists was a thin one. Everett Tucker had concluded that the moderates could not run as integrationists and win, and, in fact, he found the segregationist position comfortable: "I had no trouble adopting this posture, having been born on a cotton plantation and grown up in this part of the country, and sincerely at that time I know, speaking for myself, I felt that the best educational program for both races was possible through the kind of education we had had." School board lawyer Archie House later wrote of Tucker that he came "from a long line of farmers who condemn Lincoln's Proclamation and, as I understood, his basic ideas were in accord with those of A. Guthridge et al." According to Irving Spitzberg, Tucker had voted against integration and for closing the schools in the September election. Billy Rector, who was later described by Arkansas Council of Human Relations executive director Nat Griswold as "a real Tory," wrote to Adolphine Terry in 1960 that he would not "participate in any program for the gradual desegregation of any facilities in our community."[24]

When the election results were tallied, Little Rock found itself with a school board split 3–3 on the issue of compliance with federal court orders to integrate the schools. Tucker, Matson, and Lamb represented the moderates; McKinley, Rowland, and Laster represented the segregationists. Whatever their position on integration, the women candidates for the school board went down to defeat. One of the defeated moderates, Billy Rector, blamed the WEC for his loss. Vivion Brewer related that in a meeting after the election, he "suddenly rose to point an accusing finger at my astonished face: 'You are the one who defeated me,' he shouted and he left unceremoniously." Years later, he repeated the accusation to Mrs. Terry at a dinner party at her house. She replied, "Young man, for your information, the only votes you got were from my women." She added that those women supported him with great reluctance. According to Everett Tucker,

Rector lost because he had gotten into a well-reported public dispute with Orval Faubus a few months before the election.[25]

The school board chose Ed McKinley as its new president and appointed Terrell Powell, the principal of Hall High School, as its new superintendent. In Powell, they got an administrator who was more conservative than Blossom and more inclined to defer to the moderates on the school board. At the same time, Powell was a professional educator who, like his predecessor, was dedicated to maintaining academic standards in the schools.[26]

In late December 1958 the new school board fired Archie House and the Rose, Meek, House, Barron & Nash law firm and replaced them with the firm of Mehaffy, Smith & Williams. According to Harry Ashmore, the school board released House because he would not allow the board to collude with Faubus in his efforts to use the state courts to secure a delay. House knew the courts would not grant a delay: "You'd be trying intermissions cases until doomsday." When the board fired House, Ashmore "was outraged, and wanted to make [an] issue out of his dismissal, but Archie would have no part of any public complaint." The former editor charged that the change in law firms meant that they were "sending to court lawyers more given to temporizing than the one who was being proved right at every critical juncture." Gaston Williamson of the Rose law firm explained the board's decision in terms of its desire to make peace with Faubus, who was also represented by the Mehaffy firm: "They claimed [House] was getting too old and claimed he was not flexible enough to know how to handle Faubus. Hell, the only way you could handle Faubus was with a two-by-four right between the eyes. That's all he understood. That's what Eisenhower eventually applied."[27]

The new school board immediately faced new litigation in the ongoing desegregation case. In early January, the NAACP and the Justice Department asked Judge Miller to order the school board to desegregate the schools immediately. Miller refused, directing the board to present a new desegregation plan instead. In turn, the board petitioned to be allowed to reopen the schools on a segregated basis. Miller denied this petition but also denied a request by the Justice Department that the board be declared in contempt of court if it did not immediately move to open desegregated schools. Persuaded that Miller was unsympathetic to their position, the NAACP initiated a new lawsuit to challenge the school closing law. Once again, the Justice Department entered with an *amicus* brief and offered informal assistance with the NAACP's briefs.[28]

Soon, the segregationists let it be known that they aimed to fire teachers and administrators whose stand on integration offended them. On February 9, Faubus told reporters that Central High School Principal Jess Matthews and Vice Principals J. O. Powell and Elizabeth Huckaby should not be rehired. McKinley approached school superintendent Terrell Powell to persuade him not to rehire teachers and administrators who had displeased the segregationists. Powell refused. Two weeks later, McKinley asked him to go with him to meet with Faubus. When Powell declined, McKinley threatened to have the school board fire him.[29]

Faubus attempted to help the segregationist cause by introducing a bill in the state legislature giving him the power to appoint three additional members to the Little Rock School Board. This board-packing bill, which was sponsored by T. E. Tyler of Pulaski County, was defeated in early March by a filibuster orchestrated by other Pulaski County representatives. Horrified at this proposed interference in their local affairs, the Pulaski County representatives were aware of the growing public hostility to such tactics. In its first official action since the crisis over desegregation began, the executive committee of the Little Rock PTA joined the WEC, the AAUW, and others in opposing Faubus's bill. Such an extension of gubernatorial power at the expense of local government made many legislators uneasy. For the first time, Faubus failed to have his way on a school issue in the state legislature.[30]

While Faubus worked to impede school desegregation and the school board tried to avoid compliance with the federal order for immediate desegregation, the WEC continued its organizational work. At the outset, it had determined to increase its membership substantially. Each member was urged to recruit ten new members and the wives of Chamber of Commerce members were targeted for special appeals to join. Within two weeks of the integration election the WEC had eight hundred members. The reality of closed schools contributed to the WEC's success in recruiting new members, although many Little Rock women still refused to join. Some women cited other commitments or their husbands' fears of business or job loss. A few women joined on condition of anonymity, some refusing even to have mailings sent to their homes.[31]

Lorraine Gates has argued that the women of the WEC were able to take a public stance because their position as middle-class women who had the financial support of their husbands shielded them from the economic reprisals that men would face. As she points out, only the husbands of women in leadership positions lost jobs and customers as a consequence of their wives' participation in WEC. Vivion Brewer's husband, who lost his job with the federal government, blamed segregationists for his firing. Irene Samuel's husband, a doctor, lost many patients as a consequence of her participation in the WEC. Her friends teased her about being the only poor doctor's wife they knew. The WEC leaders' husbands were singled out in part because it was difficult for the opposition to secure the names of rank-and-file members and because the large numbers of women who joined provided a safety in numbers that made it much more difficult to target individuals. As shall be seen, keeping its membership list secret was a critical goal of the WEC.[32]

Of course, the women's sacrifices were hardly insignificant. Some WEC members found that their participation in the organization had strained their relations with their husbands. Some marriages did not withstand the stress and the women found no alternative to divorce. Others lost valued friendships because of their political stance. When asked many years later how she felt about the friendships she lost during the crisis years, Irene Samuel said, "I still cry about it." Vivion Brewer said that it was particularly hard "to combat the loss of friendships and the breaks in family ties." The crisis in personal relations also bred distrust. When Brewer received anonymous hate mail with her first name spelled correctly, she believed it came from former friends. Clearly, middle-class women were more willing to strain and even jeopardize their family and personal relations than the men were to take risks in the masculine domains of business and politics.[33]

Although it tried to broaden support for its views in white working-class areas, the WEC had few members with the requisite neighborhood and workplace ties to such constituencies and never understood the working class well enough to find a common position. Whether a different political vocabulary would have helped is not certain. Because of his populist appeal, Faubus was extremely influential with working-class Arkansans. The unions divided over the school integration issue. The crafts unions generally supported segregation and the industrial unions (historically more

open to blacks) supported the public schools. Moreover, when the WEC
went door to door in the poorer white neighborhoods, its message was not
well received. According to Irene Samuel, the woman who canvassed these
areas reported that she got "all the hard-core insults." Margaret Morrison,
a segregationist activist, believed that the WEC viewed its opponents
through the lens of class stereotypes: "They tried to imply that we were
ignorant, uneducated white trash." Morrison herself felt the sting of their
contempt and told Sara Murphy later that "The women on the other side
felt superior. They left the impression, 'You're just white trash.'"[34]

Morrison was largely correct. The WEC understood school closure primarily in relation to the needs of *middle-class* white students. Adolphine
Terry later wrote that "Those who suffered the most, I knew, would be
the young people whose college credits would be put in jeopardy." In its
campaign to open the public schools, the WEC stressed the costs of private
education, emphasizing in particular the inability of middle-class parents
to afford private schooling for their children. This focus on the middle
class recurred in the television appearances and speeches organized by the
WEC. That high school was the end of the educational road for many
working-class students and thus had a different meaning in their lives did
not enter into or shape the WEC's discussions, even though the organization was aware that many working-class students, black and white, were
completely denied access to schools in the 1958–1959 academic year. The
WEC's appeal to unquestioned middle-class values and concerns was taken
for granted within the organization. Virgil Blossom also equated educational quality with the needs of white middle-class students.[35]

In order to direct its message to "the moderates . . . [and] the segregationists who yet realized the importance of public education," the WEC excluded
blacks from membership. A subject of ongoing controversy among WEC
leaders, this decision reflected their conviction that they would not receive a
hearing in the white community if they broke the taboo on interracial cooperation. As Vivion Brewer put it later: "*We could afford no hint of being an
integration group if we were to win any election* in the hysterical atmosphere
which our governor knew so well how to foment." In addition, they removed
Velma Powell as secretary lest her association with the interracial Arkansas
Council of Human Relations discredit the group.[36]

As did the male moderates, WEC leaders took for granted black community support for moderate candidates and positions on issues related to

the schools. Unlike the male business elite, however, WEC leaders did work behind the scenes and individually with black leaders. Only the personal loyalty that Daisy Bates, president of the Arkansas NAACP, felt for Adolphine Terry kept her and other blacks from denouncing the WEC. In effect, however, the WEC's actions—as well as the actions of other white moderates (particularly those on the school board), segregationists, and the Eisenhower administration—reinforced the view that race relations were a dispute among whites over what to do about blacks. Indeed, the construction of the legitimate political community as white was a critical feature of the early years of crisis in Little Rock.[37]

Although it denied that it took a position on integration, in fact, the WEC offered tacit support to a program of very gradual (token) integration. In a November 1958 letter, WEC activist Anne Helveston revealed that "With a more favorable public opinion, ultimately the Committee hopes to promote the opening of our public schools following the Court-approved [Blossom] Plan." The gradualism of their approach served to bridge the racial liberalism of many WEC leaders and the segregationist beliefs of some of the members. Indeed, their program of gradual integration indicated the ways in which the politics of the WEC entailed an ongoing set of compromises within the group and in relation to other constituencies.[38]

Although WEC leaders were much more willing than their male allies to take a public stand on open schools, they mirrored the timidity of the business leaders in their unwillingness to endorse desegregation or to break publicly with dominant white views on race. Having organized and mobilized middle-class white women who were concerned about providing open public schools for their children, WEC founders then followed a politics of racial caution at odds with their initial motives for starting the organization. They did so in reaction to the racial conservatism of many of their members and because they believed that confronting race relations directly and publicly would not only harm their goal to open schools but would also impede racial progress.[39]

At the same time, the leadership worked privately to expose its members to more egalitarian views of race and to support the creation of public interracial community boards. The former effort included everything from teaching the members how to say "Negro" to providing speakers and other resources on race relations. On behalf of the organization, Anne Helveston worked to develop a library of films and books that members could use. In the "Letter from Little Rock" sent by many WEC members with their holiday cards in December 1958, they stated that "If the schools open, the education work of the Committee will be needed more than ever to counteract the hatreds and prejudices already awakened."[40]

One untitled piece in the WEC library, for example, questioned the prejudices and hypocrisies of white, Christian, Americans. It stated that "all being white makes me is a member of a minority group that is distrusted by the masses." It criticized those who professed democracy but failed to support equality and freedom and to advocate for others when their rights were being denied. Finally, it stated that "To be a real Christian you have to love your neighbor. You have to help those who are not as fortunate and be tolerant of those who are different." Finally, it asked that they "join the human race" by renouncing their "silly prejudices."[41]

The WEC tried on various occasions to implement these views by broadening the community's role in local decision making. In 1958, for example, it launched an effort to create an interracial public body to address problems of race relations directly and to facilitate communication between African American and white leaders. The WEC leaders' proposal was essentially a conservative one that reserved important powers for elected officials. They envisioned an advisory group to local governmental bodies, including the City Board of Managers, which would select its members, and the Little Rock School Board. Even that idea, however, was too drastic for local leaders to endorse.[42]

As before, African Americans found little space to articulate the needs of black students or the black community. Confronted with an accelerated campaign of red baiting and legal harassment designed to render blacks suspect as political actors and to deny them access to the courts that could protect their constitutional rights, the NAACP fought for its right to participate in the political process. At the same time, the vast majority of white activists and policymakers continued to avoid any public association with African Americans or the NAACP, convinced that their own credibility was predicated on the perception that they did not speak for or to blacks about public issues. As a result, most whites continued to frame the discussion of school issues in terms of the needs of white students and white interests, particularly those of the business community. In fact, the alternative institutional arrangements made during the year of school closure were designed specifically to accommodate white students, while African American children paid a disproportionate amount of the social costs of whites' resistance to desegregation. Moreover, the debates among whites over school policies focused primarily on the meanings of particular plans for white students.

Early in 1959, Vivion Brewer, president of the WEC, met with Little Rock City Attorney Joseph Kemp in response to an attempt by city officials to force her organization to provide a list of its members and donors. Brewer, who was well connected socially to many of the men who controlled local institutions, was no stranger to the corridors of state power. Even so, for Brewer the meeting symbolized the inadequacy of women's power and resources compared to the power wielded by local male elites: "The curtains were drawn; the lights were dim. He sat behind a handsome mahogany desk. The entire plush atmosphere was such a shocking contrast to the make-shift, harried, crowded decor of the W.E.C. office that I suddenly felt as though I must be dreaming."[43]

The meeting also signified the vulnerability of the women's organization to state sanctions. In an attempt to subject members of moderate and liberal organizations to various forms of public retaliation, the state of Arkansas and some municipalities, including Little Rock, had passed laws requiring organizations to provide membership and contributor lists to local officials. Modeled on laws passed throughout the South that targeted the NAACP, the Little Rock ordinance proved useful to segregationists worried that the WEC's advocacy of open public schools threatened their strategies of massive resistance to desegregation. When Kemp asked for the WEC list, Brewer refused to turn it over and denied that the organization had such a list. She asked him whether he realized that the reason for the legal requirement was "for harassment, for reprisals" and then asserted, "I will not make this possible—not for one single woman if I can help it." Kemp agreed to demur if she would send him a letter attesting that the WEC did not keep a membership list. She did not do so. Thereafter, city officials threatened to arrest WEC secretary, Dottie Morris, but desisted, apparently unwilling to take on a civic group as well connected as the WEC.[44]

The WEC found a new ally when Grainger Williams became president of the Little Rock Chamber of Commerce. The president of an insurance company, Williams believed strongly that "had it not been for the [public school] system I would never have gotten through college." He had sent his

daughter and niece to live with his wife's mother in North Carolina so that
they could continue their education when Little Rock's high schools were
closed. He was willing to take risks to bring the business community out
of hiding on the issue of support for public education. Substantially more
liberal than most of his peers on racial issues, Williams believed in the moral
necessity for desegregation and had joined the Urban League in the mid-
1950s. Thereafter, he continued to participate in interracial groups. In his
inaugural address to the Chamber of Commerce on January 14, 1959,
Williams stated his conviction that they needed to consider the cost of the
lack of public schools to the community and work to achieve an atmosphere of open communication on the issues raised by the crisis over desegregation. On January 26, the Chamber of Commerce approved a statement that encouraged the development of "a climate of communication
through which all citizens can discuss the problem with understanding
and respect for one another" and encouraged the completion of all legal
and legislative matters relating to the crisis.[45]

On the same day, the Chamber of Commerce supported the school
board's request that the courts allow it to reopen the schools on a segregated basis and submit a new plan for desegregation in August. When the
courts denied this request, the Chamber of Commerce polled its members,
asking them to express their preference between closed schools and schools
reopened "on a controlled minimum plan of integration acceptable to
the Federal Courts." A substantial majority favored the latter course, so the
businessmen's group began to advocate for desegregation based on the
state's pupil assignment law. The Chamber of Commerce announced its
position in a newspaper ad on March 25, 1959, claiming that Virginia's
massive resistance campaign had failed to withstand judicial scrutiny while
North Carolina's use of pupil assignment law had "worked in controlling
integration." The ad declared the members' support for private schools, the
renewal of teacher contracts, and the passage of new federal laws to "return
the operation of public schools to each individual school district." Significantly, the Chamber of Commerce omitted from the ad a claim from an
earlier draft that the NAACP was "setting back the progress of the Southern Negro by insisting on the overthrow of the South's natural social system and traditions."[46]

As a result of its stand on a controlled minimum plan of integration, the
Chamber of Commerce lost about 20 percent of its members, the loss re-

flecting white middle-class divisions over race relations. The criticism it received from its own members reflected the business community's conservatism on race and its caution in the face of controversy. The Chamber of Commerce compensated for the loss in income by raising the dues and continued operating as usual.[47]

In May 1959, the actions of the segregationist faction on a bitterly divided school board finally gave the moderate male leaders in Little Rock the kind of unassailable issue they needed to come out of hiding. After a lengthy and acrimonious meeting whose dynamics were exemplified in a long series of 3–3 votes, the three moderates on the school board walked out, declaring that there was no quorum. The remaining three members, all segregationists, voted to fire forty-four teachers whom they believed to have supported integration if only by disciplining segregationist students. Board president Ed McKinley said that the teachers fired would be reinstated if they made a statement "that they support the public policy of racially separate schools" and charged that integrationists were "injecting extraneous academic issues in a frantic attempt to stampede our people into capitulating to the NAACP." The segregationist faction of the board included on its list of dismissed teachers many educators with long service in the Little Rock schools who were beloved in the community. Not surprisingly, the list of discharged teachers included the principal, two vice principals, and twenty-two teachers from Central High School.[48]

Finally segregationists' anger over the racial "treason" of some of their children's teachers had found an outlet. Convinced that the people in power were treating segregationists and their children disrespectfully, segregationist leaders struck back. The result, they hoped, would be a reinstatement of authority over their own children unchallenged by "integrationist" politicians and educators.

Their actions, however, shook many moderates profoundly. Using a law passed at the urging of Faubus, the WEC joined a group of male civic leaders to launch a petition drive for a school board recall election aimed at the three segregationist members. The men formed STOP (Stop This Outrageous Purge), and threw their prestige and their money into the fray. The WEC spearheaded the campaign, providing hundreds of effective volunteers, the voter registration lists they had developed for previous elections, and their already considerable organizational experience. At no point, however, did anyone acknowledge that the WEC was actually running the

show or, indeed, even participating in it. The women's invisibility rankled
WEC president Vivion Brewer, but it enabled them to take the political
heat for the Little Rock male establishment and encouraged more men to
come out of hiding.[49]

The WEC leaders ran a series of ads using pictures of the fired teachers
accompanied by biographical statements attesting to their long affiliations
with Little Rock public schools, local churches, and civic groups. At this
point, the issue was not integration but rather the undermining of a policy
of hiring based on merit and the retention of qualified (and indeed beloved) teachers for the public school system. The PTAs, whose member-
ships included many WEC activists, convened meetings about the purge.
WEC members packed the meetings, passing fiery resolutions in support
of their teachers. As school board chair Ed McKinley gave a speech at one
of the schools, the wife of school superintendent Terrell Powell led a walkout to protest the firings. Her husband was sitting on the platform with
McKinley.[50]

The women activists received much more community support than
they had in the past. The Chamber of Commerce, the American Association of University Women (AAUW), and some labor unions joined in
denouncing the firings. A WEC account of the situation stated: "Thank-
fully we learned that other citizens—MEN of Little Rock—were irate over
this purging." The account described WEC members' reaction to the For-
est Park PTA meeting: "It was a thrill to those of us who had felt so alone
and yes, even scorned, before this, to see the auditorium packed" and to
witness the passage of a resolution to recall the three segregationist school
board members pass "Amid resounding applause."[51]

Unlike the segregationists, the moderates had at their disposal the WEC,
which by that time was a highly developed political machine that could
and did deploy hundreds of volunteers overnight. Given that they had only
slightly more than two weeks after the recall petitions had been filed to
mobilize their constituency for the election, the moderates could hope to
claim victory only because of the work of the WEC before and during that
particular crisis. Indeed, the vocal support of the PTAs developed largely
because the WEC leaders had strongly encouraged their members to run
for PTA offices the previous fall.[52]

The segregationists, who quickly organized as the Committee to Retain
Our Segregated Schools (CROSS), immediately took the offensive against

their critics. As CROSS leader Rev. M. L. Moser later noted, the election was a referendum on the "question of who was going to control the schools." After witnessing the quick organization of the opposition forces through groups as diverse as the PTA and the Chamber of Commerce, Capital Citizens' Council leader Amis Guthridge charged that "communist fronters" were assisting the WEC and the Chamber of Commerce to run "a race-mixing campaign." He charged that five of the PTA meetings had included "rigged communist-like demonstrations" and that "a few top left-wing PTA leaders are attempting to hoodwink the 13,000 members." While such rhetoric may have motivated some segregationist leaders, it did not address the concerns of an electorate increasingly concerned about the future of the public schools.[53]

Segregationist leaders also appealed to class antagonisms to motivate working-class voters to support the recall of the school board moderates. In an ad run in the *Arkansas Gazette*, they used a city map to illustrate that the greater proportion of African Americans lived in neighborhoods occupied by working-class whites than in neighborhoods that included moderate leaders. Class privilege, the ad claimed (with some justification), protected affluent whites from widespread integration of their children's schools: "If you don't have to live with integration—as none of the STOP ringleaders would have to do, because [of] the almost non-existent Negro population in the silk stocking 'Country Club' Ward 5 area... it doesn't really affect you! For the large majority of Little Rockians, however, it is a different story." In a televised speech, Governor Orval Faubus stated that the moderates' recall campaign had begun "to look like the charge of the Cadillac brigade, with many good, honest, hard working negroes in the front as shock troops."[54]

After voting, WEC activist Sara Murphy went to New York City with her husband. At midnight, they found a copy of a tabloid with the headline "Faubus Loses." Overcome with joy and disbelief, she said to the vendor, "I worked in that election, but I never thought this would happen. You don't know how happy this makes me." He offered his congratulations. Back in Little Rock, Central High School Vice Principal Elizabeth Huckaby and other teachers on the purge list shared her elation. The next day many of the educators wore the orchids they had received a few days before at a tribute lunch sponsored by the American Association of University Women.[55]

The symbolic significance of the teacher purge cannot be overstated. By firing dedicated and effective teachers on purely political grounds, the segregationists exposed the irresponsibility at the heart of their punitive politics and offended many Little Rock voters and civic leaders. Because it threatened the long-term viability of the public schools, the teacher purge also mobilized those citizens who were tired of closed schools and attacks on public education. Sara Murphy later concluded that the election "was a major turning point because the citywide grass roots effort caused citizens to reject not only the teacher purge but also the increasing repression that it signified."[56]

The moderates won because their supporters had the political capital to generate an extremely high voter turnout among the African Americans and middle-class whites who supported their position. That high turnout combined with a low voter turnout in working-class white neighborhoods sealed the victory. According to Henry Woods, who assisted the WEC in the campaign, "If they'd [the segregationists] have got out their vote, they'd have beat our butts." The most important of the moderates' resources in the election were the women of the WEC, who had mobilized the political expertise and assistance of their members and many in the Little Rock establishment. They employed the labor of hundreds of women who had the free time and the income to put in the long hours necessary for a successful political campaign. They also deployed other women's organizations, including the AAUW, the League of Women Voters, and the PTA on behalf of their cause. As Orval Faubus admitted later, he had believed that the anger of the mothers mobilized by the WEC would last for a little while and then dissipate. He was profoundly wrong.[57]

The political legacies of this election were contradictory. As Sara Murphy noted later, the school board members she supported "had won by a hair." In Little Rock's working-class neighborhoods support for segregation remained strong, but had not been mobilized effectively because the CROSS campaign was poorly funded and politically inept. The time, money, and political expertise that the segregationists could rally were inferior to those available to their adversaries. The STOP victory, in short, derived in part from the class and race privileges of the whites who supported the moderates' cause. For their part, African American leaders, who organized their own campaign in the recall election, took their first steps toward the political autonomy they would develop in the next few years. Ironically, their path to autonomy was paved in part by their work with a broad coalition of white activists, particularly those in the WEC, whose tactics they would emulate in the future.

In the meantime, securing and extending the victory in the school board recall election would require further activism. It would also test the fragile coalition of middle-class white women, African Americans, labor leaders, businessmen, and educators whose concerted efforts had enabled the defeat of the die-hard segregationists in that election. These groups, however, continued to disagree over fundamental priorities and goals and over how to oppose segregationists' actions and threats. As Little Rock's voters and the courts undermined legal strategies for massive resistance to desegregation, Governor Orval Faubus and the state's segregationists would find themselves facing more limited choices. What would they do? How would white moderates and African Americans respond?[58]

CHAPTER SIX

Politics as Usual: Reviving the Politics of Tokenism

> The federal forces may eventually win the battle of Little Rock, but it is these local citizens who will have to win the war. It will be a very long and very cold one.
> —Dan Wakefield[1]

For Little Rock's citizens, the summer of 1959 was an anxious one. In June, the Ku Klux Klan received incorporation papers from the state of Arkansas, signaling the beginning of public recruitment efforts in the state. The Little Rock School Board's statement later that month that it would open the city's public high schools in the fall relieved parents worried about their children's future. At the same time, some segregationists reacted with anger and voiced their determination to prevent any form of desegregation in the schools. Many citizens worried about the social discord and potential for violence that the school board's announcement had generated. Daisy Bates, who had been receiving threats in her role as president of the Arkansas NAACP, had a bomb explode in her yard on July 7.[2]

The next few months and years would prove pivotal in determining the future of race relations and school politics in Little Rock. Some segregationists would adopt violent strategies that placed supporters of segregated schools on the defensive. Would the Capital Citizens' Council denounce violent segregationists and their actions or would it stand by them? How would moderate business leaders respond to violent actions? Who would prevail in the continuing standoff involving African American leaders, the NAACP, the WEC, and the school board over its politics of tokenism in school integration?

When the U.S. District Court ruled in June 1959 that the state's school closing and school vouchers laws were unconstitutional, segregationists lost crucial tools in their campaign of massive resistance. In its case against the state, the NAACP alleged that the laws were designed specifically to undermine the U.S. Supreme Court's decision in *Cooper v. Aaron*, which had found that impermissible state actions in Arkansas were impeding lawful compliance with the *Brown* decisions and ordered the school board to implement desegregation immediately. In 1959 the federal district court agreed with the NAACP, ordering the members of the Little Rock School Board (and their successors) to execute their plan of integration. The court's decision points to the critical role played by the NAACP and African American litigants in undermining segregationist legislation and in assisting Little Rock's moderates to open the schools. Despite the need to remove these legislative barriers to open schools, the moderates on the Little Rock School Board and their allies did not support the suit in any way.[3]

Governor Orval Faubus responded sharply to the court's decision. "Federal force" and "live ammunition" would be necessary, he claimed, to support any attempts to integrate Little Rock's schools. The *Atlanta Constitution* called his remark "one of the most shocking statements ever made in America by a public official. It can accomplish nothing other than to create a climate for the violence of which he speaks. That seems to be what he wants." The editorial went on to note the poor timing of his comments: "At the very time there is an all-important need for wise, cool-headed leadership, Faubus frantically is issuing what amounts to a blanket invitation to the hot-headed, hoodlums and any others who can be aroused to resist the law by brute force. Peace in Little Rock? Not if Faubus can help it."[4]

Despite the governor's rabble-rousing rhetoric, the moderate male leadership in Little Rock was more interested in placating him than in confronting him. Balancing their awareness of the threat of violence with their desire to make free public education available to all students, Little Rock's moderates worked to secure a peaceable reopening of the public high schools and to keep state government from further efforts to obstruct local control of the schools. School officials joined with other moderates to find a compromise solution acceptable to the governor and his segregationist allies. They attempted to get Faubus to endorse the school board's policies of tokenism and gradualism in integration, pointing out that the governor had supported and signed the pupil placement law they intended to employ in order to minimize desegregation. Instead, the governor continued to claim that tokenism ultimately meant widespread integration: "Six this year, 60 next year and 600 the next."[5]

As the day to reopen the schools approached, the Little Rock School Board used the pupil placement law to eliminate fifty-four of the sixty African Americans who had applied for transfer to the three previously all-white high schools. To defuse segregationist criticism that Hall High School, which was located in the more affluent western area of the city, had not been desegregated, the school board assigned three African American students to Hall and three to Central High. In response, the NAACP filed suit, alleging that the school board had used the new pupil placement law in a racially biased fashion to evade its obligation to follow the Blossom Plan. Neither the Blossom Plan nor the 1956 decision in *Cooper v. Aaron* had discussed the application of screening or placement mechanisms, although the school board had used them throughout the desegregation process. School board president Everett Tucker, Jr., claiming that the board's policies were legally proper, stated that Little Rock's blacks, "who were the principal victims of the school closings, should be gratified that the School Board is making it possible for Negro children to resume their interrupted education." Instead, he noted, "they elect to attack us in court." Tucker conveniently failed to note that it was the successful NAACP suit against school closing and school vouchers laws that had in fact enabled the board to reopen the schools.[6]

Tucker's tone of injured rectitude did not move African American leaders in Little Rock, who voiced their determination to fight the school board's unilateral and paternalistic approach to desegregation. In August I. S. McClinton, who headed the Arkansas Democratic Voters Association and had worked amicably with Little Rock's power structure for years, suggested that increasing the numbers of transfers to a total of about twenty would reduce the possibility of legal actions. The Little Rock School Board, however, preferred to invite a lawsuit rather than admit more blacks to "white" schools. The NAACP expressed the anger of blacks over their treatment and charged that the school board had treated African American students who sought to attend previously white schools "as if they were 'presumptive disease-carriers' who require 'screening' before release from the quarantine of 'jim-crow' schools."[7]

Prior to opening day in the public schools, NAACP field secretary Clarence Laws called Little Rock "the testing ground for the South." Claiming that events in Little Rock would "set the pace and pattern from here on and could go a long way toward making or breaking the entire desegregation program in the South," he urged the Justice Department to get tough with anyone who interfered with desegregation there, even if it meant throwing Governor Faubus in jail.[8]

Conversely, Little Rock's moderates wanted to negotiate with Faubus, not incarcerate him. In the summer of 1959, the Little Rock School Board and its allies pursued a plan that would allow it to provide financial support for the private, white-only Raney High School. Devised by the ubiquitous Herbert Thomas, who served as a middle man between the school board and Faubus, the plan was designed to placate segregationists, to keep the student trouble makers out of the public high schools, to provide Faubus with a face-saving way to desist from further obstructionist actions, and thus to enable the reopening of all the public schools in Little Rock in the fall. In a closed meeting held at the Chamber of Commerce offices, the school board approved a plan to lease and operate Raney High under the guise of a "voluntary segregation plan." Legally, this was a high-risk strategy, given that a federal court had enjoined the board in the fall of 1958 from using public funds or facilities for private segregated schools. As board president Everett Tucker explained later, they wanted to provide a segregated school as a "safety valve" for those who "were just so adamant and so opposed to any form of integration."[9]

The school board members explored this means to a dual system despite the opposition of their lawyers, who advised them that the courts would not permit their involvement in such a scheme, and despite the opposition of other moderates, including the Committee for the Peaceful Operation of Free Public Schools (CPOFPS), a new organization formed by Little Rock's male business elite. This opposition so incensed Thomas that he wrote to Gaston Williamson, chairman of CPOFPS, that it was his "personal opinion that neither Harry Ashmore, Ed Dunaway or Henry Woods represents the moderate thinking of Little Rock." Clearly, Thomas and most of the business leadership believed the proposal for a dual system could be the means to get Faubus and other state leaders to leave the fate of Little Rock's schools to local decision makers. To that end, the Little Rock Chamber of Commerce drafted a letter to Faubus urging him "to now take the leadership in the reopening of our High Schools."[10]

Liberal school board member Ted Lamb opposed the Raney scheme. As a result, he got calls from all his major Arkansas clients urging him to go along. Many people in the business community were not only enthusiastic about the plan but were also more than willing to emulate the segregationists in the use of economic pressure to achieve their political goals. The business elite of Little Rock remained untroubled by the exclusionary politics it employed in devising and debating the plan. While incorporating a wide network of male business leaders in its discussions of the issue, the school board excluded the women of the WEC and African American leaders, who were unlikely to offer support. As before, it made significant decisions in private. No mention of the abortive plan appeared in any official school board minutes.[11]

The school board's dubious proposal was undermined by the unexpected announcement in early August 1959 that Raney High School was no longer receiving large private donations and thus did not have the funds to continue operations. After yet another secret meeting, the school board had dispatched board member J. H. Cottrell to the state Capitol with a letter to Faubus announcing its plan to incorporate Raney High into the public school system. Emissaries from the board reached Cottrell at the Capitol before he handed over the letter. Even so Thomas continued to believe it important to publicize the school board's commitment to the Raney plan as a means to avert any attacks on the schools that Faubus might attempt.[12]

The announcement that Raney High would be closing caught many people in Little Rock by surprise, including prominent segregationist leaders, who viewed Raney as the cornerstone of a new, all-white private school system. The school, after all, was adding new classrooms at the time of the announcement that it did not have the money to continue operations. According to Amis Guthridge, some people doubted that Raney actually lacked funds and blamed Faubus for its demise. Given the school's continued high enrollments and its announcement that it would charge tuition, their skepticism is understandable. For some, the dream of a private all-white school supported at least in part by state funds died hard. Malcolm Taylor, who was the president of the Capital Citizens' Council and treasurer of the Little Rock Private School Corporation, resigned from corporation's board in early 1960 because he was "unalterably opposed to the closing of Raney High School."[13]

The school vouchers system created under Arkansas law did not require public accountability from private schools whose students received stipends.

Several months before the closure of Raney High, some Mothers' League leaders contacted the Arkansas State Police to allege that influential male segregationists had taken money raised for the school and used it for their own personal purposes. The final audit for the Little Rock Private School Corporation revealed that the administration at Raney High had spent an average of $313.72 per pupil in its one year of operation (1958–59), compared to $322.75 per pupil in the public high schools in 1957–58. For undisclosed reasons, Raney's "general control" costs, which included administrative salaries, had been far higher per pupil than the "general control" costs reported for the public schools.[14]

The day after the audit revelation, the Little Rock School Board followed with its own surprise. On August 5, it announced a plan devised by Ted Lamb to open the high schools on August 12, almost a month ahead of schedule. The surprise announcement was intended to catch the segregationists off guard and to prevent the governor from calling a special session of the legislature in order to block the opening of the schools. In the meantime, city officials announced their intention to insure public order as the school sessions got underway.[15]

Shortly before opening day of school, some former Raney High School students held a car wash to raise money for the defunct white-flight school. Most of the students told reporters that they would rather not have any school than attend an integrated one. One girl put the issue squarely, stating: "I would rather be stupid than go to school with a nigger." The defiant teens declared that they would attend Hall or Central only if their parents forced them to do so.[16]

The day before classes were to start, eighteen lawyers from the Legal Committee of the CPOFPS announced they were ready to seek court injunctions against anyone who caused trouble. The moderates' willingness to act against anyone who tried to prevent the execution of a federal court order marked a departure from their earlier inaction. Previously they had feared that a strong stance against public disorders would intensify segregationist resistance and weaken political support for the moderates. The moderates' reversal also implied that they had accepted some of the assumptions advanced by the NAACP in the 1958 hearing on the school board's request for a delay in desegregation. The civil rights organization had charged that the school board's lax discipline at Central High and its unwillingness to seek injunctions against students who harassed or abused the African American students had encouraged violent resistance. At that time, the school board's position was that law enforcement was not its responsibility.[17]

Meanwhile, the plan to fund the private, all-white Raney High School with state funds had widened the divide between the WEC and Little Rock's business leadership. WEC leader Vivion Brewer called Raney "a makeshift school" and concluded that the scheme "could have been a betrayal leading to ruin." When Adolphine Terry suggested at a June meeting of WEC and STOP leaders that the school board sue for the $71,000 the state had spent on Raney High, STOP chairman Will Mitchell disagreed, citing the need for harmony. He proposed that there be new leadership in all the public organizations, an obvious attack on Vivion Brewer's position as president of the WEC. Brewer speculated in her memoir that maybe they had "antagonized, even frightened the power structure, for we stubbornly refused to be silent." As Sara Murphy concluded later, the "women's seat at that table proved to be a not altogether comfortable one." It was hardly their last unnerving interaction with their erstwhile allies.[18]

Other moderate male leaders in Little Rock acted on the assumption that the realm of formal politics now belonged only to them. They believed that their victory in the recall election—which was made possible by the labor of the WEC and the support of African Americans—would now provide them with their opportunity to silence the WEC forever. Some moderates in the business community had decided that the leaders of the women's organization were too liberal on racial issues and that their public stance could hamper moderate men's efforts to manage segregationist resistance and run the schools and the community as they saw fit. To that end, some of the more conservative moderate men formed the Committee for the Peaceful Operation of Free Public Schools (CPOFPS) mentioned earlier. Although CPOFPS included some women members, its leaders engaged in the usual behind-the-scenes decision making that excluded women. Its legislative subcommittee included no women and aspired to take over the lobbying role in the state legislature that had been effectively managed by the WEC. The exclusionary practices were blatant. In the summer of 1959, for example, volunteers from the WEC were used to call men for a men-only meeting of the new organization.[19]

Claiming he was speaking for others as well as himself, business leader Herbert Thomas wrote to Vivion Brewer in June 1959, asking the WEC not to place ads in newspapers anymore because, he asserted, people had accepted the opening of the public schools and ads "would irritate the extreme segregationists and possibly the Governor." He added, "the less we say publicly that could irritate anybody, the more quietly we could work, (if the other side will permit us), the more successful the school opening will be." Brewer wrote back, expressing her belief that requests for the WEC to demobilize and silence itself were premature. She stated that many people were pessimistic regarding the opening of the schools and that "mothers seek our advice, trying to weigh probabilities, worried to the point of discussing moving out of Arkansas in order to educate their children." She questioned the moderate males' long-term policy of silence and inactivity and reiterated her determination to maintain the WEC's strength. In July, Thomas responded to a proposal that various civic groups, including the WEC, issue public statements in support of the school board's decision to open all schools in the fall, suggesting that the WEC volunteer its clerical help, but not make any public announcements.[20]

At this point, Thomas assumed segregationist mobilization could be retarded if the visibility of racial issues in the community diminished. He wrote to local newspapers urging them to downplay stories about the schools, except as they involved coverage of upcoming athletic events. Sports, he believed, not race, should be on the front page of local newspapers. He noted that moderates in North Carolina, who had been successful in advancing their politics of tokenism in school integration, had used a similar strategy.[21]

Despite their differences with some of the moderates, Sara Murphy later concluded that the WEC at that time "was moving into a partnership that gave it a voice in setting the fragile policy that would steer the community onto a better course." Achieving that goal, she believed, required "the magic of the men's names and their experience and prestige," as well as the "good, sound thinking and effort of the women." Vivion Brewer was not quite as sanguine, noting that the formation of the new pro-public schools movement "gave our ink-stained office force another job." Certainly the new movement could not have organized so rapidly without the assistance of the WEC.[22]

In the WEC's surveys of community concerns it found that the possibility of public disorders associated with school desegregation was the most important issue. In mid-July, the WEC issued a statement expressing its "utmost confidence that Little Rock is a law abiding city and that adequate protection for the peaceful opening of our schools will be provided." Within days, the former leaders of the Stop This Outrageous Purge (STOP) campaign formed CPOFPS and the school board asked that the city police deal "firmly and quickly" with any disturbances.[23]

In response, the City Board of Directors issued a statement that it had "instructed the Police Department to deal firmly and quickly in the protection of life and property" should problems arise in conjunction with the opening of the schools. Police Chief Gene Smith confirmed his intention to arrest anyone who created disturbances in the vicinity of Central High School. The *New York Times* declared that it was unlikely that a "riotous outbreak," such as had occurred in 1957, would happen again in Little Rock because civic leaders and voters supported the policies of the school board and the city police.[24]

In August, the WEC published the results of its study of the effects of the crisis over desegregation on local businesses. This report, which documented the loss of new business investments and of middle-class professionals who moved their families elsewhere, made it clear that the failure to handle school desegregation effectively had harmed significant economic interests. This news, the WEC hoped, would embolden its fearful allies in the business community to act more forcefully on the issue of desegregation. As WEC leader Pat House cynically noted: "If the Chamber of Commerce falls, the whole world falls, as far as they were concerned." The WEC's study of the business effects of the Little Rock crisis circulated throughout the South and influenced public debates on the question of massive resistance to desegregation.[25]

Caught off guard by the events of early August, segregationists offered no clear response to moderate successes. Faubus, who was tentatively planning to call a special session of the legislature, would not say whether he would try to block the reopening of Little Rock's high schools. Asked about accounts of impending violence, he said, "I have no concrete reports at this time." He denied that he had ordered the closing of Raney High School so that troublemakers could return to public schools and impede integration there. Certainly, some segregationist students were unhappy with the prospect of returning to a desegregated Central High School. The daughter of Mothers' League leader Margaret Jackson had "publicly declared that if she returned to Central her only purpose would be to 'agitate.'" Elizabeth

Huckaby, who noted the enrollment of rabble-rousers from the 1957–1958 school year in her journal, observed that many of them were "bitter because of not being able to go to Raney."[26]

On behalf of the WEC, Velma Powell, the wife of Central Vice Principal J. O. Powell, drafted recommendations for a well-organized desegregation. The proposal included efforts "to prepare students, parents and teachers to adjust" to the resumption of integration; the creation of a special department to handle discipline at Central High; the systematic enforcement of strict rules; and the use of monitors and intercoms in the hallways, cafeteria, and other areas where trouble might occur. They also suggested that the school board desegregate all three white high schools, appoint a bi-racial advisory committee, solicit support from and work closely with community organizations, and encourage bi-racial meetings of teachers and guidance counselors.[27]

The women's organization submitted its proposals to school superintendent Terrell Powell and met with board members Everett Tucker, Russell Matson, and Ted Lamb. The inclusiveness and interracial cooperation envisioned by the WEC, however, reflected values and political goals quite at odds with those held by the business leadership and its representatives on the school board. Interracial cooperation was in fact quite frightening to male moderate leaders who believed that such a policy would incite segregationist mobilization. Despite the apparent futility of its efforts, the WEC devised a similar set of suggestions in 1961 as the district planned for the desegregation of its junior high schools. The women's organization did not choose to make its views on these issues public.[28]

The debates among the men—whether to continue trying to support at least some segregation in the schools or to rely on pupil placement laws— were substantially more conservative than the concerns of the WEC at this time. By 1960, the majority of WEC members reported their own support for school integration, while only 31 percent expressed the desire to use pupil placement laws to minimize the number of blacks admitted to previously all-white schools. These results placed them squarely in support of more systematic change than was desired by the business elite, for whom tokenism represented the most extreme position they would accept.[29]

Not surprisingly, the furor over desegregation had long since halted all talk of equalizing African American schools. In Little Rock, as elsewhere in the South, separate remained unequal. The city's still segregated elementary schools registered a pupil–teacher ratio of 31:1 for African American students and 26:1 for white students as school opened in 1959. In the secondary schools, the ratio was 22:1 for all students. Hall High School showed the lowest average at 19:1. These discrepancies received no public discussion.[30]

The desire of male moderates to seek a rapprochement with the governor was not shared by the WEC or by school board member Ted Lamb. By mid-September, Lamb was questioning the insistence of other board members that they attempt to pacify segregationists by working with Faubus. In the light of the board's success in opening the schools and holding strong against protestors, he concluded that they should openly confront all adversaries, including the governor[31]

As the schools prepared to open, some segregationist resisters were once again tempted to use violence to secure their goals. At the same time, they faced the likelihood that local police powers would be turned against them while state officials did nothing. Lacking the legal and political grounds to intervene, Faubus could only join in his allies' denunciations of the actions of local authorities. Frustrated by events, a few segregationists engaged in acts of violence while others resuscitated the politics of threat and intimidation.

The most important target for racist retribution was NAACP leader Daisy Bates. After explosives were thrown in her yard on July 7, she telegraphed the White House asking for protection. Despite other attacks on her house in the past, local police had been unable to identify the persons responsible or to stop the threats to her safety. The Eisenhower administration, however, deemed the matter to be purely local and thus outside federal jurisdiction. Thereafter, she relied on volunteer guards made up of local black citizens such as Isaac Mullen, a deputy sheriff. In August, Arkansas State Police arrested Mullen; Ellis Thomas, the father of Jefferson Thomas; and Dr. Garman Freeman on charges of carrying concealed weapons in their automobiles. After the arrests, Daisy Bates contacted the White House. Once more, federal officials did not act.[32]

Hoping to place himself once again at the center of the crisis and perhaps to declare an emergency in Little Rock requiring his intervention, Governor Faubus asked two members of the Little Rock Governing Board to write him asking that state police help preserve the peace on the first day of school. In refusing they conveyed the moderates' conviction that the governor was better understood as an instigator of violence than as a "preservator of peace." Still, some national observers and authorities in Little Rock worried, as did *Time* magazine, that Faubus's "backwoods segregationist supporters might yet descend on the city in force." In anticipation, the Justice Department sent an attorney to assist U.S. Attorney Osro Cobb in case violations of federal laws or court orders should occur. As events unfolded, it would become clear that Little Rock had its own "backwoods."[33]

On the eve of the opening of Little Rock's schools, the city's segregationist leaders asked their supporters to turn out the next day "to pay tribute to our great governor and to tell him that we need and want his continued leadership in our fight against federal dictatorship." Their almost desperate pleas revealed their dependence on Faubus and on state-sanctioned weapons of resistance if they were to have any hope of success, particularly given their recent defeat in the school board recall election.[34]

The governor's reply heartened moderates more than it did the segregationists who turned to him for assistance. In response to his partisans, Faubus gave a last-minute television address urging them to lawfulness and pragmatism in their response to the school opening. Reminding his followers in Little Rock that they had failed to retain segregationist school board members in the recall election, he exhorted them to "resolve to continue the struggle for freedom" in future elections. Although he offered the standard condemnation of his opponents in Little Rock as "integrationists" and "puppets of the federal government," he told opponents of desegregation that there was no reason for them to be "beaten over the head today by the forces in the field, or to be jailed."[35]

The next morning, as three African American girls—Effie Jones, Elsie Robinson, and Estella Thompson—entered Hall High School without incident, segregationists held a rally at the Capitol. While supporters waved Confederate and American flags and hoisted signs that announced "Arkansas is for Faubus" and "Follow Faubus for Freedom," the governor and supporters of segregation gave speeches. After tear gas was found in a car near the rally, local law enforcement officers arrested three youths, including one of the leading troublemakers at Central High in 1957–1958. The police believed segregationists planned to volley the gas into the crowd and then accuse the police of using it against the demonstrators. Indeed, Dr. Malcolm Taylor, president of the Capital Citizens' Council, had charged a few days before that the school board had asked the police to use tear gas to break up the crowds at the Capitol on opening day. According to Roy Reed, the canisters were ultimately "traced to the state police via connections in the Citizens' Council." The state police, which had jurisdiction at the Capitol grounds, released the persons arrested by the city police in the tear gas incident.[36]

When a group at the rally followed Robert Norwood, president of Little Rock's States' Rights Council, and marched to Central High School, they found a resolute Police Chief Gene Smith and other public safety officers ready to respond with force. When the marchers tried to break through police lines at the school, officers used fire hoses at part pressure to disperse them. In addition, officers arrested twenty-one protestors, including Norwood, on charges ranging from disturbing the peace to assaulting a police officer. That evening, when liberal board member Ted Lamb received harassing phone calls labeling him a "nigger-lover," he twitted his antagonists with the response "What's the matter, did you get wet this afternoon?"[37]

In the meantime, Jefferson Thomas, a veteran of Central High's earlier race wars, anxiously awaited the news of events at the school with his parents and a few other supporters in the safety of his home. As they listened to radio reports on the confrontations at Central High, Mrs. Thomas worried that it would not "be safe to walk the streets" that night. Daisy Bates shared her fear: "They'll be red hot after having had the hose turned on 'em. Oh, they'll be out tonight with bombs and machine guns." Despite their worries, Jefferson Thomas, accompanied by Elizabeth Eckford, entered school that afternoon without incident.[38]

Moderates praised the Little Rock police for maintaining order and enabling a relatively calm school opening, while segregationists accused Little Rock police officials of resorting to "Hungarian Gestapo tactics" against protestors who were only "attempting to assemble peacefully." Governor Faubus claimed that Police Chief Smith was guilty of "blackjacking" a woman in the melee at Central High. At a news conference called by Amis Guthridge and Wesley Pruden, the latter announced he would be serving as treasurer for a "freedom fund" to pay the defense expenses of those arrested. After a newspaper photographer asked him if some of the money "could be used to repair my camera that one of your 'goons' smashed yesterday," the segregationist minister expressed regret but did not offer reimbursement. In a published statement, CPOFPS declared that the protestors had been handled "with the minimum force necessary" and that many of the demonstrators were "not citizens of this school district."[39]

Meanwhile, business leaders looked forward to new economic possibilities presented by the peaceable reopening of the schools. On September 3, 1959, the *Arkansas Gazette* ran an editorial cartoon entitled "No. 1 Attraction" that pictured signs touting an "orderly community and its public schools system" and that invited developers to "invest with us" and "locate your industrial plant here." Before it could open any more "factory sites in pleasant surroundings," however, the city received another blow to its public image as bombs exploded in several locations on Labor Day, September 7. The targets selected by the bombers—a city-owned automobile driven by the fire chief, an office housing the mayor's construction company, and the school board offices—revealed segregationists' anger at the public authorities they blamed for school desegregation.[40]

State and local leaders responded to the violence in a predictable fashion. Governor Faubus denied that segregationists were responsible for the violence and called the crimes "sickening and deplorable." Arkansas Attorney General Bruce Bennett affirmed his belief that the Communist Party was to blame. The Little Rock Chamber of Commerce stated that the violence had "damaged the city's reputation beyond measurement." The business leaders' organization also issued an appeal for a reward fund, raising over $20,000 in contributions within a few days.[41]

In the same period of time, Little Rock police arrested five white men and charge them with the bombings. Defendant E. A. Lauderdale, the owner of a lumber and roofing company, was a member of the board of the Capital Citizens' Council and had run twice for the City Manager Board, losing both times. He had served as chair of the arrangements committee for the August 1957 visit of Governor Marvin Griffin of Georgia that was sponsored by the Citizens' Council. Truck driver J. D. Sims, another of the accused and a member of the Ku Klux Klan, told the police that he did not want his daughter "to go to school with niggers." Trial testimony revealed that Lauderdale had approached Sims and car salesman John Coggins at KKK meetings to recruit them for the bombings. Coggins in turn enlisted Samuel Beavers, a carpenter. The fifth defendant, truck driver Jessie Perry, was also recruited at KKK meetings.[42]

Capital Citizens' Council leaders were quick to defend Lauderdale, one of their own, and to allege that the charges against him were a plot to discredit the segregation movement. Dr. Malcolm G. Taylor, president of the Capital Citizens' Council, praised Lauderdale as "a hard-working Christian patriot" whose arrest revealed the machinations of despotic local leaders. According to Taylor, "If Mr. Lauderdale can be selected as the scape goat and railroaded to prison, then no American can dare voice his honest resentment to police state tactics nor hope to find refuge in the time-honored laws and constitutional rights of this once-great land." Angry that police had followed Lauderdale from his home to Broadmoor Baptist Church in order to arrest him, Wesley Pruden, the pastor at Broadmoor, said that they had done so in order to "make a production and smear the Church and smear me." Amis Guthridge, who provided legal assistance to some of the defendants, accused the prosecutors of charging Lauderdale "because of his prominence as a segregation leader."[43]

Alleging that the power of Little Rock's Chamber of Commerce and the local media extended even into the jury room, several of the defendants asked for a change of venue. They claimed that extensive newspaper coverage had linked the defendants to the crimes, making it impossible for them to receive a fair trial in Pulaski County. According to their petition, virtually every businessman in the county belonged to the Chamber of Commerce, which was overrepresented in the petit jury panels. Their petition alleged that the Chamber of Commerce's statements and newspaper accounts had linked the bombings "with the attempt to reopen the public schools... on an integrated basis, and have publicly charged these defendants with being members of organizations opposed to the integration of the public schools." The judge denied their petition and Little Rock jurors convicted all five defendants in the late fall of 1959. All but Beavers, who received a suspended sentence for health reasons, were sentenced to prison terms of three to five years.[44]

Neither the social profile of those convicted of the bombings nor their published statements provide a clear explanation of their motives or intentions. They were clearly not drawn from Little Rock's most impoverished white citizens. For the most part, they had stable work and had families to support. In short, they had something to lose. So, why did they risk it in this way?

The timing of the bombings and their connections to a newly formed Ku Klux Klan operation in Little Rock offer clues. Clearly, the Klan directives that summer had emphasized the need to use violence because nonviolent strategies had failed to prevent school desegregation. The local Citizens' Council was in some disarray. It was losing members and the leadership seemed to have no solutions. Lauderdale had claimed to the others that the violence would cause public officials to back off from their support for desegregated schools. A few clandestine attacks on property would thus show that the dissidents' power exceeded the power of the local authorities they despised. Their acts, in short, could offer a model of successful defiance and could shore up a flagging segregationist movement.[45]

At the same time, the nascent Klan had not forged the ties of solidarity and trust that might have prevented the whole thing from unraveling after the first arrest. The defendants barely knew each other. After his arrest, Sims confessed and named all of the others who were involved. Amis Guthridge complained that he had not been allowed access to the defendant but in fact Sims refused to have a lawyer. Caught off guard, the defendants did not try to turn the trial into a political event in which they defended their racial politics or their use of violence to secure segregation.[46]

As their actions demonstrated, the line between respectable resistance and violent defiance was a thin one in Little Rock and Arkansas. The trials revealed the segregationists' use of the KKK and its "confidential squad" for their "disreputable" resistance to desegregation. If their goal was to insulate the Citizens' Council from any association with violence, they failed because Lauderdale's active role in both groups created public suspicion that the two organizations were closely connected. Indeed, *Washington Post* reporter Robert E. Baker concluded that with the arrests, the Citizens' Council's "last vestige of respectability was gone." Others believed that the bombings were the logical outcome of the defiance of federal law preached by Faubus and others in the massive resistance camp. In a letter to the *Arkansas Gazette*, for example, retired General Hugh Cort linked the refusal of segregationist public officials to support federal law to the violence: "When government officials sworn to uphold law and order, by their utterances or lack of action, breed contempt for one law, they sow the seeds for violation of all laws."[47]

The bombings also point to the inadequate response of law enforcement to the threat of violence beginning in 1957. Blossom had testified in 1958 regarding a conversation he had had with Guthridge about a group of men who advocated violence. Although Guthridge had denied any involvement with violent groups, it is not clear how much knowledge he had about them. In this period the Arkansas State Police spent many of its resources investigating teachers and integrationists and too little of its resources following through on the threat of violence that Faubus had ridden to a third term. Similar investigative inaction by the Little Rock police reflected the racist convictions of many police officers and the politics of the city administration in the period before the recall elections of spring 1959.[48]

The conviction of all five defendants comforted local leaders that the city had demonstrated to the world its revulsion at such lawlessness and its determination to end it. The *Arkansas Gazette* claimed that "the city's critics outside can contemplate the reality of justice done and order protected." Thus, the city could reclaim "its proper image." In fact, public officials at all levels had been more lucky than vigilant in their responses to the segregationists' use of violent threats. The failure of officials to investigate threats and a surveillance strategy that focused on civil rights activists had heightened the risk of public violence.[49]

After the bombers were sent to prison, some segregationists campaigned to persuade Governor Faubus to grant clemency to Lauderdale and some of his co-conspirators. E. A. Walker, for example, claimed that Lauderdale was "a fine christian [*sic*] man," adding that it was "not very fair to have him serve a sentence in the penitentiary like a criminal when he is such a high type man." These segregationists' ethical framework defined moral worth in terms of membership in a particular Christian community and, by implication, contributions to white supremacy movements and racial separation. Letters to Faubus supporting pardons generally did not claim that those convicted were innocent of the crimes or that they were penitent about their actions. One is left to conclude that those segregationists supporting pardons elevated the support for racial hierarchy to the highest moral plane, making questions of guilt irrelevant. For them, the pardons would have exonerated the violence they deemed necessary for the defense of segregation. The letters and the inaction of the Citizens' Council to Lauderdale's involvement in the bombings put to the lie to earlier assertions by council leaders that they would deal harshly with those in their organization who committed acts of violence.[50]

Some segregationists also rationalized violence as the logical outcome of federal coercion. The governor, for example, stated before the arrests that if segregationists were responsible, the "underlying cause of the violence [was] the federal government's policy on racial integration." An anonymous letter to the *Arkansas Gazette* expressed the view that when "any law offends over 75 per cent of a nation, that law is an abomination, and spawns the unholy rebellion that causes good people to commit acts of violence they would not if reason prevailed."[51]

Faubus commuted the sentences of three of the Labor Day bombers, justifying his decision by claiming that the courts had used a racial double standard favoring blacks. He reduced Lauderdale's sentence to time served and granted executive clemency to Perry and to Coggins, who had backed out of the plot after dynamite was loaded into the cars. Sims, whose initial confession had implicated Lauderdale and the others in the crime, got no break from the governor. Sims spent almost two years in prison. Lauderdale, Perry, and Coggins each spent a little over five months in prison.[52]

In the meantime, Little Rock's white moderates hoped to allay white anxieties about desegregation by touting the school board's policy of token integration carefully controlled through the Arkansas pupil placement act. The *Arkansas Gazette*, for example, published an editorial in late June noting favorably the obstacles the law placed in the way of African American applicants for transfers to previously all-white schools. These obstacles included an assessment of the morality, behavior, and psychological profile of African American students. CPOFPS president Gaston Williamson assured Little Rock citizens that the school board's pupil placement policy included a consideration of applicants' "scholastic aptitude," their "psychological qualification... for the type of associations involved," and the effects of the transfer of African American students to previously white schools on the academic progress of white students. The pupil placement law made it difficult for students who objected to their assignment to launch class action lawsuits and forced them to go through a cumbersome appeal process before they could seek redress through the courts. It explicitly put the burden of enforcing the *Brown* decision on black students and their families at the same time as it erected barriers to their success.[53]

Moderate leaders continued to misread African Americans in Little Rock as well as the intentions of the NAACP. In private discussions, leaders of the STOP campaign prepared resolutions (unadopted) to present to the school board. The resolutions stated that the "basic issue in the Negro community is over recognition of equal dignity rather than over the offering of specific courses." Tokenism, therefore, would serve black leaders' goals as well as the goals of the school board: "A few Negro pupils given recognition of equal dignity can serve as a satisfactory symbol for the whole community." In order to improve communication with the African American community, the resolution suggested the formation of a black organization to support the school board's plan. The board's liaison with the group, however, was to be private and informal.[54]

The moderates, whose commitment to tokenism was intense, confronted an African American community equally resolute in its desire to contest tokenism with whatever tools it had available. Many blacks objected to the use of pupil assignment law as evasive and destined to fail. At first, African American leaders and their white allies sought to increase the number of black students in Little Rock's high schools by coaching students through the interrogation process and by contesting the low numbers of black students that the Little Rock School Board wanted to approve for transfer. When school officials accepted only six blacks for admission to white high schools out of sixty applicants, nineteen students filed protests and eighteen students, including Thelma Mothershed and Melba Pattillo, decided to stay out of school until they were admitted to the schools of their choice.[55]

African American leaders criticized the decision of the school board and mobilized black community support for desegregation in order to increase the number of black students assigned to previously all-white schools. Daisy Bates expressed doubts that the school board had acted in good faith. To inform black students of their legal rights and to devise strategies so that more might successfully negotiate the board's arcane review procedure, African American community leaders organized a meeting at the Dunbar Center for the transfer applicants. As a response to school authorities' politicization of the assignment process, the meeting symbolized blacks' refusal to submit to the politics of racial deference so critical to school board members.[56]

According to Everett Tucker, the school board screened black applicants "very conscientiously, trying to make it work." Emphasizing the academic component of the screening process, he stated that the board sought black students who were "on a par academically and intellectually, IQ and so on, with their peers so that it would work—emotionally and this sort of thing." He did not admit that they compared black students only to the best white students while admitting all white students to schools based on residence in the schools' attendance areas. The school board's reviews of African American students included subjective judgments regarding a student's attitude and politics. Indeed, a willingness to acquiesce to white authority, especially the authority exercised by the board itself, was a crucial precondition for a positive decision. WEC leader Vivion Brewer later revealed that she had gotten a letter from a friend in Washington, D.C., charging that the board deliberately chose students who would not be able to endure the pressures associated with their roles as token black students.[57]

Interrogations of black applicants for transfers to Central High and Hall High were intended to insure that the students' motives for transfer did not reflect egalitarian aspirations and that their behavior did not imply, as Minnijean Brown's had, that they were there by right. They questioned black students in particular about their attendance at the Dunbar Center community meeting and their motives for refusing to attend Mann High School when so assigned by the school board. Board members also queried them about their ability to control their temper, still assuming that anger management skills were a requisite for any black attending an integrated school. They did not apply similar criteria to white students. Virgil Blossom's observation in his 1959 book that "all of the Negro students except one behaved well—almost stoically—under severe provocation" partly because "they were serving a cause" reveals the shortsightedness of the school board's efforts to exclude those students motivated by that very cause.[58]

The screening process was also designed to discipline black aspirations. When African American applicants for transfer stated that the curriculum at Mann High was insufficient to meet their educational or career goals or that Central High offered courses not available at Mann, they were told that those courses would be offered at Mann if sufficient students could be found to take them. If not, they would apparently be out of luck. When applicants for transfer stated that they would stand a better chance for college admission or a scholarship if they attended Central High, they were told that Mann, Central, and Hall High Schools all had the same rating from the North Central Association or that students from Mann also went to college and received scholarships. In short, they received standard responses from the school board denying any differences in academic standing or suggesting remedies within the confines of segregation. School board attorney Leon Catlett's remark in the 1956 hearing in *Aaron v. Cooper* that Hall High School would be for college-bound students and that Mann had a different mission reveals the hypocrisy of the board's professions of good faith.[59]

The school board used social and psychological criteria to justify negative decisions in applications for transfer and to ensure tractable students
for token desegregation. Although the board consistently turned down applicants with poor academic records, the fact that it disqualified other applicants so that they could stay with their friends in segregated schools
suggests that the maintenance of a dual system of schools far outweighed
academic considerations in school assignment decisions. Little Rock's
history of school segregation belied any claims that basing assignment
decisions on students' ability to maintain friendships was racially neutral.
Moreover, the board's expectation that black students would have to withstand racist abuse stoically continued the policy of extorting a high personal
price for change from African American students and their families.[60]

The school board was sometimes divided on assignment decisions; Ted
Lamb voted in the minority in several cases. The divisions were most pro-
nounced in the case of Sybil Jordan, an academically gifted student who
had attended the meeting at the Dunbar Center and refused to enroll at
Mann after her initial assignment there by the school board. The board
admitted her to Central over the strenuous opposition of new members
J. H. Cottrell and B. Frank Mackey. Claiming that Jordan "was a ringleader in a 'strike' against board regulations," Cottrell stated emphatically
that "Defiance of duly constituted authority should never be rewarded.
This is true whether that 'duly constituted authority' be a federal court or
a school board. Furthermore I do not believe that this board should ca-
pitulate to threats, intimidation, strikes or any other form of coercion from
any student." Some people believed that the board approved the transfer of
Jordan and two other African American students, James Henderson, Jr.
and Sandra Johnson, in order to strengthen its position in the NAACP
lawsuit against pupil placement laws.[61]

The WEC, which agreed with African American leaders regarding the
board's misuse of pupil placement law, met in November 1959 with board
member Russell Matson to interrogate him on the issue. According to
Vivion Brewer, "Some of the questions flung at Mr. Matson were sharp, a
few little short of rude." Matson, who called the pupil placement laws the
"salvation of the Little Rock schools," claimed that the school board
"treated all students and parents alike in the assignments hearings." His
conviction that any significant presence of African American students in

Little Rock's previously all-white schools jeopardized academic standards in the schools differed dramatically from the views of WEC activists.[62]

In an attempt to claim a greater public role in the controversy, representatives of the black community suggested at a school board meeting in September 1959 that the board assign a liaison to meet regularly with a committee chosen by local African Americans in order to improve communication with the board. School board president Everett Tucker responded that the board had no problems with communication with any group in the community and that the board "was not consciously communicating with one group more than another." He declared that African Americans could come to the public school board meetings. At the same time, his reply indicated the board's fear of legitimating opinions generated independently by the black community or representatives chosen from within it. In response, the Rev. James T. McCullum of the Steele Memorial Baptist Church said that the board had "closed minds already."[63]

The African American community then decided that the only solution was to elect a black member to the school board. At a series of community meetings, Little Rock blacks expressed their considerable disaffection with the temporizing of the moderates. Many blacks claimed that the moderates were as committed to segregation as those individuals sympathetic to the Capital Citizens' Council and more effective than them in securing its retention. For their part, the moderates told black leaders that their plan to run an African American for the school board would jeopardize white moderate candidates and threaten the future of public schools. Dr. M. A. Jackson expressed an interest in running for the board, but under pressure from white liberals and African American leaders to withdraw his candidacy, he ultimately decided not to run, citing family reasons.[64]

Tensions intensified between the WEC, which was still a white-only organization that supported the election of the school board moderates, and African Americans. In the fall of 1959, WEC leaders believed they would lose political influence with white voters if they integrated their organization. In a letter to Muriel Lokey of the organization HOPE (Help Our Public Education) in Atlanta, Billie Wilson said that WEC members were "still 'untouchables'" whose political work had to be done quietly and with no credit. She also expressed her conviction that a black candidate or one from the WEC would only divide the moderate vote and allow a segregationist to be elected to the school board. Such an outcome would jeopardize the most important goal shared by the diverse women whose labor sustained the WEC—the goal of open public schools. WEC leaders held to this position despite their growing conflicts with local moderate leaders. Many women in the organization's leadership were, in the words of Sara Murphy, developing "into confirmed integrationists."[65]

After the opening day confrontations, African American students at Hall and Central continued the work of racial integration pioneered by their predecessors from 1957 to 1958. Although they did so with less harassment and intimidation from racist white students, they still faced ostracism, racial epithets, and physical persecution. In early September, Vice Principal Elizabeth Huckaby noted in her journal that she and another teacher were "disturbed at what is to be allowed at school re harassment of Negroes." Although Principal Jess Matthews had already counseled some white boys, including one heavily involved in the 1957–1958 harassment of Jefferson Thomas, segregationist students continued to target Thomas, who was for a while the only black in the student body at Central.[66]

When Thomas asked to be transferred to other classes at Central to avoid his harassers, Matthews refused his request, noting that he could not do so because students who had invoked their right under state law to attend all-white classes would then have to be reassigned. Ellis Thomas reported his son's difficulties to school officials and to the NAACP. In mid-September, Wiley Branton wrote to school board attorney Herschel Friday to complain that school officials were doing nothing about the harassment of Thomas. Noting that the NAACP had not made note of such intimidation in its legal actions in the past, trying "to stay out of the disciplinary problems at the school and permit the school officials to handle these problems," he warned that "if they [the school board] cannot, or will not, do so, then we will have no alternative other than to ask the aid of the Court in this regard." Soon thereafter, Ellis Thomas lost the job he had held for ten years at International Harvester. The harassment of Jefferson Thomas and the other African American students at Central continued intermittently, although not on the scale experienced in 1957–1958.[67]

Unlike the first year of desegregation at Central, segregationists' use of the media to rally support for "victimized" white students declined in 1959 as did threats to go to the courts in response to school administrators' disciplinary actions. In late October, however, a classroom fight involving black student Sandra Johnson and one of the white girls who had caused trouble in 1957 led the *Arkansas Democrat* to charge that white students were being abused. Daisy Bates reported the incident to the NAACP as follows:

> Sandra Johnson, a girl who weighs about 90 pounds, beat the h... out of a girl in her study hall a few weeks ago. This girl... started on Sandra the first day she entered school by name-calling and striking her. This day she... struck her again with her fist. Sandra quietly put her books down and beat the devil out of her.... Since that time, she has had no physical violence—just veiled threats.

Significantly, school authorities did not discipline Johnson for retaliating against her tormentor. Elizabeth Huckaby reported in her journal that the white girl "seemed sorry" for her part in the conflict.[68]

Despite some improvement, Vice Principal Elizabeth Huckaby still spent time counseling African American girls who were experiencing harassment and disciplining resistant white students. In October, she noted some changes from the past in her journal: "New angle this year—some who do things sorry later." Whether these responses were sincere or opportunistic, they did reflect a changed political context for student conduct.[69]

Some white students still experienced peer pressure to conform to prevailing segregationist ideas and practices. These pressures came from students who encompassed a much wider social and political spectrum than the working-class activists who harassed black students at Central. A white girl who had attended Hall in 1959 reported years later the hostile treatment she received for her support for integration. After she lent a few cents to an African American student at lunch, "The whole cafeteria got quiet. I went back to my seat. I felt like people just followed me with their eyes." Seeking safety she sat down beside her boyfriend, who "immediately got up and left. I had a boy grab me, somebody I had gone to school with all my life, and said, don't ever speak to a nigger again. I said, I'll speak to a black anytime I want to." As she left, "this whole line of guys started going, nigger lover, nigger lover, nigger lover. I went straight to the bathroom and sobbed." Although the behavior of her friends and peer group occasioned a great deal of pain for her, she remained clear that African Americans "were as equal as anybody else, it had nothing to do with the color of their skin."[70]

In December 1959, Congressman Charles C. Diggs visited Little Rock to investigate the treatment of African American students in the city's desegregated high schools. He complained that black students continued to experience mistreatment at Central and that city police were not offering Daisy Bates sufficient protection. City Manager Dean Dauley called Diggs' complaints "completely erroneous." He said police routinely checked Daisy Bates' home and found no trouble. He also said he had received no reports from the schools about mistreatment of black students. Speaking for the school board, Everett Tucker claimed that Congressman Diggs' statement was "just another example of somebody who is politically motivated and who is attempting to interfere with the orderly operation of the schools for his own selfish political purposes. If the children are harassed they or their parents should let the school authorities know about it." The students who were being harassed and at least one parent had complained, with mixed results. To maintain Little Rock's image as a peaceable community with harmonious race relations, Tucker and other school officials continued to downplay black students' difficulties.[71]

By December, Daisy Bates could no longer bear the burden she had assumed. Still tormented by personal threats and still negotiating on a regular basis for the safety and rights of the black students at Central and Hall High Schools, she collapsed under the accumulated pressures. In December, she underwent a ten-day hospitalization for stress-related symptoms. Shortly before her collapse, she and her husband had lost the *Arkansas State Press*, which finally folded after timorous advertisers capitulated to segregationist bullies who had orchestrated a boycott of the newspaper in response to the support the desegregation cause received from Daisy and L. C. Bates. Even though the NAACP and other friends in the national civil rights community had been providing financial assistance to the journal since the beginning of the crisis over desegregation, it was no longer sufficient to offset the losses occasioned by the boycott.[72]

On May 30, 1962, Sybil Jordan graduated from Central High School. As she walked to the podium at the graduation ceremony, where she was recognized as one of 52 honor graduates in her class of 523, she heard a "long, jeering whistle" from the stands. Going back to her seat, she heard

classmates say: "Here comes the nigger now. I guess Black Beauty's happy—
she's got her scholarship." Jordan had received a four-year scholarship to
attend Earlham College in Indiana. Despite her almost complete isolation
at school, close contact with whites in class had changed one of her racial
assumptions: "I didn't think there'd be so many poor students among
them. I realized they weren't a super race." One of her white peers also
changed her own views on race and ability, commenting that "I've gotten
to know that some Negroes are pretty smart."[73]

At the time, Jordan's friend Jacquelyn Faye Evans, a junior at Hall High
School, was still facing the racial challenges imposed by token integration.
For Evans, one of the most frustrating aspects of attending a school that
was integrated in name only was her inability to participate in extracurricular events. School officials at Hall had refused her admission to the
National Beta Club, an honor society, on the grounds that the club's char-
ter forbade the admission of African Americans. Evans had a straight A
average. The Y-Teens Club refused her also, despite its self-professed mission as a "fellowship of women and girls devoted to the task of realizing in
our common life the ideals of personal and social living to which we are
committed by our faith as Christians." School administrators supported
these exclusionary practices. For them, progress in racial equality was evidenced by the fact that black students could attend athletic events at their
schools even though the teams remained all-white.[74]

School officials' gradualist approach to black student participation in
extracurricular activities was mirrored in their continuing caution regarding the admission of African American students to previously all-white
schools. In 1961–62, with 15,403 white students and 6,166 African
Americans attending schools in the Little Rock school district, only 45
blacks were enrolled in previously all-white junior and senior high schools.
The school board increased the number to 78 the following year, but kept
elementary schools completely segregated. Ted Lamb continued his opposition to token integration, voting to transfer 96 of the 103 black applicants in 1962: "I say once you've let *one* Negro youngster into a white
school, you've lost the segregationists, so forget about them. I believe in
integration. The problem will never be solved in the South until the people
recognize that segregation is immoral as well as impractical."[75]

The segregationists had a contrary view. In 1962, as before, Margaret
Jackson of the Mothers' League linked states' rights to racist ideologies that

claimed white moral superiority: "I feel more strongly than ever that desegregation is unconstitutional. We know how many Negroes would attend Central if they had a chance. Their morals are not as high, they carry
knives and ice picks and they try to date white girls." Faubus, now serving
his fourth term as governor, agreed, invoking a paternalist concern for the
well-being of African Americans and whites: "Negroes don't have funerals
or treat marriage the same as white people. Their attitudes clash. That's not
to say one is better than the other. The damage to the white majority by
forced integration would be far more than forced segregation to the Negro
minority because *it would ruin both*."[76]

The continuing success of the Little Rock Nine was ideologically important to the national civil rights community, which used the academic
success of the African American students to bolster the case for school desegregation. To enable these students to reap the reward of their academic
achievement, the NAACP set up a scholarship fund, managed by some of
the parents, to offset the costs of their college educations. After their high
school graduations, all nine started college, most in the north. In November 1961, Daisy Bates reported to the NAACP that all but Melba Pattillo
were in college and making good grades, adding that "for the most part I
am very proud of the Little Rock Nine, so far no babies, no scandals or
anything that would reflect on the struggle or the organization."[77]

The Little Rock School Board received yet another unfavorable court
decision in March 1961 when the appellate court found that Little Rock
officials had used the pupil placement law in a discriminatory fashion and
urged them to support "integration in more than a token fashion." The
appellate court ordered the school board to use residence as the initial cri-
terion for school assignments. It noted that the Blossom Plan approved by
the court had included such a provision and decided that school board
members could not use the pupil placement law "for the purpose of impeding, thwarting, and frustrating integration." The actions of school officials prompted Ted Lamb, the one liberal on the school board, to charge
that the board had paid "more attention to a handful of bigots and racists
than to those who work for justice and righteousness in our city," that it
had wasted public money in futile litigation, and that it had "never seriously sought to rally the forces of Christianity and good will in our town
to enter into compliance with the court on a moral basis." Under pressure,

the school board extended desegregation to the junior high schools in 1961 and to the elementary schools in 1963 but, in defiance of the court decision, it continued to use pupil placement to minimize the numbers of African American students in desegregated schools.[78]

Despite the 1961 legal victory in the pupil assignment case, by 1963 liberals began to despair that the school board would ever decide to advance meaningful desegregation. Arkansas Council for Human Relations chair Nathan Griswold wrote to Wiley Branton in April 1963 that those individuals who supported substantive conformity to federal court decisions had been "defeated in the enforcement of the law by increasingly bold and arrogant school officials." In 1964, Lamb continued to complain about the school board's lack of good faith compliance as he tried "to discredit... [the] unconstitutional use of the pupil assignment law by the board."[79]

The passage of the 1964 Civil Rights Act threatened the loss of federal funds at educational institutions that continued massive resistance to school desegregation and it set timetables for compliance. It is unlikely that the 1964 act would have strengthened federal enforcement authority so significantly without the lessons that federal authorities drew from the history of massive resistance and moderate equivocation that preceded it in Little Rock and elsewhere. As Attorney General Robert F. Kennedy testified in 1963, providing federal assistance to private lawsuits and imposing penalties for noncompliance had become essential both to prevent further delay in enforcing the legal mandate in *Brown* and to shield individual litigants from the harassment they had experienced in the South.[80]

The 1964 Civil Rights Act prompted politicians in Little Rock and in Arkansas to move beyond token integration. On the advice of its lawyers, the Little Rock School Board adopted the freedom of choice plan acceptable to the federal government in 1964–65, by which parents could choose their children's schools. In the South, physical and economic coercion of African Americans negated the freedom promised in such programs. Although the school board continued to devise evasive strategies for compliance thereafter, the pace of desegregation accelerated rapidly, especially at the high school level. From 1964 to 1965 the number of African Americans attending desegregated schools in Little Rock jumped from 213 to 621 and the number of desegregated districts in Arkansas increased from

24 to 152. By 1967–68, there were 415 African Americans enrolled at Central, 142 at the Metropolitan Vocational School, but only 5 at Hall High School. Massive resistance to desegregation was dead in Arkansas.[81]

Throughout the South, proponents of massive resistance had rested their hopes for success on state government action. In Arkansas, Governor Faubus had promised whites they could retain segregated public schools for their children. The federal courts, however, had dealt blow after blow to the evasive laws he had sponsored to keep that promise. Although Faubus's tactics were never as tyrannical as some of the tactics employed in the states of the Deep South, he did try to use state law and state agencies to hinder the NAACP's ability to have recourse to the courts and to repress alternative political opinions. In the long run, these efforts by Faubus were no more successful than his school closing laws.

So in the fall of 1959 the governor and segregationists in the state legislature—their backs against the wall—introduced an amendment to eliminate the constitutional requirement that Arkansas children receive free public schooling. In 1960, with Amendment 52 scheduled for a November vote of the Arkansas electorate, the men of the CPOFPS sought the assistance of the women of the WEC in mobilizing voters against the amendment. In fact, the WEC was already focused on the threat posed by the "school destruction" amendment and offered crucial state-wide leadership in the campaign to secure its defeat. The women's group organized informational workshops for its members, sent speakers and informational materials throughout the state, developed and funded advertising, and worked with other organizations to defeat the measure.[82]

Even with the enthusiastic support of Faubus and the state's segregationist leaders, the measure to abolish the constitutional guarantee of free public schools went down to a resounding defeat. The measure was defeated because the governor encountered a powerful statewide coalition of opponents loosely organized as the Committee Against Amendment 52. The committee included women's organizations, religious groups, unions, the Arkansas Farmers' Union, Parent Teacher Associations, teachers' groups, business leaders, and numerous other groups and individuals. The defeat of Amendment 52 in 1960 robbed Faubus and his allies of their most important weapon by demonstrating emphatically that white Arkansas voters were not willing to destroy public schools in order to keep segregation. Equally important, it pulled the rug out from under the white majoritarian ideology that had propped up the governor since September 1957. No longer could Faubus claim to speak for a white electorate committed to segregation at all costs.[83]

Despite the WEC's stunning success in this campaign, it did not change the reactive nature of the women's relationship to the state: they always found themselves responding to initiatives from the men who dominated formal politics. After the defeat of Amendment 52, the WEC continued to fight against initiatives threatening to the schools that continued to emanate from state leaders. In the early 1960s, the WEC fought against pension reductions for public school teachers, a measure introduced as retribution against the teachers' role in the defeat of the amendment; against state laws providing for quick votes on amendments, designed to rush citizens to a decision; and against school finance proposals that the women deemed harmful.[84]

In order to improve the situation in the state legislature, the WEC also worked hard to elect legislators who were supportive of its position. In 1960, WEC mobilized sixty volunteers to work long hours for Jim Brandon's campaign against Willie Oates for the state senate. Oates, who stood for the legislature after she was recruited by allies of Governor Faubus, had served on the Raney High School board and had voted for Faubus's school board bill in the spring of 1959. Brandon, an advertising executive who worked for Ted Lamb, defeated the establishment incumbent largely as a result of the civic labor of the women of the WEC. Thereafter, he worked closely with its leadership.[85]

Women activists in Arkansas worked to guarantee a secret ballot and to reform Arkansas voter registration law in order to remove the potential for corruption. The changes they supported were particularly unsettling to eastern Arkansas planters who were used to "voting" their workers by paying their poll taxes and watching them vote. All of the voter reforms they proposed or supported, including the "one man, one vote" decision of the U.S. Supreme Court in *Baker v. Carr*, threatened traditional power arrangements in state politics.

When the American Association of University Women (AAUW) in Arkansas took on these voter reform issues, it encountered the opposition of veteran legislator Paul Van Dalsem. The powerful representative from eastern Arkansas tried to prevent the testimony of AAUW leader Eleanor Reid in the state legislature, storming out when he was overruled. At a meeting of the Optimists Club in Little Rock, he offered his own recommendations for dealing with women's activism in Arkansas politics:

> We don't have any of these university women in Perry County, but I'll tell you what we do up there when one of our women starts poking around in something she doesn't know anything about. We get her an extra milk cow. And then if that's not enough, we get her pregnant and keep her barefoot.

When redistricting measures gave Van Dalsem's district a large number of voters from Pulaski County, he found that he had entered WEC/AAUW territory. The "university women" he had so disparaged came out *en masse* to unseat the powerful state legislator. Given their success in passing the voter reform legislation he opposed, he should not have been surprised. [86]

The WEC had no influence over the governor, who continued to lead segregationist forces in the state, but it did become a visible and relatively effective presence in the legislature. The WEC sent representatives to lobby lawmakers daily, ensuring that the legislators would not allow the issue of open public schools to languish because of caution or conservatism. By 1960 many legislators, fearful that the WEC would use its large volunteer membership against them in upcoming elections, were careful to assure the women's organization that they supported public schools even as they continued to temporize on school desegregation. In 1961, for example, segregationist state representative Glen Walther wrote to the WEC to assure its leadership that he planned to vote against some of the bills they opposed: "You ladies have been under the impression that I am opposed to public education. I trust that you have discovered that this is not true." In fact, several legislators lost their seats when they incurred the wrath of the WEC, including Tom Tyler, the sponsor of a school board packing bill. By this time, the women's persistence and effectiveness as lobbyists had become clear. The *Southern Patriot* reported that the "Visits of the women to the Statehouse were reported to be 'driving the men out at the Legislature crazy.'"[87]

When Everett Tucker ran against Jim Brandon for the state legislature in 1964, the power of an emerging liberal coalition in Little Rock became evident. According to AFL-CIO president Bill Becker, Tucker's supporters "raised the race issue and distributed hate literature in the working class wards. They conducted the most vicious and vile campaign seen for many years in Pulaski County." In that literature, Tucker damned his opponent for having supported Blanche Evans, an African American woman, for the school board against moderate W. C. McDonald, a white man. In an ad paid for by the "Committee for Racial Peace," Tucker's supporters claimed Evans was "closely identified with the race extremists who . . . would, if they could, keep this community in a state of constant turmoil." Although the newspapers did not report Tucker's appeal to racism directly, they did print Brandon's remark at an AAUW forum that his opponent's speech was "of such a nature that I am surprised that he is not at [Alabama] Governor [George] Wallace's rally tonight." Despite the reluctance of the press to report critically on racism in local elections, Tucker's tactics backfired, offending many whites. Brandon won easily, revealing the perils of overt appeals to racism in Little Rock politics.[88]

Notwithstanding the WEC's persistent efforts to defeat the governor himself, the women's group could not bring about his political demise. For some women in the organization, removing him from power became an obsession. One woman was heard "comparing herself jestingly to Javert, Victor Hugo's detective who spent so much of his life in the dogged pursuit of Jean Valjean. She remembers clearly what she has against Orval Faubus" and vows, "I'm going to get him if it takes all my life." Various former leaders of the WEC would work hard on the campaign of Republican Winthrop Rockefeller, who finally ended Faubus's long gubernatorial tenure in 1966. Until then, a number of factors had supported Faubus: the power of eastern Arkansas planters in state politics, the governor's willingness to offer the planters his support for segregation in exchange for advancing his other goals for the state, the effective disfranchisement of African Americans in the rural areas of Arkansas, and Faubus's own increasing recourse to race baiting. The race baiting, however, rang the death knell for any national political ambitions the governor may have harbored.[89]

As segregationist leaders' enthusiasm for the enactment of more laws to oppose federally mandated segregation abated, the *Arkansas Gazette* assessed the costs and consequences of the seventeen acts passed in the 1958 special session of the state legislature. According to its 1961 tally, three of the acts had been declared unconstitutional, four were still in the courts, one had been repealed, three had been used sparingly, and two were routine measures. The costs were $167,017 in appropriated funds that were merely a part of "the enormous economic cost to Little Rock of that year of disrupted education, several remaining laws of doubtful constitutionality, the bitter memories and the bad name." The accounting did not include the costs of defending in court laws whose constitutionality was suspect.[90]

The early to mid-1960s witnessed subtle but significant shifts in black political consciousness and organization in Arkansas and Little Rock: the erosion of NAACP membership and leadership in the community; the formation of new organizations, including the Student Non-Violent Co-ordinating Committee (SNCC); and the internal strife made it difficult to develop cohesive and effective alliances. Act 10, which required educators to reveal their membership in political and civic groups, had an especially harmful effect on the NAACP, which lost many members in Arkansas, most of them public school teachers who were afraid they would lose their jobs if they continued their involvement in the organization. Competition between the NAACP and SNCC for the mantle of leadership and for the allegiance of young African Americans became heated and impeded community cooperation.[91]

In the fall of 1960, a group of young male professionals formed the Council on Community Affairs (CCA) to coordinate the activities of the various African American organizations and to provide leadership in the ongoing struggle to desegregate Little Rock schools. Its leaders sought to operate independently from the politics of white pressure and patronage that had characterized the relationship of black political leaders to Little Rock's establishment in the past. The CCA emulated the tactics of the WEC and the League of Women Voters in interviewing candidates to elected office regarding their positions, identifying citizens who supported their candidates' positions, and getting out the vote for their candidates. They phoned, ran sweeps through the housing projects on election day, and made sure voters had a ride to the polls. According to black activist Ozell Sutton, "It was that coming together of liberals, blacks and unions that really brought the change that was made in this city and in this state." Several women from the WEC, including Adolphine Terry and Pat House, worked with the CCA in these activities.[92]

In March 1960, students at Philander Smith College organized sit-ins in downtown Little Rock to force the desegregation of business facilities. Authorities responded forcefully, arresting and convicting the demonstrators under a variety of new state laws passed in the late 1950s. Speedy trials and heavy fines and sentences made dissent quite costly. When students appealed their convictions, the judge handed out stiffer penalties. The students resumed their protests in the fall of 1962.[93]

The CCA worked with the student demonstrators, initiating discussions with white business leaders and joining with SNCC representatives in meetings with the local power structure. Fearful that adverse publicity would attend continuing demonstrations, business leaders headed by banker James Penick had organized the Downtown Negotiating Committee in late 1962. Over time, the businessmen's conviction that resistance to desegregation would ultimately prove futile and might extort substantial costs to them promoted their reluctant acquiescence in a plan to provide equal access to public accommodations in Little Rock's central business district.[94]

Black activists' growing autonomy from white sponsors and white officeholders in this period did not reflect a politics of separatism. CCA leader Dr. W. H. Townsend worked with various white and interracial organizations, including the Arkansas Council on Human Relations. He credited the latter with facilitating new interracial communication that was important to political collaborations "because there were a lot of walls built up on both [sides] that were artificial and unrealistic and all that was needed was coming together" to talk. These collaborations would be fraught with racial tension and conflicts over priorities and tactics, especially in the early years, and were shadowed by the enduring power of the business elite in Little Rock.[95]

By 1962, some WEC board members had concluded "that the 'king makers' in the industrial community should not be permitted to make selections for the entire city," and that the WEC should consider running its own candidates for the school board. Incumbent school board president Everett Tucker had indicated that he would step down if the "right" candidate offered to run. So Sara Murphy decided to throw her hat in the ring for the seat occupied by Tucker. After he met with Murphy, who did not reveal her affiliation with the WEC, Tucker announced his decision to run for another term. He did so despite advice from some powerful moderate men, including Hugh Patterson and Gaston Williamson, that he step aside.

Murphy and others in the WEC believed that Tucker, who was the industrial development manager for the Little Rock Chamber of Commerce, was only representing economic interests and doing nothing to create meaningful change. Indicating displeasure at being unpaid and disempowered workers for the power structure, the women of the WEC noted that Tucker "was elected, not by his own efforts, but by a tremendous amount of hard work by any number of leaders better qualified to represent [Little Rock's] viewpoint." Moreover, Tucker had supported "hopeless but expensive" lawsuits so that he could claim he was forced into desegregation by the federal government. In short, the WEC claimed, his "actions had not been in accord with the general thinking of our Board for a peaceful and progressing school system."[96]

According to Murphy, the local business community galvanized into action to defeat her candidacy. At a meeting of businessmen supporting Tucker, one of the men reportedly said, "We've got a fire and we've got to put it out." To douse the fire, Tucker and his supporters, who included many of the school board members elected with the assistance of the WEC, used their financial clout and exploited the tensions between the all-white WEC membership and the black community. The strategy was particularly effective given the WEC's refusal to support the candidacy of Dr. M. A. Jackson, an African American, to the school board because it had already promised support to his opponent. The tactics of Tucker's allies were particularly cynical, given that Tucker used racial epithets and freely expressed his segregationist views in private conversations. An oral history given by Tucker in the early 1970s confirms his racist views: "But even if I had been in favor of segregation to the bitter end, I would have had to say we've got to have the schools open, if it takes having some nigger children admitted that's what we have to do to get the schools open." Despite ads signed by prominent black leaders urging her election, Murphy lost the black vote and the election.[97]

During the campaign, the *Arkansas Gazette* defended Murphy's decision to run against criticism coming from "some businessmen who are bitter about the WEC's endorsement of the opponent of School Board President Everett Tucker." Noting that the women's organization had been "very effective," the editorial asserted that its "outspoken stands have made the WEC a villainess at the Statehouse and may have caused some more conservative 'moderates' to think they would like to see the WEC broken." After mentioning that Tucker had thrown his hat in the ring very late, the editorial concluded, "if the board of the WEC felt that Mrs. Murphy had the better qualifications or that a woman ought to be on the board, then it had every right to endorse her."[98]

African American candidates ran for the school board and Board of City Managers positions in 1962 and 1963, but failed to win even when "moderate" white men divided on their candidates. When Blanche Evans ran for the school board in 1963, she was a member of the WEC executive board and easily secured its support for her candidacy. She came within two thousand votes of unseating moderate W. C. McDonald. Her candidacy and relatively strong showing symbolized the growing alliance between African Americans and many white women in the WEC.[99]

Sara Murphy's earlier decision to run for the school board indicated how far the WEC had come since the fall of 1958, when it assisted the traditional male leadership in recruiting a "businessmen's slate" to run for the board. From the outset, the business elite's terms for partnership with the WEC required the invisibility and subordination of the women. Ironically, the activist women had developed the electoral base for moderate white male success in Little Rock politics but the men they had empowered saw them as tainted by their open advocacy for shared moderate goals. Murphy's defeat suggests the obstacles middle-class white women faced when they tried to exercise political power directly.[100]

The contested, limited, and local power of the WEC was insufficient to implement all the policies its leadership espoused. It exerted little influence over national policymakers, although it sometimes benefited from timely federal court decisions. The Little Rock School Board continued to drag its feet on desegregation, despite pressures from the WEC and the black community to move beyond token integration. The WEC's inability to unseat moderates who dominated the school board after the 1959 recall election and its continuing strained relations with Little Rock business leadership limited women's influence over school policies. Even at the local level, therefore, white women's ability to translate activism into power was limited, particularly when they sought to redefine race relations. Finally, in November 1963, with the crisis over closed schools apparently over and the leadership deeply divided over issues and candidates, the WEC folded.[101]

Disputes between the WEC and local business leaders had politicized many WEC activists after 1958. Initially intent on encouraging and enabling the traditional male elite to solve the problem of closed schools, many WEC members ultimately extended their political vision to encompass improved race relations and the conviction that blacks had to claim a larger public role in the community. In a 1960 letter to a public schools

226CHAPTERSIX

activist in Atlanta, Billie Wilson described an interracial meeting of the Conference on Community Unity (CCU) she had attended with her husband as "one of the most rewarding experiences of our lives." She compared the blacks in the CCU to the politicians they were opposing and concluded that the state was ill served by "overlooking well educated, clear thinking, qualified tax-payers who happen to have a dark skin color." She further noted:

> Of course this is the type of thing I have felt all along we had failed to do and one the W.E.C. has urged the city fathers, the Chamber of Commerce and any other interested group to do. No one would touch it. It is all very strange as I am afraid I was definitely a moderate until the segregationists pushed me too far—I guess I am now definitely a liberal.[102]

Women in the WEC leadership also participated in CCU meetings during this period. Initiated by the Arkansas Human Rights Council in association with American Friends Service Committee representative Thelma Babbitt, the CCU received substantial support from a loose coalition of African American activists, liberal whites, and religious leaders. The CCU was designed to encourage better communication across racial divides and to change public discourse on race and the schools. Its meetings were not usually linked directly to politics. In late 1960, however, CCU marshaled its religious leaders and used religious ideals to criticize the local school board publicly for its use of pupil placement policies to limit desegregation to a few token blacks in otherwise all-white schools. The school board responded with injured indignation at the suggestion that it had not acted in a moral and impartial fashion. It suggested that the religious leaders, though well intentioned, did not fully understand the situation and in their focus on African American students had not taken into account the best interests of whites who attended Little Rock schools. The CCU had little immediate effect on local politics. As Susan Lynn has argued, its primary legacy was "to cement an alliance between [liberal] whites and the black community that would remain in place when the civil rights revolution swept through Little Rock in the early 1960s."[103]

At the same time, the organization of the WEC as a woman-only movement and its liberal leadership had helped to push many of its members to a more critical stance regarding the values and prerogatives of the local business elite and to the perils of racial division. Many of the women continued to participate in local and state politics long after the WEC disbanded in 1963. Moreover, their tense alliance with African American leaders in the early 1960s solidified once blacks developed their own political organizations and could find their own voice in Arkansas politics. Ironically, the more solid alliance between politicized white middle-class women and African American leaders was probably aided by the demise of the WEC, whose political caution and whites-only membership policy rankled many black leaders. National events—the passage of the 1964 Civil Rights Act and the 1965 Voting Rights Act—combined with a new political assertiveness by African Americans locally to offer new possibilities for the liberal alliance that the WEC helped to form in the years of the crisis over desegregation. The leadership of African Americans and (former) WEC women in the 1970s and 1980s sustained various forms of activism and may have helped to move politics in Arkansas in a more progressive direction than occurred in other southern states in this period.[104]

Despite the strength of this coalition, male business leaders retained their hold on the school board. Indeed, in 1968 Adolphine Terry complained to a friend that "under the leadership of the real estate people, who are usually wrong, we have chosen a reactionary school board and city administration—although we have just elected our first negro member of the City Board of Directors." In the following years, Little Rock experienced a pattern of white flight from the city, court-ordered busing, and the continuation of de facto segregation in Little Rock's schools. In short, by the 1970s Little Rock's school politics resembled those of the rest of the nation. A civic elite hostile to racial change and dedicated to the reproduction of its own power forged the path to that end.[105]

CONCLUSIONS

Little Rock and the Legacies of *Brown v. Board of Education*

> Together we look to the time when the citizens of this land
> will erase the shame of Little Rock, when the Constitution
> of the United States will embrace every man regardless of
> his color, when brotherhood will be more than a mere topic
> for an annual church sermon.
>
> —Daisy Bates[1]

Decades after the admission of African American students to Central High, black students and teachers who had been involved in the crisis over desegregation expressed disaffection with the poor quality of education African American children still received in Little Rock and the nation. In August 1987, Daisy Bates wrote to Elizabeth Huckaby that she was "truly unhappy about the condition of the Little Rock schools." She expressed her surprise and disappointment that school officials had yet to commit to "the quality of education for all children." In a 1987 interview Elizabeth Eckford wondered "What good does it do to desegregate the schools if they're only going to serve one or two classes of people?" Minnijean Brown Trickey worried in 1979 that desegregation had left too many blacks behind and had eroded the cultural traditions and strengths important for viable communities: "Were the changes that I helped bring about in the South all good for the blacks? Perhaps we blacks did lose something with integration, something of our traditions and culture. I don't know." Little Rock's black schools, which taught African American history, had nurtured in some students a sense of possibility and a culture of dissent from the ruling political and social system.[2]

As the reflections of these individuals suggest, the legacy of the *Brown* decision is contradictory. Some scholars note that the courage and moral strength of civil rights activists enabled the growth of an African American middle class, greater legal protection and social acceptance for nondiscriminatory employment practices, and the expansion of voting rights in the United States. The legacy they stress is the expansion of freedoms, rights, and opportunities for all Americans as a result of the postwar civil rights struggles. As Patricia Williams has stated, African Americans trusted in the idea of civil rights "so much and so hard that we gave them life where there was none before. We held onto them, put the hope of them into our wombs, and mothered them—not just the notion of them. We nurtured rights and gave rights life." Other scholars, however, have emphasized the persistence of racist ideas (often encoded in images and in discourses about crime, dependency, and sexuality), the poor quality of the still-segregated schools attended by most children of color, and the despair and deprivation engendered by widespread poverty in communities of color. Derrick Bell, for example, noted that while Americans celebrate the anniversaries of the demise of "separate but equal," they find that "the passwords for gaining judicial recognition of the still viable property right in being white include 'higher entrance scores,' 'seniority,' and 'neighborhood schools.'"[3]

Those passwords indicate the power of a neo-liberal ideology of "race neutrality" in contemporary American politics, law, and society. The ideology of "race neutral" law, however, was not created after the civil rights movement had passed its zenith, as some scholars assume. It was, in fact, given much of its contemporary form by southern moderates who wished to claim that they were complying with the Supreme Court's rulings against state-based racial segregation in the *Brown v. Board of Education* cases while working hard to evade them. The strategies, political rhetoric, and public policies fashioned by Little Rock's civic establishment in the years from 1954 to 1964 reveal with particular clarity the racial roots of "race-blind" legal theory and institutional practices in the postwar era. They also demonstrate the political and legal efficacy of a language of euphemism designed to sound inclusive without actually being so.[4]

Even before 1954, Little Rock's leaders fashioned housing, education, and other public policies designed to construct patterns of racial segregation that would enable them to evade the intent of future school desegregation decisions. The practice of minimizing public funding for African American education, evidenced in the partial privatization of costs for black schools and materials, continued in the desegregation era as less money was spent on Mann High School than on Hall High School and student–teacher ratios remained higher in black schools. The rhetoric of educational quality that school officials used in court partially masked their intent to safeguard a system of educational inequality based on class and race while claiming to comply with the rulings in *Brown v. Board of Education*. The courts' acceptance of this reasoning and their support for pupil placement laws demonstrated the symbiotic relationship between moderates' legal strategies and federal courts' institutionalization of ostensibly race neutral laws that operated in racially discriminatory ways.[5]

The political dynamics of the Little Rock crisis over desegregation disclose the centrality of the courts to American political culture and its system of social relations. In a political system in which the courts have the right of judicial review, legal action is political action, as all participants in the Arkansas school dilemma realized. The state government and local school boards in Arkansas spent scarce public funds defending ill-conceived laws and policies as they attempted to bury *Brown v. Board of Education* in a never-ending barrage of litigation. In the meantime, their schools remained woefully underfunded.

At the same time, black litigants and civil rights activists in Little Rock, along with the NAACP, pushed the courts to support a program of substantive compliance with *Brown*. Their persistence compelled the Warren Court to assert its authority adamantly in *Cooper v. Aaron* and brought the dilatory evasions of local school officials to the attention of federal judges and lawmakers. Their courtroom successes would reduce the options available to other southern communities as well as those of Little Rock officials. Ultimately, the U.S. Congress and the Supreme Court would decide that leaving the issue in the hands of southern moderates had resulted not in gradual compliance but in the flouting of federal authority and the denial of constitutionally protected rights. If federal court decisions and legislation had a significant effect on local outcomes in Arkansas and elsewhere in the nation, the actions of local activists also supported and motivated those decisions.[6]

The symbolic importance of Little Rock guaranteed that school politics there would be enacted under the gaze of the nation and the world. The small southern city had in fact become the "canary in the mine" for people on all sides of the school segregation issue. The rise of television and the culture of the visual made the images of the conflict critical to the formation of political consciousness locally, nationally, and internationally. Indeed, the Little Rock crisis reflected a new politics of visibility, perception, and accountability that resulted from the growing role of television in American culture. Although the meanings of exhortations to "Remember Little Rock" were subject to considerable dispute, they helped to set the terms of debate in the critical years leading up to the 1964 Civil Rights Act. Whether white southerners decided that they wanted to avoid federal troops at all cost or worked hard to keep northern capital flowing south or knowingly agreed to enroll in another "Lost Cause," they could not be oblivious to events in Little Rock and neither could federal officials.[7]

A reluctant warrior for federal authority, President Dwight D. Eisenhower equivocated on the propriety of the *Brown* decisions and worried about how to extricate his administration from an active and public role in the Little Rock crisis over desegregation. Meanwhile, his administration examined the broad issues raised by overt defiance of the federal courts in the South. As authorities in the Attorney General's office anticipated the Supreme Court decision in *Aaron v. Cooper* in September 1958, for example, they observed that in the past the federal courts had always been able to rely on "the entirely proper premise that the community itself will support adherence to the law" when they ordered remedies through equity procedures. Facing an unprecedented and systematic defiance of judicial authority in the South, Justice Department officials believed that the strength of the resistance there would require federal action whenever the courts requested it.[8]

No one feared further federal interventions more than Little Rock's business leaders, who desperately wanted both to maintain their dominance in local politics and to persuade companies to relocate their businesses to their city. Of necessity, they also were very aware of the political weight attached to school politics in their community. They could only sustain their economic and political power if they managed the volatile politics of race, gender, and class entailed by the issue of school desegregation sufficiently well to retain their local legitimacy and provide the social stability and open schools required by outside investors. This put them on a collision course with the arch segregationists and with African Americans.

Their most direct opposition came from African Americans committed to integration and willing to volunteer their children as racial pioneers. From the 1956 lawsuit brought by the local NAACP to their later challenges to segregationist laws and school board policies, Little Rock's blacks refused to be intimidated. White resistance to desegregation, whether from the Capital Citizens' Council and Mothers' League or from equivocating moderates, only increased their resolve. Despite the harassment endured by the students at Central High, African American citizens' support for desegregation remained strong in all social classes. In the first few years, Daisy Bates and the local NAACP worked, with mixed success, to keep the pressure on Little Rock's timorous school board and to protect the African American students in desegregating schools.[9]

In Little Rock and elsewhere, African Americans had almost no recourse except private litigation, coordinated and funded primarily by the NAACP, as the means to secure their constitutional rights. As University of Texas law professor Charles Alan Wright noted in 1958, this gave southern states every advantage. Then as now, lawsuits were very expensive and the NAACP's funds were "a pittance compared to what Southern legislatures [were] willing to appropriate from otherwise-impoverished state treasuries for the cause of preserving segregation." In Arkansas and elsewhere in the South, resisters relied heavily on state laws passed to support segregation and on a confusing welter of litigation and political maneuvering to provide legitimacy to their refusal to comply with federal court orders and to force African Americans to challenge an unending parade of segregation statutes.[10]

Over time, a new African American leadership emerged, more broadly based and committed to securing an independent voice and political base in Little Rock. This leadership moved from the behind-the-scenes political negotiations of blacks with local power brokers in the preceding decades to a strategy that also included autonomous political organizing and coalition building. In doing so, they worked with some activists in the Women's Emergency Committee and emulated the voter mobilization tactics of the women's organization. The uneasy relationship between the women activists and the African American leadership, especially in the early years, set limits on their effectiveness.[11]

At the same time, former WEC leaders continued to press the business elite regarding its racial politics. In December 1968, Adolphine Terry wrote to a friend complaining that "under the leadership of the real estate people, who are usually wrong, we have chosen a reactionary school board and city administration." A few months later, she wrote to business leaders William

McLean and Everett Tucker condemning the behind-the-scenes influence of realtor Billy Rector, whom she accused of block busting and steering: "his agents take [clients] to additions in the far west and assure them that 'there will never be a nigger in the schools your children will attend.'" Billy Rector's support for white flight, she stated, prompted "Billy's School Board" to oppose progressive school proposals in favor of a neighborhood school plan that served his business purposes and racial prejudices. Her letter to Tucker, the former head of the school board, combined praise for him with condemnation of Rector: "I can't understand why you follow Billy's lead. You have better brains, more . . . and better manners." The WEC founder ended her letter bitterly: "I cannot bear to see my town ruined by the stupidity (or is it the cupidity?) and indifference of its citizens."[12]

Tucker, who was a close friend of Rector, was not fooled by her flattery. He particularly took issue with Terry's description of Rector "as a throwback to the 19th century," claiming that her remark revealed "a complete lack of understanding and appreciation of what makes Little Rock move forward." He praised his friend as a leader who was "habitually in the forefront of all undertakings—civic, economic, cultural, education, social or whatever." He also defended Rector's remunerative business practice of racial steering by claiming that "the majority of home buyers insist on being as far removed as possible from the sort of chaos that has characterized integration at Central, West Side and other schools where the ratio of black to whites has escalated." Tucker, and many like him, continued to believe that progress required the retention of white supremacy. In justifying Rector's business practices, Tucker also reiterated the civic elite's longheld assumption that a large presence of African Americans in a school automatically led to declining quality of education. He did not entertain the view that local leaders bore any responsibility for white flight or for the inadequacies of black schools.[13]

Tucker's disagreements with Terry over the definition of progress and the politics of race also reiterated old gender disputes and demonstrated the enduring power of Little Rock's male elite. Their disagreements also revealed the ways that the structure of the WEC as a women-only organization had signified and deepened gender conflicts between many of its activists and the city's leaders. Despite the hesitant and conflict-ridden emergence of a more liberal coalition in the 1960s, moderate men managed to hold on to power in city and school politics. The institutional basis and the incentives for the businessmen's assiduous state-building activities, which were fully developed before the school crisis, survived the crisis and guarded the political strength of men into the future. The women's mobilization, based in a more local and situated sense of the connections between their personal interests and state policies, did not endure. In the end, the informal associational power deployed by the WEC could not counter the formal political and economic power wielded by men at all levels of government. They also could not match the civic elite's commitment to the goal of political dominance.[14]

Ironically, the political acumen and activism of the WEC enabled the male leadership to prevail when its power was most tenuous. The WEC enabled the male leadership because its members brought to politics a set of resources derived from their own class privilege: expertise, skill, a network of potential political allies, access to the political establishment, time, and money. The reputation of the women who participated and the mobilization strategies adopted by the organization gave the opposition to massive resistance a legitimacy in the white community that it otherwise would have lacked. The WEC provided a strong voice to those in Little Rock who were not willing to pay the costs entailed in defiance of the federal courts: closed schools, public disorder, and lost business. The demise of the WEC, however, meant that the ability of middle-class white women to challenge "business as usual" in local politics was diminished.

Whatever private ideals motivated the WEC's leaders, they compromised them too fundamentally and for too long to offer a meaningful alternative to the power of the male elite. Their willingness to defer to the segregationist convictions of many of their own members and to the political wishes of male business leaders made them poor allies for African Americans seeking racial justice. Ultimately, WEC leaders acted from a class-based conviction that the "better classes" should hold power and that public education should particularly serve the needs of college-bound students. Their elitism also fueled the class resentments of their working-class segregationist adversaries.

For its part, the Mothers' League of Central High School sought to achieve many of the same goals—political legitimacy and electoral clout—

for the staunch segregationists that the WEC did for the moderates. The relatively small number of working-class women who participated in the Mothers' League, however, could not mobilize the kind of resources their adversaries in the WEC had. As working mothers, they had less time for political action. As a result, the Mothers' League worked primarily to encourage student resistance at Central High School and to arouse the feeling in white students and parents that they were being victimized by African Americans, the federal government, and local leaders. They assumed that voters, most of whom shared their segregationist sentiments, would express those values and their anger at the polls. The League's decision to focus more on mobilizing resentment than on mobilizing voters, however, limited its political reach, as did its inability to understand the importance of public schools to many Little Rock voters.

At the same time, the Mother's League influenced events in Little Rock out of proportion to its numbers and helped to keep the moderates in a state of panic and fear through most of the crisis. It mobilized children as political actors and politicized their treatment when they were disciplined by school administrators so effectively that the moderates backed off from effective protection for the African American students. By serving as symbols of white victimization and as political actors who generated racial and sexual fears, mistrust of local elites, and a sense of virtuous rage, the members of the Mothers' League kept the focus on race as the key issue in school politics and put the moderates on the defensive. The moderates embraced the politics of extreme caution even more fervently in the face of the resistance generated by the Mothers' League.

Gender affected massive resistance, and the social relations in which resistance was embedded, in complex ways. It is hard to say whether the working-class roots of massive resistance in Little Rock made the presence and activism of women more necessary to segregationists' attempts to construct a credible and peaceable politics of resistance, but it seems likely. Segregationists used women to claim respectability and nonviolence for a movement that relied on the idea of a spontaneous and potentially violent popular racism, and thus used women to justify state resistance to federal court orders. Symbolically, women also stood in as archetypal victims, enabling men to enact the protector role while obscuring their own inability as men to defend either their personal or state sovereignty. The 1959 bombings, however, radically reduced the credibility of the claims by the Mothers' League and the Capital Citizens' Council that the resistance movement represented a respectable and nonviolent "Christian" movement.

The opposition of local elites to the arch segregationists' search for power made the massive resistance movement more dependent on state government and in particular on Governor Orval Faubus. As Sara Diamond has commented, success in "'massive resistance' would require the development of organizations committed to more respectable tactics and facilitated, not repressed, by local elites." For his part, Faubus acted to pressure Little Rock's business interests so that they put more effort into attempts to evade compliance than to support it. Many of the governor's actions, from using the National Guard to impede desegregation to closing the schools, put him at odds with the development goals of Little Rock's business leaders. Ultimately, the federal courts invalidated Faubus's most important resistance legislation and Little Rock voters favored open schools, thus undermining the governor's claims that he could provide publicly supported and segregated schools and that he represented majority sentiment (at least in Little Rock).[15]

The actions of the segregationists in Little Rock put the Supreme Court decision in *Brown II* to its most important test. Their resistance to the federal mandate to desegregate public schools threatened the political power of the business elite. The harassment campaign they orchestrated at Central High School disrupted education for many students. Both factors prompted the school board to resist pressures from the WEC and from African Americans to move more rapidly and systematically toward desegregation. Instead, the school board filed a lawsuit asking for a lengthy delay in the implementation of desegregation. The resulting decision in *Cooper v. Aaron* marked the Supreme Court's first expression of anger at southern officials for evading the spirit and intent of the 1954 decision in *Brown v. Board of Education*.[16]

That did not mean, however, that the federal courts had moved away from their own efforts to give the South time and latitude to desegregate schools. In his 1956 decision, Judge John E. Miller implicitly incorporated the South's dual system of education into the standard for admitting students to schools on a "nonracial" basis. The open admission by School Superintendent Virgil Blossom that the Little Rock School Board planned to draw attendance lines on the basis of race received no notice in Miller's finding that the board's gradual plan for integration demonstrated that it had made a "prompt and reasonable start toward full compliance with the requirements of the law." During the hearing, Blossom contended that only socially homogeneous classrooms would provide progressive educators with "teachable" students. The Little Rock school superintendent had implicitly converted racial segregation in schools from an unconstitutional policy into a tool necessary for educational progress. By accepting his reasoning, Miller paved the legal path for systematic resistance to meaningful racial change. The history of the school board's actions reveals institutional racism to be the intentional result of local choices endorsed by federal court decisions.[17]

When the U.S. Supreme Court upheld state placement laws in 1958, it gave the South a powerful tool for evasion and further incorporated race into the construction of "race-neutral law." In the 1958 decision in *Shuttlesworth v. Birmingham*, the Court sanctioned such pupil placement laws so long as they were applied in a race-neutral fashion. In fact, doing so was impossible. By design, African Americans occupied an inferior and racialized place in the so-called race-neutral domain crafted by such laws, which had incorporated racial prejudices into their fundamental premises and practices. As Derrick Bell has perceptively concluded, the Court's recourse to an abstract formalism in school decisions sought to undo *Plessy* without addressing the profound consequences of segregation in American political culture and race relations. This legal formalism implicitly constructed American law as "that which fixes racism rather than that which participates in its consolidation."[18]

In the Little Rock case, the NAACP fought the legal formalism and racial subtexts implicit in the school board's policies, particularly in regard to pupil placement laws and practices and in the federal courts' approach to desegregation. Its briefs detailed the racist intentions, methods, and outcomes of the placement law and of those who implemented it. Although the legal position of the NAACP was premised on formal equality under the law, federal court decisions in cases like *Shuttlesworth*, not the NAACP's position, built southern evasion of full integration on a foundation of legal formalism that skillfully avoided compliance with the spirit and intent of the law. Throughout the desegregation process, Little Rock school officials used pupil placement laws as an overt mechanism of discrimination. They continued to do so even after a 1961 court decision ordering them to desist. Weak oversight of the implementation of desegregation by federal

courts, in Little Rock and elsewhere, and the acceptance of unsubstantiated claims of race neutrality left an ambiguous legacy for the future.

Other private and government institutions also upheld practices that
sustained racial and other inequalities. The custodians of the nation's urban
growth machines, including the businessmen who ran Little Rock, embraced state-mandated, publicly funded urban renewal policies as a means
to strengthen residential segregation and to claim city spaces for developers
and other business interests. Industrial recruiters in the South marketed
local workers' tractability and poverty upheld with the aid of state laws
designed to impede unionization and subsidize corporate moves to their
cities. Employers worked hard to ensure that, until 1964, their racial and
other forms of job discrimination were perfectly legal.[19]

The New South dream of new industrial jobs to cure the region's poverty was surprisingly vague. Its architects did not discuss publicly the de-
mographics of the labor force, the effects of different kinds of industries
on opportunity structures, or the likelihood that a low wage development
strategy would simply recreate poverty in an urban form. As a result, the
new industrial jobs created in Little Rock, like those throughout the
South, went almost entirely to whites. In 1960, African Americans, who
were 25 percent of the city's workers, made up 15.6 percent of craftsmen,
operatives, and driver positions. In Arkansas, black median income went
from 43.6 percent of white median income in 1949 to 39.7 percent in
1959.[20]

Ultimately, the political agenda embraced by Little Rock's traditional
civic elite lacked moral content, evaded the issue of race, and fueled resistance from residents who saw federal authority as a threat to their dignity
and independence. The business leaders' insistence that they be forced to
desegregate through publicly visible legal actions so that (they hoped) they
themselves would not be held personally accountable for desegregation
extorted huge costs in litigation, social conflict, and in a politics of delay
that ultimately contributed to "white flight." Business leaders embraced an
ideology that conflated their power and economic well being with the public good and thus sanctioned their exclusionary, secretive, and self-interested
political agenda. Their commitment to an ideology of progress grounded in
laissez-faire professions, government subsidies to business, uncontested employer power over workers, and expectations of political deference from all
others in the community foreshadowed and helped to construct the neo-
liberal political order that followed.

In the final analysis, the study of the Little Rock desegregation impasse and its aftermath is fraught with irony. A moderate governor of Arkansas, Orval Faubus, fought to maintain segregation (and his political career) against a president whose views on race were, at that time, more conservative than his own. It was also true that Faubus's moderate opponents in Little Rock often differed but little with him on issues of race. Their political interests, however, put them on opposite sides on virtually all matters related to the schools, including the need for at least a minimal compliance with federal court orders to desegregate. Little Rock's moderates, moreover, were almost as busy as the arch segregationists in the pursuit of expensive and fruitless litigation designed to defer or deny desegregation. Together, they pioneered the conservative abuse of the courts to undermine, attenuate, and delay the effects of progressive laws and court decisions.

For their part, segregationist men and women deployed a moral discourse of sexualized racial danger that derived equally from racial prejudice, class anxieties, fundamentalist religious teachings, and the "moral panic" they experienced with changes in postwar social mores. Their anxieties regarding their moral status intensified as some of Little Rock's white high school girls, like many across the nation, dropped out of school because they were pregnant. Sammie Dean Parker, the white student who had tried hard to stage the racial threat her elders associated with school integration, married an appropriate white suitor at the age of eighteen and ended up as a battered wife. In the 1950s, young white women's sexual reputations and physical safety were more threatened by white men than by men of any other race. As parents (particularly fathers) fought to retain control of their daughters' sexuality, they used race to express their sense of disempowerment while representing their daughters as innocent victims rather than as potentially defiant sexual agents. An examination of sexual politics in white families reveals the displacements and evasions at work in fashioning the sense of threat so central to the racial crisis.[21]

Having invested their families' moral integrity and their own dignity in the fight against desegregation, segregationists saw Little Rock's business establishment as their class enemy in a racial war. For segregationists, the idea that their children could be forced to attend school with African Americans reflected the local elite's disdain for the working class and their lack of power in city politics. Little Rock's arch segregationists also believed that the admission of any blacks to "their" high school portended moral decline as the civic elite chose them to be "sacrificed" to desegregation.[22]

Wedded to a political culture of defiance and resentment, the segregationists' anger and religious zeal inclined them to serious miscalculations
throughout the crisis. Their missteps, which included the threat and use of
violence, the teacher purge, and the closing of the schools, alienated voters,
who came to see their cause as disreputable or socially dangerous. Their
actions, however, derived directly from the emotional culture and the gendered racial and religious groundings of their movement. Committed to a
binary moral universe and a politics of righteous retribution, they brooked
no compromise with those who stood in their way. Their politics of reprisal
represented not only a strategic method; it also expressed the anger and
vengeance at the heart of their political culture. Although segregationist
leaders' refusal to condemn those responsible for the 1959 bombings harmed
their cause, it also reflected a deep loyalty to their partisans occasioned by
shared political zeal and common religious affiliations.

Segregationists and moderates alike went from claiming in the 1950s
that laws were inadequate as a means to racial change because they could
not change private feelings and actions to a fervent embrace of law as the
only domain that had to change in order to create racial justice. The two
positions were not that far apart in their social vision, as the development
of a new "race-neutral" law covertly incorporated most of the racial assumptions and discriminatory practices shared by the South's arch segregationists and moderates. The legacies of 1950s moderate successes in foster-
ing delay in desegregation while touting tokenism in school integration
ultimately enabled the creation of white flight and of private schools that
allowed white middle-class parents to isolate their children from working-
class and minority children. [23]

The marriage of the religious fundamentalism embraced by the arch
segregationists and the capitalist fundamentalism embraced by male moderates ultimately paved the way for the formation of the New Right. Ironically, the path to success for the New Right was steeper in Arkansas, where
the mobilization of white middle-class women and African Americans left
a successful oppositional legacy that endured for a generation. Thereafter,
questions of economic inequities and political exclusions receded to the
political margins as public discussions of morality came to center almost
exclusively on religion, gender, and sexuality.

Increasingly, any government action beyond the enactment of "race-
neutral" laws, especially anything labeled affirmative action, came to be

denounced as an un-American "reverse" discrimination. Indeed, "race neutrality" replaced racial justice in public discourse and as the normative standard for private institutions as well as public policies. The focus on abstract law serves conservative ideological purposes by touting the values of a now "race-neutral" culture. Conservative distaste for the actual enforcement of civil rights laws, especially Title VII of the 1964 Civil Rights Act, belies the profession that changing laws eliminates discriminatory practices. In most cases, the law proves to be a useful tool only when determined litigants, who also happen to be fortunate in the lawyers, bureaucrats, juries, and judges associated with their cases, persist in seeking justice.[24]

Despite this, white Americans' sense of lost rights and opportunities has fueled the backlash against African Americans and those politicians perceived to be their advocates. This backlash has targeted successful blacks (who are denounced as undeserving beneficiaries of affirmative action) as well as unsuccessful blacks (who are viewed as parasitic dependents living off of welfare). As Beth Roy has brilliantly shown, white Americans use race to explain their failure to realize the American dream in part because they lack a vocabulary for discussing class or critiquing corporate practices and are unwilling to jettison their belief in an ideology of individualism. Race, which whites have deployed for a very long time as a comforting explanation for their fears and disappointments, continues to serve that function despite and because of the civil rights gains of the 1960s. As Roy notes, "Concepts of race are deeply imbedded in American culture, constituting a language that works somehow to explain the anomalies created by our classed classlessness." Racism, indeed, allows whites to communicate a sense of oppression and powerlessness "that somehow goes unexpressed in other forms."[25]

By centering different actors and examining documents in a new light, this study seeks to illuminate the political and ideological conflicts that shaped the politics of race and schools at the local and national levels in the decade after the *Brown* decisions. In Little Rock, those struggles occurred within and among groups that were neither homogeneous nor clearly bounded from one another. Their relationships were marked by opposition to and dependence on each other, shared aims (often unacknowledged), and bitter differences. Arch segregationists and moderates alike resented the federal government and generally supported segregation. They differed profoundly, however, on the priority given to segregation in their political goals. The moderates denounced the NAACP as "extremist" but relied on it to get the school closing laws declared unconstitutional and on black voters to secure electoral success for moderates. They won over black voters by relying on the likelihood that the threats posed by arch segregationists would persuade blacks to accept moderate candidates as the lesser of two evils.

How did gender matter in all of this? White men from both classes experienced cognitive dissonance when their experiences of political limitation and subordination clashed with highly gendered expectations of political efficacy. White male moderates worried that they had been unmanned by an authoritarian populism embodied by Orval Faubus and by the power of a remote and inaccessible federal government. At the same time, segregationist men worried about their subordination to a dictatorial federal government in alliance with local elites. They also tried to retain white supremacy as a talisman against lost family powers and economic uncertainties.

White women activists also faced gendered dilemmas as they mobilized politically, changed political discourses, and threatened conventional power arrangements. Both the Mothers' League of Central High School and the Women's Emergency Committee claimed to be acting in the best interests of children, thus revealing the power of gender in their political values and in their performance of a citizenship gendered as feminine. Class differences between the two women's organizations affected the emotional culture of their movements, their resources, political ideologies, and political efficacy. Ultimately, those disparities meant defeat for the segregationists in local elections as the WEC could deliver the vote much more effectively than the Mothers' League.

The WEC, by contrast, focused particularly on shifting public discourse to the issue of open schools and on strategies to maximize voter turnout and to secure the support of the business elite for their position. Behind the scenes, its leaders also sought to change the racial attitudes of white women at the same time that it promoted interracial interactions only outside the WEC. Moreover, WEC leaders brought to politics a set of resources that derived from their own class and race privilege: expertise, skill, a network of potential political allies created by the long history of civic activism many members brought to the new cause, the ability to hire African American women at low wages to do their domestic work, some access to the political establishment, and money to use on behalf of the WEC. The difficulties of their relationships with African Americans and the class divide that separated these women from many working-class people set important limits to their ability to forge an effective coalition of dissidents.

Despite the political clout that they wielded by the early 1960s, WEC leaders lacked the internal cohesion or independent resources to contest directly the "king makers" of Little Rock, however fervently some of them wished to do so. However much they appreciated the assistance of the WEC, business leaders feared the political priorities of its leaders and tried to direct the organization's activism solely to goals defined by male leaders. Nonetheless, moderate control of local government in the key years of the crisis over desegregation derived directly from the activism, resources, and political acumen of WEC members.

The fate of women who ran in school board elections after the disorders of September 1957 reveals the means by which men managed to keep a monopoly on political offices in a period of significant political mobilization by women. Women candidates from each class faced opposition not only from their ideological opponents but also from men who ostensibly embraced their general position but nonetheless ran directly against them. Even when the votes of their constituencies were not divided, women contenders consistently lost their races in elections to the school board, thus reflecting the sexism of some Little Rock voters. The support of the business establishment for Everett Tucker's deceptive and corrupt 1962 campaign against Sara Murphy revealed the degree to which gendered differences in material interests, political ideologies, political resources, and norms about civic culture shaped electoral outcomes.[26]

Ironically, the outcomes of the disputes in Little Rock would sow the seeds for both the civil rights revolutions that culminated in the 1960s and 1970s and the counterrevolution that began gathering strength at the same time. Some Little Rock activists, particularly African Americans and white middle-class women, found themselves changed by their participation in the electoral process. They moved into civil rights, feminist, and educational activism, formed important alliances, and sought broad changes in American society and culture. The political mobilization of a religious identity and a rhetoric centered on sexuality pioneered by the arch segregationists in Little Rock and elsewhere would resurface at the center of

New Right politics in the 1970s and 1980s. The desire to capture the state so that it would enforce religiously sanctioned social inequalities would achieve a surprising legitimacy in the following half century, fueled in part by an anxiety over the socialization of children in a time when traditional ideas about sexuality and gender were changing. The moral fears engendered in the New Right were closely related to those expressed in the massive resistance movement to desegregation. The encoding of racism in new legal and political ideologies forged by the South's moderates as they fought racial change would endure even longer than Little Rock's school desegregation case, which was still active in the 1990s.[27]

America's culture wars have deep and densely entangled historical roots. Exploring their connections to the politics of race and schools in the decade after the *Brown* decisions illuminates the centrality of education to the contested social visions of Americans, the inadequacies of legal formalism as a means to end social and political inequalities, and the enduring significance of questions of class, gender, and sexuality in American politics. In Little Rock as elsewhere, race was not and is not a singular social relation disconnected from others. Yet the power of racial thinking evident in its school crisis and its institutional practices typified the response to the challenge of *Brown v. Board of Education* not only in the South but in the nation. Ultimately, Little Rock became the nation's story.

Abbreviations

ACHR	Papers of the Arkansas Council on Human Relations
AHC	Arkansas History Commission
AS	Alphabetical Subseries
AWF	Ann Whiteman File
Bates Papers	Daisy Bates Papers
Brown Papers	Papers of Robert Brown
Cartwright Papers	Papers of the Rev. Colbert S. Cartwright
CF	Classified File
CUOHP	Columbia University Oral History Project
DC	Daily Correspondence
DDE	Papers of Dwight D. Eisenhower
DDED	DDE Diary Series
DDEL	Dwight D. Eisenhower Library, Abilene, Kansas
EFM Diary	Diary of E. Frederic Morrow
EP Huckaby Papers	Elizabeth Paisley Huckaby Papers
FBI	Little Rock Central High Integration Crisis, Federal Bureau of Investigation Records, Investigative Reports, 1957
GF	General File
H. Ashmore Papers	Papers of Harry Ashmore
Hays Papers	Papers of L. Brooks Hays
Johnson Papers	Papers of Jim Johnson
League Papers	Records of the League of Women Voters of Arkansas

LC   Library of Congress

LRHA   Little Rock Housing Authority Papers

LRSB   Records of the Little Rock School Board

Morrow Papers   Papers of E. Frederic Morrow

Morrow–MS Papers   Papers of E. Frederic Morrow re *Black Man in the White House, 1952–1963*

Murphy Papers   Papers of Sara Murphy

NA   National Archives

NAACP Papers   Papers of the National Association for the Advancement of Colored People

OF   Official File

OSS   Office of the Staff Secretary

Powell Papers   Velma and J. O. Powell Collection

PPUS   Papers as President of the United States

Rogers Papers   William P. Rogers Papers

SHSW   State Historical Society of Wisconsin

SS   Subject Series

Terry Papers   Fletcher–Terry Papers

Thomas Papers   Papers of Herbert Thomas

UAF   University of Arkansas–Fayetteville

UALR   University of Little Rock Archives and Special Collections, UALR Library

UCSB   University of California at Santa Barbara

WEC   Papers of the Women's Emergency Committee

White Papers   Files of W. Wilson White, Assistant Attorney General, Civil Rights Division, 1958–1959, Record Group 60

WHO   White House Office

Williams Papers   Papers of Grainger Williams

WPR   William P. Rogers: Papers, 1938–1962

Notes

INTRODUCTION: NOT HERE, NOT NOW, NOT US

1. Virgil T. Blossom, *It Has Happened Here* (New York: Harper & Brothers, 1959), p. 4.

2. Interview with Wesley Pruden by John Luter, December 28, 1970, Columbia University Oral History Project [hereafter cited as CUOHP], OH-264, Dwight D. Eisenhower Library, Abilene, Kansas [hereafter cited as DDEL].

3. Daisy Bates, *The Long Shadow of Little Rock: A Memoir* (New York: David McKay Company, Inc., 1962), p. 73.

4. Bates, *The Long Shadow of Little Rock*, pp. 65–71; Grif Stockley, *Daisy Bates: Civil Rights Crusader from Arkansas* (Jackson: University Press of Mississippi, 2005), p. 123.

5. *Arkansas Gazette*, September 5, 8, 1957; *New York Times*, September 5, 1957; *Time*, September 16, 1957; FBI, Interviews with Carlotta Walls, Elizabeth Eckford, Ernest Green, Minnie Jean [*sic*] Brown, Gloria Ray, Jefferson Thomas, Terrence Roberts, and Thelma Mothershed, September 4, 1957, FBI, Box 1, UALR Archives and Special Collections, UALR Library, University of Arkansas at Little Rock [hereafter cited as UALR]; Bates, *The Long Shadow of Little Rock*, pp. 64–76; Ben Fine, Audiotape, Daisy Bates Papers [hereafter cited as Bates Papers], University of Arkansas–Fayetteville [hereafter cited as UAF]. In a statement that she refused to sign, Melba Pattillo told the FBI that she did not attempt to go to school on September 4 because she feared for her safety. In her narrative of her year at Central, however, she describes arriving on the periphery of the crowd with her mother, witnessing the treatment of Eckford, and then barely escaping from a small group of whites who ran after her and her mother, brandishing a rope. FBI Interview, Melba Joyce Pattillo, September 5, 1957, FBI, Box 1, UALR; Melba Pattillo Beals, *Warriors Don't Cry: A Searing Memoir of the Battle to Integrate Little Rock's Central High* (New York: Pocket Books, 1994), pp. 46–51.

6. *Arkansas Gazette*, September 11, 1957; Mary L. Dudziak, *Cold War and Civil Rights: Race and the Image of American Democracy* (Princeton, NJ: Princeton

University Press, 2000), p. 120; Elizabeth Huckaby, 1957 Year Book, September 4, 1957, Elizabeth Paisley Huckaby Papers, MC 428 [hereafter cited as EP Huckaby Papers], UAF; "Notes on Pupils Involved, 1957–1958," EP Huckaby Papers, UALR; Beth Roy, *Bitters in the Honey: Tales of Hope and Disappointment across Divides of Race and Time* (Fayetteville: University of Arkansas Press, 1999), p. 184. Hazel Bryan Massery commented years later that with that picture she had become "the poster child for the hate generation, trapped in the image captured in the photograph, and I knew that my life was more than that moment." Will Counts, *A Life Is More Than a Moment: The Desegregation of Little Rock's Central High* (Bloomington: Indiana University Press, 1999), p. 41.

7. Huckaby, Year Book, September 3 and 4, 1957, EP Huckaby Papers, UAF, Box 1; Roy, *Bitters in the Honey*, pp. 171–196.

8. Numan V. Bartley, *The Rise of Massive Resistance: Race and Politics in the South during the 1950s* (Baton Rouge: Louisiana State University Press, 1969), pp. 127–47, 193, 212–21; David R. Goldfield, *Black, White, and Southern: Race Relations and Southern Culture 1940 to the Present* (Baton Rouge: Louisiana State University Press, 1990), pp. 62–116; William H. Chafe, *Civilities and Civil Rights: Greensboro, North Carolina, and the Black Struggle for Freedom* (New York: Oxford University Press, 1980); Adam Fairclough, *Race and Democracy: The Civil Rights Struggle in Louisiana, 1915–1972* (Athens: University of Georgia Press, 1999).

9. Fairclough, *Race and Democracy*, pp. 223, 235.

10. *Brown v. Board of Education et al.*, 347 U.S. 483 (1954); Harry S. Ashmore, *The Negro and the Schools* (Chapel Hill: University of North Carolina Press, 1954).

11. John A. Kirk, *Redefining the Color Line: Black Activism in Little Rock, Arkansas, 1940–1970* (Gainesville: University Press of Florida, 2002), p. 95; *Brown v. Board of Education* (*Brown II*), 349 U.S. 294 (1955).

12. Kirk, *Redefining the Color Line*, pp. 86{{n}}138.

13. Unlike the African Americans in Indianapolis studied by Richard Pierce, Little Rock's activist leaders did not turn down an NAACP request that they become a test case. Instead, they moved more quickly than the national organization desired and took the initiative in a way that literally changed history not only in Little Rock but nationally. Richard B. Pierce, *Polite Protest: The Political Economy of Race in Indianapolis, 1920–1970* (Bloomington: Indiana University Press, 2005), p. 21. As Tony Freyer has cogently noted in a recent book, the lawsuit filed by the local NAACP against the Little Rock School Board fostered the political mobilization of Little Rock's African Americans. Freyer also concludes that this reflected the "synergy" between litigation and activism that characterized the civil rights struggle in the South. Tony A. Freyer, *Little Rock on Trial:* Cooper v. Aaron *and*

School Desegregation (Lawrence: University of Kansas Press, 2007), especially pp. 4–5, 32–33, 213–14, 237.

14. Elizabeth Jacoway, "Understanding the Past: The Challenge of Little Rock," in Elizabeth Jacoway and C. Fred Williams, eds., *Understanding the Little Rock Crisis: An Exercise in Remembrance and Reconciliation* (Fayetteville: University of Arkansas Press, 1999), pp. 1–22. When arch segregationist Jim Johnson ran for governor in 1956, for example, he promised to "remove colored students from our colleges." Jim Johnson to A. B. Hanks, May 8, 1956, Papers of Jim Johnson [hereafter cited as Johnson Papers], Box 4, Arkansas History Commission [hereafter cited as AHC]. Other Arkansans, by contrast, liked to point to the integration of the state's colleges as a sign that whites could be trusted to approach racial matters in progressive ways. Orval Faubus, Speech, September 2, 1957, Faubus Papers, Box 496, UAF; Herbert L. Thomas, A Statement Prepared for a Conference of Protestant Church Leaders, May 13–14, 1958, Papers of Robert Brown [hereafter cited as Brown Papers], A-81, Box 1, UALR.

15. Sen. John Sparkman to the President, October 4, 1957, DDE, Central Files, Official File, Box 732, DDEL; Goldfield, *Black, White, and Southern*, p. 64; *Arkansas Gazette*, January 17, 1959; Robert R. Brown, *Bigger Than Little Rock* (Greenwich, CT: Seabury Press, 1958) p. 25; Osro Cobb, *Osro Cobb of Arkansas: Memoirs of Historical Significance*, ed. Carol Griffee (Little Rock: Rose Publishing Company, 1989), pp. 176, 226–34.

16. Sheldon Hackney, "Southern Violence," in Hugh Davis Graham and Ted Robert Gurr, *The History of Violence in America: Historical and Comparative Perspectives* (New York: Frederick A. Praeger, 1969), pp. 505–25, quote on p. 525.

17. M. Watson to editor of *Arkansas Gazette*, June 30, 1955; Brown, *Bigger Than Little Rock*, p. 20; Speech, September 2, 1957, Faubus Papers, Box 496, UAF. At critical moments in United States history, powerful whites have built unity among themselves at the expense of African Americans' freedoms, rights, and well being. Gary Nash, *The Forgotten Fifth: African Americans in the Age of Revolution* (Cambridge, MA: Harvard University Press, 2006); David W. Blight, *Race and Reunion: The Civil War in American Memory* (Cambridge, MA: Harvard University Press, 2001).

18. Laura McEnaney, *Civil Defense Begins at Home: Militarization Meets Everyday Life in the Fifties* (Princeton, NJ: Princeton University Press, 2000); Ruth Feldstein, *Motherhood in Black and White: Race and Sex in American Liberalism, 1930–1965* (Ithaca, NY: Cornell University Press, 2000); Elaine T. May, *Homeward Bound: American Families in the Cold War Era* (1988); Stephanie Coontz, *The Way We Never Were: American Families and the Nostalgia Trap* (1992); F. G. Friedmann, "Background for Little Rock," *The Humanist* (1958): 3–11; Pete Daniel, *Lost Rev-*

olutions: The South in the 1950s (Chapel Hill: University of North Carolina Press, 2000), pp.121–75; Phoebe Godfrey, "Bayonets, Brainwashing, and Bathrooms: The Discourse of Race, Gender, and Sexuality in the Desegregation of Little Rock's Central High," *Arkansas Historical Quarterly* 62 (Spring 2003): 42–67.

19. Goldfield, *Black, White, and Southern*, pp. 77–78. Teenagers contributed to the nation's rapid decline in age of first marriage. This occurred, according to historian Stephanie Coontz, because "Young people were not taught how to 'say no'—they were simply handed wedding rings." Coontz, *The Way We Never Were*, quote on p. 39; Beth L. Bailey, *From Front Porch to Back Seat: Courtship in Twentieth-Century America* (Baltimore: Johns Hopkins University Press, 1988); Rickie Solinger, *Wake Up, Little Susie* (New York: Routledge, 1992).

20. *Arkansas Democrat Gazette*, October 5, 1997, http://www.ardemgaz.com/ prev/central/effigy05.html, accessed on July 20, 2004.

21. Tony A. Freyer, *The Little Rock Crisis: A Constitutional Interpretation* (Westport, CT: Greenwood Press, 1984); Freyer, *Little Rock on Trial*.

22. Joseph Crespino, *In Search of Another Country: Mississippi and the Conservative Counterrevolution* (Princeton, NJ: Princeton University Press, 2007); Kevin M. Kruse, *White Flight: Atlanta and the Making of Modern Conservatism* (Princeton, NJ: Princeton University Press, 2005); and Matthew D. Lassiter, *The Silent Majority: Suburban Politics in the Sunbelt South* (Princeton, NJ: Princeton University Press, 2006).

23. Sandra S. Vance and Roy V. Scott, "Sam Walton and Wal-Mart Stores, Inc.: A Study in Modern Southern Entrepreneurship," *The Journal of Southern History* 58, no. 2 (May 1992): 231–52. On conservative law breaking in the domain of labor law, see Patricia Cayo Sexton, *The War on Labor and the Left: Understanding America's Unique Conservatism* (Boulder: Westview Press, 1991).

24. Jeannie M. Whayne, *A New Plantation South: Land, Labor, and Federal Favor in Twentieth-Century Arkansas* (Charlottesville: University Press of Virginia, 1996), pp. 219–34; S. Charles Bolton, "Turning Point: World War II and the Economic Development of Arkansas," *Arkansas Historical Quarterly* 61 (Summer 2002): 123–51; Bruce J. Schulman, *From Cotton Belt to Sunbelt: Federal Policy, Economic Development, and the Transformation of the South, 1938–1980* (Durham: Duke University Press, 1994); James C. Cobb, "The Lesson of Little Rock: Stability, Growth, and Change in the American South," in Jacoway and Williams, *Understanding the Little Rock Crisis*, pp. 107–22.

25. Jacoway, "Understanding the Past," p. 9; Irving J. Spitzberg, Jr., *Racial Politics in Little Rock* (New York: Garland Publishing, Inc., 1987).

26. Fliers from Industrial Department, Little Rock Chamber of Commerce, including Little Rock's Advantages for Manufacturing and Labor—The Foremost Consideration in Plant Location Today, Box 17, Blossom Papers, UAF.

27. Spitzberg, *Racial Politics in Little Rock*; Sara Alderman Murphy, *Breaking the Silence: Little Rock's Women's Emergency Committee to Open Our Schools, 1958–1963* (Fayetteville: University of Arkansas Press, 1997), pp. 58–60.

28. Deborah Kerfoot, "The Organization of Intimacy: Managerialism, Masculinity and the Masculine Subject," in Stephen M. Whitehead and Frank J. Barrett, eds., *The Masculinities Reader* (Cambridge, UK: Polity Press, 2001), pp. 233–52, quote on p. 234.

29. Daniel, *Lost Revolutions*, pp. 1, 251; C. Fred Williams, "Class: The Central Issue in the 1957 Little Rock School Crisis," *Arkansas Historical Quarterly* 56 (Autumn 1997): 341–44; David L. Chappell, "Editor's Introduction," *Arkansas Historical Quarterly* 56 (Autumn 1997): ix–xvi.

30. Virginia Scharff, *Twenty Thousand Roads: Women, Movement, and the West* (Berkeley and Los Angeles: University of California Press, 2003), p. 140; Schulman, *From Cotton Belt to Sunbelt*; Dudziak, *Cold War Civil Rights*.

31. Carl Abbott does note the importance of analyzing the role of diverse actors in forging the outcomes of desegregation in Norfolk, as does Andrew Lewis in his study of school politics in Charlottesville. Carl Abbott, "The Norfolk Business Community: The Crisis of Massive Resistance," in Jacoway and Colburn, *Southern Businessmen and Desegregation*, pp. 98–119. This study follows the advice of historians Matthew Lassiter and Andrew Lewis by examining the South's movement from massive resistance to token compliance in terms of "the political conflict and historical contingency which marked that moment in time," rather than seeing the transition as a "relatively seamless" process. Andrew B. Lewis, "Emergency Mothers: Basement Schools and the Preservation of Public Education in Charlottesville," in Matthew D. Lassiter and Andrew B. Lewis, eds., *The Moderates' Dilemma: Massive Resistance to School Desegregation in Virginia* (Charlottesville: University Press of Virginia, 1998), pp. 72–103; Matthew D. Lassiter and Andrew B. Lewis, "Massive Resistance Revisited: Virginia's White Moderates and the Byrd Organization," in Lassiter and Lewis, *The Moderates' Dilemma*, p. 4. For a review of the literature on businessmen and desegregation, see Tony Badger, "Review Essay: Segregation and the Southern Business Elite," *Journal of American Studies* 18 (1984): 105–9. I examine these issues more fully in Karen Anderson, "The Little Rock School Desegregation Crisis: Moderation and Social Conflict," *Journal of Southern History* 70 (August 2004): 603–36.

32. Stephen M. Whitehead, "Man: the Invisible Gendered Subject?" in Stephen M. Whitehead and Frank J. Barrett, eds., *The Masculinities Reader* (Cambridge, UK: Polity Press, 2001), pp. 351–68; Michael S. Kimmel, "Invisible Masculinity," in Michael S. Kimmel, ed., *The History of Men: Essays on the History of American and British Masculinities* (Albany: State University of New York Press, 2005), pp. 3–15, quote on p. 4; Anthony Rotundo, *American Manhood: Transfor-*

mations in Masculinity from the Revolution to the Modern Era (New York: Basic Books, 1993). As Kathleen Brown has noted, "A gender history of men may also help to deconstruct the false opposition of human (male) experience to the particular gendered experience of women." Kathleen M. Brown, "Brave New Worlds: Women's and Gender History," *William and Mary Quarterly* 50 (April 1993): 311–28, quote on p. 325. Despite the congruence between prescriptions for normative manhood and institutional practices in American history, these insights occupy a specialized by-way in American historical scholarship. As Rotundo noted, men's dominance in American institutions meant that "many of our institutions have men's needs and values built into their foundations, [and] many of our habits of thought were formed by male views at specific points in historical time." Rotundo, *American Manhood*, pp. 9, 196; Kristin Hoganson, "What's Gender Got to Do with It? Women and Foreign Relations History," *OAH Magazine of History* 19 (March 2005): 14–18.

33. Kimmel, "Invisible Masculinity," pp. 3–15; Joane Nagel, "Nation," in Michael S. Kimmel, Jeff Hearn, and R. W. Connell, eds., *Handbook of Studies on Men and Masculinities* (London: Sage Publications, 2005), pp. 397–413.

34. Brown, *Bigger Than Little Rock*, pp. 7–8; Kimmel, "Invisible Masculinity," pp. 3–15; Robert Dean, *Imperial Brotherhood: Gender and the Making of Cold War Foreign Policy* (Amherst: University of Massachusetts Press, 2001); Blossom, *It Has Happened Here*. Male moderates were particularly subject to the 1950s ideology of economic success. As C. Wright Mills observed in 1951, "If men are responsible for their success, they are also responsible for their failure." C. Wright Mills, *White Collar: The American Middle Classes* (London: Oxford University Press, 1951), p. 283. On Civil War memorialization, see Blight, *Race and Reunion* and David Goldfield, *Still Fighting the Civil War: The American South and Southern History* (Baton Rouge: Louisiana State University Press, 2002). These outstanding works, however, have not taken fully into account the volatile mix of sex, race, and gender (particularly that centered on manhood) that has shaped the culture of memory so important not only to memorialization but also to southern white political mobilizations.

35. Solinger, *Wake Up, Little Susie*; Feldstein, *Motherhood in Black and White*; Godfrey, "Bayonets, Brainwashing, and Bathrooms," pp. 42–67; Brown, *Bigger Than Little Rock*, p. 146.

36. The silencing of liberal ministers, in fact, constitutes a critical legacy of massive resistance to postwar American political culture.

37. Lorraine Gates, "Power from the Pedestal: The Women's Emergency Committee and the Little Rock School Crisis," *Arkansas Historical Quarterly* 55 (Spring 1996): 26–57; Elizabeth Jacoway, "Down from the Pedestal: Gender and Regional Culture in a Ladylike Assault on the Southern Way of Life," *Arkansas Historical*

Quarterly 56 (Autumn 1997): 345–352; Spitzberg, *Racial Politics in Little Rock.* Graeme Cope, for example, views the Mothers' League as a political irritant and not as a central actor in the Little Rock dispute. Graeme Cope, "'A Thorn in the Side'? The Mothers' League of Central High School and the Little Rock Desegregation Crisis of 1957," *Arkansas Historical Quarterly* 57 (Summer 1998): 160–90; Graeme Cope, "'Honest White People of the Middle and Lower Classes'? A Profile of the Capital Citizens' Council during the Little Rock Crisis of 1957," *Arkansas Historical Quarterly* 61 (Spring 2002): 36–58; Williams, "Class: The Central Issue in the 1957 Little Rock School Crisis," pp. 341–44. Chappell reads Williams' article as a demonstration that class "may sometimes shape the world in which race and gender conflicts take place more than vice-versa." Chappell, "Editor's Introduction," pp. ix–xvi, quote on p. xii. Roy Reed, *Faubus: The Life and Times of an American Prodigal* (Fayetteville: University of Arkansas Press, 1997); Elizabeth Jacoway, "Taken By Surprise: Little Rock Business Leaders and Desegregation," in Elizabeth Jacoway and David R. Colburn, eds., *Southern Businessmen and Desegregation* (Baton Rouge: Louisiana State University Press, 1982), pp. 15–40. Beth Roy does analyze the gendered class ideologies and actions of white girls who attended Central High School during 1957–58. Roy, *Bitters in the Honey.*

CHAPTER ONE. MAPPING CHANGE: LITTLE ROCK FORGES A DESEGREGATION PLAN

1. Colbert S. Cartwright, "Failure in Little Rock," *The Progressive* (June 1958): 12–15; Papers of the Rev. Colbert S. Cartwright, MC 1026 [hereafter cited as Cartwright Papers], UAF.

2. *Arkansas Gazette*, February 5, 1953; *Arkansas Democrat Magazine*, August 26, 1954; Nathan Griswold, "The Second Reconstruction in Little Rock," n.d., Book II, Ch. 3, pp. 2–4, Murphy Papers, Box 11, UAF.

3. Griswold, ibid.; Oral History Interview, E. Grainger Williams, December 29, 1970, CUOHP, UALR; Sara Murphy Interview with Harry Ashmore, June 13, 1994, Murphy Papers, Box 1, UAF. According to school board member Wayne Upton, Blossom was "a driver, just always on the go, always trying to get something done, and always with the idea in mind of improving the quality of public education." Oral History Interview with Wayne Upton, CUOHP, May 11, 1972, UAF.

4. For a fuller discussion of the moderates, see Karen Anderson, "The Little Rock School Desegregation Crisis: Moderation and Social Conflict," *Journal of Southern History* 70 (August 2004): 603–36.

5. Scott DH [Hamilton] to Virgil Blossom, February 10, 1953, Blossom Papers, MS 1364, Box 1, UAF; Dave Grundfest to Virgil Blossom, December 28,

1953, Blossom Papers, Box 1, UAF; Glenn A. Green to Virgil Blossom, March 31, 1954, Blossom Papers, Box 1, UAF; Herbert L. Thomas, Jr. to John A. Riggs, Jr., July 28, 1955, Blossom Papers, Box 1, UAF; Everett Tucker, Jr. to Virgil T. Blossom, February 1, 1956, Blossom Papers, Box 1, UAF.

6. Irving J. Spitzberg, Jr., *Racial Politics in Little Rock* (New York: Garland Publishing, Inc., 1987), pp. 38–42; Oral History Interview with Everett Tucker, August 16, 1971, CUOHP, UAF; Oral History Interview with Wayne Upton, December 29, 1971, CUOHP, UAF; Virgil T. Blossom, *It Has Happened Here* (New York: Harper & Brothers, 1959), pp. 191–93; Author's interview with Harry Ashmore, February 5, 1995; Virgil T. Blossom to R. A. Lile, July 12, 1956, Blossom Papers, Box 1, UAF. School board members generally came from business backgrounds. *Arkansas Gazette*, November 14, 1954.

7. Author's interview with Georg Iggers, September 4, 2002; Georg Iggers and Wilma Iggers, *Zwei seiten einer geschichte: lebensbericht aus unruhigen zeiten* (Göttingen: Vandenhoeck & Ruprecht, 2002).

8. Author's interview with Georg Iggers, September 4, 2002; John A. Kirk, *Redefining the Color Line: Black Activism in Little Rock, Arkansas, 1940–1970* (Gainesville: University Press of Florida, 2002), pp. 63–64.

9. *Arkansas Gazette*, March 1–4, 1953; Griffin Smith, Jr., "Localism and Segregation: Racial Patterns in Little Rock, Arkansas, 1945–54" (MA thesis, Columbia University, April 29, 1965), pp. 56–65; Sara Alderman Murphy, *Breaking the Silence: Little Rock's Women's Emergency Committee to Open Our Schools, 1958–1963* (Fayetteville: University of Arkansas Press, 1997), pp. 20–24.

10. *State Press*, May 23, 1952, August 15, 1952. White women activists were very active supporters of the city's 1950 initiative for urban renewal and a 1955 campaign for slum clearance. *Arkansas Democrat*, April 27, 1950, February 13, 1955, February 20, 1955; *Arkansas Gazette*, May 8, 1950. Private developers and lending agencies supported private home construction for blacks, but only on the far east side. *Arkansas Gazette*, September 25, 1955. Little Rock's enthusiastic use of federal funds to support urban renewal projects was replicated in other southern cities. *Mobile Register*, January 16, 1952, in the Little Rock Housing Authority Papers [hereafter cited as LRHA], UALR.

11. Harry Ashmore, *The Negro and the Schools* (Chapel Hill: University of North Carolina Press, 1954); James D. Anderson, *The Education of Blacks in the South, 1860–1935* (Chapel Hill: University of North Carolina Press, 1988); Faustine Childress Jones, *A Traditional Model of Educational Excellence: Dunbar High School of Little Rock, Arkansas* (Washington, DC: Howard University Press, 1981); Marci K. Bynum, "Scholastic Achievement in the Segregation Era: Dunbar High School of Little Rock, Arkansas," 1995, p. 36, UALR.

12. *Arkansas Democrat*, September 24, 1952, February 27, 1953; *Arkansas Gazette*, March 1–4, 1953; Griffin Smith, Jr., "Localism and Segregation: Racial Patterns in Little Rock, Arkansas, 1945–54" (MA thesis, Columbia University, April 29, 1965), pp. 56–65; Murphy, *Breaking the Silence*, pp. 20–24.

13. Little Rock Council on Schools, "A Study on Equality under Segregation in the Little Rock Public School System," [1952], Papers of Georg Iggers, B-1, UALR; Georg C. Iggers, "The Race Question in Little Rock's Schools before 1956," in Wilson Record and Jane Cassels Record, eds., *Little Rock, U.S.A.: Materials for Analysis* (San Francisco: Chandler Publishing Company, Inc., 1960), pp. 283–91. School board data showed that the educational gap between white and African American sixth graders had declined from two years and five months to one year and five months between 1945 and 1955. I. Q. Ranges School Population Little Rock School District, Blossom Papers, Box 3, UAF.

14. Little Rock Council on Schools, "A Study on Equality under Segregation in the Little Rock Public School System," [1952], Papers of Georg Iggers, B-1, UALR.

15. Iggers, "The Race Question," pp. 283–91; Author's interview with Georg Iggers, September 4, 2002.

16. Harry A. Little to the board, February 20, 1952, Blossom Papers, Box 3, UAF; *Arkansas Gazette*, February 18, 1953; *Arkansas Gazette*, February 20, 1952; Iggers, "The Race Question," pp. 283–91. The trade laundry course, which was required for girls attending Dunbar, was widely disliked. Bynum, "Scholastic Achievement in the Segregation Era," p. 36, UALR.

17. Iggers, "The Race Question," pp. 283–91.

18. *Arkansas Democrat*, May 17, 1954, in Blossom Papers, Box 19, UAF; *Arkansas Democrat*, May 18, 1954.

19. *Arkansas Democrat*, May 17, 1954.

20. Minutes of Little Rock Board of Education Meeting, May 20, 1954, Blossom Papers, Box 12, UAF.

21. Ch. 2, page 2 in JAM to Virgil [Blossom], n.d., Blossom Papers, Box 2, UAF; Virgil T. Blossom, "The Untold Story of Little Rock: 'Where Does the Governor Stand?,'" *Saturday Evening Post*, May 30, 1959, p. 27; Interview with R. A. Lile, August 19, 1971, CUOHP, OH-219, DDEL; Junior League Provisional Training Course in Ruth A. and Buck Moore to Wayne Upton and Virgil Blossom, November 11, 1958, Blossom Papers, Box 11, UAF; Tony A. Freyer, *The Little Rock Crisis: A Constitutional Interpretation* (Westport, CT: Greenwood Press, 1984), pp. 16–18. Blossom evaded responsibility for mobilizing community sentiment in favor of desegregation even as some liberals warned that delay and silence would create the political space for significant opposition to develop. Irene

Osborne, Development of Community Responsibility for Integration, n.d., Blossom Papers, Box 3, UAF.

22. Wiley A. Branton to William G. Cooper, August 21, 1954, Blossom Papers, Box 3, UAF; Legal Redress Committee, September, 1954, Blossom Papers, Box 3, UAF; *Arkansas Gazette*, June 16, 1954, August 26, 1954, September 10, 1954, *Arkansas Democrat*, August 26, 1954; Sara Murphy Telephone Interview with Mrs. Daisy Bates, August 23, [1992], Murphy Papers, Box 1, UAF.

23. *Arkansas Democrat*, March 20, 1955, in Blossom Papers, Box 3, UAF. The editorial also noted its surprise that "the biggest cry for government surplus food for down-and-out families should have come from Eastern Arkansas, where farm land is richest."

24. Minutes, Little Rock School Board Meeting, March 31, 1955, Little Rock School District Office. Pulaski County population grew by 11.1 percent between 1950 and 1953. *Arkansas Business Bulletin* 21 (February 1954): 1–7, Blossom Papers, Box 15, UAF. Farm workers were left out of much of the New Deal's safety net, including the unemployment and pension provisions of the 1935 Social Security Act. Suzanne Mettler, *Dividing Citizens: Gender and Federalism in New Deal Public Policy* (Ithaca, NY: Cornell University Press, 1998).

25. *Arkansas Gazette*, August 4, 1955; Vernon McDaniel, "The Status of Desegregation in Arkansas—Some Measures of Progress," n.d., Papers of the National Association for the Advancement of Colored People [hereafter cited as NAACP Papers], Group II, Box B-136, Library of Congress [hereafter cited as LC]; United Committee for Better Schools, News Release to County Newspapers, December 1, 1954, Blossom Papers, Box 3, UAF.

26. *Arkansas Gazette*, May 18, 1954.

27. Kirk, *Redefining the Color Line*, p. 90; L. D. Poynter to Orval E. Faubus, August 31, 1957, Blossom Papers, Box 7, UAF.

28. Pre-press conference notes, September 3, 1957, DDE, PPUS, AWF, DDED, Box 27, DDEL; Diary, July 24, 1953, DDE, PPUS, AWF, DDED, Box 9, DDEL; James C. Duram, *A Moderate Among Extremists: Dwight D. Eisenhower and the School Desegregation Crisis* (Chicago: Nelson-Hall, Inc., 1981), pp. 53–71, 108–15.

29. According to Morrow, Eisenhower had initially opposed integrating the armed forces because he had consulted with his high-ranking friends in the military. Dwight D. Eisenhower to Lothaire S. Green, October 4, 1957, Classified Files, Office Files, Box 732, DDEL; Oral History of E. Frederic Morrow, January 31, 1968, CUOHP, OH-92, #1, DDEL; Duram, *A Moderate Among Extremists*, pp. 60–69.

30. Memo for Governor Adams, April 29, 1953, DDE, Classified Files [hereafter cited as CF], Official File [hereafter cited as OF], Box 731, DDEL; Telegram, Roy Wilkins to Pres. DDE, September 25, 1957, DDE, CF, OF, Box 732, DDEL;

Maxwell M. Rabb to Governor Adams, October 11, 1957, DDE, CF, OF, Box 732, DDEL; William G. Nunn to Maxwell Raab [sic], October 28, 1955, CF, General File [hereafter cited as GF], Box 42, DDEL; Maxwell M. Rabb to William G. Nunn, October 31, 1955, CF, GF, Box 42, DDEL; Rev. Martin L. King et al., for the Southern Negro Leaders Conference to the President, February 14, 1957, CF, GF, Box 912, DDEL; Louis R. Lautier to Governor Adams, February 17, 1958, DDE, CF, OF, Box 731, DDEL; B. C. Coleman to President Dwight D. Eisenhower, February 11, 1958, NAACP Papers, Box A 113, LC. Among those Eisenhower put off was Daisy Bates. Memo, SW to Mr. Rabb, October 21, 1957, DDE, CF, OF, Box 731, DDEL.

31. March 14, 1956 and April 4, 1956, Papers of E. Frederic Morrow re *Black Man in the White House, 1952–1963*, [hereafter cited as Morrow-MS Papers], Box 1, DDEL.

32. Thurgood Marshall to Dwight D. Eisenhower, September 6, 1956, CF, General Files, Box 916, DDEL.

33. Herbert Brownell with John P. Burke, *Advising Ike: The Memoirs of Attorney General Herbert Brownell* (Lawrence: University Press of Kansas, 1993), pp. 204–5.

34. Michal R. Belknap, *Federal Law and Southern Order: Racial Violence and Constitutional Conflict in the Post-Brown South* (Athens: University of Georgia Press, 1987), pp. 32–34; Robert Fredrick Burk, *The Eisenhower Administration and Black Civil Rights* (Knoxville: University of Tennessee Press, 1984), pp. 166–70, quote on p. 170.

35. John Pagan Interview with Forrest Rozzell, December 29, 1972, Murphy Papers, Box 3, UAF; Oral History Interview with Everett Tucker, CUOHP, August 16, 1971, UAF; Griswold, "The Second Reconstruction in Little Rock," p. 3, Murphy Papers, Box 11. UAF.

36. Urban League of Greater Little Rock Report Of Education Committee Meeting with Mr. Virgil T. Blossom, May 18, 1955, Blossom Papers, Box 3, UAF.

37. Colbert S. Cartwright to Virgil Blossom, November 22, 1954, Blossom Papers, Box 1, UAF.

38. Little Rock Board of Education, Plan of Integration, n.d. [before March 1955], Blossom Papers, Box 3, UAF; Blossom, "The Untold Story of Little Rock: 'Where Does the Governor Stand?,'" p. 82; Ernest Q. Campbell and Thomas F. Pettigrew, *Christians in Racial Crisis: A Study of Little Rock's Ministry* (Washington, DC: Public Affairs Press, 1959), pp. 179–81; *Arkansas Gazette*, August 9, 1959.

39. *Arkansas Democrat*, May 31, 1955; *Arkansas Democrat*, June 1, 1955; Oral History Interview with Wayne Upton, CUOHP, December 29, 1971, UAF.

40. *Arkansas Gazette*, November 1, 1958, in Blossom Papers, Box 30, UAF; *Arkansas Gazette*, November 1, 1958, in Blossom Papers, Box 30, UAF; Dale Al-

ford and L'Moore Alford, *The Case of the Sleeping People (Finally Awakened by Little Rock School Frustrations)* (Little Rock: 1959), p. 110; Opinion, John E. Miller, *John Aaron et al. v. William G. Cooper et al.* In the United States District Court, Eastern District of Arkansas, Western Division, Civil Action No. 3113, [143 F. Supp. 866], Blossom Papers, Box 3, UAF. The Blossom Papers, which include minutes from all other board meetings in these years, do not include any minutes from May 24, 1955.

41. Author's Interview with Paul Fair, May 28, 1996; Blossom, "The Untold Story of Little Rock: 'Where Does the Governor Stand?,'" p. 82.

42. Blossom, ibid.; Junior League Provisional Training Course in Ruth A. and Buck Moore to Wayne Upton and Virgil Blossom, November 11, 1958, Blossom Papers, Box 11, UAF; Murphy, *Breaking the Silence*, p. 35. The transfer policy was in place by February 1956. A. F. House to Attorney Group, February 15, 1956, Blossom Papers, Box 3, UAF. The *Arkansas Gazette* published a map in late June 1955 designating the racial composition of neighborhoods and noting the location of black schools. The caption read: "Part of the Integration Problem is Geographical." *Arkansas Gazette*, June 26, 1955.

43. *Arkansas Gazette*, May 11, 1954, August 26, 1954.

44. Joel Spring, *The Sorting Machine: National Educational Policy Since 1945* (New York: David McKay Company, Inc., 1976); Griswold, "The Second Reconstruction in Little Rock," p. 3, Murphy Papers, Box 11, UAF.

45. Alexander Frazier, "How to 'Keep Them in Their Place,'" *School Review* 55 (1947): 339–44.

46. Minutes of Little Rock Board of Education Meeting, November 17, 1954, Blossom Papers, MS 1364, Box 12, UAF; [Virgil Blossom], "Where We Go?," n.d., Blossom Papers, Box 4, UAF. In the 1958 trial on the school board's petition for a delay to desegregation, Blossom testified that "Socio-economic background materially affects the ability [of students] to accept teaching and the ability of the teacher to dispense knowledge." *Arkansas Gazette*, n.d. [June 1958], EP Huckaby Papers, UALR. John Kirk concludes that the decision in *Brown II* caused the board to change to a more conservative approach, without noting that the date on the plan (May 24, 1955) predated *Brown II*. Kirk, *Redefining the Color Line*, p. 96. Because there was no written plan before the summer of 1955 and Blossom was vague and contradictory in his public remarks about how those zones would be used, it is difficult to conclude, as Georg Iggers did in the late 1950s, that Blossom originally intended to use attendance zones to enable systematic integration within their boundaries. Iggers, "The Race Question," p. 287.

47. Colbert S. Cartwright, "Lesson from Little Rock," *Christian Century*, October 9, 1957 in Cartwright Papers, UAF; Oral history interview with Nat R. Griswold, August 21, 1971, Little Rock desegregation crisis, 1957–1959, Oral

history interview transcripts, 1972–1973, MS L720 310 Little Rock, UAF; Sara Murphy Interview with Fred Darragh, November 24, 1993, Murphy Papers, Box 1, UAF.

48. Deborah Kerfoot, "The Organization of Intimacy: Managerialism, Masculinity and the Masculine Subject," in Stephen M. Whitehead and Frank J. Barrett, eds., *The Masculinities Reader* (Cambridge, UK: Polity Press, 2001), pp. 233–52, quote on p. 238; R. W. Connell, *Gender and Power: Society, the Person and Sexual Politics* (Cambridge, UK: Polity Press), p. 107.

49. Roland Smith to Dr. Virgill [*sic*] Blossom, November 11, 1955, Blossom Papers, Box 3, UAF; Virgil T. Blossom to Rev. Roland Smith, November 25, 1955, Blossom Papers, Box 3, UAF; Virgil T. Blossom to Rev. Roland Smith, January 27, 1956, Blossom Papers, Box 3, UAF.

50. John Pagan Interview with Forrest Rozzell, December 29, 1972, Murphy Papers, Box 3, UAF; Upton Oral History, UAF; Robert R. Brown, *Bigger Than Little Rock* (Greenwich, CT: Seabury Press, 1958), p. 48.

51. Sara Murphy Interview with Harry Ashmore, June 13, 1994, Murphy Papers, Box 1, UAF. Grif Stockley contends that Bates supported the Blossom Plan unequivocally, alienating some in the African American community, mostly those who felt disempowered by her conspicuous leadership role during the crisis. More likely, she supported the school board plan when it appeared strategically necessary to her. Grif Stockley, *Daisy Bates: Civil Rights Crusader from Arkansas* (Jackson: University Press of Mississippi, 2005), p. 191.

52. Charles B. Pyles to Virgil Blossom, July 22, 1955, Blossom Papers, Box 1, UAF.

53. Elizabeth Williams, "Little Rock Footnote," n.d., Murphy Papers, Box 5, UAF.

54. Cartwright, "Failure in Little Rock," Cartwright Papers, UAF.

55. Freyer, *The Little Rock Crisis*, pp. 41–62; Author's Interview with Wilma Iggers, September 5, 2002; Author's Interview with George Iggers, September 4, 2002; Tony A. Freyer, *Little Rock on Trial:* Cooper v. Aaron *and School Desegregation* (Lawrence: University Press of Kansas, 2007), p. 7. The new building for African American students was originally to be a junior high but, according to Blossom, it was changed to a high school to provide "adequate attendance areas that would serve the needs of the children under the state [stated] principles of this program." Testimony of Virgil Blossom, *Aaron v. Cooper*, Office Court Reporter's Transcript of Proceedings Taken Before Hon. John E. Miller, August 15, 1956, Blossom Papers, Box 5, UAF. In 1957, Daisy Bates claimed that the plan the school board submitted to the court in 1956 provided for desegregation to be completed in twelve years. Telephone Interview, Mrs. L. C. Bates, October 4, 1957, Bates Papers, State Historical Society of Wisconsin [hereafter cited as SHSW], Box 5.

56. Freyer, *The Little Rock Crisis*, pp. 41–62, quote on p. 49; John Pagan Interview with A. F. House, August 15, 1972, Murphy Papers, Box 1, UAF.

57. Freyer, ibid.; A. F. House to Attorney Group, April 3, 1956, Blossom Papers, Box 3, UAF.

58. Kirk, *Redefining the Color Line*, pp. 98–100.

59. A. F. House to Henry Spitzberg, July 6, 1956, Blossom Papers, Box 3, UAF; Junior League Provisional Training Course in Ruth A. and Buck Moore to Wayne Upton and Virgil Blossom, November 11, 1958, Blossom Papers, Box 11, UAF; A. F. House to Attorney Group, February 13, 1956, Blossom Papers, Box 3, UAF.

60. Brooks Hays, *A Southern Moderate Speaks* (Chapel Hill: University of North Carolina Press, 1959), p. 216; *Aaron v. Cooper*, Office Court Reporter's Transcript of Proceedings Taken Before Hon. John E. Miller, August 15, 1956, Blossom Papers, Box 5, UAF.

61. *Aaron v. Cooper*, Office Court Reporter's Transcript of Proceedings Taken Before Hon. John E. Miller, ibid.

62. Opinion, John E. Miller, *John Aaron et al. v. William G. Cooper et al.* In the United States District Court, Eastern District of Arkansas, Western Division, Civil Action No. 3113, Blossom Papers, Box 3, UAF.

63. Marvin M. Hamilton to the School Board Members of Little Rock, August 16, 1956, Blossom Papers, Box 3, UAF; Woodruff Faculty to Virgil T. Blossom, August 31, 1956, Blossom Papers, Box 1, UAF; Staff at Centennial School to Virgil T. Blossom, September 11, 1956, Blossom Papers, Box 1, UAF; "A Citizen of Little Rock" to School Adminstrative [*sic*] Office, n.d., Blossom Papers, Box 3, UAF.

64. Roy Reed, *Faubus: The Life and Times of an American Prodigal* (Fayetteville: University of Arkansas Press, 1997), pp. 172–74; Harry S. Ashmore, *Civil Rights and Wrongs: A Memoir of Race and Politics, 1944–1994* (New York: Pantheon Books, 1994), p. 113.

65. Reed, *Faubus*, pp. 172–74; *Life*, July 25, 1955, pp. 29–31; John T. Elliff, *The United States Department of Justice and Individual Rights, 1937–1962* (New York: Garland Publishing, Inc., 1987, reprint of Ph.D. dissertation, Harvard University, 1967), pp. 407–20; *New York Times Magazine*, September 25, 1955; Freyer, *The Little Rock Crisis*, p. 65; *Arkansas Gazette*, September 18, 1955. Fayetteville and a few other communities in Arkansas had desegregated quietly without eliciting such a backlash. Kirk, *Redefining the Color Line*, p. 87.

66. Reed, ibid.; Elliff, ibid.; *New York Times Magazine*, September 25, 1955; Freyer, ibid. The *Arkansas Gazette* reporter in Hoxie refused to publish the sexualized and violent rhetoric of the segregationists there because they were "unfit for publication." Griswold, "The Second Reconstruction in Little Rock," n.d., quote in chap. 1, p. 29, Murphy Papers, Box 11, UAF. Elizabeth Jacoway's characteriza-

tion of segregationists primarily as advocates of local control obscures the connections between segregationists' understandings of race, sex, and gender and their
enthusiasm for local power, then a monopoly of white men. She herself concludes
that the "trouble with the Jim Johnsons of the world was that they believed the
things they said about integration leading inevitably to miscegenation." Jacoway
does not ask why this was so nor does she investigate its relationship to their advocacy of states' rights. Elizabeth Jacoway, "Jim Johnson of Arkansas: Segregationist Prototype," in Ted Ownby, ed., *The Role of Ideas in the Civil Rights South* (Jackson: University Press of Mississippi, 2002), pp. 137–55.

67. *Arkansas Gazette*, August 14, 21,1955.

68. *Hoxie v. Brewer* (137 F. Supp. 364) in *Race Relations Law Reporter* 1 (April
1956), 299–304; Freyer, *The Little Rock Crisis*, pp. 63–73.

69. *New York Times Magazine*, September 25, 1955; Reed, *Faubus*, pp. 172–
74; Osro Cobb, *Osro Cobb of Arkansas: Memoirs of Historical Significance*, ed.
Carol Griffee (Little Rock: Rose Publishing Company, 1989); pp. 171–72; *Arkansas Gazette*, September 14, 1955, August 30, 1957.

70. Elliff, *The United States Department of Justice and Individual Rights, 1937–
1962*, p. 438.

71. Michal Belknap, *Federal Law and Southern Order*, p. 38.

72. Reed, *Faubus*, pp. 172–74; Jacoway, "Jim Johnson of Arkansas," p. 148;
Adam Fairclough, "The Little Rock Crisis: Success or Failure for the NAACP?"
Arkansas Historical Quarterly 56 (Autumn 1997): 371–75. See Reed interview
with Johnson, UAF.

73. Reed, *Faubus*, pp. 172–74; Blossom, *It Has Happened Here*, p. 38; Interview with Amis Guthridge, August 19, 1971, CUOHP, OH-186, DDEL.

74. Reed, *Faubus*, pp. 174–81; Freyer, *The Little Rock Crisis*, pp. 63–82; *Arkansas Gazette*, September 7, 1955, September 10, 1955; Interview with Amis Guthridge, CUOHP, OH-186, August 19, 1971, DDEL; *Arkansas Faith*, November,
1955, Johnson Papers, Box 2, AHC. The same issue featured an article by Johnson
assuring his supporters that violence was not necessary to the victory of their
cause.

75. Phil [Stratton] to Virginia [Johnson], n.d. [March 1956], Johnson Papers,
Box 4, AHC. Little Rock's Capital Citizens' Council took the extreme step of removing three members, including Robert Ewing Brown, because of their close
embrace of anti-Semitism. Clive Webb, *Fight Against Fear: Southern Jews and
Black Civil Rights* (Athens: University of Georgia Press, 2001), p. 48.

76. Charles Morrow Wilson, "ORVAL FAUBUS—How Did He Get That Way?"
Reader's Digest, February 1959, pp. 78–84; Reed, *Faubus*, pp. 1–88.

77. Reed, *Faubus*, pp. 78–80. Henry Woods referred to Faubus's 1957 actions
as a Faustian deal. Author's Interview with Henry Woods, June 29, 1995.

78. Reed, *Faubus*, pp. 174–81; *Arkansas Gazette*, September 7, 1955, September 10, 1955; Interview with Amis Guthridge, August 19, 1971, CUOHP, OH-186, DDEL; Freyer, *The Little Rock Crisis*, pp. 63–82.

79. Freyer, *The Little Rock Crisis*, pp. 78–82; Griswold, "The Second Reconstruction in Little Rock," bk. 1, chap. 2, pp. 1–27, Murphy Papers, Box 11, UAF.

80. Untitled, "In the statement... ," n.d., Blossom Papers, Box 5, UAF.

81. Reed, *Faubus*, pp. 174–81; Freyer, *The Little Rock Crisis*, pp. 63–82; *Arkansas Gazette*, September 7, 1955, September 10, 1955; Interview with Amis Guthridge, August 19, 1971, CUOHP, OH-186, DDEL; *Blytheville Courier News*, April 11, 1977, Papers of Harry Ashmore, MSS 155 [hereafter cited as H. Ashmore Papers], Box 4, University of California at Santa Barbara [hereafter cited as UCSB].

82. Faubus claimed erroneously that one of the two who had not signed the Manifesto was defeated in his next electoral try. In fact, of the three senators and twenty-two congressmen who refused to sign, only two, both from North Carolina, were defeated in their reelection campaigns. Anthony J. Badger, "The White Reaction to Brown: Arkansas, the Southern Manifesto, and Massive Resistance," in Elizabeth Jacoway and C. Fred Williams, eds., *Understanding the Little Rock Crisis: An Exercise in Remembrance and Reconciliation* (Fayetteville: University of Arkansas Press, 1999), pp. 83–97, quotes on pp. 95, 96; John Ward Interview with Orval Faubus and Brooks Hays, Fayetteville, June 4, 1976, Hays Papers, Box 45, UAF; Oral History Interview with Brooks Hays, June 27, 1970, CUOHP, UALR; Southern Manifesto, http://www.cviog.uga.edu/Projects/gainfo/manifesto.htm, accessed on May 25, 2003. According to Hays, when New York Congressman Adam Clayton Powell introduced an amendment to a 1956 bill forbidding federal aid to districts that practiced segregation, southerners' fear of federal intervention intensified, as did their resistance to desegregation. Hays, *A Southern Moderate Speaks*, p. 88.

83. Brown, *Bigger Than Little Rock*, p. 10; Reed, *Faubus*, p. 178; Freyer, *The Little Rock Crisis*, pp. 76–97.

84. Arthur B. Caldwell to Warren Olney III, July 24, 1957, Papers of Arthur Caldwell, MS C-127, University of Arkansas, Fayetteville, Box 5; *U.S. News and World Report*, September 28, 1956; Cartwright, "Failure in Little Rock," Cartwright Papers, UAF; Author's Interview with Roy Reed, June 19, 1995; JAM to Virgil [Blossom], n.d., Blossom Papers, Box 2, UAF; Interview with R. A. Lile by John Luter, August 19, 1971, CUOHP, DDEL, OH-219.

85. Tony Badger, "'The Forerunner of Our Opposition': Arkansas and the Southern Manifesto of 1956," *Arkansas Historical Quarterly* 56 (Autumn 1997): 353–60, quote on p. 360.

86. Brown, *Bigger Than Little Rock*, pp. 21–22. For use of Citizens' Council symbols in Little Rock, see Citizens' Council ad, "Shall the School Board Deprive

Children of an Education Because They Opposed Race-Mixing?" n.d., EP Huckaby Papers, Box 2, Special Collections, UAF.

87. Kirk, *Redefining the Color Line.*

88. Rev. Wesley Pruden to Virgil Blossom and Members of Little Rock School Board, July 6, 1957, Blossom Papers, Box 4, UAF; Minutes of the Little Rock Board of Education Meeting, June 27, 1957, Records of the Little Rock School Board Minutes, Box 1, UALR. Ultimately, the board decided against allowing black students to participate in any extracurricular school activities.

CHAPTER TWO. "OCCUPIED ARKANSAS": CLASS,
GENDER, AND THE POLITICS OF RESISTANCE

1. Speech, September 26, 1957, Faubus Papers, Box 496, Special Collections, UAF.

2. Colbert S. Cartwright, "Lesson from Little Rock," *Christian Century*, October 9, 1957, p. 1193.

3. Interview Report, Mrs. Clyde Thomason, September 4, 1957, FBI, File Number 44–12284, "Integration in Public Schools in Little Rock," MS 1027, Little Rock Central High Integration Crisis, Federal Bureau of Investigation Records, Investigative Reports, 1957 [hereafter cited as FBI], UAF; Mrs. Abby Edwards to Jim Johnson, April 28, 1958, Johnson Papers, AHC, Box 6. Blossom also denied the request of Margaret Jackson, president of the Mothers' League, to transfer her two daughters from Central. Interview Report, Mrs. Margaret Jackson, September 6, 1957, FBI, File Number 44–341, FBI, UALR.

4. Interview Report, Mrs. Clyde Thomason, September 4, 1957, FBI, File Number 44–12284, FBI, UAF; Tony A. Freyer, *The Little Rock Crisis: A Constitutional Interpretation* (Westport, CT: Greenwood Press, 1984), pp. 101–2; *Arkansas Gazette*, August 28, 1957; Graeme Cope, "'A Thorn in the Side'? The Mothers' League of Central High School and the Little Rock Desegregation Crisis of 1957," *Arkansas Historical Quarterly* 57 (Summer 1998): 160–90. William Smith, Faubus's lawyer, and others associated with the governor were involved in initiating the suit. Roy Reed, *Faubus: The Life and Times of an American Prodigal* (Fayetteville: University of Arkansas Press, 1997), p. 199.

5. *Arkansas Gazette*, August 28, 30, 1957, September 3, 4, 8, 1957; Graeme Cope, "'Honest White People of the Middle and Lower Classes'? A Profile of the Capital Citizens' Council during the Little Rock Crisis of 1957," *Arkansas Historical Quarterly* 61 (Spring 2002): 36–58; Huckaby Oral History, CUOHP, EP Huckaby Papers, UALR; Sewell, notes, September 30, 1957, White House Office, Office of the Staff Secretary, Subject Series: Alphabetical Subseries, Box 13, DDEL.

6. Reed, *Faubus*, pp. 274–75.

7. Reed, *Faubus*, pp. 206–23; Freyer, *The Little Rock Crisis*, pp. 96–109. For a slightly different version of this section, see Karen Anderson, "Massive Violence, and Southern Social Relations: The Little Rock, Arkansas School Integration Crisis, 1954–1960," in Clive Webb, ed., *Massive Resistance: Southern Opposition to the Second Reconstruction* (New York: Oxford University Press, 2005), pp. 203–20.

8. Irving J. Spitzberg, Jr., *Racial Politics in Little Rock* (New York: Garland Publishing, Inc., 1987), pp. 38–42; Oral History Interview with Everett Tucker, August 16, 1971, CUOHP, MS 720 310, UAF; Oral History Interview with Wayne Upton, December 29, 1971, CUOHP, MS 720 310, UAF; Virgil T. Blossom, *It Has Happened Here* (New York: Harper & Brothers, 1959), pp. 31, 191–93; Author's Interview with Harry Ashmore, February 5, 1995; Author's Interview with Harry Ashmore, February 3, 1997; Sara Alderman Murphy, *Breaking the Silence: Little Rock's Women's Emergency Committee to Open Our Schools, 1958–1963* (Fayetteville: University of Arkansas Press, 1997), pp. 43–49; Oral History Interview with Wesley Pruden, December 28, 1970, CUOHP, OH-264, DDEL; Oral History Interview with James T. Karam, 1973, CUOHP, OH-215, DDEL; Freyer, *The Little Rock Crisis*, pp. 90–91.

9. Blossom, *It Has Happened Here*, pp. 47–131; Reed, *Faubus*, pp. 193–263; Outline of Publicity, n.d., FBI, A-39, Box 1, UALR.

10. FBI Investigation Instituted at Request of Judge Ronald L. Davies, FBI, A-39, Box 1, UALR; *Arkansas Gazette*, August 30 and 31, 1957; Michal R. Belknap, *Federal Law and Southern Order: Racial Violence and Constitutional Conflict in the Post-Brown South* (Athens: University of Georgia Press, 1987), p. 46.

11. Arthur B. Caldwell to Warren Olney III, July 24, 1957, Caldwell Papers, Box 5, UAF; Blossom, *It Has Happened Here*, pp. 53–54; *Arkansas Gazette*, August 18, 1957; Freyer, *The Little Rock Crisis*, pp. 99–100; A. F. House, Oral History, 1971, CUOHP, OH-299, DDEL.

12. Freyer, ibid.; Blossom, *It Has Happened Here*, pp. 52–54; *Arkansas Gazette*, August 21 and 22, 1957; FBI, Interview Report, Virgil Blossom, September 7 and 8, 1957, FBI, A-39, Box 1, UALR; Arthur B. Caldwell to Warren Olney III, August 30, 1957, Caldwell Papers, Box 5, UAF; Wayne Upton to William P. Rogers, September 9, 1958, William P. Rogers: Papers, 1938–1962 [hereafter cited as WPR], Daily Correspondence [hereafter cited as DC], Box 54, DDEL; Transcript, *John Aaron et al. v. William G. Cooper et al.*, in the United States District Court, Eastern District of Arkansas, Western Division, Blossom Papers, Box 5, UAF.

13. Blossom, *It Has Happened Here*, pp. 53–54; *Arkansas Gazette*, August 18, 1957; Freyer, *The Little Rock Crisis*, pp. 99–100; Arthur B. Caldwell to Warren Olney III, August 30, 1957, Papers of Arthur B. Caldwell, C-127, Box 5, UAF; Nat R. Griswold, Interview, August 21, 1971, CUOHP, UAF.

14. Freyer, ibid.; Osro Cobb, *Osro Cobb of Arkansas: Memoirs of Historical Significance*, ed. Carol Griffee (Little Rock: Rose Publishing Company, 1989), p. 181; Interview with A. F. House by John Luter, August 17, 1971, CUOHP, OH-299, DDEL; Archie House to Arthur Caldwell, July 21, 1958, Caldwell Papers, Box 5, UAF; *Arkansas Gazette*, August 24, 1957. Miller prosecuted African Americans after whites attacked and murdered many blacks in Elaine, Arkansas in 1919 even though he knew that police had beaten them to secure confessions. Grif Stockley, *Daisy Bates: Civil Rights Crusader from Arkansas* (Jackson: The University Press of Mississippi, 2005), pp. 79–80. In a letter to Herbert Thomas the following spring, Miller revealed his conviction that if all parties cooperated it was possible to handle the school issue "without disturbing and upsetting the traditional way of life in the South." John E. Miller to Herbert L. Thomas, Sr., March 31, 1958, Papers of Herbert Thomas, MC 437 [hereafter cited as Thomas Papers], Box 4, UAF.

15. *Arkansas Gazette*, August 23, 1957; Reed, *Faubus*, pp. 196–97; Blossom, *It Has Happened Here*, pp. 55–56; Harry S. Ashmore, *Civil Rights and Wrongs: A Memoir of Race and Politics, 1944–1994* (New York: Pantheon Books, 1994), pp. 125–26; Interview with Orval Faubus, 1971, CUOHP, OH-215, DDEL. For the Georgia resistance plan, see Kevin M. Kruse, *White Flight: Atlanta and the Making of Modern Conservatism* (Princeton, NJ: Princeton University Press, 2005), p. 132.

16. Amis Guthridge, Interview, 1971, CUOHP, OH-215, DDEL; James T. Karam, Interview, 1973, CUOHP, OH-215, DDEL; Reed, *Faubus*, pp. 207, 213; *Look*, November 12, 1957; FBI, Interview Report, Hugh Lynn Adams, September 13, 1957, FBI, Box 1, UALR; FBI, Interview Report, Billie LeRoy Shaw, September 13, 1957, FBI, Box 1, UALR. Attorney Amis Guthridge refused to discuss any knowledge he had regarding threats of violence with the FBI because he served as attorney for the Capital Citizens' Council and could not divulge privileged information. FBI, Interview Report, Amis Guthridge, September 7, 1957, FBI, UAF. Apparently, the FBI did not follow up on any of these reports.

17. FBI Investigation Instituted at Request of Judge Ronald N. Davies, FBI, Box 1, UALR; FBI, Interview Report, L. D. Poynter, September 9, 1957, FBI Records, UALR, A39, Box 1; FBI Investigation Instituted at Request of Judge Ronald L. Davies, FBI Records, UALR, A39, Box 1; Amis Guthridge to Orval E. Faubus, August 28, 1957, Box 589, Faubus Papers, UAF. The CCC rhetoric regarding violence resembled that in other parts of the South. David R. Goldfield, *Black, White, and Southern: Race Relations and Southern Culture 1940 to the Present* (Baton Rouge: Louisiana State University Press, 1990), pp. 82–84.

18. Arthur B. Caldwell to Warren Olney III, August 30, 1957, Papers of Arthur B. Caldwell, C-127, Box 5, UAF; Robert Fredrick Burk, *The Eisenhower Administration and Black Civil Rights* (Knoxville: University of Tennessee Press, 1984), pp. 176–77.

19. Tony A. Freyer, "The Little Rock Crisis Reconsidered," *Arkansas Historical Quarterly* 56 (Autumn 1997): 361–70; Orval Faubus, CUOHP, 1971, OH-215, DDEL; Burk, *The Eisenhower Administration*, pp. 174–89.

20. Arthur B. Caldwell to Judge Archie F. House, Caldwell Papers, Box 5, UAF.

21. FBI, Interview Report, Virgil Blossom, September 5, 1957, FBI, A-39, Box 1, UALR; Blossom, *It Has Happened Here*, pp. 52–53; Nathan Griswold, Oral History, 1971, CUOHP, UAF; John Luter Interview with Orval Faubus, August, 1971, CUOHP, DDEL.

22. Speech, September 2, 1957, Faubus Papers, Box 496, UAF; Arthur B. Caldwell to Warren Olney III, August 30, 1957, Caldwell Papers, Box 5, UAF.

23. Speech, September 2, 1957, Faubus Papers, Box 496, UAF; FBI Investigation Instituted at Request of Judge Ronald N. Davies, FBI, Box 1, UALR.

24. Sidney McMath, Oral History, CUOHP, 1970, UAF; Reed, *Faubus*, pp. 222–23.

25. Local NAACP leaders had concluded in May that the superintendent's procedures were at odds with the desegregation plan approved by the court and "seemed only to instill a feeling of inferiority, fear and intimidation." They asked that school officials cease using them. Report of Conference between Little Rock School superintendent and NAACP Representatives, May 29, 1957, NAACP, Group III, Box A98, LC.

26. Henry Louis Gates, Jr., *Colored People: A Memoir* (New York: Vintage Books, 1994), pp. 25–27.

27. *Arkansas Gazette*, September 4, 1957; Pre-press conference notes, September 3, 1957, Papers of Dwight D. Eisenhower [hereafter cited as DDE], Papers as President of the United States [hereafter cited as PPUS], Ann Whiteman File [hereafter cited as AWF], Box 27, DDE Diary Series [hereafter cited as DDED], DDEL.

28. *Time*, September 16, 1957; Reed, *Faubus*, p. 239.

29. *Arkansas Gazette*, September 6, 1957; Interview with Henry Woods, December 8, 1972, CUOHP, UALR; Sidney McMath, Interview, CUOHP; Huckaby to Bill, September 8, 1957, EP Huckaby Papers, UALR, Letters to Bill File.

30. *Arkansas Gazette*, September 6, 1957; Interview with Henry Woods, December 8, 1972, CUOHP, UALR; Interview with Wayne Upton, December 29, 1971, CUOHP, UAF; Interview with Sidney McMath, December 30, 1970, CUOHP, OH-202, UAF.

31. Telegram, Orval E. Faubus to the President, September 4, 1957, CF, OF, Box 733, DDEL; Dwight D. Eisenhower to Orval E. Faubus, September 5, 1957, CF, OF, Box 733, DDEL; *Arkansas Gazette*, September 5, 1957.

32. Telegram, Orval E. Faubus to the President, September 4, 1957, CF, OF, Box 733, DDEL; Wayne Upton, Oral History, 1971, CUOHP, MS 720 310, UAF. A scholarship on masculinity, southern culture and identity, and white racial

privilege is now beginning to emerge. See Kari Frederickson, "'As a Man, I Am Interested in States' Rights': Gender, Race, and the Family in the Dixiecrat Party," in Jane Dailey, Glenda Elizabeth Gilmore, and Bryant Simon, eds., *Jumpin' Jim Crow: Southern Politics from Civil War to Civil Rights* (Princeton, NJ: Princeton University Press, 2000), pp. 260–74; Nancy Bercaw, ed., *Gender and the Southern Body Politic: Essays and Comments* (Jackson: University Press of Mississippi, 2000); Ted Ownby, *Subduing Satan: Religion, Recreation, and Manhood in the Rural South, 1865–1920* (Chapel Hill: University of North Carolina Press, 1990); Bryant Simon, "The Appeal of Cole Blease of South Carolina: Race, Class, and Sex in the New South," in Martha Hodes, ed., *Sex, Love, Race: Crossing Boundaries in North American History* (New York: New York University Press, 1999), pp. 373–98.

33. John T. Elliff, *The United States Department of Justice and Individual Rights, 1937–1962* (New York: Garland Publishing, Inc., 1987, reprint of Ph.D. dissertation, Harvard University, 1967), pp. 468–72.

34. Telephone calls, September 11, 1957, DDE, PPUS, AWF, DDED, Box 27, DDEL.

35. Reed, *Faubus*, pp. 217–19; Diary, Notes dictated by the President on October 8, 1957, DDE, PPUS, AWF, DDED, Box 27, DDEL.

36. Statement by the President, September 14, 1957 and Statement by the Governor of Arkansas, DDE, PPUS, AWF, AWD, Box 9, DDEL.

37. Pre-Press Conference, October 9, 1957, DDE, PPUS, AWF, Box 27, DDEL; Reed, *Faubus*, p. 233; Interview by John Luter with Orval Faubus, CUOHP, August, 1971, DDEL.

38. Telephone calls, September 20, 1957, DDE, PPUS, AWF, Box 27, DDEL; DDE to General Alfred M. Gruenther, September 24, 1957, DDE, PPUS, AWF, DDED, Box 26, DDEL; Robert R. Brown, *Bigger Than Little Rock* (Greenwich, CT: Seabury Press, 1958), p. 38; Reed, *Faubus*, p. 222. Eisenhower thought that the FBI report confirmed Faubus's political opportunism because it revealed no specific evidence of impending violence. Diary, September 14, 1957, DDE, PPUS, AWF, AWD, Box 9, DDEL.

39. Untitled, n.d., "Governor Faubus advised...," WPR, DC, Box 16, DDEL; *Arkansas Democrat*, September 20, 1957; Reed, *Faubus*, p. 222.

40. Sara Murphy Interview with Edwin Dunaway, August 18, 1992, Murphy Papers, Box 1, UAF. In my interview with Ashmore, he said that if Gene Smith "looked across the table and said he would kill me, I'd believe him." Author's interview with Harry Ashmore, February 3, 1997.

41. *New York Times*, September 24, 1957; *Arkansas Gazette*, September 24, 1957; *Washington Post*, September 23, 1957 in FBI, Box 1, UALR; Reed, *Faubus*, p. 224; *Time*, September 30, 1957; Interview with Robert E. Baker, September

25, 1957, FBI, Series V, Box 1, UALR; Investigation to Determine Leaders and Instigators of Violence at Central High, FBI, Box 1, UALR.

42. *New York Times*, September 24, 1957; *Arkansas Gazette*, September 24, 1957; Blossom, *It Has Happened Here*, p. 50.

43. Burk, pp. 184–86; Elliff, *The United States Department of Justice and Individual Rights*, pp. 477–79; *Arkansas Gazette*, September 24, 1957.

44. Virgil T. Blossom, "Situation Out of Control," *Saturday Evening Post*, June 13, 1959.

45. *Arkansas Gazette*, September 25, 1957; Telegram, Mayor Mann to the President, Sept. 24, 1957, White House Office, Office of the Staff Secretary, Subject Series; Alphabetical Subseries, Box 17, DDEL.

46. *Arkansas Democrat*, October 25, 1957; *New York Times*, September 24, 1957.

47. Reed, *Faubus*, p. 226; *Chicago Defender*, October 5, 1957; *New York Times*, September 24, 1957. In a *New York Post* article reprinted in the *Arkansas Gazette*, Murray Kempton described women demonstrating against integration in Nashville as "on parade, in sweat socks one, in formless cotton sacking others" sending "up their tribal cries." *Arkansas Gazette*, September 16, 1957. The picture of Hazel Bryan shouting hatefully at Elizabeth Eckford elicited a great deal of negative response. *Arkansas Gazette*, September 11, 1957; Elizabeth Huckaby, 1957 Yearbook, September 4, 5, 1957, EP Huckaby Papers, Box 1, UAF.

48. *Arkansas Democrat*, October 25, 1957.

49. *Arkansas Gazette*, August 23, 28, 1957.

50. Interview with Mrs. Margaret Jackson, September 6, 1957, FBI Report, FBI, A-39, Box 1, UALR; Interview with Mrs. A. T. Forbess, September 7, 1957, FBI Report, FBI, Box 1, UALR; Interview with Mrs. T. H. Dame, September 8, 1957, FBI, Box 1, UALR.

51. John Edgar Hoover, Memorandum for Mr. Tolson et al., October 7, 1957, FBI Record on Orval Faubus, unprocessed collection, UAF. One police officer at the school commented that he was surprised that a minister would use "such strong language" as he heard from one who participated in the mob. Interview with Thomas Owen, September 24, 1957, FBI, UALR.

52. Interview with Mrs. Margaret Jackson, September 6, 1957, FBI Report, FBI, A-39, Box 1, UALR; Interview with Mrs. A. T. Forbess, September 7, 1957, FBI Report, FBI, A-39, Box 1, UALR; Phoebe Christina Godfrey, "'Sweet Little Girls'? Miscegenation, Desegregation and the Defense of Whiteness at Little Rock's Central High, 1957–1959," (Ph.D. dissertation, Binghamton University, State University of New York, 2001), pp. 139–58, 174; *Arkansas Gazette*, August 28, 30, 1957; John Wyllie, "Conversations in the South," March 3, 1959, Faubus Papers, Box 498, UAF.

53. Pete Daniel, *Lost Revolutions: The South in the 1950s* (Chapel Hill: University of North Carolina Press, 2000), pp. 251–83; Phoebe Godfrey, "Bayonets, Brainwashing, and Bathrooms: The Discourse of Race, Gender, and Sexuality in the Desegregation of Little Rock's Central High," *Arkansas Historical Quarterly* 62 (Spring 2003): 42–67.

54. Daniel, ibid.; Godfrey, ibid.

55. Speech, September 26, 1957, Faubus Papers, Box 496, UAF; Godfrey, ibid., quote on pp. 50–51. Elizabeth Huckaby's interpretation of the picture varied considerably from that advanced by segregationists. She saw "two laughing girls, absent from school without their mothers' knowledge I found later, being moved along by soldiers with bayonets pointed toward them." Elizabeth Huckaby, *Crisis at Central High, 1957–58* (Baton Rouge: Louisiana State University Press, 1980), p. 45. In early October, federal troops removed the bayonets from their rifles. Summary Report: Arkansas, 3 October 1957, No. 24, White House Office, Office of the Staff Secretary, Subject Series; Alphabetical Subseries, Box 16, DDEL.

56. Harris concluded that "Little Rock has proved to the crazy bunch in Washington that they haven't got enough soldiers to station troops in every white school in the south." Speech of Roy V. Harris before Capital Citizens' Council, Little Rock, Arkansas, January 14, 1958, OEF, Box 589.

57. *Arkansas Democrat*, September 25, 1957; Brown, *Bigger Than Little Rock*, p. 22; Unsigned postcard to Virgil Blossom, January 8, 1958, Blossom Papers, Box 7, UAF. The use of little girls in another symbol popular in the South, the "Brotherhood by Bayonet" figure, illustrates the tenacity of an imagery of victimization gendered female even when the political vocabulary of equality—brotherhood—was gendered male. Removed from walls or picked up around Central H.S., 1957–58, EP Huckaby Papers, Box 2, UAF.

58. Speech, September 26, 1957, Faubus Papers, Box 496, UAF; Godfrey, "Bayonets, Brainwashing, and Bathrooms," pp. 42–67.

59. David Goldfield, *Still Fighting the Civil War: The American South and Southern History* (Baton Rouge: Louisiana State University Press, 2002), pp. 2, 28.

60. Anonymous letter and cartoon, n.d., Blossom Papers, Box 7, UAF. An unmarked copy of this cartoon can also be found in the papers of Jim Johnson. Johnson Papers, Box 48, AHC.

61. Anonymous letter and cartoon, n.d., Blossom Papers, Box 7, UAF.

62. Anon. to the president of the N.A.C.P.A. [*sic*], September 30, 1957, Bates Papers, MSS 523, Box 1, SHSW; "from one who has always helped the negros but never again" to Daisy Baites [*sic*], October 18, 1957, Bates Papers, Box 1, SHSW; "From an organizer to stop furnishing negro's [*sic*] in any way or form" to Mrs. L. C. Bates, October 2, 1957, Bates Papers, Box 1, SHSW; Carol Wood to [Daisy Bates], n.d., Bates Papers, Box 1, SHSW.

63. Terry, *Life Is My Song, Also*, p. 231, (unpublished manuscript), Series II, Subseries II, Box 2, Fletcher–Terry Papers [hereafter cited as Terry Papers], RG A-13, UALR; *Arkansas Gazette*, September 5, 1957; David Thoreau Wieck, "Report From Little Rock," *Liberation*, October 1958, pp. 4–9; *New York Times*, September 6, 1957; *Arkansas Democrat*, September 29, 1987. When Faubus later attacked Terry for her opposition to him, a friend wrote to her that Faubus was a "man of small caliber and low breeding." E. C. Dean to Mrs. Terry, July 16, 1960, Terry Papers, RG A-13, Series II, Subseries II, Box 4, UALR.

64. Gertrude Samuels, "The Silent Fear in Little Rock," *New York Times Sunday Magazine*, March 30, 1958, pp. 11, 78–79.

65. Henry Woods, CUOHP, UALR; Liz to Bill, October, 1957, File, Letters to Bill, 1957–1958, EP Huckaby Papers, UALR.

66. Author's Interview with Henry Woods, June 29, 1995.

67. *New York Times*, September 24, 1957; *New York Herald Tribune*, January 29, 30, and 31, 1958; Reed, *Faubus*, p. 231; Elliff, *The United States Department of Justice and Individual Rights*, pp. 478–79.

68. Activities of the President, September 23, 1957, DDE, PPUS, AWF, Box 27, DDE; *New York Herald Tribune*, January 30, 1958; Belknap, *Federal Law and Southern Order*, p. 49; Interview of E. Frederic Morrow by Ed Edwin, January 31, 1968, CUOHP, OH-92, #1, DDEL; Mary L. Dudziak, *Cold War and Civil Rights: Race and the Image of American Democracy* (Princeton, NJ: Princeton University Press, 2000), pp. 115–51; Azza Salama Layton, "International Pressure and the U.S. Government's Response to Little Rock," *Arkansas Historical Quarterly* 56 (Autumn 1997): 257–72. The film *Song of the South*, which is no longer available, generated controversy for its inaccurate and romanticized depictions of race relations in the plantation South.

69. *Arkansas Gazette*, November 17, 1957; Speech, September 26, 1957, Faubus Papers, Box 496, UAF; *New York Times*, September 28, 1957; Petition for Injunction and Declaratory Judgment, *Jackson v. Kuhn*, FBI, Box 1, UALR; Interview, Everett Barnes, February 7, 1958, Faubus Papers, Box 497, UAF; Godfrey, "Bayonets, Brainwashing, and Bathrooms," pp. 42–67. Judge Ronald Davies found against Jackson in the suit. She appealed to the Court of Appeals, which unanimously denied her appeal in April 1958. Investigation to Determine Leaders and Instigators of Violence at Central High School, FBI, Box 1, UALR.

70. The touchy negotiations prior to the meeting between the President and the governor, centering on who was to request the meeting and how, also bespeak the freighted emotional subtext of the encounter. Brooks Hays, *A Southern Moderate Speaks* (Chapel Hill: University of North Carolina Press, 1959), pp. 138–65.

The women of the Mothers' League also experienced federal intervention as humiliating, but did not invest it with the concern for masculine dignity and autonomy expressed by the men. Cope, "'A Thorn in the Side'?" p. 168.

71. *Arkansas Gazette*, September 20, 1957; *New York Times*, October 4, 1957; *Shreveport Journal*, September 17, 1958, Blossom Papers, Box 10, UAF; John Ward Interview with Orval Faubus and Brooks Hays, June 4, 1976, Papers of L. Brooks Hays, MS H334P [hereafter cited as Hays Papers], Series 3, Subseries 1, Box 45, UAF; Harry Ashmore, "The Untold Story Behind Little Rock," *Harper's*, June, 1958, p. 16. The Rev. Wesley Pruden, a segregationist leader, later stated that Faubus was set up in the late September meeting with President Eisenhower for the "surrender of his position." Wesley Pruden, Oral History, 1970, CUOHP, OH-264, DDEL. Former Arkansas governor Sid McMath saw Eisenhower's decision to meet with Faubus as an inappropriate elevation of the governor's status, commenting that the president "met with him and negotiated with him as if he were ambassador of some foreign country, you know, and gave him prestige and recognition—he should never have called him up there and conferred with him and given him recognition." Oral History Interview with Sidney McMath, December 30, 1970, OH-202, CUOHP, MS L720 310, UAF.

72. Investigation Instituted at Request of Judge Ronald L. Davies, FBI Records, Box 1, UALR.

73. Freyer, "The Little Rock Crisis Reconsidered," pp. 361–70.

74. *Arkansas Gazette*, August 17, 1958; NAACP, Report of the Secretary, November 10, 1958, Bates Papers, Box 4, SHSW; *Arkansas Democrat*, n.d., EP Huckaby Papers, UALR; Bruce Bennett to Oren Harris, October 3, 1958, Papers of Oren Harris, MS H242 138, 4–2-34, Gp. 3, Loc. 1140, UAF; Dale Alford and L'Moore Alford, *The Case of the Sleeping People (Finally Awakened by Little Rock School Frustrations)* (Little Rock, 1959), p. 103; Numan V. Bartley, *The Rise of Massive Resistance: Race and Politics in the South during the 1950s* (Baton Rouge: Louisiana State University Press, 1969), pp. 112–13, 212–21; Steven F. Lawson, *Running for Freedom: Civil Rights and Black Politics in America Since 1941* (Philadelphia: Temple University Press, 1991), pp. 48–49.

75. Hearings before the Subcommittee to Investigate the Administration of the Internal Security Act and Other Internal Security Laws, Committee on the Judiciary, 85th Congress, 1st Session, October 28 and 29, 1957; *Arkansas Gazette*, February 28, 1958.

76. Jane Cassels Record, *American Scholar* 26 (Summer 1957): 325–33.

77. Clive Webb, *Fight Against Fear: Southern Jews and Black Civil Rights* (Athens: University of Georgia Press, 2001), p. 46; Christ Ambassador (Mrs.) Sarah E. Williams, September 23, 1957 to (Mrs.) L. C. Bates, Bates Papers, Box 1, SHSW.

78. Author's Interview with Lee Lorch, September 5, 2002; Vivienne Mayes, "Lee Lorch at Fisk: A Tribute," *American Mathematical Monthly* 83 (November 1976): 708–11; Hearing before the Committee on Un-American Activities, House of Representatives, 83d Congress, 2d Session, September 15, 1954, pp. 6953–77. Lorch continued to hold National Science Foundation grants throughout his political travails.

79. Transcript of a conversation between Mr. Current in New York and Mrs. Bates and Mr. Laws in Little Rock, October 17, 1957, Bates Papers, Box 5, SHSW; Transcript of a conversation between Mr. Current in New York and Mr. Laws in Little Rock, October 31, 1957, Bates Papers, Box 5, SHSW; Author's Interview with Lee Lorch, September 5, 2002.

80. Reed, *Faubus*, pp. 275–84; Excerpt from TV address of Governor Orval E. Faubus, May 22, 1959, WEC Papers, Box 15, AHC.

81. Murphy, *Breaking the Silence*, p. 81.

82. Spitzberg, *Racial Politics in Little Rock*, pp. 69–81, quote on p. 80.

83. Cobb, *Osro Cobb of Arkansas*, pp. 244–45.

84. Brown, *Bigger Than Little Rock*, pp. 75–84, quote on p. 82.

85. Ernest Q. Campbell and Thomas F. Pettigrew, *Christians in Racial Crisis: A Study of Little Rock's Ministry* (Washington, DC: Public Affairs Press, 1959), pp. 26–40; Brown, *Bigger Than Little Rock*, pp. 43–44, 92–127. As Brown notes, no such reservations regarding the church's role deterred segregationist ministers at that time.

86. Oral History interview with Nat R. Griswold, August 21, 1971, CUOHP, MS L720 310, UAF. The Rev. Colbert Cartwright signed the public statement issued by the leaders of the day of prayer, but did so reluctantly, believing that it did not meet the need to "try to give some moral and theological depth to the whole turmoil." Bert to Rev. Robert D. Chambless, Christian Church, Russellville, September 23, 1957, Cartwright Papers, UAF.

87. Brown, *Bigger Than Little Rock*, pp. 92–127, quote on p. 126; William Chafe, *Civilities and Civil Rights: Greensboro, North Carolina and the Black Struggle for Freedom* (New York: Oxford University Press, 1980), pp. 3–10; Oral History interview with Nat R. Griswold, CUOHP, August 21, 1971, MS L720 310, UAF; A Statement Prepared for a Conference of Protestant Church Leaders, May 13–14, 1958, Thomas Papers, Box 5, UAF; Thomas to Frank, Thomas Papers, Box 4, UAF and see *Gazette*, August 11, 1959. Within large churches particularly, affluent businessmen exerted great pressure on their ministers to join the local elite's strategy of silence. Campbell and Pettigrew, *Christians in Racial Crisis*, pp. 63–136. Similarly, the Rev. Dr. J. H. Jackson, president of the National Baptist Convention, concluded that it was important to remember that "achieving constructive human relations and goodwill" should not be sacrificed "in a meticulous

contention for the letter of the law." Thomas to Frank, Thomas Papers, Box 4, UAF and see *Arkansas Gazette*, August 11, 1959.

88. *Christian Century*, October 2, 1957; Mrs. Emma Cooper to Orval E. Faubus, September 9, 1957, Faubus Papers, Box 530, UAF; Mrs. J. Russell Henderson to Orval E. Faubus, September 5, 1957, Faubus Papers, Box 530, UAF; Campbell and Pettigrew, *Christians in Racial Crisis*, p. 21.

89. His publications included Colbert S. Cartwright, "Lesson from Little Rock," *Christian Century*, October 9, 1957, pp. 1193–94; "The Improbable Demagogue of Little Rock, Ark.," *The Reporter*, October 17, 1957, pp. 23–24; "Failure in Little Rock," *The Progressive* (June 1958); "Hope Comes to Little Rock," *The Progressive* (August 1959). One publication appeared in the Congressional Record. Reprint of Colbert S. Cartwright, "Lesson from Little Rock," Congressional Record, 85th Congress, 2d Session, WEC, Box 6, AHC.

90. Colbert Cartwright to Dad, October 30, 1957, Cartwright Papers, UAF; Colbert Cartwright to Dr. Hayden C. Nicholson, November 2, 1957, Cartwright Papers, UAF; Colbert S. Cartwright to Dr. Harold E. Fey, October 30, 1957, Cartwright Papers, UAF; Colbert S. Cartwright to Bob, April 4, 1961, Cartwright Papers, UAF.

91. Colbert S. Cartwright to Dr. Harold E. Fey, October 30, 1957, Cartwright Papers, UAF; Colbert S. Cartwright to Thelma [Babbitt], February 9, 1961, Cartwright Papers, UAF; Colbert S. Cartwright to Rev. Robert D. Chambless, September 23, 1957, Cartwright Papers, UAF; Nathan Griswold, manuscript, Book I, Ch. II, p. 22, Murphy Papers, Box 11, UAF; Colbert S. Cartwright to Dr. and Mrs. Hunter, December 21, 1957, Cartwright Papers, UAF.

92. Robert R. Brown, "The Moderate," in Robert R. Brown to Mr. Thomas, n.d., Box 4, Thomas Papers, UAF.

93. Investigation to Determine Leaders and Instigators of Violence at Central High School, FBI, Box 1, UALR; Subjects Arrested—Little Rock, FBI Report, FBI, Box 1, UALR; Clarence A. Laws to Roy Wilkins, December 18, 1957, Bates Papers, Box 4, SHSW; Spitzberg, *Racial Politics in Little Rock, 1954–1964*, pp. 70–81; Colbert S. Cartwright to Dr. Harold E. Fey, October 30, 1957, Cartwright Papers, UAF.

94. *Arkansas Gazette*, February 20, 1958; Clipping, no cite, March 18, 1958, EP Huckaby Papers, UALR.

95. Clipping, no cite, March 18, 1958, EP Huckaby Papers, UALR; *Arkansas Gazette*, February 20, 1958.

96. *Arkansas Gazette*, February 21, 1958.

97. *Arkansas Gazette*, ibid.; *Arkansas Gazette*, February 22, 1958.

98. *Arkansas Gazette*, February 21, 1958.

99. Deborah G. Kades, "Covering the Second Fort Sumter: Newspapers and the Little Rock Crisis," (M.A. thesis, University of Wisconsin, 1992), pp. 112–14,

125–26; Harry Ashmore, "The Untold Story Behind Little Rock," *Harper's*, June 1958; *Arkansas Gazette*, February 22, 1958.

100. Ashmore, "The Untold Story behind Little Rock." Arthur Caldwell and Roy Reed agreed with Ashmore's assessment. A. B. Caldwell to Archie F. House, August 12, 1958, Caldwell Papers, Box 5, UAF; Reed, *Faubus*, pp. 231–32. John Elliff implied that the appointment of Rogers ensured that the administration would pursue weak enforcement policies in the future, noting that "Federal Judges throughout the South saw clearly the implications of Little Rock and Rogers' subsequent policy; the federal executive would not ease their burden if they followed Judge Davies' example and ordered desegregation." Elliff, *The United States Department of Justice and Individual Rights*, pp. 484–87, quote on p. 487.

101. Sara Murphy Interview with Harry Ashmore, June 13, 1994, Murphy Papers, Box 1, UAF. For a more extensive discussion of the caution of the moderates, see Karen Anderson, "The Little Rock School Desegregation Crisis: 'Moderation' and Social Conflict," *Journal of Southern History* (June 2004): 603–36.

102. Arthur B. Caldwell to Judge Archie F. House, August 1, 1958, Caldwell Papers, Box 5, UAF; Archie House to Arthur Caldwell, August 8, 1958, Caldwell Papers, Box 5, UAF; Interview of E. Frederic Morrow by Ed Edwin, January 31, 1968, CUOHP, OH-92, #1, DDEL.

103. Interview of E. Frederic Morrow by Ed Edwin, January 31, 1968, CUOHP, OH-92, #1, DDEL.

104. Archie House to Arthur Caldwell, July 21, 1958, Caldwell Papers, Box 5, UAF.

105. James Youngdahl, "The New Populism of Orval Faubus," *The Progressive*, December 1959, pp. 41–43, quote on p. 41. C. Fred Williams, "Class: The Central Issue in the 1957 Little Rock School Crisis," *Arkansas Historical Quarterly* 56 (Autumn 1997): 341–44; David L. Chappell, "Editor's Introduction," *Arkansas Historical Quarterly* 56 (Autumn 1997): ix–xvi.

106. Harry S. Ashmore to Gil Harrison, January 17, 1958, Papers of Harry Ashmore, RG H-37, Box 6, UALR; Campbell and Pettigrew; Bates, *The Long Shadow of Little Rock*, pp. 179–213; Kades, "Covering the Second Fort Sumter," p. 126.

CHAPTER THREE. UNCIVIL DISOBEDIENCE:
THE POLITICS OF RACE AND RESISTANCE AT
CENTRAL HIGH SCHOOL, 1957–1958

1. J. O. Powell to Tim Delaney, April 2, 1991, Velma and J. O. Powell Collection, Ms 1367 [hereafter cited as Powell Papers], Box 1, UAF.

2. Interview with R. A. Lile by John Luter, August 19, 1971, CUOHP, OH-219, DDEL.

3. Student records, Minnijean Brown, December 17, 1957, Microfilm edition, Reel 6, Bates Papers, SHSW; Elizabeth Huckaby, *Crisis at Central High, 1957–58* (Baton Rouge: Louisiana State University Press, 1980), pp. 103–4.

4. Round table discussion by Negro students, [1957], Bates Papers, Box 5, SHSW.

5. Beth Roy, *Bitters in the Honey: Tales of Hope and Disappointment across Divides of Race and Time* (Fayetteville: University of Arkansas Press, 1999), quotes on pp. 171, 179.

6. Scholars who have looked at the Little Rock school crisis have usually noted that the nine African American students who attended Central High School in 1957–58 endured various forms of harassment and intimidation. Some have also understood, correctly, that that treatment was part of the segregationists' efforts to drive them from the school and thus to end Little Rock's nascent experiment in desegregation. They have, however, treated the situation in the school as, at most, a sidebar to the main story. Tony A. Freyer, *The Little Rock Crisis: A Constitutional Interpretation* (Westport, CT: Greenwood Press, 1984), p. 139; Elizabeth Jacoway, "Understanding the Past: The Challenge of Little Rock," in Elizabeth Jacoway and C. Fred Williams, eds., *Understanding the Little Rock Crisis: An Exercise in Remembrance and Reconciliation* (Fayetteville: University of Arkansas Press, 1999), p. 10; Irving J. Spitzberg, Jr., *Racial Politics in Little Rock, 1954–1964* (New York: Garland Publishing, Inc., 1987). John Kirk is a partial exception to this pattern. John A. Kirk, *Redefining the Color Line: Black Activism in Little Rock, Arkansas, 1940–1970* (University Press of Florida), pp. 119–24.

7. J. O. Powell, "Central High Inside Out (A Study in Disintegration) or Remember Central High (A Study in Disintegration)," Powell Papers, MS 1367, Box 1, UAF; Melba Pattillo, 1957–1959, October 2, 1957, Bates Papers, MSS 523, Microfilm Edition, Reel 6, SHSW; Roy, *Bitters in the Honey*, pp. 171–226.

8. Melba Pattillo Beals, *Warriors Don't Cry: A Searing Memoir of the Battle to Integrate Little Rock's Central High* (New York: Pocket Books, 1994), p. 149. The other members of the Little Rock Nine were Minnijean Brown, Gloria Ray, Terrence Roberts, Jefferson Thomas, Carlotta Walls, Elizabeth Eckford, Thelma Mothershed, and Ernest Green.

9. J. O. Powell, "Central High Inside Out," Powell Papers, Box 1, UAF; Student Records, CHS, Microfilm Edition, Reel 6, Bates Papers, SHSW; Statement of the Little Rock Board of Directors, Before Midterm 1958, Blossom Papers, Box 3, UAF; Bryce Harlow to Governor, October 1, 1957, CF, OF, Box 732, DDEL; Beals, *Warriors Don't Cry*, p. 148. William P. Rogers, the new U.S. Attorney General, was also pressuring the military to remove the troops as soon as possible. Transcript of conversation between Mrs. L. C. Bates and Gloster Current, November 13, 1957, Bates Papers, SHSW, Box 5.

10. Author's interview with Ernest Green, March 12, 1996; *Arkansas Gazette*, August 26, 1957; Virgil T. Blossom, *It Has Happened Here* (New York: Harper & Brothers, 1959), pp. 57, 134.

11. Author's interview with Ernest Green, March 12, 1996.

12. J. O. Powell, "Central High Inside Out," Powell Papers, Box 1, UAF; Daily Bulletin, October 11, 1957, EP Huckaby Papers, Box 1, UAF.

13. Liz to Bill, September 1, 1957, EP Huckaby Papers, UALR.

14. *Arkansas Gazette*, March 17, 1974; Beals, *Warriors Don't Cry*, pp. 131–33.

15. Audiotape, Daisy Bates, Tapes 1 and 2, Bates Papers, UAF; Oral History Interview with Daisy Bates, October 11, 1976, Southern Oral History Project, Southern Historical Collection, University of North Carolina. In her autobiography, Bates told an apocryphal story of her mother's murder at the hands of whites. Although the truth of her mother's death cannot be discerned, the story expressed the sense of victimization and of anger at southern whites she experienced before and during the crisis. Daisy Bates, *The Long Shadow of Little Rock: A Memoir* (New York: David McKay Company, Inc., 1962), pp. 9–24; Grif Stockley, *Daisy Bates: Civil Rights Crusader from Arkansas* (Jackson: University Press of Mississippi, 2005), pp. 17–18.

16. Audiotape, Daisy Bates, Tape 2, Bates Papers, UAF; Bates, *The Long Shadow of Little Rock*; Linda Reed, "The Legacy of Daisy Bates," *Arkansas Historical Quarterly* 59 (Spring 2000): 76–83; *Baltimore Afro-American*, October 5, 1957.

17. Investigation Report, Arkansas State Police, September 23, 1957, Faubus Papers, Box 498, UAF.

18. Elizabeth Huckaby, 1957 Yearbook, September 17, 1957, EP Huckaby Papers, MC 428, Box 1, UAF; J. O. Powell, "Central High Inside Out," Powell Papers, Box 1, UAF; The White House, General Goodpaster, 2/6/58, Little Rock, Miscellaneous, Vol. II, White House Office [hereafter cited as WHO], Office of the Staff Secretary [hereafter cited as OSS], Subject Series [hereafter cited as SS], Alphabetical Subseries [hereafter cited as AS], DDEL; Student Records, 1/21/58, Bates Papers, Microfilm edition, Reel 6, SHSW; Blossom, *It Has Happened Here*, p. 151.

19. Statements of J. O. Powell, March 6, 1958, Blossom Papers, Box 4, UAF; Testimony of Elizabeth Huckaby, Transcript, *John Aaron et al. v. William G. Cooper et al.*, In the United States District Court, Eastern District of Arkansas, Western Division, Blossom Papers, Box 5, UAF; Elizabeth Huckaby, *Crisis at Central High School: Little Rock, 1957–58* (Baton Rouge: Louisiana State University Press, 1980).

20. Special Bulletin, September 4, 1957, EP Huckaby Papers, Box 1, UAF; Daily Bulletin, September 23, 1957, EP Huckaby Papers, Box 1, UAF.

21. Confidential Bulletin to Teachers, September 23, 1957, EP Huckaby Papers, Box 1, UAF; Bulletin, October 29, 1957, EP Huckaby Papers, Box 1, UAF;

Daily Bulletin, November 13, 1957, EP Huckaby Papers, Box 1, UAF; Liz to Bill, February 2, 1958, EP Huckaby Papers, UALR.

22. *Little Rock Central Tiger*, October 15, 1976; Beals, *Warriors Don't Cry*, p. 160; Author's Interview with Ernest Green, March 12, 1996. Several teachers took their objections to the presence of African American students at Central to the Arkansas State Police. Interview, Everett Barnes, February 7, 1958, Faubus Papers, Box 497, UAF; Statement of William P. Ivey to Howard Chandler, January 21, 1958, Faubus Papers, Box 497, UAF; Statement of Mrs. James E. Griffin, February 6, 1958, Faubus Papers, Box 497, UAF; Interview, Paul Magro, February 5, 1958, Faubus Papers, Box 497, UAF.

23. J. O. Powell, "Central High Inside Out," Powell Papers, Box 1, UAF; Terrence Roberts, 1957–1958, October 2, 1957, Bates Papers, Microfilm Edition, Reel 6, SHSW; Melba Pattillo, 1957–1959, October 2, 1957, Bates Papers, Microfilm edition, Reel 6, SHSW.

24. Beals, *Warriors Don't Cry*; Author's Interview with Ernest Green, March 12, 1996; *Arkansas Gazette*, May 18, 1979; *Arkansas Gazette*, May 28, 1967; *Arkansas Gazette*, January 30, 1966.

25. Some white parents decided to withdraw their children rather than have them attend school with African Americans. Powell, "Central High Inside Out," Powell Papers, Box 1, UAF; Blossom, *It Has Happened Here*, pp. 135–36; Minutes of the Little Rock Board of Education Meeting, October 18, 1957, Records of the Little Rock School Board [hereafter cited as LRSB], Box 1, UALR.

26. Powell, "Central High Inside Out," Powell Papers, Box 1, UAF.

27. *Arkansas Democrat*, December 15, 1957.

28. Elizabeth Huckaby, 1957 Yearbook, October 10, 1957, EP Huckaby Papers, Box 1, UAF; Melba Pattillo, 1957–1959, October 2, 1957, Bates Papers, Microfilm Edition, Reel 6, SHSW; *Arkansas Gazette*, May 18, 1979. Many students ignored the treatment of the black students out of a commitment to their notions of neutrality and normality. One explained to oral historian Beth Roy that she "came in the side door, went to my locker, did my thing." Roy, *Bitters in the Honey*, p. 174.

29. Elizabeth Huckaby, 1957 Yearbook, September 23, 1957, EP Huckaby Papers, Box 1, UAF; Huckaby, *Crisis at Central High*, p. 101.

30. Special Bulletin, September 4, 1957, EP Huckaby Papers, Box 1, UAF; Powell, "Central High Inside Out," Powell Papers, Box 1, UAF. By contrast, African American students at Mann High School participated in classroom discussions of school integration. *New York Times*, September 15, 1957.

31. Daily Bulletin, October 3, 1957, EP Huckaby Papers, Box 1, UAF; Report on Little Rock, 10/2/57, Little Rock Reports: Volume I, WHO, OSS, SS, AS, DDEL; Bates, *The Long Shadow of Little Rock*, pp. 117, 124–30; Transcript of a

conversation between Gloster Current, Daisy Bates, and Clarence Laws, October 1, 1957, Bates Papers, SHSW, Box 5.

32. Gloster Current of the NAACP thought they should consider swearing out warrants for the arrest of the guilty students if the school officials did not do anything. Transcript of a conversation between Gloster Current, Daisy Bates, and Clarence Laws, October 2, 1957, Bates Papers, Box 5, SHSW; Bates, *The Long Shadow of Little Rock*, pp. 126–30.

33. Transcript of a conversation between Gloster Current, Daisy Bates, Henry Moon, and Clarence Laws, October 3, 1957, Bates Papers, Box 5, SHSW; Bates, *The Long Shadow of Little Rock*, pp. 126–30.

34. Powell, "Central High Inside Out," Powell Papers, Box 1, UAF; Transcript of a conversation between Gloster Current, Daisy Bates, and Clarence Laws, October 2, 1957, Bates Papers, Box 5, SHSW.

35. Powell, "Central High Inside Out," Powell Papers, Box 1, UAF. Melba Pattillo also questioned the willingness and ability of Arkansas National Guardsmen to offer them protection. Beals, *Warriors Don't Cry*, pp. 169–72.

36. Transcript of a conversation between Gloster Current, Daisy Bates, Henry Moon, and Clarence Laws, October 3, 1957, Bates Papers, SHSW, Box 5; Huckaby, *Crisis at Central High*, p. 57.

37. Powell, "Central High Inside Out," Powell Papers, Box 1, UAF; Racial Incidents at Central High School, 1957–1958, EP Huckaby Papers, Box 2, UAF. In February, 1958, two fathers of girls attending Central came to the school charging that the "occupation troops" had stolen books from their daughters' lockers during a search for bombs. Soon the girls located the missing books "where they had left them." Huckaby, *Crisis at Central High*, p. 153.

38. Arthur Larson, Memo for the President, the White House, September 30, 1957, Little Rock, Miscellaneous, Vol. II, WHO, OSS, SS, AS, DDEL; The White House, notes, 30 Sept. 1957, Little Rock, Miscellaneous, Vol. II, WHO, OSS, SS, AS, Box 17, DDEL; Col. Sewell, 26 Sept 57, OSS, SS, AS, Box 16, DDEL; Powell, "Central High Inside Out," Powell Papers, Box 1, UAF. African American leaders in Little Rock, by contrast, lobbied to keep the federal military at the high school as long as possible. J. R. Booker and Dr. H. A. Powell to Val Washington, October 11, 1957, SF, AD-M, Box 11, DDEL; Val J. Washington to Sherman Adams, October 16, 1957 and November 14, 1957, SF, AD-M, Box 11, DDEL.

39. Transcript of a conversation between Gloster Current, Henry Moon, Clarence Laws, and Daisy Bates, October 3, 1957, Bates Papers, SHSW, Box 5.

40. Elizabeth Huckaby, 1957 Yearbook, October 30, 1957, EP Huckaby Papers, Box 1, UAF; John Pagan Interview with Ernest Green, January 26, 1973, Murphy Papers, Box 1, UAF; Huckaby, *Crisis at Central High*, p. 112.

41. Transcript of a conversation between Gloster Current, Daisy Bates, and Clarence Laws, September 30, 1957, Bates Papers, Box 5, SHSW; Transcript of a conversation between Gloster Current, Henry Moon, Daisy Bates, and Clarence Laws, October 3, 1957, Bates Papers, Box 5, SHSW.

42. Huckaby, *Crisis at Central High*, pp. 123, 155, 164–65; Student Records, Bates Papers, Microfilm Edition, Reel 6, SHSW; Liz to Bill, February 12, 1958, EP Huckaby Papers, UALR; Powell, "Central High Inside Out," Powell Papers, UAF.

43. Chronology, December 12, 1957, FBI-L.R. Crisis Reports, A-39, Box 1, UARL; Summary of Incidents, CHS, 10/2/57, Student Records, CHS, Microfilm Edition, Reel 6, Bates Papers, SHSW; Elizabeth Huckaby, 1957 Yearbook, October 7 and 10, 1957, EP Huckaby Papers, Box 1, UAF; Pre-Press Conference, October 9, 1957, DDE, PPUS, AWF, Box 27, DDEL. Faubus's penchant for referring to General Edwin Walker as the "Commander of the Little Rock Occupational Forces" in his correspondence also enraged the Army. Orval E. Faubus to the President, October 25, 1957 and Wilber M. Brucker, Secretary of the Army, to Orval E. Faubus, October 26, 1957, CF, OF, Box 733; Orval E. Faubus to the President, October 25, 1957, CF, OF, Box 733.

44. Powell, "Central High Inside Out," Powell Papers, Box 1, UAF; Elizabeth Huckaby, CUOHP, 1973, EP Huckaby Papers, UALR.

45. The White House, Wheeler, 30 Oct 57, WHO, OSS, SS, AS, Box 13, DDEL.

46. Blossom, *It Has Happened Here*, p. 160.

47. Clipping, no cite, November 24, 1957, EP Huckaby Papers, UALR; Transcript of conversation between Mrs. L. C. Bates and Gloster Current, November 13, 1957, Bates Papers, Box 5, SHSW; *New York Times*, August 13, 1959; Colbert S. Cartwright to Dr. and Mrs. Hunter, December 21, 1957, Cartwright Papers, UAF.

48. Racial Incidents at Central High School, 1957–1958, EP Huckaby Papers, Box 2, UAF; Beals, *Warriors Don't Cry*, p. 177; Huckaby, *Crisis at Central High*, p. 112; Student Records, Terrence Roberts, January 10, 1958, Microfilm edition, Reel 6, Bates Papers, SHSW; Student Records, Ernest Green, January 10, 1958, January 30, 1958, Microfilm edition, Reel 6, Bates Papers, SHSW. The girls also experienced difficulties in gym class. Student Records, Elizabeth Eckford, December 10, 1957, January 31, 1958, Microfilm Edition, Reel 6, Bates Papers, SHSW.

49. Huckaby, *Crisis at Central High*, p. 156; Beals, *Warriors Don't Cry*, p. 184; Tim Delaney to J. O. Powell, n. d., Powell Papers, Box 1, UAF.

50. J. O. Powell report, January 16, 1958, Student Reports, Minnijean Brown, Microfilm Edition, Reel 6, Bates Papers, SHSW; January 29, 1958, Student Reports, Minnijean Brown, Microfilm Edition, Reel 6, Bates Papers, SHSW; Chronology, January 31, 1958, FBI-L.R. Crisis Reports, Box 1, UARL; Huckaby, 1958

Yearbook, January 16, 1958, EP Huckaby Papers, Box 1, UAF; Elizabeth Huckaby, CUOHP, 1973, EP Huckaby Papers, UALR. Daisy Bates to Henry Lee Moon, February 18, 1958, Student Reports, Minnijean Brown, Microfilm Edition, Reel 6, Bates Papers, SHSW; *Baltimore Afro-American*, February 8, 1958.

51. Huckaby, *Crisis at Central High*, pp. 157–60.

52. Huckaby, *Crisis at Central High*, pp. 128–29, 154–59; Interview with Elizabeth Huckaby, CUOHP, 1973, UALR; Huckaby note on clipping, *Arkansas Gazette*, October 17, 1978, EP Huckaby Papers, UALR.

53. Powell, "Central High Inside Out," Powell Papers, Box 1, UAF; Statement of William P. Ivey to Howard Chandler, January 21, 1958, Faubus Papers, Box 497, UAF; Mothers' League of Central High to Jess Matthews, December 13, 1957, Blossom Papers, Box 7, UAF. It is impossible to determine whether the women's organization had heard of Matthews' comments at the staff meeting a few days earlier. It is true, however, that a Central High School teacher, William Ivey, went to the Arkansas State Police on January 20 and told them of Matthews' remarks. There is no extant evidence to suggest that Ivey or another teacher upset at the principal's decision contacted like-minded activists outside the school before January 20. Statement of William P. Ivey to Howard Chandler, January 21, 1958, Faubus Papers, Box 497, UAF.

54. "Shall the School Board Deprive Children of an Education Because They Opposed Race-Mixing?" n.d., EP Huckaby Papers, Box 2, UAF.

55. A. F. House to Board of Directors, Little Rock School District, January 23, 1958, Blossom Papers, Box 3, UAF; Huckaby, *Crisis at Central High*, pp. 125, 129, 168; Roy, *Bitters in the Honey*, p. 174; Special Bulletin, September 5, 1957, EP Huckaby Papers, Box 1, UAF; Blossom, *It Has Happened Here*, p. 139; FBI Reports, Chronology, April 1, 1958, FBI, Box 1, UALR. Students found creative ways to distribute the forbidden literature at the school. One even fastened a "ONE DOWN EIGHT TO GO" card on Jess Matthews' coat tail as he was going up a stairway. When someone pointed it out to him, he said, "I wondered what everybody was laughing at." Powell, "Central High Inside Out," Powell Papers, Box 1, UAF.

56. Huckaby, *Crisis at Central High*, pp. 51, 101–2; Elizabeth Huckaby, Diary, December 13, 1957 and December 16, 1957, EP Huckaby Papers, Box 1, UAF; Taped Interview with J. O. Powell, Bates Papers, Tape 5, UAF; Clipping, December 15, 1957, EP Huckaby Papers, UALR; Central High School, Student Discipline Records, Microfilm edition, 1980, Reel 6, SHSW; Powell, "Central High Inside Out," Powell Papers, Box 1, UAF.

57. "'Mrs' Daisy Bates Little Rock's 'Lady' of the Year," EP Huckaby Papers, Box 2, UAF; Huckaby, *Crisis at Central High*, p. 105.

58. Huckaby, *Crisis at Central High*, p. 154; Powell, "Central High Inside Out," Powell Papers, Box 1, UAF; Blossom, *It Has Happened Here*, p. 173. The

teachers' testimony would be used later when segregationists targeted some for its May 1959 "purge." *Arkansas Gazette*, May 8, 1959.

59. Huckaby, 1958 Yearbook, February 10, 1958, Box 1, UAF; Huckaby, *Crisis at Central High*, pp. 159, 162; Powell, "Central High Inside Out," Powell Papers, Box 1, UAF.

60. Clipping, no cite, January 14, 1958, EP Huckaby Papers, UALR; Chronology, January 6, 1958, FBI-L.R. Crisis Reports, A-39, Box 1, UARL.

61. Re: Elizabeth Eckford, January 10, 1958, EP Huckaby Papers, Box 2, UAF; Report to Mr. Blossom on Darlene Holloway, EP Huckaby Papers, Box 2, UAF; *Arkansas Gazette*, February 16, 1958; Huckaby, 1958 Yearbook, March 5, 1958, EP Huckaby Papers, Box 1, UAF. Elizabeth Huckaby wrote in her journal after the school board meeting on Holloway's case that she felt "like a Christian martyr thrown to lions" and that Amis Guthridge was "ignorant, lying, hateful." Huckaby, 1958 Yearbook, January 22, 1958, EP Huckaby Papers, Box 1, UAF. During her suspension, Darlene showed up in the school cafeteria at noon. When Huckaby told her to leave, she said she would have to call Citizens' Council leader Wesley Pruden about it. Huckaby, 1958 Yearbook, January 16, 1958, Box 1, UAF.

62. Statement of Policy by Board of Directors of Little Rock School District, n.d. [February 1958], Blossom Papers, Box 4, UAF; *Arkansas Gazette*; Huckaby, *Crisis at Central High*, p. 162.

63. Huckaby, ibid.

64. Oral History interview with Nat R. Griswold, August 21, 1971, Little Rock desegregation crisis, 1957–1959, Oral history interview transcripts, 1972–1973, MS L720 310 Little Rock, UAF; Nat R. Griswold to Harold Fleming, November 29, 1957, Papers of the Arkansas Council on Human Relations [hereafter cited as ACHR], Box 20, UAF; *Arkansas Gazette*, February 20, 1958; *Arkansas Gazette*, February 21, 1958; Clipping, no cite, n.d., EP Huckaby Papers, UALR.

65. Interview with R. A. Lile by John Luter, August 19, 1971, CUOHP, OH-219, DDEL; R. A. Lile to Sherman Adams, March 17, 1958, CF, OF, Box 733, DDEL.

66. Powell, "Central High Inside Out," Powell Papers, Box 1, UAF; *U.S. News and World Report*, June 20, 1958, pp. 74–86.

67. Untitled, February 6, 1958, EP Huckaby Papers, Box 2, UAF.

68. Elizabeth Huckaby, 1957 Yearbook, February 6, 1958, EP Huckaby Papers, Box 1, UAF; Student reports dated February 6, 1958 in EP Huckaby Papers, Box 2, UAF; Daisy Bates to Henry Lee Moon, February 18, 1958, Student Reports, Microfilm Edition, Reel 6, Bates Papers, SHSW; J. O. Powell report, January 20, 1958, Student Reports, Microfilm Edition, Reel 6, Bates Papers,

SHSW; file listed under student's name, Student Reports, Microfilm Edition, Reel 6, Bates Papers, SHSW.

69. Virgil T. Blossom to Mr. and Mrs. W. B. Brown, February 13, 1958 in Minutes of the Little Rock Board of Education Meeting, February 17, 1958, LRSB, Box 1, UALR; Huckaby, *Crisis at Central High*, p. 152; Ellis Thomas to Virgil T. Blossom, February 11, 1958, Blossom Papers, Box 8, UAF; Transcript of a conversation between Gloster Current, Clarence Laws, Christopher Mercer, and Mrs. L. C. Bates, February 13, 1958, Bates Papers, SHSW, Box 5.

70. Mrs. Jack Davis to Wayne Upton, February 14, 1958, Blossom Papers, Box 8, UAF; *Chicago Daily News*, February 17, 1958, Blossom Papers, Box 8, UAF. For more letters, including several from Little Rock African Americans, see Blossom Papers, Folder 2, Box 8, UAF.

71. Transcript, *John Aaron et al. v. William G. Cooper et al.*, In the United States District Court, Eastern District of Arkansas, Western Division, p. 325, Blossom Papers, Box 5, UAF.

72. Huckaby, *Crisis at Central High*, p. 159; *Arkansas Gazette*, February 19, 1958; *New York Times*, February 23, 1958.

73. Sammie Dean Parker (Summary), EP Huckaby Papers, Box 2, UAF; Roy, *Bitters in the Honey*, pp. 171–96.

74. Sammie Dean Parker (Summary), EP Huckaby Papers, Box 2, UAF; *Arkansas Gazette*, March 1, 1958; Suspension Notice, Feb. 17, 1958, EP Huckaby Papers, Box 2, UAF; Elizabeth Huckaby, CUOHP, 1973, EP Huckaby Papers, UALR; 1957 Yearbook, September 5, 1957, EP Huckaby Papers, Box 1, UAF.

75. Clipping, no cite, March 21, 1958, EP Huckaby Papers, UALR; *Arkansas Gazette*, September 29, 1957; Beals, *Warriors Don't Cry*, pp. 179–80; John Pagan Interview with Elizabeth Huckaby, n.d., Murphy Papers, Box 1, UAF; Re: Sammie Dean Parker, February 6, 1958, EP Huckaby Papers, Box 2, UAF. The FBI confirmed her meetings with the state police. Huckaby, *Crisis at Central High*, p. 163.

76. Sara Murphy Interview with Sammie Dean Hulett, December 9, 1992, Murphy Papers, Box 1, UAF; Chronology, April 29, 1958, FBI-L.R. Crisis Reports, A-39, Box 1, UARL.

77. Sammie Dean Parker (Summary), EP Huckaby Papers, Box 2, UAF; Elizabeth Huckaby, CUOHP, 1973, EP Huckaby Papers, UALR; Huckaby, *Crisis at Central High*, p. 163.

78. Minutes of the Little Rock Board of Education Meeting, February 21, 1958, LRSB, Box 1, UALR; Conference re Sammie Dean Parker, February 27, 1958, EP Huckaby Papers, Box 2, UAF.

79. Conference re Sammie Dean Parker, February 27, 1958, EP Huckaby Papers, Box 2, UAF; Huckaby, *Crisis at Central High*, pp. 170–72. Unsurprisingly,

Huckaby concluded that "Sammie Dean's mother had emotional problems. She was very hyper all the time." Sara Murphy Interview with Elizabeth Huckaby, August 18, 1992, Murphy Papers, Box 1, UAF.

80. Minutes of the Little Rock Board of Education Meeting, February 28, 1958, LRSB, Box 1, UALR.

81. Elizabeth Huckaby, 1957 Yearbook, February 26, March 4, 7, 1958, EP Huckaby Papers, Box 1, UAF; *Arkansas Gazette*, n.d., EP Huckaby Papers, UALR; Huckaby, *Crisis at Central High*, pp. 173–75.

82. *Arkansas Gazette*, February 25, 1958.

83. Powell, "Central High Inside Out," Powell Papers, Box 1, UAF; *Arkansas Gazette*, March 5, 1958. Some of her classmates remembered the incident quite differently. One reported much later that Sammie Dean "was kicking, spitting, scratching, and the policeman couldn't do anything with her, she was so out of control." Roy, *Bitters in the Honey*, pp. 171, 175.

84. Powell, "Central High Inside Out," Powell Papers, Box 1, UAF; *Arkansas Gazette*, March 5, 1958.

85. Clipping, no cite, March 9, 1958, EP Huckaby Papers, UALR; *Arkansas Gazette*, March 5, 1958; *Arkansas Gazette*, March 6, 1958; *Arkansas Gazette*, March 7, 1958.

86. *Arkansas Gazette*, March 8, 1958, March 12, 1958; Powell, "Central High Inside Out," Powell Papers, Box 1, UAF.

87. Liz to Bill, March 12, 1958, EP Huckaby Papers, UALR; Huckaby, *Crisis at Central High*, p. 184.

88. Chronology, April 29, 1958, FBI-L.R. Crisis Reports, A-39, Box 1, UARL; Re: Sammie Dean Parker, April 10, 1958, EP Huckaby Papers, Box 2, UAF; Huckaby, *Crisis at Central High*, pp. 189–90; Elizabeth Huckaby, CUOHP, 1973; Phoebe Christina Godfrey, "'Sweet Little Girls'? Miscegenation, Desegregation and the Defense of Whiteness at Little Rock's Central High, 1957–1959" (Ph.D. dissertation, Binghamton University, State University of New York, 2001), p. 217.

89. Name Withheld to the Parents (REAL Parents) of Central High Students, March 8, 1958, EP Huckaby Papers, Box 2, UAF; Elizabeth Huckaby, 1958 Yearbook, February 26, March 4, 7, 1958, EP Huckaby Papers, Box 1, UAF; *Arkansas Gazette*, n.d., EP Huckaby Papers, UALR; Huckaby, *Crisis at Central High*, p. 177.

90. John Pagan Interview with Ernest Green, January 26, 1973, Murphy Papers, Box 1, UAF; Bates, *The Long Shadow of Little Rock*, pp. 142–43.

91. Huckaby, *Crisis at Central High*, p. 163; Student Records, CHS, Microfilm Edition, Reel 6, Bates Papers, SHSW.

92. Roy, *Bitters in the Honey*, quotes on pp. 183, 184.

93. Powell, "Central High Inside Out," Powell Papers, Box 1, UAF.

94. Transcript of conversation with Gloster Current, Daisy Bates, and Clarence Laws, December 13, 1957, Bates Papers, Box 5, SHSW; Bates, *The Long Shadow of Little Rock*, pp. 113–50; Chronology, November 12, 1957 and January 31, 1958, FBI-L. R. Crisis Reports, A-39, Box 1, UARL.

95. Transcript, *John Aaron et al. v. William G. Cooper et al.*, United States District Court, Eastern District of Arkansas, Western Division, Blossom Papers, Box 5, UAF; Blossom, *It Has Happened Here*, pp. 151, 171–72.

96. Blossom, *It Has Happened Here*, pp. 86–89, 195–97, 201; Huckaby, *Crisis at Central High*, p. 168; Interview with R. A. Lile by John Luter, August 19, 1971, CUOHP, OH-219, DDEL.

97. Huckaby, *Crisis at Central High*, p. 168; Powell, "Central High Inside Out," Powell Papers, Box 1, UAF.

CHAPTER FOUR. THE POLITICS OF SCHOOL CLOSURE: MASSIVE RESISTANCE PUT TO THE TEST, 1958–1959

1. Mrs. Charles Stephens, Program to Save Our Schools [draft], September 25, 1958. Papers of the Women's Emergency Committee [hereafter cited as WEC], Box 2, AHC.

2. Tony A. Freyer, *The Little Rock Crisis: A Constitutional Interpretation* (Westport, CT: Greenwood Press, 1984), pp. 139–70.

3. Oral History Interview with Mrs. Joe Brewer, August 20, 1971, CUOHP, DDEL; Diary, Mrs. D. D. Terry, September 12, 1958, Terry Papers, Series II, Subseries II, Box 1, UALR; Personal Statement of Mrs. Joe R. Brewer, Fall of 1959, Vivion L. Brewer Collection [hereafter cited as Brewer Papers], Series I, Box I, UALR; Author's Interview with Velma Powell, March 15, 1996.

4. Oral History Interview with Mrs. Joe Brewer, August 20, 1971, CUOHP, DDEL; Sara Alderman Murphy, *Breaking the Silence: Little Rock's Women's Emergency Committee to Open Our Schools, 1958–1963* (Fayetteville: University of Arkansas Press, 1997), p. 75; Lorraine Gates, "Power from the Pedestal: The Women's Emergency Committee and the Little Rock School Crisis," *Arkansas Historical Quarterly* 55 (Spring 1996): 26–57; Vivion Lenon Brewer, "The Embattled Ladies of Little Rock," pp. 5–10, Brewer Papers, Series I, File 2, UALR.

5. *Newsweek*, June 30, 1958; *Time*, June 30, 1958; Oral History Interview with A. F. House, August 17, 1971, CUOHP, DDEL. The *Arkansas Gazette* ran a very positive description of Lemley just after the decision. *Arkansas Gazette*, June 22, 1958.

6. *U.S. News and World Report*, June 20, 1958, pp. 74–86; *Arkansas Gazette*, June 4, 1958; *Arkansas Democrat*, June 3, 1958; *Aaron v. Cooper*, 163 F. Supp. 13; Virgil T. Blossom, *It Has Happened Here* (New York: Harper & Brothers, 1959),

pp. 179–80. Elizabeth Huckaby reported in her journal that Principal Jess Matthews said that "not being allowed to testify made him feel like a heel." Elizabeth Huckaby Journal, June 5, 1958, EP Huckaby Papers, Series I, Box I, UAF.

7. *U.S. News and World Report*, June 20, 1958, pp. 74–86. For other Faubus blaming, see Blossom, *It Has Happened Here*, pp. 176–77; Woodrow Wilson Mann, "The Truth about Little Rock," *New York Herald Tribune*, January 19 and 22, 1958.

8. *Arkansas Democrat*, June 3, 1958; clipping, no cite, June 6, 1958, EP Huckaby Papers, UALR; Blossom, *It Has Happened Here*, p. 180; *Arkansas Gazette*, June 4, 1958.

9. *Arkansas Gazette*, June 4, 1958; *Arkansas Democrat*, June 3, 1958.

10. *Arkansas Gazette*, June 4, 1958; *Arkansas Democrat*, June 3, 1958; *U.S. News and World Report*, June 20, 1958, pp. 74–86; Blossom, *It Has Happened Here*, pp. 18–19.

11. *Aaron v. Cooper*, 163 F. Supp. 13; Little Rock Desegregation, June 25, 1958, Files of W. Wilson White, Assistant Attorney General, Civil Rights Division, 1958–1959, Record Group 60 [hereafter cited as White Papers], Box 2, National Archives [hereafter cited as NA]; *Newsweek*, June 30, 1958.

12. *Arkansas Gazette*, June 21, 1958, June 22, 1958; *Time*, June 30, 1958; *Newsweek*, June 30, 1958; *Wall Street Journal*, June 26, 1958; clipping, no cite, June 21, 1958, EP Huckaby Papers, UALR; *U.S. News and World Report*, June 20, 1958, pp. 74–86; Liz [Huckaby] to Bill [Paisley], June, 1958, EP Huckaby Papers, UALR. Harry Ashmore, editor of the *Arkansas Gazette*, similarly observed that "time is of value only if it is put to some practical use," in a perceptive article published in June 1958. His position in that article does not fit easily with the stance adopted by the *Gazette* at the time. Harry Ashmore, "The Easy Chair: The Untold Story Behind Little Rock," reprint from *Harper's Magazine*, June 1958, NAACP Papers, Group III, Box A 98, LC. Senator J. William Fulbright sent a brief in support of the district court decision after the NAACP appealed the finding to the Eighth Circuit Court of Appeals. Statement by Senator J. W. Fulbright, August 27, 1958, Faubus Papers, Box 497, UAF.

13. Little Rock Desegregation, June 25, 1958, White Papers, Box 2, NA; Memorandum for the Attorney General, July 22, 1958, White Papers, Box 2, NA; Memorandum, August 14, 1958, White Papers, Box 2, NA; John T. Elliff, *The United States Department of Justice and Individual Rights, 1937–1962* (New York: Garland Publishing, Inc., 1987, reprint of Ph.D. dissertation, Harvard University, 1967), pp. 602–9.

14. Memorandum for the Files, June 24, 1958, CF, OF, Box 731, DDE, DDEL; Memorandum to Mr. Wilkins from Mr. Current, June 23, 1958, NAACP Papers, Group III, Box A98, LC; A Statement to President Dwight D. Eisenhower, June 23, 1958, NAACP Papers, Group III, Box A98, LC. For Eisenhower's

reluctance to meet or act, see Frederic Morrow Diary, March 14, 1956, Morrow-MS Papers, Box 1, DDEL; Diary of E. Frederic Morrow [hereafter cited as EFM Diary], June 23, 1958, Papers of E. Frederic Morrow [hereafter cited as Morrow Papers], Box 1, DDEL; E. Frederic Morrow, *Black Man in the White House: A Diary of the Eisenhower Years by the Administrative Officer for Special Projects, the White House, 1955–1961* (New York: Coward-McCann, Inc., 1963), pp. 226–29, 233–34; Interview with E. Frederic Morrow, January 31, 1968, CUOHP, OH-92, #1, DDEL. Eisenhower denied a request that a representative of the National Council of Negro Women be included in the delegation. Morrow, *Black Man in the White House*, pp. 232–33.

15. Interview with E. Frederic Morrow, CUOHP, #1, DDEL.

16. Southern Regional Council, "A Background Report on School Desegregation for 1959–1960," August 10, 1959, WEC Papers, Box 20, AHC; Mary L. Dudziak, *Cold War and Civil Rights: Race and the Image of American Democracy* (Princeton, NJ: Princeton University Press, 2000), p. 140.

17. *Aaron v. Cooper* 257 F. 2d 33; *New York Times*, August 19, 1958.

18. Statement of Governor Faubus, August 19, 1958, Faubus Papers, UAF, Box 606.

19. Statement of Governor Faubus, August 19, 1958, Faubus Papers, UAF, Box 606; *U.S. News and World Report*, June 20, 1958; Freyer, *The Little Rock Crisis*, pp. 10–12, 75, 90–91.

20. Address to Second Extraordinary Session of the 61st General Assembly, August 26, 1958, Faubus Papers, MS F27 301, Box 496, UAF; Statement of Governor Faubus, August 19, 1958, Faubus Papers, Box 606, UAF; *Newsweek*, September 8, 1958; Author's Interview with Roy Reed, June 19, 1995.

21. Statement of Governor Faubus, August 19, 1958, Faubus Papers, UAF, Box 606; Roy Wilkins to Daisy Bates, August 20, 1958, NAACP Papers, Group III, Box A98, LC.

22. Address to Second Extraordinary Session of the 61st General Assembly, August 26, 1958, Faubus Papers, MS F27 301, Box 496, UAF; Statement of Governor Faubus, August 23, 1958, Faubus Papers, UAF, Box 606; *Newsweek*, September 8, 1958.

23. Jim Johnson to Orval E. Faubus, October 3, 1957, Faubus Papers, Box 590, UAF; *William G. Cooper et al. v. John Aaron et al.*, Appeal from the United States District Court for the Eastern District of Arkansas to United States Court of Appeals for the Eighth Circuit, November 10, 1958; the League of Women Voters of Arkansas, "Arkansas' Public Schools: Study Guide," WEC, Box 2, AHC; Southern Regional Council, "A Background Report," WEC Papers, Box 20, AHC.

24. Jeff Woods, "'Designed to Harass': The Act 10 Controversy in Arkansas," *Arkansas Historical Quarterly* 56 (Winter 1997): 443–60; Nat R. Griswold, "Rec-

ognition of WEC," January 25, 1969, Powell Papers, Box 2, UAF. Act 10 infuriated and alienated many public school teachers and university professors in Arkansas who, in the words of businessman Joshua Shepherd, "quite naturally and understandably resent having their loyalty and integrity questioned in this stigmatic [sic] manner." Joshua K. Shepherd to Orval Faubus, September 3, 1958, Faubus Papers, Box 432, UAF.

25. Statement of Governor Orval E. Faubus, September 12, 1958, Faubus Papers, Box 606, UAF; *Arkansas Gazette*, September 19, 1958.

26. AP news release of statement by President Eisenhower, August 27, 1958, Faubus Papers, Box 606, UAF; *Newsweek*, September 8, 1958; Osro Cobb, *Osro Cobb of Arkansas: Memoirs of Historical Significance*, ed. Carol Griffee (Little Rock: Rose Publishing Company, 1989), p. 261.

27. Department of Justice, Press Releases, September 11, 1958, William P. Rogers Papers [hereafter cited as Rogers Papers], Box 54, DDEL; *New York Times*, September 17, 1958.

28. *Arkansas Gazette*, November 2, 4, 1958.

29. *William G. Cooper et al. v. John Aaron et al.*, Supreme Court of the United States, August Special Term, 1958. In a concurring opinion, Justice Felix Frankfurter called the actions of the state of Arkansas an "illegal, forcible interference" with Constitutional requirements and denied that "law should bow to force." He further denied the inevitability of resistance, stating that "Experience attests that such local habits and feelings will yield… to law and education."

30. *Time*, September 29, 1958; Cobb, *Osro Cobb*, p. 268; Strom Thurmond to Orval Faubus, October 3, 1958, Faubus Papers, Box 599, UAF.

31. Brooks Hays to Sherman Adams, September 3, 1958, CF, GF, Box 919, DDE, DDEL; *New York Times*, September 17, 1958. Justice Department attorneys had been developing briefs on the constitutional issues raised by the school closings. Lawrence H. Walsh to W. Wilson White, School Closing Laws, September 12, 1958, White Papers, Box 2, NA; W. Wilson White to Lawrence E. Walsh, September, 1958, White Papers, Box 2, NA; Memorandum, September 5, 1958, White Papers, Box 2, NA; Memorandum, September 19, 1958, White Papers, Box 2, NA.

32. "Personal Statement of Mrs. Joe. R. Brewer," Fall, 1959, Brewer Papers, UALR, Series 1, Box 1; Brewer, "The Embattled Ladies of Little Rock," pp. 6–7, Brewer Papers, Series I, File 2, UALR; Terry, *Life Is My Song, Also*, p. 231, Terry Papers, RG A-13, UALR; *Arkansas Gazette*, July, 1960, WEC, Box 2, AHC.

33. David L. Chappell, *Inside Agitators: White Southerners in the Civil Rights Movement* (Baltimore: Johns Hopkins University Press, 1994), pp. 97–121.

34. Blossom, *It Has Happened Here*, pp. 181–83; "Letter From Little Rock," WEC, Box 1, AHC; Author's Interview with Harry Ashmore, February 5, 1995;

Author's Interview with Velma Powell, March 15, 1996; *Pine Bluff Commercial*, November 5, 1963; Minutes, Board, Women's Emergency Committee, September 5, 1962, WEC, AHC, Box 2. On this I differ with Elizabeth Jacoway, who has investigated the "behind-the-scenes" efforts of some businessmen to seek a solution to the problem. In my view, a decision to operate only in private meant that public leadership and activism was partially ceded to other social groups in the community. Elizabeth Jacoway, "Taken By Surprise: Little Rock Business Leaders and Desegregation," in Elizabeth Jacoway and David R. Colburn, eds., *Southern Businessmen and Desegregation* (Baton Rouge: Louisiana State University Press, 1982), pp. 15–40; "Letter From Little Rock," WEC, Box 1, AHC; Brewer, "The Embattled Ladies of Little Rock," p. 3, Brewer Papers, Series I, File 2, UALR; *Arkansas Gazette*, June 15, 1966.

35. Daisy Bates, *The Long Shadow of Little Rock: A Memoir* (New York: David McKay Company, Inc., 1962), pp. 179–213; Author's Interview with Pat House, June 28, 1995; Dan Wakefield, "Siege at Little Rock: The Brave Ones," *Nation*, October 11, 1958, pp. 204–6; Gertrude Samuels, "The Silent Fear in Little Rock," *New York Times Sunday Magazine*, March 30, 1958, pp. 11, 78–79.

36. Anonymous to Mrs. D. D. Terry, September 18, 1958, Terry Papers, Series II, Subseries II, Box 4, UALR; Author's interview with Pat House, June 28, 1995. For the importance of sexuality to segregationist thought, see also many of the letters to Daisy Bates in Bates Papers, MSS 523, SHSW, Box 1.

37. Author's Interview with Velma Powell, March 15, 1996; Author's Interview with Pat House, June 28, 1995; Author's Interview with Irene Samuel, June 30, 1995; Terry, *Life Is My Song, Also*, pp. 60–61, Terry Papers, UALR. For hate mail received by the WEC see Box 16, WEC Papers, AHC.

38. Terry, *Life Is My Song, Also*, Series II, Subseries II, Box 2, Terry Papers, UALR; Author's Interview with Velma Powell, March 15, 1996. My view that the leaders of the WEC had more racially egalitarian politics than the membership differs from that advanced by Lorraine Gates. Gates, "Power from the Pedestal," p. 40. The activities of Adolphine Terry and Velma Powell prior to the crisis and the activism of Pat House, Vivion Brewer, Sara Murphy, and others after the crisis suggest that the leaders were more committed to racial change than the members. Brewer, "The Embattled Ladies of Little Rock," p. 275, Brewer Papers, Series I, UALR; Author's Interview with Velma Powell, March 15, 1996.

39. Personal History Characteristics of the Members of the Women's Emergency Committee for Public Schools, WEC, Box 1, AHC; *Arkansas Democrat*, June 27, 1960; Author's Interview with Irene Samuel, June 30, 1995; Author's Interview with Pat House, June 28, 1995. Very few members of the Junior League joined the WEC. Sara Murphy Interview with Jean Gordon, June 16, 1992, Murphy Papers, Box 1, UAF. In 1960, the median school years completed for women

in Arkansas was 9.5 years. A little over 3 percent of women in the state had completed four or more years of college. U.S. Department of Commerce, Bureau of the Census, "Census of Population: 1960," Volume 1, Part 5, pp. 274–77.

40. G [Grace] to Vivion, August 15, 1960, WEC Papers, Box 4, AHC.

41. Brewer, "The Embattled Ladies of Little Rock," p. 3, Brewer Papers, UALR, Series I, File 2; Author's Interview with Irene Samuel, June 30, 1995; Vivion Brewer to Mrs. Guerdon Nichols, October 27, 1959 and April 2, 1959, WEC Papers, Box 4, AHC; Mrs. Byron House, Jr. To Mrs. Douglas J. Romine, WEC Papers, Box 4, AHC. The League of Women Voters of Arkansas did not get publicly involved in the school crisis until February, 1958, when they passed a resolution in favor of opening the public high schools of Little Rock. Minutes, League of Women Voters of Arkansas, February 23, 1958, Records of the League of Women Voters of Arkansas, MC 476 [hereafter cited as League Papers], Box 11, UAF.

42. *Pine Bluff Commercial*, February 22, 1966; Author's Interview with Harry Ashmore, February 5, 1995; Profile of Mrs. Brewer, WEC Papers, Box 1, AHC; *Arkansas Gazette*, June 15, 1966; *Arkansas Gazette*, June 22, 1969; Murphy, *Breaking the Silence*, pp. 1–25.

43. Letter From Little Rock, December, 1958, WEC, Box 1, AHC.

44. Letter From Little Rock, December, 1958, WEC, Box 1, AHC; Author's Interview with Jim Childers, June 28, 1995.

45. *Arkansas Gazette*, September 22, 1958; "Letter from Little Rock," WEC Papers, Box 1, AHC; *New York Times*, September 21, 1958; *Time* called the ad "the most significant rebellion of all." *Time*, September 29, 1958. One of the first tasks of the WEC was to write letters of appreciation to each lawyer who signed the ad, thanking him for his willingness to risk the loss of clients in support of public schools. Ronald A. May to Mrs. Joe R. Brewer, November 21, 1958, WEC Papers AHC; Brewer, "The Embattled Ladies of Little Rock," pp. 20–23, UALR.

46. *Arkansas Gazette*, September 19, 1958; "History of Women's Emergency Committee to Open Our Schools," WEC Papers, Box 15, AHC. Faubus later received information offering a very different view of the situation in the Washington schools. Benjamin Muse to Rolla Fitch, July 27, 1959, with enclosure, Southern Regional Council, Report No. L-6, "The 'Davis Report' and the Truth about the Public School Situation in Washington, D. C., Faubus Papers, Box 498, UAF. The SRC report can also be found in WEC Papers, Box 3, AHC.

47. WEC Papers, AHC; Women's Emergency Committee to Open Our Schools, Bates Papers, MSS 523, Box 5, SHSW.

48. Program to Save Our Schools, September 25, 1958, WEC Papers, Box 2, AHC. The others on the program were attorney John E. Coates, the Rev. Dale Cowling, and Mrs. Charles Henry, a former teacher.

49. Oral History Interview with Pat House, August 22, 1971, CUOHP, OH-193, DDEL; Author's Interview with Pat House, June 28, 1995. David Goldfield has noted that in the south "schools were much more than educational facilities. They were extensions of family life, of community and individual values." David Goldfield, *Black, White, and Southern: Race Relations and Southern Culture 1940 to the Present* (Baton Rouge: Louisiana State University Press, 1990), p. 77.

50. *Arkansas Gazette*, September 28, 1958; Elizabeth Huckaby Journal, September 27, 1958, EP Huckaby Papers, Series I, Box I, UAF; Irving J. Spitzberg, Jr., *Racial Politics in Little Rock, 1954–1964* (New York: Garland Publishing, Inc., 1987), p. 85; *Time*, October 6, 1958. According to Spitzberg, the Hall High School picket was staged by Jimmy Karam.

51. *Arkansas Gazette*, September 28, 1958; "Letter from Little Rock," WEC Papers, Box 1, AHC; David Thoreau Wieck, "Report from Little Rock," *Liberation*, October 1958, pp. 4–9; Author's Interview with Jim Childers, June 28, 1995.

52. *Time*, September 29, 1958; *Arkansas Gazette*, September 21, 1958; *Arkansas Democrat*, October 16, 1982; "History of the Women's Emergency Committee to Open Our Schools" WEC Papers, Box 15, AHC [says their poll was of Hall HS].

53. "Letter From Little Rock," WEC, Box 1, AHC; Oral History Interview with Vivion Brewer, CUOHP, OH-193, DDEL; Oral History Interview with Pat House, CUOHP, DDEL; Author's Interview with Irene Samuel, June 30, 1995; Author's interview with Pat House, June 28, 1995; Brewer, "The Embattled Ladies of Little Rock," Brewer Papers, UALR. The WEC's efforts to infiltrate the PTAs had only begun so that the PTA Council of Little Rock was not ready to take a stand on the election. Author's Interview with Irene Samuel, June 30, 1995; Brewer, "The Embattled Ladies of Little Rock," pp. 20–23, Series I, UALR.

54. *Pine Bluff Commercial*, February 22, 1966; Brewer, "The Embattled Ladies of Little Rock," pp. 82–83, Series I, UALR; Address by Mrs. John Samuel, June 11, 1963, WEC Papers, Box 6, AHC; "Letter from Little Rock," WEC Papers, Box 1, AHC.

55. Brewer, "The Embattled Ladies of Little Rock," Brewer Papers, UALR; Herbert L. Thomas to Mrs. D. D. Terry, September 26, 1958, Thomas Papers, Box 4, UAF; *Pine Bluff Commercial*, February 22, 1966; Brewer, "The Embattled Ladies of Little Rock," Series I, UALR; Address by Mrs. John Samuel, June 11, 1963, WEC Papers, Box 6, AHC; "Letter from Little Rock," WEC Papers, Box 1, AHC. At the same time, Powell shared in the veneration for these ideas, characterizing the leadership of the Capital Citizens' Council as laughable because they "were the long standing anti-progress people in the community." Velma Powell, untitled, manuscript, n.d., Powell Papers, MS 1367, Box 2, UAF; Sara Murphy Interview with Harry Ashmore, June 13, 1994, Murphy Papers, Box 1, UAF.

56. Sara Murphy Interview with Parma Basham, September 24, 1992, Murphy Papers, Box 1, UAF; Sara Murphy Interview with Pat House, July 7, 1992, Murphy Papers, Box 1, UAF; Sara Murphy Interview with Irene Samuel, August 14, 1993, Murphy Papers, Box 3, UAF; Brewer, "The Embattled Ladies of Little Rock," Brewer Papers, UALR. Indeed, the Capital Citizens' Council was correct when it charged that there were "big moneybags" behind the WEC. Capital Citizens' Council to Dear Member, n.d., ACHR, MC Ar4, Box 34, UAF.

57. Memorandum to Little Rock School Board [prepared by its attorney], September, 1958, White Papers, Box 2, NA; Memorandum, Use of public school buildings by private schools, September 5, 1958, White Papers, Box 2, NA; Blossom, *It Has Happened Here*, p. 186; Elliff, *The United States Department of Justice and Individual Rights*, pp. 610–12; *Time*, November 3, 1958.

58. *Rebel Rouser*, January 18, 1959, WEC Papers, Box 13, AHC; Donations by State, October, 1958 Through February, 1959, Faubus Papers, Box 531, UAF; Existing Private Schools, WEC Papers, Box 13, AHC; *Arkansas Democrat*, n.d., EP Huckaby Papers, UALR; clipping, no cite, November 17, 1958, EP Huckaby Papers, UALR; *Arkansas Gazette*, November 2, 1958; Oral History Interview of Wayne Upton, December 29, 1971, CUOHP, UAF; J. Harvey Walthall, Jr., "A Study of Certain Factors of School Closing in 1958 as They Affected the Seniors of the White Comprehensive High Schools in Little Rock, Arkansas" (Ed.D. dissertation, University of Arkansas, 1963), p. 36. Less than half of Raney's teachers met minimum state educational standards for public school teachers. *Washington Post*, May 18, 1959, WEC, Box 14, AHC.

59. Existing Private Schools, 1958, WEC, Box 13, AHC. Little Rock University was willing to admit white students for its spring semester provided they had the right combination of test scores and high school and correspondence course credit hours. Clipping, no cite, November 16, 1958, EP Huckaby Papers, UALR.

60. Oral History Interview with Grainger Williams, CUOHP, UALR; From "Our Town Column," *Arkansas Gazette*, May 24, 1959, WEC, Box 17, AHC; Author's Interview with Jim Childers, June 30, 1995; Elizabeth Huckaby Journal, September 2 and 26, 1958, EP Huckaby Papers, Series I, Box I, UAF; Brewer, "The Embattled Ladies of Little Rock," p. 34, Brewer Papers, Series I, File 2, UALR; *Arkansas Gazette*, March 19, 1959, April 19, 1959; Gene Fretz to Bishop Brown, October 6, 1958, Brown Papers, UALR, A-81, Box 1; Transcript for Documentary Film on Little Rock Crisis shown in Atlanta, 1959, WEC, Box 1, AHC.

61. Existing Private Schools, 1958, WEC, Box 13, AHC; Oral History Interview of Wayne Upton, December 29, 1971, CUOHP, MS L720 310, UALR; Pat House's comments on visits to legislators, 1959, WEC, Box 2, AHC.

62. Mrs. Gordon N. Wilson, Transcript for Documentary Film on Little Rock
Crisis show in Atlanta 1959, WEC Papers, Box 1, AHC; Cobb, *Osro Cobb*, p. 266;
Author's Interview with Jim Childers, June 30, 1995; Suggested Letter of Trans-
mittal, n.d., WEC Papers, Box 15, AHC; Transcript for Documentary Film on
Little Rock Crisis shown in Atlanta, 1959, WEC, Box 1, AHC.

63. Author's Interview with Linda Childers Suffridge and Carol Ervren, June
30, 1995. Nyna Seeton, whose daughter attended the same school in Searcy, reported that her daughter thought her year there was "awful. The rules were
strict.... It was painful for her, and it was terrible for me." Sondra Gordy, "Empty
Classrooms, Empty Hearts: Little Rock Secondary Teachers, 1958–1959," *Arkansas Historical Quarterly* 56 (Winter 1997): 427–42, quote on p. 440.

64. Summary Report, Little Rock Scholarship Fund, October 19, 1957 to May
14, 1963, WEC Papers, Box 13, AHC; John A. Morsell to Phelps Phelps, December
19, 1958, NAACP Papers, Group III, Box A98, LC; John A. Morsell to Daisy Bates,
December 9, 1958, NAACP Papers, Group III, Box A 98, LC; Cobb, *Osro Cobb*,
p. 266; Brewer, "The Embattled Ladies of Little Rock," p. 80, Series I, UALR.
Mrs. L. C. Bates to Gloster B. Current, December 31, 1958, Bates Papers, Box 4,
SHSW; NAACP, Report of the Secretary, November 10, 1958, Bates Papers, Box 4,
SHSW. Some black parents were upset at the poor quality of schooling their children received in Pulaski County high schools. Mann High School, in fact, had
attracted students from outside the district who chose to pay tuition there so that
they could get a better education. Report on Little Rock, n.d., ACHR, Box 1, UAF;
Gordy, "Empty Classrooms, Empty Hearts," pp. 427–42. Nancy Popperfuss, a
teacher at Hall High School, participated in a brief experiment in offering television
courses to displaced students, was surprised to learn that Mann High School students were using old textbooks provided to them when the white high schools had
abandoned them. Gordy, "Empty Classrooms, Empty Hearts," pp. 430–31.

65. Mrs. L. C. Bates to Gloster B. Current, December 31, 1958, Bates Papers,
Box 4, SHSW.

66. John A. Morsell to Phelps Phelps, December 19, 1958, NAACP Papers,
Group III, Box A98, LC; John A. Morsell to Daisy Bates, December 9, 1958,
NAACP Papers, Group III, Box A 98, LC; Cobb, *Osro Cobb*, p. 266; *Arkansas
Gazette*, November 3, 1958; Brewer, "The Embattled Ladies of Little Rock," p. 80,
Series I, UALR; Henry Lee Moon to Editors, Scripps–Howard newspapers, De-
cember 5, 1958, NAACP Papers, Group III, Box A 98, LC; *Arkansas Gazette*,
January 18, 1959. Branch offices of the NAACP assumed the responsibility for
raising money for correspondence courses for the six black students scheduled to
continue at Central. Memorandum from Mr. Wilkins to Mr. McClain, November 21, 1958, NAACP Papers, Group III, Box A 98, LC.

67. E. C. Gathings to Orval Faubus, October 3, 1958, Faubus Papers, Box 588.

68. Bates, *The Long Shadow of Little Rock*, p. 160; [Daisy Bates] to Aida Hunter, August 17, 1959, Bates Papers, Box 2, SHSW; Daisy Bates to Carlotta Walls, May 26, 1959, Bates Papers, Box 2, SHSW; *Arkansas Gazette*, n.d. [1987], EP Huckaby Papers, UALR. For the liabilities and costs of correspondence courses, see Gordy, "Empty Classrooms, Empty Hearts," pp. 440–41.

69. Walthall, "A Study of Certain Factors of School Closing," pp. 43–58, 91; clipping, no cite, December 8, 1959, EP Huckaby Papers, UALR.

70. Walthall, ibid.

CHAPTER FIVE. THE POLITICS OF FEAR AND GRIDLOCK

1. Sara Alderman Murphy, *Breaking the Silence: Little Rock's Women's Emergency Committee to Open Our Schools, 1958–1963* (Fayetteville: University of Arkansas Press, 1997), p. xiii.

2. Daisy Bates, *The Long Shadow of Little Rock: A Memoir* (New York: David McKay Company, Inc., 1962), pp. 195–212; William Hadley, Jr. to Daisy Bates, January 6, 1961, Bates Papers, Box 2, SHSW; Mrs. L. C. Bates to Gloster B. Current, December 31, 1958, Bates Papers, Box 4, SHSW; Author's Interview with Velma Powell, March 15, 1996.

3. Bates, *The Long Shadow of Little Rock*, pp. 195–212; William Hadley, Jr. to Daisy Bates, January 6, 1961, Bates Papers, Box 2, SHSW.

4. C. Wright Mills, *White Collar: The American Middle Classes* (London: Oxford University Press, 1951), p. 283. See William Hollingsworth Whyte, *The Organization Man* (New York: Simon and Schuster, 1956) and Mills, *White Collar* for critiques of men who abandoned the ostensible independence of self-employment for the deference required within corporate structures.

5. Irving J. Spitzberg, Jr., *Racial Politics in Little Rock* (New York: Garland Publishing, Inc., 1987), p. 171. Mills, for example, claimed that the new economy rewarded men who relied on a "generalized knack of handling people, rather than on moral integrity, substantive accomplishments, and solidity of person." Mills, *White Collar*, p. 263.

6. NAACP, Report of the Secretary, November 10, 1958, Bates Papers, Box 4, SHSW; *Arkansas Democrat*, n.d., EP Huckaby Papers, UALR.

7. *Arkansas Gazette*, August 17, 1958; NAACP, Report of the Secretary, November 10, 1958, Bates Papers, Box 4, SHSW; *Arkansas Democrat*, n.d., EP Huckaby Papers, UALR; Bruce Bennett to Oren Harris, October 3, 1958, Papers of Oren Harris, MS H242 138, 4-2-34, Gp. 3, Loc. 1140, UAF.

8. Hearing Before the Special Education Committee of the Arkansas Legislative Council, December 16–18, 1958, NAACP Papers, Group III, Box A 98, LC;

Numan V. Bartley, *The Rise of Massive Resistance: Race and Politics in the South during the 1950s* (Baton Rouge: Louisiana State University Press, 1969), pp. 187–89. In 1964, Bennett wrote to Faubus, without any apparent ironic intent, that he was glad the state had not formed a civil rights commission because, he claimed, such agencies "breed an 'informer' psychology" and construct a "spy system [that] has every hallmark of a police state." Bruce Bennett to Orval E. Faubus, June 24, 1964, Faubus Papers, Box 582, UAF.

9. *Time*, September 29, 1958; Unsigned letter to Drew Pearson, n.d., Blossom Papers, Box 11, UAF; *Arkansas Gazette*, September 1, 1957; Donald Parks to Orval E. Faubus, September 22, 1958, Faubus Papers, Box 530, UAF; *Arkansas Gazette*, October 14, 1958; Ernest Q. Campbell and Thomas F. Pettigrew, *Christians in Racial Crisis: A Study of Little Rock's Ministry* (Washington, D. C.: Public Affairs Press, 1959), pp. 112–13.

10. Campbell and Pettigrew, ibid.; *Arkansas Gazette*, September 2, 1957; *Arkansas Gazette*, September 13, 1957; *New York Times*, September 27, 1959.

11. Howard Chandler to Alan R. Templeton, May 13, 1959, Faubus Papers, Box 540, UAF; Inter-Office to Governor, May 23, 1959, Faubus Papers, Box 597, UAF; Roy Reed, *Faubus: The Life and Times of an American Prodigal* (Fayetteville: University of Arkansas Press, 1997), pp. 272–84, quote on p. 284. On the NAACP, see reports in Faubus Papers, Box 582, File 1, UAF.

12. *Arkansas Gazette*, September 20, 1958. In the rural areas and small towns, Mothers' League activists and others had trouble getting women's signatures for segregationist initiatives because many women were not registered to vote. Mrs. Ira Smith to Jim Johnson, March 5, 1958, Johnson Papers, Box 6, AHC; Emile Metcalfe to Jim Johnson, n.d., Johnson Papers, Box 6, AHC.

13. The States Rights Amendment, Johnson Papers, Box 6, AHC; Mrs. Abby Edwards to Jim Johnson, April 22, 1958, Johnson Papers, Box 6, AHC; Mrs. Abby Edwards to Jim Johnson, April 28, 1958, Johnson Papers, Box 6, AHC; Mrs. Abby Edwards to Jim Johnson, June 19, 1958, Johnson Papers, Box 6, AHC. The Johnson Amendment was ruled unconstitutional by the Arkansas State Supreme Court.

14. Oral History Interview with Sidney McMath, December 30, 1970, CUOHP, UALR; *Arkansas Gazette*, August 3, 1958; Spitzberg, *Racial Politics in Little Rock*, pp. 89–90; Dale Alford and L'Moore Alford, *The Case of the Sleeping People (Finally Awakened by Little Rock School Frustrations)*, (Little Rock, 1959), pp. 67–79.

15. *Arkansas Gazette*, November 8, 1958; Spitzberg, *Racial Politics in Little Rock*, p. 75; J. W. Fulbright to the Hon. Brooks Hays, November 22, 1958, Papers of J. William Fulbright MSF 956, BCN 105, Box A564, UAF; Randall

Woods, *Fulbright: A Biography* (Cambridge: Cambridge University Press, 1995), pp. 228–37.

16. Woods, *Fulbright*, pp. 228–37.

17. Interview with Terrell E. Powell, November 20, 1972, CUOHP, MS L720 310, UAF; Interview with R. A. Lile, August 19, 1971, CUOHP, OH-219, DDEL; Interview with A. F. House, August 17, 1971, CUOHP, OH-299, DDEL; Interview with Wayne Upton, December 29, 1971, CUOHP, MS L720 310, UAF; clipping, no cite, n.d., EP Huckaby Papers, UALR; John T. Elliff, *The United States Department of Justice and Individual Rights, 1937–1962* (New York: Garland Publishing, Inc., 1987, reprint of Ph.D. dissertation, Harvard University, 1967), p. 612; Tony A. Freyer, *The Little Rock Crisis: A Constitutional Interpretation* (Westport, CT: Greenwood Press, 1984), pp. 157–58.

18. Oral History Interview with Terrell E. Powell, November 20, 1972, CUOHP, MS L720 310, UAF; Oral History Interview with R. A. Lile, August 19, 1971, CUOHP, OH-219, DDEL; Oral History Interview with A. F. House, August 17, 1971, CUOHP, OH-299, DDEL; Oral History Interview with Wayne Upton, December 29, 1971, CUOHP, MS L720 310, UAF; clipping, no cite, n.d., EP Huckaby Papers, UALR; David Thoreau Wieck, "Report From Little Rock," *Liberation* (October 1958): 4–9; Spitzberg, *Racial Politics in Little Rock*, p. 95.

19. Spitzberg, *Racial Politics in Little Rock*, pp. 96–98; Oral History Interview with Terrell E. Powell, November 20, 1972, CUOHP, MS L720 310, UAF; Virgil T. Blossom, *It Has Happened Here* (New York: Harper & Brothers, 1959), pp. 191–93; *Arkansas Democrat*, November 15, 1958. Virgil Blossom's choice of a title for his book bespeaks his conviction that they were experiencing the power of a populist fascist. *It Has Happened Here* referenced Sinclair Lewis's 1935 novel, *It Can't Happen Here*, a tale of a small town editor whose warnings about the impending loss of freedom in America were met with the confident response of local businessmen: "It can't happen here." Sinclair Lewis, *It Can't Happen Here* (Garden City, NY: Sun Dial Press, Inc., 1935).

20. Brewer, "The Embattled Ladies of Little Rock," Brewer Papers, UALR; Murphy, *Breaking the Silence*, pp. 102–7.

21. Spitzberg, *Racial Politics in Little Rock*, pp. 97–98; Oral History Interview with Nat Griswold, August 21, 1971, CUOHP, MS L720 310, UAF; Oral History Interview with Everett Tucker, August 16, 1971, CUOHP, MS L720 310, UAF; Murphy, ibid.

22. Oral History Interview with Everett Tucker, August 16, 1971, CUOHP, MS L720 310, UAF; *Arkansas Gazette*, November 14 and November 23, 1958; clippings, no cite, November 11 and November 17, 1958, EP Huckaby Papers, UALR; clipping, no cite, n.d., EP Huckaby Papers, UALR; advertisement, [December,

1958], WEC Papers, Box 7, AHC. Vivion Brewer referred to Morrison as "a member of the screaming Mothers' League." Brewer, "The Embattled Ladies of Little Rock," pp. 44–46, Brewer Papers, Series I, File 2, UALR.

23. Freyer, *The Little Rock Crisis*, p. 159; Howard Chandler to Alan R. Templeton, November 18, 1958, Faubus Papers, Box 280, UAF; 917 to 901, December 8, 1958, Faubus Papers, Box 280, UAF; Howard Chandler to Alan R. Templeton, January 15, 1959, Faubus Papers, Box 280, UAF. School Board member Wayne Upton later suggested that Pruden was profiting from his involvement in the segregationist cause. Oral History Interview with Wayne Upton, December 29, 1971, CUOHP, MS L720 310, UAF.

24. Spitzberg, *Racial Politics in Little Rock*, p. 85; Oral History Interview with Nat Griswold, August 21, 1971, CUOHP, MS L720 310, UAF; W. F. Rector to Adolphine Terry, March 16, 1960, Terry Papers, Series I, Box 2, UALR; Oral History Interview with Everett Tucker, CUOHP, August 16, 1971, MS L720 310, UAF; Murphy, *Breaking the Silence*, pp. 102–7. House further wrote of Tucker that his mother, Marion Williams, "was as rabid a segregationist as could be found and I am sure she brooked no opposition in the Tucker home." Archie House to Harry Ashmore, June 26, 1979, H. Ashmore Papers, Box 3, UCSB.

25. Brewer, "The Embattled Ladies of Little Rock," pp. 46–47, Brewer Papers, UALR; Oral History Interview with E. Grainger Williams, December 29, 1970, CUOHP, UALR; Oral History Interview with Everett Tucker, August 16, 1971, CUOHP, MS L720 310, UAF. The segregationists documented this dispute in their ads for their candidates. "The Daisy Chain," n.d., WEC, Box 7, AHC.

26. Minutes of the Little Rock Board of Education Meeting, December 18, 1958; Oral History Interview with Everett Tucker, CUOHP, August 16, 1971; Oral History interview with Nat R. Griswold, August 21, 1971, CUOHP, UAF.

27. Minutes of the Little Rock Board of Education Meeting, December 28, 1958; Oral History Interview with A. F. House, August 17, 1971, CUOHP, OH-299, DDEL; Interview with Edwin Dunaway, August 18, 1992, Murphy Papers, Box 1, UAF; John Pagan Interview with A. F. House, August 15, 1972, Murphy Papers, Box 1, UAF; Interview with Gaston Williamson, December 10, 1993, Murphy Papers, Box 5, UAF; Harry S. Ashmore, "A Delayed Tribute to Archie House," in *Arkansas Lawyer*, enclosure in Gaston Williamson to Harry Ashmore, October 31, 1992, H. Ashmore Papers, MSS 155, Box 5, UCSB. The Dollarway School District, which was also under NAACP pressure to desegregate, also hired the Mehaffy firm to handle its case. *Southern School News*, March 1959.

28. Freyer, *The Little Rock Crisis*, p. 159; Elliff, *The United States Department of Justice*, pp. 612–13.

29. Spitzberg, *Racial Politics in Little Rock*, pp. 14–15.

30. *New York Times*, May 30, 1958; Clipping, no cite, March 4 and 5, 1959, EP Huckaby Papers, UALR; Spitzberg, *Racial Politics in Little Rock*, pp. 107–8.

31. "Letter From Little Rock," WEC, Box 1, AHC. By December 1958, they had over 1,000 members.

32. Lorraine Gates, "Power from the Pedestal: The Women's Emergency Committee and the Little Rock School Crisis," *Arkansas Historical Quarterly* 55 (Spring 1996): pp. 26–57; author's interview with Irene Samuel, June 30, 1995.

33. Gates, "Power from the Pedestal," pp. 37–38; Preliminary Survey Results, September 28, 1960, WEC, Box 1, AHC; Personal statement of Mrs. Joe R. Brewer, WEC Papers, Box 1, AHC; other cites from Murphy Papers; Author's Interview with Irene Samuel, June 30, 1995; Author's Interview with Mamie Ruth Williams, October 31, 1996. Velma Powell, whose friendships were largely with those who agreed with her, experienced her only serious disagreement with her father. She later recalled that he "reached a point where he wouldn't even talk to me." Author's Interview with Velma Powell, March 16, 1996.

34. Author's interview with Irene Samuel, June 30, 1995; Sara Murphy, Telephone Interview with Margaret Morrison, June 10, 1992, Murphy Papers, Box 2, UAF.

35. "Program To Save Our Schools," KATV, September 25, 1958, WEC, Box 2, AHC; Terry, *Life Is My Song, Also*, pp. 237–38, Terry Papers, Series II, Subseries II, Box 2, UALR; Sara Murphy Interview with Harry Ashmore, June 13, 1994, Murphy Papers, Box 1, UAF; "Women's Emergency Committee Activities During Recall Election," n.d., WEC, Box 1, AHC; Kathie Wood to Mrs. Samuel, June 17, 1968, WEC, Box 4, AHC; Author's Interview with Pat House, June 28, 1995. Given the high birth rates in the 1950s, the issue of cost was particularly salient, even in middle-class households.

36. Brewer, "The Embattled Ladies of Little Rock," pp. 9–10, 52–53, Brewer Papers, UALR (emphasis in original); Nat R. Griswold to Dr. Henry Alexander, September 16, 1960, ACHR, Box 3, UAF; Author's Interview with Pat House, June 28, 1995.

37. Brewer, "The Embattled Ladies of Little Rock," pp. 52–53, Brewer Papers, UALR; Minutes, WEC Board, April 18, 1962, WEC, Box 2, AHC. The school board also decided that it could not deal openly with the NAACP (or other blacks) if it was to have credibility in the community. Oral History Interview with R. A. Lile, August 19, 1971, CUOHP, DDEL. The Eisenhower administration also deliberately excluded African Americans from the political community, particularly with respect to race relations. This was particularly the case during the Little Rock crisis. Maxwell M. Rabb to Governor Adams, October 11, 1957, DDE, CF, OF, Box 732, DDEL. Eisenhower, for example, told a reporter that he

would not meet with white and black leaders in the South because such meetings lead to expectations of action. EFM Diary, March 14, 1956, Morrow-MS Papers, 1952–1963, Box 1, DDEL.

38. *Time*, September 29, 1958; Pat House Interview, CUOHP, DDEL; Anne Helveston to Carrie Chapman Catt Memorial Fund Inc., November 13, 1958, WEC Papers, Box 15, AHC; Preliminary Survey Results, September 28, 1960, WEC, Box 1, AHC.

39. When the idea of admitting blacks was broached by some people on another committee on which she was involved, Adolphine Terry noted, "I was adamant on that point—*no*—we are attempting to squirt around the Balm of Gilead not fire water." Mrs. D. D. Terry, Diary, May 16, 1958, Box 1, Terry Papers, UALR.

40. Anne Helveston to Carrie Chapman Catt Memorial Fund Inc., November 13, 1958, WEC Papers, Box 15, AHC; "Letter from Little Rock," WEC Papers, Box 1, AHC; Oral History Interview with Pat House, CUOHP, DDEL.

41. Untitled, ["Let's Join the Human Race"], WEC Papers, Box 2, AHC.

42. Mrs. D. D. Terry, Diary, April 11, 17, May 8, 1958, Terry Papers, Series II, Subseries II, Box 1, UALR; Brewer, "The Embattled Ladies of Little Rock," Series I, Brewer Papers, UALR; Mrs. Joe R. Brewer to Board of Directors, City of Little Rock, December 17, 1958, WEC Papers, Box 5, AHC; *Arkansas Gazette*, September 14, 1963.

43. Brewer, "The Embattled Ladies of Little Rock," Brewer Papers, Series I, UALR.

44. Brewer, ibid.; Letcher Langford to Mrs. Woodridge E. Morris, April 25, 1959, WEC Papers, Box 17, AHC; Murphy, *Breaking the Silence*, pp. 129–33. Brewer lied to Kemp about the lists. For copies of the lists, see WEC Papers, Box 1, AHC.

45. Oral History Interview with E. Grainger Williams, CUOHP, December 29, 1970, UALR; *Arkansas Gazette*, March 25, 1959; E. G. W.'s remarks on Public Schools at Annual Meeting of Little Rock Chamber of Commerce, January 14, 1959, Papers of Grainger Williams [hereafter cited as Williams Papers], A-33, Box 1, UALR. Williams, who had been serving as the vice president of the Chamber, automatically moved up to the presidency in early 1958. He was not chosen for his views on race and integration.

46. *Arkansas Gazette*, March 25, 1959; Interview with Grainger Williams, December 29, 1970, CUOHP, UALR; Suggested Draft, Statement of Policy on the Little Rock School Crisis, Williams Papers, Box 1, UALR. Herbert Thomas had suggested to Williams that he conduct the poll of Chamber members. Herbert Thomas to Grainger Williams, February 19, 1959, Thomas Papers, Box 5, UAF.

47. Oral History Interview with E. Grainger Williams, CUOHP, December 29, 1970, UALR; George Dwyer to E. Granger [*sic*] Williams, March 5, 1959, Williams Papers, Box 1, UALR; Ben C. Isgrig, Jr. to E. Grainger Williams, March 4, 1959, Williams Papers, Box 1, UALR; "A friend of the poor" to E. Grainger Williams and the Little Rock Chamber of Commerce, n.d., Williams Papers, Box 1, UALR; Mrs. Joe R. Brewer to Grainger Williams, January 16, 1959, Williams Papers, Box 1, UALR.

48. *Arkansas Democrat*, May 10, 1959. There was some suspicion that the Legislative Council from the state legislature, which was headed by Representative Paul Van Dalsem, had used the interviews of teachers done by the Arkansas State Police in a Faubus-inspired "investigation" of integration to draw up the list of teachers to be purged. *Arkansas Gazette*, May 8, 1959.

49. "WEC Part in STOP," WEC, Box 7, AHC; "Women's Emergency Committee Activities During Recall Election," n.d., WEC, Box 1, AHC; Brewer, "Embattled Ladies," pp. 124–26, Brewer Papers, UALR; Henry M. Alexander, "The Little Rock Recall Election" (Rutgers, Eagleton Institute, 1960), Brewer Collection, UALR, File 14; Author's Interview with Irene Samuel, June 30, 1995.

50. "This Teacher Was Purged," WEC, Box 7, AHC; "WEC Part in STOP," WEC, Box 7, AHC; Author's interview with Irene Samuel, June 30, 1995; *Arkansas Gazette*, May 8, 1959; John Pagan Interview with Terrell Powell, August 22, 1972, Murphy Papers, Box 3, UAF. The PTAs in Virginia organized in a similar fashion. Memorandum for the Attorney General, July 22, 1958, White Papers, Records of the Department of Justice, Box 2, NA.

51. *Arkansas Gazette*, May 8, 1959. Labor's support for the STOP campaign was based on the issue of unfair firing. After STOP, however, unions quickly became disillusioned with the new school board as it responded "with a posture of arrogance" to a labor committee request that it honor the right of public employees to join a union. James Youngdahl, "The New Populism of Orval Faubus," *The Progressive*, December 1959, pp. 41–43.

52. Author's Interview with Henry Woods, June 1995; "WEC Part in STOP," WEC, Box 7, AHC; Murphy, *Breaking the Silence*, pp. 157–84.

53. John Pagan Interview with M. L. Moser, January 4, 1973, Murphy Papers, Box 2, UAF; *Arkansas Gazette*, May 11, 1959.

54. *Arkansas Gazette*, May 24, 1959; History of the Women's Emergency Committee to Open Our Schools, May 22, 1959, WEC, Box 15, AHC; Reed, *Faubus*, p. 255.

55. Murphy, *Breaking the Silence*, pp. 181–84; Elizabeth Huckaby, Yearbook, May 26, 1959, EP Huckaby Papers, UALR.

56. Murphy, ibid.

57. Sara Murphy Interview with Orval Faubus, August 19, 1992, Murphy Papers, Box 1, UAF; Author's Interview with Henry Woods, June 29, 1995.

58. Murphy, *Breaking the Silence*, pp. 181–84; Author's Interview with Henry Woods, June 29, 1995.

CHAPTER SIX. POLITICS AS USUAL: REVIVING THE POLITICS OF TOKENISM

1. Dan Wakefield, "Siege at Little Rock: The Brave Ones," *The Nation*, October 11, 1958.

2. *New York Times*, June 9, 1959.

3. *John Aaron et al. v. Ed. Il McKinley, Jr. et al.*, June 18, 1959, U.S. District Court, NAACP Papers, Box J7, Group III, LC; *Arkansas Gazette*, June 19, 1959; Tony A. Freyer, *The Little Rock Crisis: A Constitutional Interpretation* (Westport, CT: Greenwood Press, 1984), p. 162; *Arkansas Gazette*, February 3, 1959. Thomas tried to persuade Faubus to join the Little Rock School Board in an appeal of the decision against Acts 4 and 5 despite the fact that the school board had indicated no interest in such an appeal. Herbert Thomas to William J. Smith, June 23, 1959, Thomas Papers, MC 437, Box 4, UAF.

4. Editorial from the *Atlanta Constitution* probably in *Arkansas Gazette*, July 8, 1959; Sara Alderman Murphy, *Breaking the Silence: Little Rock's Women's Emergency Committee to Open Our Schools, 1958–1963* (Fayetteville: University of Arkansas Press, 1997), p. 185.

5. Herbert Thomas to William J. Smith, June 23, 1959, Thomas Papers, MC 437, Box 4, UAF; Little Rock School Board to Orval E. Faubus, draft, n.d., enclosed in Herbert Thomas to Everett Tucker, August 3, 1959, Thomas Papers, MC 437, Box 4, UAF; Herbert Thomas to J. Gaston Williamson, August 10, 1959, Thomas Papers, MC 437, Box 4, UAF; *Arkansas Gazette*, August 4, 1959.

6. *Arkansas Gazette*, August 9, 1959; *Arkansas Democrat*, n.d. [1959], EP Huckaby Papers, UALR.

7. Plaintiff's Brief, *John Aaron et al. v. Everett Tucker Jr. et al.*, NAACP Papers, Group III, Box J7, LC; *Arkansas Gazette*, August 5, 1959.

8. *Chicago Defender*, August 8, 1959.

9. Herbert Thomas to William J. Smith, June 23, 1959, Thomas Papers, MC 437, Box 4, UAF; Little Rock School Board to Orval E. Faubus, draft, n.d., enclosed in Herbert Thomas to Everett Tucker, August 3, 1959, Thomas Papers, MC 437, Box 4, UAF; Herbert Thomas to J. Gaston Williamson, August 10, 1959, Thomas Papers, MC 437, Box 4, UAF; Herbert Thomas to Orval E. Faubus, April 9, 1959, Thomas Papers, Box 4, UAF; Orval E. Faubus to Herbert L. Thomas,

June 24, 1959, Thomas Papers, Box 4, UAF; Herbert Thomas to Orval E. Faubus, June 29, 1959, Thomas Papers, Box 4, UAF; Orval E. Faubus to Dr. T. J. Raney, July 1, 1959, Thomas Papers, Box 4, UAF; Oral History Interview with Everett Tucker, August 16, 1971, CUOHP, MS L720 310, UAF; *WEC Newsletter*, November, 1961, WEC Papers, Box 12, AHC; *Arkansas Gazette*, August 5, 1959; Daisy Bates, *Long Shadow of Little Rock: A Memoir* (New York: David McKay Co., 1962), pp. 51–52; John Pagan Interview with Everett Tucker, August 25, 1972. Murphy Papers, Box 5, UAF. As evidence of the moderate conviction that segregationists needed an alternative to integrated public schools, the *Arkansas Gazette* stated in an editorial on the closing of Raney High that Little Rock needed a private school. *Arkansas Gazette*, August 6, 1959.

10. Herbert Thomas to J. Gaston Williamson, August 10, 1959, Thomas Papers, Box 4, UAF; unsigned letter to Faubus, n.d., Thomas Papers, Box 4, UAF.

11. Irving J. Spitzberg, Jr., *Racial Politics in Little Rock* (New York: Garland Publishing, Inc., 1987), p. 113. Minutes of the Little Rock Board of Education Meeting, July 29, 1959, LRSB, Box 3, UALR; Minutes of the Little Rock Board of Education Meeting, August 4, 1959, LRSB, Box 3, UALR.

12. *Arkansas Gazette*, August 5, 1959; Spitzberg, ibid.; Roy Reed, *Faubus: The Life and Times of an American Prodigal* (Fayetteville: University of Arkansas Press, 1997), p. 256; Herbert Thomas to Everett Tucker, August 3, 1959 and enclosed letter to Orval E. Faubus, Thomas Papers, Box 4, UAF.

13. History of the Women's Emergency Committee to Open Our Schools, June 21 and June 29, WEC Papers, Box 15, AHC; *Arkansas Gazette*, August 5, 1959; *Time*, August 17, 1959; John Luter interview with Amis Guthridge, CUOHP, OH-186, August 19, 1971, DDEL; Malcolm G. Taylor to Dr. Thomas J. Raney, February 8, 1960, Murphy Papers, Box 3, UAF. At the same time, some of the other church-based private schools folded. Mark Newman, "The Arkansas Baptist State Convention and Desegregation, 1954–1968," *Arkansas Historical Quarterly* 56 (Autumn 1997): 294–313.

14. Howard Chandler to Alan R. Templeton, November 18, 1958, Faubus Papers, Box 280, UAF; Howard Chandler to Alan R. Templeton, January 15, 1959, Faubus Papers, Box 280, UAF; Murphy, *Breaking the Silence*, p. 127; *Arkansas Gazette*, October 3, 1959; *Arkansas Gazette*, October 25, 1959. Raney, which had received $71,907.50 in Act 5 funds in the previous year, would no longer be able to look to the state for this assistance. *John Aaron et al. v. Ed. Il McKinley Jr. et al.*, June 18, 1959, U.S. District Court, NAACP Papers, Box J7, Group III, LC.

15. *Arkansas Gazette*, August 5, 1959; Murphy, *Breaking the Silence*, p. 195.

16. *Arkansas Gazette*, August 8, 1959; *Chicago Defender*, August 15, 1959.

17. Transcript, *John Aaron et al. v. William G. Cooper et al.*, United States District Court, Eastern District of Arkansas, Western Division, Blossom Papers, Box

4, UAF; *Southern School News*, September, 1959; *New York Times*, September 13, 1959.

18. Murphy, *Breaking the Silence*, pp. 187–89; Vivion Lenon Brewer, "The Embattled Ladies of Little Rock," Brewer Papers, Series I, UALR.

19. Murphy, *Breaking the Silence*, pp. 182, 192; Herbert Thomas to William J. Smith, June 23, 1959, Thomas Papers, Box 4, UAF; Little Rock School Board to Orval E. Faubus, draft, n.d., enclosed in Herbert Thomas to Everett Tucker, August 3, 1959, Thomas Papers, Box 4, UAF; Herbert Thomas to J. Gaston Williamson, August 10, 1959, Thomas Papers, Box 4, UAF; "To the Members of the Arkansas General Assembly," n.d., Thomas Papers, Box 4, UAF; CPOFPS, Legislative Subcommittee, Suggestions about the Meeting, Thomas Papers, Box 4, UAF; Executive Committee Meeting, July 15, 1959, WEC Papers, Box 2, AHC. Sara Murphy saw improvement in women's representation in CPOFPS because they had more representatives than they had had in STOP. Murphy, *Breaking the Silence*, p. 192.

20. Herbert L. Thomas to Mrs. Joe Brewer, June 24, 1959, Thomas Papers, Box 5, UAF; Mrs. Joe R. Brewer to Herbert L. Thomas, June 30, 1959, Thomas Papers, Box 5, UAF; Herbert Thomas to Eugene R. Warren, July 13, 1959, and enclosures, Thomas Papers, Box 4, UAF. Sara Murphy wrote later that the WEC board decided to continue running its ads, but Brewer wrote to Thomas that they would desist for the moment but consider the issue from week to week. Murphy, *Breaking the Silence*, pp. 188–89; Mrs. Joe R. Brewer to Herbert L. Thomas, July 1, 1959, Thomas Papers, UAF. Brewer understood that Thomas's wife believed that the WEC should disband. Brewer, "The Embattled Ladies of Little Rock," Brewer Papers, Series I, UALR.

21. Herbert Thomas to Eugene R. Warren, July 13, 1959, and enclosures, Thomas Papers, MC 437, Box 4, UAF.

22. Murphy, *Breaking the Silence*, pp. 193, 197; Brewer, "The Embattled Ladies of Little Rock," p. 151, Brewer Papers, Series I, UALR.

23. Murphy, *Breaking the Silence*, pp. 189, 191; *Southern School News*, August 1959, p. 6, in Record and Record, *Little Rock, U.S.A.*, p. 158.

24. *Southern School News*, August 1959, p. 6, in Record and Record, *Little Rock, U.S.A.*, p. 158; *New York Times*, July 24, 1959; *Arkansas Democrat*, July 20, 1959.

25. "Little Rock Report," WEC, Box 15, AHC; Pat House Interview, CUOHP, DDEL. The Citizens' Council felt compelled to rebut the idea that business losses and closed schools represented a threat to community well-being, contending in a newsletter that "business is better in Little Rock with the schools closed than it is in the northern cities that have been conned into unholy race-mixing." Capital Citizens' Council Newsletter, No. 2, Johnson Papers, Box 45, AHC. The WEC

also sent Christmas letters annually throughout the nation describing the situation in Little Rock. Mrs. Joe R. Brewer to William M. Lightsey, March 12, 1959, WEC, Box 6, AHC. The women in the public schools movements in the South, who kept in touch regarding strategies, commiserated with one another about the lack of public support from male leaders in their communities. Mrs. Hollis J. Wiseman to Irene [Samuel], June 15, 1963, WEC, Box 4, AHC.

26. *Arkansas Gazette*, August 8, 1959; *New York Times*, August 10, 1959 in WEC Papers, Box 14, AHC; Huckaby, Yearbook, August 4 and 7, 1959, EP Huckaby Papers, UALR.

27. *New York Times*, August 10, 1959 in WEC Papers, Box 14, AHC; Murphy, *Breaking the Silence*, p. 189; WEC Recommendations, L. R. Desegregation, n.d.; Suggestions Concerning Desegregation of Little Rock Schools, 1959, WEC Papers, Box 1, AHC

28. Murphy, ibid.; Suggestions Concerning Desegregation of Little Rock Schools, March, 1961, WEC Papers, Box 1, AHC.

29. Mrs. Joe R. Brewer, Oral History, CUOHP, OH-171, MS 720 310, DDEL; Pat House, Oral History, August 22, 1971, CUOHP, OH-193, DDEL; Murphy, *Breaking the Silence*, pp. 80, 101; Fliers, WEC Papers, Boxes 1, 16, AHC; Preliminary Survey Results, September 28, 1960, WEC, Box 1, AHC. The anonymous survey was mailed to each member of the WEC (which then numbered around 1700) with 720 returning it.

30. *Arkansas Gazette*, October 25, 1959.

31. Gertrude Samuels, "Act III Opens in Little Rock," *New York Times*, September 13, 1959.

32. The incident occurred when a suspicious car with Georgia license plates (which turned out to be an undercover state police car) followed Thomas as he was leaving the Bates' residence. Garman and Mullen decided to follow the car because they had seen it drive by the house several times previously. Bates, *Long Shadow of Little Rock*, pp. 161–69; *Arkansas Gazette*, October 28, 1959.

33. *Arkansas Gazette*, August 12, 1959; *Time*, August 17, 1959; *Time*, August 24, 1959.

34. *Arkansas Gazette*, August 11, 1959; *Arkansas Gazette*, August 12, 1959.

35. Murphy, *Breaking the Silence*, pp. 196–97; Reed, *Faubus*, p. 256; *Arkansas Democrat*, August 12, 1959.

36. Murphy, ibid.; *Arkansas Gazette*, August 8, 1959; Reed, *Faubus*, p. 256; *Southern School News*, September 1959, WEC Papers, Box 21, AHC; *New York Times*, August 13, 1959.

37. Reed, *Faubus*, p. 256; Oral History Interview with Everett Tucker, CUOHP, August 16, 1971; *Arkansas Gazette*, August 13, 1959; *Time*, August 24, 1959. When interviewed by state police, all of those arrested claimed they had no idea

how the tear gas got into the car. Howard Chandler to Paul R. McDonald, August 12, 1959, Faubus Papers, Box 540, UAF. Dewey Coffman paid for segregationist literature. "The Daisy Chain," WEC, Box 7, AHC.

38. *New York Times*, August 13, 1959.

39. Ibid.; *New York Times*, August 14, 1959.

40. *Arkansas Gazette*, September 3, 1959.

41. Reed, *Faubus*, pp. 256–57; *Time*, September 21, 1959; Murphy, *Breaking the Silence*, pp. 201–2; Robert E. Baker, "Passions Calmer in Little Rock, [*Washington Post*], WEC Papers, Box 14, AHC; *Arkansas Gazette*, September 9, 1959.

42. *Arkansas Gazette*, September 10, 1959; *Arkansas Gazette*, September 12, 1959; *Arkansas Gazette*, October 10, 1959; *Arkansas Democrat*, November 3, 1959; *Arkansas Gazette*, October 28, 1959.

43. *Arkansas Gazette*, September 11, 1959; *Arkansas Democrat*, October 28, 1959; *Arkansas Gazette*, November 28, 1959; *Arkansas Democrat*, July 10, 1961; *Arkansas Gazette*, September 10, 1959; *Arkansas Gazette*, October 30, 1959.

44. *Arkansas Gazette*, October 20, 1959; *Arkansas Gazette*, October 29, 1959.

45. *Arkansas Gazette*, September 11, 1959; *Arkansas Gazette*, October 29, 1959.

46. *Arkansas Gazette*, September 10, 11, 1959; *Arkansas Gazette*, October 29, 1959.

47. *Arkansas Gazette*, September 9, 1959; *Arkansas Gazette*, October 29, 1959; Baker, "Passions Calmer in Little Rock"; Clipping, no cite [probably *Arkansas Gazette*, June 18, 1958], EP Huckaby Papers, UALR; *New York Times*, November 29, 1959.

48. FBI Investigation Instituted at Request of Judge Ronald N. Davies, FBI, Box 1, UALR; Murphy, *Breaking the Silence*, p. 197.

49. *Arkansas Gazette*, October 30, 1959.

50. J. E. Walker to Orval E. Faubus, March 25, 1961, Faubus Papers, Box 592, UAF; Petition from Hebron Baptist Church, Little Rock, for E. A. Lauderdale, Sr., March 18, 1961, Faubus Papers, Box 592, UAF; Roy T. Morrison to Orval Faubus, March 19, 1961, Faubus Papers, Box 592, UAF; Margaret E. Morrison to Orval Faubus, March 19, 1961, Faubus Papers, Box 592, UAF.

51. *Arkansas Gazette*, September 9, 1959; *Arkansas Gazette*, October 1, 1959.

52. Orval E. Faubus to A. C. Moore, April 12, 1961, Box 592, Faubus Papers, UAF; Brewer, "The Embattled Ladies of Little Rock," p. 196, Brewer Papers, UALR; *Arkansas Democrat*, October 28, 1959; *Arkansas Gazette*, November 28, 1959; *Arkansas Democrat*, July 10, 1961; *Arkansas Democrat*, September 14, 1961. Alleged irregularities in the Lauderdale trial are discussed in Dissenting Opinion, Sam Robinson, Associate Justice, *E. A. Lauderdale Sr. v. the State of Arkansas*, February 13, 1961, Faubus Papers, Box 592, UAF.

53. *Arkansas Gazette*, June 21, 1959, cited in Murphy, *Breaking the Silence*, p. 186; *Arkansas Gazette*, July 19, 1959; *Arkansas Gazette*, July 30, 1959; *Arkansas Gazette*, June 28, 1959; *New York Times*, September 26, 1959.

54. Unadopted recommendations drawn up by Little Rock citizens for the Little Rock School Board, n.d. [1959], Records of the Arkansas Council on Human Relations, MS Ar4 ACHR, Box 8, UAF; John A. Morsell to Lester Markel, September 23, 1959, NAACP Papers, Group III, Box A98, LC. See also *New York Times*, September 13, 1959.

55. *Southern School News*, September 1959, WEC Papers, Box 21, AHC; Some Concerns of and Suggestions from Negro Citizens to the School Board, n.d., ACHR, Box 20, UAF.

56. *Southern School News*, September 1959, WEC Papers, Box 21, AHC. A May 1958 study by the Southern Regional Council had revealed strong African American support for desegregation from both working-class and middle-class blacks in Little Rock. Indeed, working-class blacks reported that they wanted more from their social class assigned to previously all-white schools. SRC, "Some General Observations in the Negro Community of Little Rock, Arkansas," May 1958, WEC, Box 20, AHC.

57. John Pagan Interview with Everett Tucker, August 25, 1972, Murphy Papers, Box 5, UAF; Untitled, n.d. [Report on reassignment hearings before school board], Bates Papers, SHSW; Brewer, "The Embattled Ladies of Little Rock," p. 208, Brewer Papers, UALR.

58. Minutes of Little Rock School Board, Box 3, UALR; Virgil T. Blossom, *It Has Happened Here* (New York: Harper & Brothers, 1959), p. 159.

59. Minutes of Little Rock School Board Special Meeting, September 2, 1959, Box 3, UALR; Minutes of Little Rock School Board Special Meeting, September 4, 1959, Box 3, UALR; Untitled, n.d. [Report on reassignment hearings before school board], Bates Papers, SHSW; *Aaron v. Cooper*, Office Court Reporter's Transcript of Proceedings Taken Before Hon. John E. Miller, August 15, 1956, Blossom Papers, Box 5, UAF. In October, the *Arkansas Gazette* claimed proudly that Central High School had "already enjoyed something of a national reputation before 1957, but this was with professional educators who recognized in the institution one of the largest and—by almost every test—one of the finest in the land." It made no such claims for Mann High School. *Arkansas Gazette*, October 20, 1959.

60. Untitled, n.d. [Report on reassignment hearings before school board], Bates Papers, SHSW.

61. Minutes of Little Rock School Board Executive Meeting, September 14, 1959, Box 3, UALR; *Arkansas Democrat*, September 16, 1959; *Arkansas Gazette*, September 17, 1959.

62. Murphy, *Breaking the Silence*, pp. 194, 208; Brewer, "The Embattled Ladies of Little Rock," pp. 208–10, Brewer Papers, UALR.

63. *Arkansas Gazette*, September 30, 1959; Minutes, Little Rock School Board, September 29, 1959, LRSB, B-5, Box 3, UALR.

64. Untitled, [begins "On November 10, 1959"], n.d., WEC Papers, Box 12, AHC; John A. Kirk, *Redefining the Color Line: Black Activism in Little Rock, Arkansas, 1940–1970* (Gainesville: University Press of Florida, 2002), p. 140; Southern Regional Council, "Some General Observations in the Negro Community of Little Rock, Arkansas," May, 1958, WEC Papers, Box 20.

65. Murphy, *Breaking the Silence*, p. 207; Billie Wilson to Muriel Lokey, October 31, 1959, Murphy Papers, Box 5, UAF.

66. Huckaby, Yearbook September 5, 1959, EP Huckaby Papers, UALR. The others who had been assigned to Central were Elizabeth Eckford, who found that she had accumulated enough credits to graduate, and Carlotta Walls, who could not meet the early start date at Central because she had not finished her summer school courses in Colorado. The school board added Sybil Jordan, James Franklin Henderson, and Sandra Johnson in September. *Arkansas Gazette*, August 11, 1959; *Arkansas Gazette*, September 16, 1959.

67. Ellis Thomas to Jesse Matthews, August 18, 1959; Ellis Thomas to Jesse Matthews, cc: Terrel Powell, September 9, 1959; Wiley A. Branton to Herschel H. Friday, Jr., September 11, 1959; Ellis Thomas to Brooks McCormick, International Harvester Co., Chicago, October 6, 1959; Brooks McCormick to Ellis Thomas, November 9, 1959; Daisy Bates [apparently] to Roy Wilkins and the Board of Directors, November 19, 1959; all in Bates Papers, Microfilm Edition, Reel 6, SHSW. It seems highly likely that Thomas's firing was instigated by moderates, who were the only ones with information regarding his actions.

68. Huckaby, Yearbook, October 28 and 29, 1959, EP Huckaby Papers, UALR; Daisy Bates [apparently] to Roy Wilkins and the Board of Directors, November 19, 1959, Bates Papers, Microfilm Edition, Reel 6, SHSW.

69. Huckaby, Yearbook, October 15, 1959, and passim, EP Huckaby Papers, UALR.

70. Sara Murphy Interview with Sharon Adair, December 9, 1992, Murphy Papers, Box 1, UAF.

71. *Chicago Defender*, December 26, 1959; *Arkansas Democrat*, n.d., EP Huckaby Papers, UALR.

72. Bates, *The Long Shadow of Little Rock*, pp. 170–78; Daisy Bates to William H. Hadley, Jr., December 10, 1959, Bates Papers, Box 2, SHSW.

73. Gerald Walker, "Little Rock—Five Years Later," *Redbook*, November 1962, pp. 75, 129–33, WEC Papers, Box 25, AHC.

74. Walker, ibid., WEC Papers, Box 25, AHC.

75. Walker, ibid., WEC Papers, Box 25, AHC.

76. Walker, ibid., WEC Papers, Box 25, AHC.

77. Mrs. Daisy Bates to Mr. Roy Wilkins, November 28, 1961, Bates Papers, Box 2, SHSW; George W. Lee to Mr. L. C. Bates, September 11, 1961, Bates Papers, Box 2, SHSW.

78. Freyer, *The Little Rock Crisis*, p. 163; Walker, "Little Rock—Five Years Later," 75, 129–33, WEC Papers, Box 25, AHC; *Arkansas Gazette*, March 3, 1961; Statement Released on March 4, 1961 by Ted Lamb, Cartwright Papers, UAF; Nathan Griswold, "The New Situation in Little Rock," n.d., Cartwright Papers, UAF; Paul W. Masem, "Resegregation: A Case Study of an Urban School District" (Ed. D. dissertation, Vanderbilt University, 1986), p. 4; Floyd Parsons to Mr. Griswold, March 14, 1962, WEC Papers, Box 13, AHC; *New York Times*, March 12, 1961.

79. Nat R. Griswold to Wiley A. Branton, April 26, 1963, ACHR, Box 31, UAF; Minutes of the Little Rock School District Board of Directors Regular Meeting, May 21, 1964, LRSB, B-5, Box 9, UALR. Jennifer Hochschild has concluded that these kinds of incremental policies to desegregate schools can leave "minorities and Anglos... worse off" than if nothing had been done and achieve "less than full-scale, rapid, extensive—but unpopular—change to improve race relations, achievement, and community acceptance and to minimize white flight." Jennifer L. Hochschild, *The New American Dilemma: Liberal Democracy and School Desegregation* (New Haven: Yale University Press, 1984), p. 91.

80. Testimony of Attorney General Robert Kennedy, House Committee on the Judiciary, 88th Congress, 1st Session, 1963.

81. Oren Harris to Herschel H. Friday, April 14, 1965, Faubus Papers, Box 540, MS F27 301, UAF; Allen Lesser to Oren Harris, April 9, 1965, Faubus Papers, Box 540, MS F27 301, UAF; General Statement of Policies Under Title VI of the Civil Rights Act of 1964, Faubus Papers, Box 540, MS F27 301, UAF; Oral History Interview with Everett Tucker, August 16, 1971, CUOHP, UAF; Masem, *Resegregation*, pp. 58, 74, 81–83; Statistical Results of Desegregation in Little Rock Schools, 1957–1963, WEC Papers, Box 17, AHC; *Arkansas Gazette*, September 17, 1965; School Desegregation, Fall 1965, Records of Burke Marshall, RG 60, Box 1, NA; A Review of the Activities of the Department of Justice in Civil Rights in 1964, Records of John Doar, RG 60, Box 1, NA. For the status of desegregation in Little Rock in 1963, see Basic Information on Little Rock, n.d., ACHR, Box 20, UAF, and in the state, see Arkansas Advisory Committee to the United States Commission on Civil Rights, "Public Education in Arkansas, 1963: Still Separate and Still Unequal," WEC Papers, Box 13, AHC. Freedom of choice plans did not work well in other parts of the South. Southern Research Council,

"School Desegregation: Old Problems under a New Law," September 1965, WEC Papers, Box 20, AHC.

82. Gaston Williamson to Mrs. Wilson, January 18, 1960, Murphy Papers, Box 5, UAF; History of the WEC, n.d., WEC Papers, Box 6, AHC; Buzz Session Schedules–Week of April 18, 1960 and Week of May 2, WEC Papers, Box 10, AHC; Work Program and Advertising Schedule, WEC, Box 10, AHC; To the School Patrons of the Special School District of Little Rock, November 7, 1960, WEC Papers, Box 10, AHC; VLB [Vivion Brewer] to Frances Farrar, May 23, 1960, WEC Papers, Box 10, AHC; Murphy, *Breaking the Silence*, pp. 210–12.

83. Mrs. Byron House, Jr. to [supporters], WEC, January 10, 1961, Box 10, AHC; Murphy, ibid. At the end of the campaign against Amendment 52, WEC membership peaked at over 2,000.

84. Mrs. Byron House, Jr. to legislators, February 14, 1961, WEC Papers, Box 10, AHC; Mrs. Byron House, Jr. to Jim Brandon, March 9, 1961, WEC Papers, Box 10, AHC; Statement of Eugene Warren on Proposed Bond Issue, May 20, 1961, WEC Papers, Box 10, AHC.

85. Sara Murphy Interview with Willie Oates, August 24, 1992, Murphy Papers, Box 3, UAF; Women who helped in Jim Brandon's campaign, n.d., WEC Papers, Box 9, AHC; Jim Brandon to Mrs. Byron House, Jr. February 15, 1961, WEC Papers, Box 10, UAF; Mrs. Byron House, Jr. to Jim Brandon, March 9, 1961, WEC Papers, Box 10, AHC.

86. Robert Thompson, "Barefoot and Pregnant: The Education of Paul Van Dalsem," *Arkansas Historical Quarterly* 57 (Winter 1998): 377–407, quote on p. 392.

87. *WEC Newsletter*, June 1, 1961, WEC Papers, Box 15, AHC; Glen F. Walther to Mrs. Byron House, Jr., February 3, 1961, WEC Papers, Box 10, AHC; Jim Brandon to Mrs. Byron House, Jr., February 3, 1961, WEC Papers, Box 10, AHC; *Southern Patriot*, April 1959, WEC Papers, Box 19, AHC; Pat House's Comments on visits to legislators, 1959, WEC Papers, Box 2, AHC; Nat Griswold, "Arkansans Organize for Public Schools," *New South* (June 1959): 3–7, WEC Papers, Box 20, AHC.

88. Oral History Interview with J. Bill Becker, August 16, 1971, CUOHP, UALR; "Political Birds of a Feather… ," Murphy Papers, Box 9, UAF; *Arkansas Gazette*, July 15, 1964.

89. *Arkansas Gazette*, January 7, 1962; Murphy, *Breaking the Silence*, pp. 222–23, 236; Oral History Interview with Pat House, August 22, 1971, OH-193, CUOHP, DDEL; Charles Morrow Wilson, "ORVAL FAUBUS—How Did He Get That Way?" *Reader's Digest*, February 1959, pp. 78–84. Faubus was one of the first to use attacks on AFDC to discredit African Americans. *Arkansas Gazette*, September 6, 1959; clipping, "The ADC Program: Does It Subsidize Sin?" WEC Papers, Box 8, AHC.

90. *Arkansas Gazette*, February 10, 1961, WEC Papers, Box 2, AHC.

91. Kirk, *Redefining the Color Line*, pp. 139–62; *Arkansas Gazette*, August 14, 1961; L. C. Bates to Gloster B. Current, Field Secretary's Reports for Periods Ending March 25, 1960; April 25, 1960; May 7, 1960; and May 25, 1960, NAACP Papers, Group III, Box C222.

92. Kirk, ibid., pp. 150–67; Spitzberg, *Racial Politics in Little Rock*, pp. 134–75; *Arkansas Gazette*, September 14, 1963; Sara Murphy Interview with Ozell Sutton, September 20, 1993, Murphy Papers, Box 3, UAF.

93. Kirk, ibid., pp. 139–62

94. Kirk, ibid., pp. 156–58; Spitzberg, *Racial Politics in Little Rock*, pp. 142–49.

95. Sara Murphy Interview with Dr. W. H. Townsend, July 23, 1992, Murphy Papers, Box 4, UAF.

96. Procedure [Minutes of WEC Board meeting, September 5, 1962], WEC Papers, Box 2, AHC; Unsigned draft letter to Mr. Reasoner, n.d., WEC, Box 4, AHC; WEC minutes, August 22, 1962, WEC Papers, Box 2, AHC; Spitzberg, *Racial Politics in Little Rock*, pp. 85, 137.

97. Procedure, [Minutes of WEC Board meeting, September 5, 1962.] WEC Papers, Box 2, AHC; Unsigned draft letter to Mr. Reasoner, n.d., WEC, Box 4, AHC; Murphy, *Breaking the Silence*, pp. 224–30; Henry Woods to Sara Murphy, n.d. [December 1962], Murphy Papers, Box 2, UAF; Vote for Sara Murphy, Murphy Papers, Box 5, UAF; Flyer, LITTLE ROCK SCHOOL BOARD ELECTION, December 4, 1962, Murphy Papers, Box 5, UAF; Ad for Everett Tucker, n.d., Murphy Papers, Box 2, UAF; Interview with Edwin Dunaway, October 15, 1992, Murphy Papers, Box 1, UAF; Henry Woods to Sara Murphy, n.d. [1962], Murphy Papers, Box 2, UAF; *Arkansas Gazette*, December 8, 1962. A member of Atlanta's HOPE organization wrote to Billie Wilson after a visit there by Tucker that "You—or Irene Samuel—are right in thinking Tucker is an avowed segregationist; his conversations in private fairly curled my liberal hair." Fran [Breeden] to Billie [Wilson], November 30, 1959, Murphy Papers, Box 5, UAF. WEC leaders worried in 1959 when Tucker was to appear on *Face the Nation* that he might slip up, so they delegated various men to talk to him. Nathan Griswold contacted Gaston Williamson of STOP to suggest to Tucker that "if he couldn't learn to pronounce 'Negro' to just say 'colored people.'" Irene [Samuel] to Vivion [Brewer], August 1959, Brewer Papers, Box 1, UALR. When interviewed in 1971, Tucker could not name one woman in the WEC. Without their labor, he would never have been elected. Oral History Interview with Everett Tucker, August 16, 1971, CUOHP, UAF.

98. *Arkansas Gazette*, December 8, 1962.

99. Spitzberg, *Racial Politics in Little Rock*, pp. 135–39; Murphy, *Breaking the Silence*, p. 208.

100. Those who define moderation as support for token integration put in place to protect public schools and business development narrow moderation to a specific response to particular set of historical circumstances rather than seeing it

as a broader set of assumptions and commitments. They also eclipse any disagreements among moderates by defining it in the terms employed by the winners of those disputes. Freyer, *The Little Rock Crisis*, p. 15; Matthew D. Lassiter and Andrew B. Lewis, "Massive Resistance Revisited: Virginia's White Moderates and the Byrd Organization," in Matthew D. Lassiter and Andrew B. Lewis, eds., *The Moderates' Dilemma: Massive Resistance to School Desegregation in Virginia* (Charlottesville: University Press of Virginia, 1998), pp. 1–21.

101. Murphy, *Breaking the Silence*, pp. 185, 230–36; Author's Interview with Mamie Ruth Williams, October 31, 1996; Sara Murphy Interview with Carroll Holcomb, August 24, 1994, Murphy Papers, Box 1, UAF.

102. Billie Wilson to Fran [Breeden], March 2, 1960, Murphy Papers, Box 5, UAF.

103. Fourth Conference on Community Unity, Planning Committee Meeting, November 1, 1960, Cartwright Papers, MC 1026, microfilm, UAF; Planning Committee of the Fourth Community Unity Conference, November 28, 1960, Cartwright Papers, UAF; *Arkansas Gazette*, November 23, 1960. Susan Lynn, *Progressive Women in Conservative Times: Racial Justice, Peace, and Feminism, 1945 to the 1960s* (New Brunswick: Rutgers University Press, 1992), p. 79. Ultimately, the Rev. Colbert Cartwright, the group's main leader, concluded that the meetings had come to naught and might have been "just producing a little wider basis for cynicism in our community." Colbert S. Cartwright to Thelma [Babbitt], February 9, 1961, Cartwright Papers, UAF.

104. Sara Murphy Interview with Irene Samuel, July 21, 1992, Murphy Papers, Box 3, UAF; Sara Murphy Interview with Jo Jackson, June 3, 1992, Murphy Papers, Box 2, UAF; Sara Murphy Interview with Jean Ann Schmutz, June 11, 1992, Murphy Papers, Box 3, UAF; Sara Murphy Interview with Dr. W. H. Townsend, July 23, 1992, Murphy Papers, Box 3, UAF; *Arkansas Gazette*, September 14, 1963; Memorandum to Edwin Dunaway from Irene G. Samuel, November 17, 1966, WEC Papers, Box 8, AHC.

105. Author's Interview with Paul Fair, May 28, 1996; Adolphine Terry to Francis Goodell, December 10, 1968, Terry Papers, Box 2, UALR.

CONCLUSIONS: LITTLE ROCK AND THE
LEGACIES OF *BROWN V. BOARD OF EDUCATION*

1. Daisy Bates, *The Long Shadow of Little Rock: A Memoir* (New York: David McKay Company, Inc., 1962), p. 225.

2. Daisy Bates to Elizabeth P. Huckaby, August 18, 1987, EP Huckaby Papers, UALR; *Arkansas Democrat*, January 2, 1977, EP Huckaby Papers, UALR; *Arkansas Gazette*, August 19, 1979, EP Huckaby Papers, UALR.

3. Patricia J. Williams, "Alchemical Notes: Reconstructing Ideals from Deconstructed Rights," in Richard Delgado, ed., *Critical Race Theory: The Cutting Edge* (Philadelphia: Temple University Press, 1995), p. 91; Derrick Bell dissenting in Jack M. Balkin, ed., *What* Brown v. Board of Education *Should Have Said: The Nation's Top Legal Experts Rewrite America's Landmark Civil Rights Decision* (New York: New York University Press, 2001), pp. 185–200.

4. Kevin K. Gaines, *Uplifting the Race: Black Leadership, Politics, and Culture in the 20th Century* (Chapel Hill: University of North Carolina Press, 1996), p. xi–xii. The latest entries in the vocabularies of political euphemism include "No Child Left Behind" and "ownership society."

5. Other scholars of the South place the origins of the neo-liberal order in the 1970s when it actually began in the postwar period. Joseph Crespino, *In Search of Another Country: Mississippi and the Conservative Counterrevolution* (Princeton, NJ: Princeton University Press, 2007); Kevin M. Kruse, *White Flight: Atlanta and the Making of Modern Conservatism* (Princeton, NJ: Princeton University Press, 2005); and Matthew D. Lassiter, *The Silent Majority: Suburban Politics in the Sunbelt South* (Princeton, NJ: Princeton University Press, 2006).

6. Adam Fairclough, Race *and Democracy: The Civil Rights Struggle in Louisiana, 1915–1972* (Athens: University of Georgia Press, 1999), p. 235.

7. Michael J. Klarman, *From Jim Crow to Civil Rights: The Supreme Court and the Struggle for Racial Equality* (New York: Oxford University Press, 2004), pp. 419, 422–23; Mary L. Dudziak, *Cold War Civil Rights: Race and the Image of American Democracy* (Princeton, NJ: Princeton University Press, 2000), pp. 115–51, 166; Southern Regional Council, "A Background Report on School Desegregation for 1959–60," August 10, 1959, WEC Papers, Box 20, AHC.

8. Support of the Courts by the Department of Justice, September 1958, White Papers, Box 2, NA. Justice Department officials also informed the Supreme Court of their plans to use federal marshals to support orderly desegregation in Little Rock in September 1958. J. Lee Rankin to James R. Browning, September 10, 1958. Encloses for the Supreme Court, Attorney General William P. Rogers to Dean Dauley, Little Rock City Manager, September 7, 1958 and Rogers to Wayne Upton, President of the Little Rock School Board, September 7, 1958, Records of the U.S. Supreme Court, RG 267, Box 2602, NA. In 1960 they concluded that the attorney general had the authority to seek injunctive or other relief to eliminate race discrimination or to initiate or support private lawsuits challenging race discrimination even without legislative authorization from the 1957 and 1960 Civil Rights Acts. Harold R. Tyler, Jr. to Philip Marcus, September 21, 1960, White Papers, Box 2, NA.

9. Southern Regional Council, "Some General Observations in the Negro Community of Little Rock, Arkansas," May 1958, WEC Papers, Box 20, AHC;

John Pagan Interview with Ernest Green, January 26, 1973, Murphy Papers, Box 1, UAF.

10. Charles Alan Wright, "School Integration: An Almost Lost Cause," *The Progressive* (August 1958) in Record and Record, *Little Rock, U.S.A.*, pp. 268–71. Southern states' strategy of "conservative lawbreaking" required the use of "'legal' methods" of resistance that entailed the "violation of [federal] law through properly constituted authority," usually state governments. David R. Goldfield, *Black, White, and Southern: Race Relations and Southern Culture 1940 to the Present* (Baton Rouge: Louisiana State University Press, 1969), pp. 79–81. Responsibility for effective enforcement of Title VII of the 1964 Civil Rights Act passed also to private litigants as employer resistance and relative federal inaction left those who experienced continuing discrimination few alternatives. Herbert Hill, "The Equal Employment Opportunity Commission: Twenty Years Later," *Journal of Intergroup Relations* 11 (Winter 1983): 45–72.

11. John A. Kirk, *Redefining the Color Line: Black Activism in Little Rock, Arkansas, 1940–1970* (Gainesville: University Press of Florida, 2002), pp. 139–84; Sara Murphy Interview with Dr. W. H. Townsend, July 23, 1992, Murphy Papers, Box 4, UAF; Sara Murphy Interview with Harry Ashmore, June 13, 1994, Murphy Papers, Box 1, UAF; Sara Murphy Interview with Ozell Sutton, September 20, 1993, Murphy Papers, Box 3, UAF; Sara Murphy Telephone Interview with Mrs. Daisy Bates, August 23 [no year], Murphy Papers, Box 1, UAF; Henry Woods to Sara Murphy, n.d. [December 1962], Murphy Papers, Box 2, UAF.

12. Adolphine Terry to Francis Goodell, December 10, 1968, Terry Papers, Box 2, UALR; Adolphine Terry to Wm. H. McLean, March 9, 1970, Terry Papers, Box 6, UALR; Terry Papers, Box 2, UALR; Adolphine Terry to Everett Tucker, March 10, 1970, Terry Papers, Box 6, UALR. In another letter, Terry agreed that "the definition of Urban Renewal as 'negro removal' which it certainly has been in this town" was an apt one. Adolphine Terry to Carol Parsons, May 23, 1969, Terry Papers, Box 2.

13. Everett Tucker, Jr. to Mrs. David D. Terry, Sr., March 6, 1970 and March 20, 1970, Terry Papers, Box 6, UALR.

14. John R. Logan and Harvey L. Molotch, *Urban Fortunes: The Political Economy of Place* (Berkeley and Los Angeles: University of California Press, 1987).

15. Sara Diamond, *Roads to Dominion: Right-Wing Movements and Political Power in the United States* (New York: Guilford Press, 1995), p. 69.

16. Klarman, *From Jim Crow to Civil Rights*, pp. 326–29.

17. Ibid., pp. 329–43.

18. Untitled, "In the statement... ," n.d., Blossom Papers, Box 5, UAF; Derrick Bell dissenting in Balkin, *What* Brown v. Board of Education *Should Have Said*, pp. 185–200; Klarman, *From Jim Crow to Civil Rights*, pp. 325–43; Derrick

Bell, "Property Rights in Whiteness—Their Legal Legacy, Their Economic Costs," in Delgado, *Critical Race Theory*, p. 81. Bell's "interest convergence theory," which is based on the idea that whites support racial advances only when it serves their own interests, assumes that white interests are monolithic and that racial hierarchy is the most important political priority of whites. Although the Little Rock case offers important support for his thesis, it also complicates it by revealing differences among whites and underscoring the centrality of questions of power relations among whites to the politics of race.

19. Thomas Sugrue, *The Origins of the Urban Crisis: Race and Inequality in Postwar Detroit* (Princeton, NJ: Princeton University Press, 1995); Logan and Molotch, *Urban Fortunes*; Lydia R. Otero, "Conflicting Visions: Urban Renewal, Historical Preservation and the Politics of Saving a Mexican Past" (Ph.D. dissertation, University of Arizona, 2003). At the local and state level, the moderate architects of "progress" have recruited low wage and environmentally hazardous industries to the South where employers still find workers who are sufficiently poor and disempowered to accept those conditions. James C. Cobb, *Industrialization and Southern Society, 1877–1984* (Chicago: Dorsey Press, 1988); Robert D. Bullard, *Dumping in Dixie: Race, Class, and Environmental Quality* (Boulder: Westview Press, 1990).

20. Excerpts from Urban League of Greater Little Rock, "A Study of the Social and Economic Conditions of the Negro in Greater Little Rock—1963," n.d., WEC Papers, Box 17, AHC; Cobb, *Industrialization and Southern Society*.

21. Elizabeth Huckaby, Yearbook, 1959, October 26, 1959, EP Huckaby Papers, UALR.

22. Phoebe Godfrey, "Bayonets, Brainwashing, and Bathrooms: The Discourse of Race, Gender, and Sexuality in the Desegregation of Little Rock's Central High," *Arkansas Historical Quarterly* 62 (Spring 2003): 42–67.

23. As Robert Burk notes, in the 1960s law and order went from a moderate ideology of racial equivocation to a mainstream vocabulary for denouncing African Americans and setting limits to Americans' sense of commitment to racial change. Robert Fredrick Burk, *The Eisenhower Administration and Black Civil Rights* (Knoxville: University of Tennessee Press, 1984), p. 265. The old "race neutral" law, of course, was that validated in the decision in *Plessy v. Ferguson* upholding segregation.

24. Herbert Hill, "The Equal Employment Opportunity Commission: Twenty Years Later," *Journal of Intergroup Relations* 11 (Winter 1983): 45–72; Dan Carter, *From George Wallace to Newt Gingrich: Race in the Conservative Counterrevolution, 1963–1994* (Baton Rouge: Louisiana State University Press, 1996); Jane Mayer and Jill Abramson, *Strange Justice: The Selling of Clarence Thomas* (Boston: Houghton Mifflin, 1994); Steve Watkins, *The Black O: Racism and Redemption in an American Corporate Empire* (Athens: University of Georgia Press, 1997).

25. Beth Roy, *Bitters in the Honey: Tales of Hope and Disappointment across Divides of Race and Time* (Fayetteville: University of Arkansas Press, 1999), pp. 11, 317–84, quotes on p. 337, 11; Toni Morrison, *Playing in the Dark: Whiteness and the Literary Imagination* (Cambridge, MA: Harvard University Press, 1992). The accusation that African Americans were indolent and prone to public dependence took root in the resistance to civil rights in the 1950s and soon developed as a potent national ideology of race. Indeed, Orval Faubus was one of its architects. "Facts on Welfare," December 11, 1961, WEC Papers, Box 8, AHC; Winifred Bell, *Aid to Dependent Children* (New York, 1965); Rickie Solinger, *Wake Up Little Susie: Single Pregnancy and Race before* Roe v. Wade (New York, 1992).

26. Orval Faubus asked Margaret Morrison to withdraw her candidacy for the school board in 1958 so that the segregationist vote would not be divided. Sara Murphy, Telephone Interview with Margaret Morrison, June 10, 1992, Murphy Papers, Box 2, UAF.

27. Henry Woods and Beth Deere, *Arkansas Law Review* 44 (1991): 971–1006.

Index

Brown, Kathleen, 251*n*32

Brown, Minnijean (later Trickey): on community traditions, 228; complaints about federal troops, 105; at delay hearing, 129*f*; on harassment campaign, 117; harassment of, 94–95, 109–10, 115–16; at Little Rock Nine anniversary, 136*f*; suspensions/expulsion, 94, 111, 116–17; Thanksgiving dinner, 128*f*

Brown, Robert Ewing, 6, 38, 84–85, 87, 261*n*75

Brown v. Board of Education, overview, 4–5. *See also specific topics, e.g.,* delay *entries;* NAACP

Brown II: and Blossom Plan, 33, 258*n*46; components of, 4–5; and presidential intervention reluctance, 31; resistance strategies summarized, 236; and school integration election, 146–47; Virginia's response, 49

Brownell, Herbert, 31, 67, 68, 69

Bryan, Hazel (later Massery), 2–3, 117, 135*f*, 247*n*6

bulletin approach, Matthews', 100, 103, 105

Burns, Lucy, 152

business impact report, WEC's, 198, 302*n*25

business leadership: overview, 9–14; Ashmore's criticisms, 90; Blossom Plan, 38; bomb explosion response, 203; Caldwell's criticisms, 91; churches, 272*n*87; dual system proposal, 193–94; gender assumptions, 196–97; and harassment campaign, 114; intimidation tactics, 178; and school board elections, 174–75, 223–24; school board recall campaign, 185–86; and school board resignations, 173–74; school closure campaign, 155, 157–58; silence response, 77–78, 83–84, 88, 151, 174, 287*n*34; traditional community roles, 20–23, 167–68. *See also* Chamber of Commerce

Butler, Richard, 140

Byrnes, Jimmy, 30

cafeteria harassment, 94–95, 109–10, 115–16

Caldwell, Arthur, 59–61, 62–63, 91

Campbell, Ernest, 86

Capital Citizens' Council: anti-Semitism, 261*n*75; and bomb explosion, 203–4, 205, 206; Capitol Building Rally, 201–2; as class representation, 78; economic development perspective, 290*n*55; harassment defense, 111; mobilization rally, 61; Parker's expulsion, 120; private school monies, 175–76; violence rhe-toric, 61, 62, 64. *See also* Citizens' Council of Arkansas; Guthridge, Amis

Capitol Building rally, 133*f*, 201–2, 303*n*37

Carpenter, Claude, 176

Cartwright, Colbert: Blossom Plan, 33, 37, 39; on CCU meetings, 310*n*103; desegregation support, 86–87; prayer day, 272*n*86

Catlett, Leon, 41–42, 209

CCA (Council on Community Affairs), 222–23

CCU (Conference on Community Unity), 226, 310*n*103

Central High School: closure, 131*f*; commencement ceremonies, 127*f*, 214–15; education reputation, 305*n*59; enrollment statistics, 218; entrance attempts, 1–3, 65–67, 69–70, 135*f*, 247*n*5; entrance success, 98, 130*f*; lease proposal, 154, 159; photos, 128*f*, 130–31*f*; in pupil screening process, 192, 209, 210; reopening of, 202–3; school integration election, 157; walkouts, 99, 101–2. *See also* harassment campaign

Chafe, William, 85

POLITICS AND SOCIETY IN TWENTIETH-CENTURY AMERICA